The Wooster Group Work Book

Described by Ben Brantley in *The New York Times* as "America's most inspired company," The Wooster Group has consistently challenged audiences and critics alike with their extraordinary performance works, many of which are now recognized as classics of the contemporary stage.

The Wooster Group Work Book accesses, often for the first time, the company's rehearsal methods and source materials, as well as the creative thinking and reflections of director Elizabeth LeCompte and her main artistic collaborators. Focusing on five performance pieces, *Frank Dell's The Temptation of St. Antony* (1987), *Brace Up!* (1991), *Fish Story* (1994), *House/Lights* (1999) and *To You, the Birdie! (Phèdre)* (2002), this new volume gathers together an astonishing range of archival material to produce a vivid and personal account of how the company makes its work.

This book's intricate layering of journal extracts, actors' notes, stage designs, drawings, performance texts, rehearsal transcriptions, stage managers' logs and stunning photographs traces a unique documentary path across the practice of The Wooster Group, one that will be an indispensable resource for all those with an interest in contemporary performance and its impact on contemporary culture.

Highly accessible to the student, scholar, theater-goer and practitioner, and including a contextualizing introduction and conclusion by Andrew Quick, this book offers a series of remarkable insights into the working practices of one of the world's leading performance companies.

Andrew Quick is a Senior Lecturer in Theatre Studies at Lancaster University. He is also a founder member of Leeds-based performance company, imitating the dog, where he writes and directs.

The Wooster Group Work Book

Andrew Quick

With photographs by Paula Court and Mary Gearhart

Routledge
Taylor & Francis Group
NEW YORK AND LONDON

The Wooster Group Work Book is supported by
Arts & Humanities Research Council

First published 2007 by Routledge
270 Madison Avenue, New York, NY 10016

Simultaneously published in the UK by Routledge
2 Park Square, Milton Park, Abingdon, Oxon OX14 4RN

Routledge is an imprint of the Taylor & Francis Group, an informa business

Editorial Adviser: Clay Hapaz, Archivist for The Wooster Group
Typeset in Bliss by Lewis Nicholson
Publication designed by Lewis Nicholson
Printed and bound in Great Britain by Bell & Bain Ltd., Glasgow

British Library Cataloguing in Publication Data
A catalogue record for this book is available from the British Library

Library of Congress Cataloging in Publication Data
A catalog record for this book has been requested

ISBN10: 0-415-35333-5 (hbk)
ISBN10: 0-415-35334-3 (pbk)
ISBN13: 978-0-415-35333-5 (hbk)
ISBN13: 978-0-415-35334-2 (pbk)

Contents

Acknowledgements

The idea for this publication grew out of a two-day symposium on The Wooster Group held by the *London International Festival of Theatre* in 2002. Many thanks go to Rose Fenton, Lucy Neal, Adrian Heathfield and The Wooster Group for hosting this event and supporting this publication at its inception. I am especially grateful to Elizabeth LeCompte and Kate Valk, who have given this project their constant support, encouragement and valuable time. Their participation has been immense and this publication could not have been completed without their input. Equally important is the contribution made by Clay Hapaz, archivist for The Wooster Group, who has also been the editorial advisor for this book. His energy, acumen, creativity and generosity of spirit have guided this project at every step. Special thanks go to Cynthia Hedstrom, who has provided continual assistance and advice. From The Wooster Group, I would also like to thank Yvan Greenberg, Joel Bassin, Roy Faudree, Sheena See, Ari Fliakos, Scott Shepherd, Geoff Abbas, Joby Emmoms, Teresa Hartmann, Gabe Maxson, Ken Kobland, Reid Farrington, Bozkurt "Bozzy" Karasu, Shannon Sindelar, Kristin Abbas and Kaneza Schaal for making my time spent researching in The Performing Garage an unforgettable experience.

I also owe a great debt to Lewis Nicholson who, as the designer of this book, has been a major collaborator. His commitment, intelligence and artistry can be felt on every page. I am also deeply grateful to the photographers whose extraordinary images appear in this publication, especially Paula Court and Mary Gearhart.

This publication has received extensive support from the UK Arts and Humanities Research Council (AHRC). This includes a Small Grant in the Creative and Performing Arts, which funded initial archival research in New York and a Research Leave Scheme Award that enabled the project's completion. I would also like to thank Lancaster University for providing additional funds for permissions, scans, travel and accommodation.

All documents provided by The Wooster Group are reproduced with its permission and The Wooster Group retain the copyright to all its documentary contributions to this volume. All photographs are reproduced courtesy of the photographers Paula Court, Mary Gearhart, Louise Oligny and Bob van Dantzig and each retain the copyright to all their respective images in this publication. Pages and excerpts from Gertrude Stein's *Doctor Faustus Lights the Lights* are reproduced with permission granted by the Estate of Gertrude Stein, through its Literary Executor, Mr. Stanford Gann, Jr. of Levin & Gann, PA. Permission to reproduce excerpts from Paul Schmidt's translation of *Three Sisters*, originally published in *The Plays of Anton Chekhov* (1998) is granted by Harper Perennial (Harper Collins). Pages and excerpts from Paul Schmidt's translations of *Three Sisters* and *Phèdre* are also reproduced with permission granted by Helen Merrill LLC, 295 Lafayette Street #915, New York, NY. With regards to Paul Schmidt, all rights including, but not limited to, professional, amateur, recording, motion picture, recitation, lecturing, public reading, radio, and television broadcasting, and the rights of translation into foreign language are expressly reserved. Particular emphasis is placed on the question of reading and all uses of these plays by educational institutions, permission for which must be secured from the author's representative. Permission to reproduce textual and visual excerpts from *Olga's House of Shame* and from the "Something Weird Catalogue" is granted by Something Weird Video, Inc., who retains the copyright to this material.

Of course, in completing a project of this size there are many people to thank and it is impossible to include them all. At Routledge I would like to thank Talia Rodgers for her unflagging patience and belief in the book. Thanks also go to Geraldine Martin for her invaluable advice and support during the lead up to this volume's publication. At Theatre Studies, Lancaster University, I owe many thanks to my colleagues Elaine Aston, Gerry Harris, Karen Juers-Munby, Carl Lavery, Ola Johansson and Nigel Stewart, who have given time, advice and help while I have been working on this book. I am especially grateful to Jackie Stacey for her close readings and responses to my writing and thanks also go to Peter Petralia for keeping a watchful eye on my wandering punctuation. Many people have made my visits to New York possible and I would especially like to thank Fiona Templeton, Anna Köhler, Lenora Champagne, Lois Weaver, Peggy Shaw and Siobhan Liddell for making me feel so at home in the city. I am also very grateful to Sandra Booth for all her help, humor and accuracy. Most important of all, I owe an incalculable debt to Alice Booth, who has lived every moment of this book's creation. Her intelligence, wit and faith have been inspirational.

—**Andrew Quick**

Introduction

Andrew Quick

> FRANK Sue, can you stay an extra hour? I'm gonna need a little help.
> SUE Why, did you find that tape with the answer to everything on it?
> (*Frank Dell's The Temptation of St. Antony*: "Episode 1: The Monologue")

The photograph on the front cover of this book is taken by Paula Court of *Frank Dell's The Temptation of St. Antony*, which was first staged by The Wooster Group in 1987. It captures a beautiful and humorous moment that occurs towards the end of the penultimate episode in which the character of Frank Dell (played by Ron Vawter) attempts to stage a death defying escape routine as part of a hastily arranged magic show. At the start of this scene the stage is filled with smoke. The performers, seemingly surprised by having to take part, attempt to disguise their confusion by enacting improvised dances or by desperately rushing around the stage as if involved in the creation of some grand finale that might ward off Frank Dell's imminent psychological and physical disintegration. At the center of this photograph, we see the raised body (a dummy in a white shroud), held in place by a silhouetted performer (Kate Valk), apparently frozen in response to the mesmerizing hands of Frank Dell. Something in this image captures both the promise and in-built failure of theater. This stilled moment evokes the potential for a theatrical event to transcend the ordinary—that a transformative act might occur before us, that the living be induced into a state of death and then be brought back to life. Yet, at the same time, behind the illusionary appearance of things, we can see that theater is little more than an elaborate arrangement of barely hidden ropes, sleights of hands and a series of tricks. It is all a sham.

As the following documents and interviews bring to light, this apparent contradiction is one of the most important preoccupations in the work of The Wooster Group—the search for a profound form of experiential reality that challenges the ordinary, which is, paradoxically, always negotiated and filtered via the very artistry and artificiality of performance itself. The photograph also prompts me to recognize one of the contradictions that haunts the pages of this book. This is the potential for a collection of documents and interviews to assume that they can miraculously breathe life once again into dead works of theater, that they can somehow resurrect the past before us in order that we might establish where the origins of an event began. The notion that the document "houses" origins is, of course, one of the fantasies (or fevers, as the philosopher Jacques Derrida puts it) that a close proximity to the archive generates: the dream that we might be able to gain access to the actual source and beginning of things.[1] As Carolyn Steedman warns us in her excellent analysis of the practice of "archivisation" nothing begins its life in the archive, although, as she comments, "things certainly end up there." Rather, she observes, the archive houses "stories caught half way through: the middle of things; discontinuities."[2] In short, as is implied in the citation taken from *Frank Dell's The Temptation of St. Antony* that opens this introduction, it is not possible to find the tape "with the answer to everything on it."[3] In the course of my research for this book, I have watched hours and hours of tapes and searched through boxes and boxes of documents. While watching recordings of rehearsals and performances and reading the many and diverse forms of documentation that make up the Group's archive, I have sometimes been seduced into thinking that the actual mechanisms and processes of how particular performances were put together were tantalizingly within my reach. And yet, I was also always conscious that so much is missed or excluded in all forms of documentation. A great deal happens off the screen and, of course, many important parts of the process never make the page. As such, it is impossible to grasp the totality of how a particular work is put together and it is necessary to acknowledge that the interpretive acts that are generated by an engagement with the archive are always speculative. Perhaps, we have to approach the documentary sections and interviews that make up this book in the manner of a detective (but one with little hope of solving the mystery). We have to be prepared to piece together the scattered traces left in the wake of a work's creation, to imagine and speculate upon the events stilled in the many beautiful and evocative black and white photographs of the performances and be alert to the fact that words spoken in interviews are always partial and subjective accounts of what occurred. Perhaps most important of all, we have to be aware of the fact that the various notes, drawings, interviews, transcriptions, photographs, performance and technical scores that make up this publication can never stand in for the fullness, the plenitude and the sensuous reality of the live event itself.

Yet, looking closely at the spidery network of scribbles and words that are layered into the photograph that introduces us to this book, it is possible to surmise that these notations are the very origin of performance, that this frozen moment of *Frank Dell's The Temptation of St. Antony* was born out of these enigmatic and highly coded markings. Indeed, many of the documents in the pages that follow reveal the ways in which the various practices of documentation play a key role in The Wooster Group's making process. Transcription, forensic reconstruction of documentary material (drawn from recordings of their own rehearsals, television, film, the performance work of others, interviews, telephone calls, meetings and so forth), the intricate construction of scores by performers, technicians, assistant directors, stage managers, all indicate the multiple ways in which documentation is not only a residue of their process but also a vital component of the Group's creative practice. In short, as I explore in more detail in the concluding chapter of this book, documents are not solely a way of accounting for what took place but are often an instrument in the work's construction and performance to audiences. These documents might not have begun their life in the archive, but The Wooster Group often turn to its tapes, its various and multiple forms of documentation as an important resource and stimulus for the creative process.

Seen in a different light, however, the photograph appears to be disappearing under the weight of cryptic writing. Rather than emerging from the etched surface of frantically arranged phrases, numbers and drawings, the photograph looks as if it is being submerged under a wash of information. From this perspective the image suddenly becomes a telling reminder that a book can never rigidly fix the event of performance, which, in its original incarnation, always presents itself as a series of fleeting moments that occur in a particular space and time with and before living bodies. Consequently, as the following pages bear testimony, all we are left with are the documentary relics of the performances and our fickle memories of having witnessed their particular stagings. It would seem then, that we have to engage with the documentary material that makes up this book with a certain caution, accepting the fact that documents cannot fully represent the complex reality of The Wooster Group's work while all the time understanding that they offer us key insights into the making processes of one of the North America's most enduring and influential performance companies.

Establishing The Wooster Group

As is well documented in other publications, The Wooster Group began by working within the organizational set-up of The Performance Group in New York, which had been established by Richard Schechner in 1967.[4] Elizabeth LeCompte, who has been the Director of The Wooster Group since the first piece *Sakonnet Point* premiered in 1975, joined Schechner's company in 1970 as Assistant Director for his production of *Commune* (1971). While assisting Schechner on a number of productions (which she has likened to serving an apprenticeship) and sometimes performing in Performance Group pieces (Sam Shepard's *Tooth of Crime* in 1972; Bertolt Brecht's *Mother Courage* in 1974; *The Marilyn Project* in 1975; *Cops* in 1978), LeCompte began to develop a theater aesthetic that broke away from Schechner's more ritualistic and psychologically based style. Drawing on the improvisational techniques and approaches to texts that she had observed while working with Schechner and taking inspiration from innovative work that was being made and shown in New York, LeCompte, along with other collaborators from both inside and outside of The Performance Group (these included Spalding Gray, Ron Vawter, Libby Howes, Willem Dafoe, Jim Clayburgh, Peyton Smith and Kate Valk) began experimenting with and pursuing a markedly different approach to making theater.[5] Schechner's methodology primarily placed an emphasis on the performer's emotional and psychological state as a mode of communication. This performer-centered approach was also wedded to the interrogation and exposing of particular social and political conditions that could be potentially transformed through creating what Schechner believed was an authentic relationship between performer and spectator, which often involved direct physical and verbal interaction between player and viewer. Naming this form of performance "Environmental Theater," Schechner sought to break through what he considered to be the illusory and aesthetic condition of theater itself in order to make contact with the more real experience that might arise through a genuine social exchange between performer and spectator and between the space of theater and the spaces of everyday reality (primarily the street). His aim, in short, was to create a reality that might challenge the dominant ideological order.[6]

In contrast, but clearly informed by her work with Schechner, LeCompte sought to position the performer within a shifting array of frameworks in which autobiography, found materials, documentary and fictional texts, improvised and reconstructed action, sat within what she has sometimes called an overarching "architectonic" structure.[7] Unlike Schechner's work, there is no place for a physical interaction between performer and viewer. The audience is always spatially separated from the scenic landscapes that she constructs. This is particularly evident in the performance pieces that make up this book where the dividing-line between the spaces of performing and spectating is explicitly marked by a metal rail (*House/Lights* [1997]), raised platforms (*Frank Dell's The Last Temptation of St. Antony*; *Brace Up!* [1991]; *Fish Story*; *To You, the Birdie! (Phèdre)* [2002]) and/or movable metal frameworks that operate as a kind of skeletal safety curtain (*Brace Up!*; *House/Lights*; *Fish Story*; *To You, the Birdie! (Phèdre)*): these are often named "dummy" and "stupid" in the documentation. The spectator's role, as she expresses in an interview with David Savran, is to witness events, rather than become an active or equivalent participant in their performance of them.[8] LeCompte's approach in these earliest works (*Sakonnet Point, Rumstick Road* [1977], *Nayatt School* [1978] and *Point Judith (an epilog)* [1979]) placed an emphasis on encountering material, rather than seamlessly representing or embodying character and/or the landscape in which the dramatic action takes place. As she comments in an interview that directly relates to this period, "I circle around ideas, rotate the viewpoint."[9] This circling and rotating has always involved negotiating the mediating mechanisms of performance and the technologies of meaning production that exist both in the theater and also in popular culture (including the various technologies of communication—sound, video, televisual, as well as pictorial, cinematic and choreographic modes of expression). Equally significant is the fact that LeCompte immediately began building each piece in relation to the previously completed work. Gestures, physical and musical motifs, scenic references, the biographical history of Spalding Gray and the various responses to this material produced by the other performers, are repeated across a series of pieces that are constructed in direct relation to each other. This body of work eventually formed a trilogy, which was linked under the title of *Three Places in Rhode Island* and was concluded by the performance of *Point Judith (an epilog)* in 1979.

If *Point Judith (an epilog)* marked a certain completion in a cycle of The Wooster Group's work (LeCompte has described it as being a piece that staged a "gentle goodbye" to "the character" of Spalding Gray), it also coincided with a number of changes that began to take place within the wider community of The Performance Group.[10] In 1980 Schechner left The Performance Group, which then formally disbanded. The Performance Group had purchased The Performing Garage on Wooster Street in SoHo, a Downtown district in New York, in 1968, and the ownership of the space was carried forward to The Wooster Group, under LeCompte's artistic direction, where she has continued to make the work ever since. The function of The Performing Garage as a home and rehearsal/performance space has been one of the most important factors in ensuring the long-term survival of The Wooster Group. In the concluding interview of this book, LeCompte describes how crucial a studio-based practice is to her way of working and the great debt she owes to both Schechner and Gray for introducing her to a collective based methodology for making performance. She comments, "In many ways it's thanks to Richard (Schechner) that I'm here—Spalding, as well. They showed me that I could do with other people what I had previously tried to do on my own. They took me here" (p. 268). Across the interviews it becomes clear that this approach to performance making is founded on the fact that the Group has unrestricted access to this building. On simple economic grounds, it would be commercially impossible to rent spaces for the lengthy rehearsal periods that the methodology of constructing the work demands. The Garage, LeCompte explains, makes available the time and space to thoroughly play with and meditate upon the material generated in rehearsals. It is the constant access to the space that creates a regular working structure for the Group. The every day use of the space permits the Group to pursue a form of practice that is based on problem solving, on being able continually to layer and re-organize the material over the required time it takes to complete a work. It allows LeCompte to gather a core group of collaborators that can participate and share in a history of making performance that can run for years, which often includes presenting unfinished versions, as works-in-progress, to the general public before they are finally completed. The Performing Garage also provides an administrative and archival home for the Group and houses parts of the sets, the costumes, the props and other materials that are continually returned to and re-engaged with across the different performance works that are made there.

Performance signatures

In a sense, it is The Performing Garage that creates the authorial space that has established LeCompte as one of the most significant figures in the field of contemporary performance. As I examine in more detail in the conclusion, it is possible to locate the scenic footprint of The Performing Garage in all the works that The Wooster Group have created to date. This footprint not only continually replays and refashions the history of the Group and the shifting relationships of all those who work within the company but it also repeatedly bears the mark of LeCompte's directorial signature. In the following interviews LeCompte avoids being cast as an auteur, preferring to emphasize and explain the collaborative nature of the work. She describes how it is constructed out of who and what is in the room, how it is always filtered through the different personalities that have changed over the years, by those individuals whom she describes as being "closest to the center of making the work" at any particular time (p. 268). And, as the various documents that dominate this book reveal, it is clear that LeCompte is able to harness and frame an extraordinarily diverse and skilled range of energies in the process of composing the Group's performances. Depending on the nature of the piece, she is able to make room for a great deal of individual creative input. Her description of Chris Kondek's contribution to how *Brace Up!* was composed is one particular example of the complex relationship that clearly exists between LeCompte, as the primary shaper of the material, and an individual who is able to bring her/his creative energies into play in the work's construction. Recalling how Kondek brought important video and sound material into the rehearsal process, she describes how crucial his intuitive approach was to arriving at the final layering of video and sound sources that formed one of the key components in the scenic structure of *Brace Up!*: "Chris had no fear of interfering with anything I was doing. He would just come in with anything at any time" (p. 109). LeCompte also acknowledges how problems arise in rehearsals when ideas and inputs are not forthcoming: "Every time I approach a project, I am like "Why?" Then, the people in the room tell me why. If they're not there, I am not there" (p. 265). Indeed, LeCompte points out that the impetus to explore the different texts that are negotiated and performed in the Group's work rarely comes from her. As she explains, "I get taken to things. Often, the things I do for myself just aren't as interesting" (p. 268).

However, despite this apparent dependence on others, LeCompte, as Valk points out, is the pivotal creative and organizational presence: the figure through whom all the material is finally filtered and structured, the person who has a sense of the "whole." LeCompte attends almost all of The Wooster Group's rehearsals and is rarely absent from any public performance. Even when a piece first opens to an audience, as Valk explains, it is "not finished." According to Valk, it is LeCompte's "work of art, so she gets her hands in there, tweaking and tuning and changing and manipulating whatever she needs, until it is realized for her" (p. 158). While LeCompte goes to great lengths to acknowledge the collective process involved in the making of each performance, I think it would be a mistake to underestimate her role in "authoring" the work of The Wooster Group. Perhaps, one of the key reasons for her success as a director rests on her ability to allow space for individual creative expression and input while all the time setting up particular structural frameworks and scenic landscapes that situate this activity within a coherent and often challenging aesthetic—one that we recognize as being the work's signature. This may be at the root of the "architectonic idea" that LeCompte has spoken of as being a key starting point for her in the making of any performance. This architectonic idea is the larger structural and scenic/spatial framework (she also sometimes speaks of this framework in musical terms) within which the work of others can exist and reverberate. It is a framework that often declares or reveals itself structurally in the performance. This, it seems, is very much what LeCompte is in control of. The specific nature of LeCompte's role is difficult to define, even to herself, reflecting the complex function and status she has within the Group. However, what LeCompte makes clear in the interviews is that she is not necessarily the originator of ideas. What she sets up are systems and environments that generate material, which is then filtered through a set of frameworks that she establishes, frameworks that are always in some dialogue with whom and what is in the room with her and the history of the Group itself. As she explains in an interview from 1984, "I am the central vessel, or vehicle, or last circuit that everything must pass through." In order to hold a group together, she adds, "You have to have a central vortex." According to LeCompte, this is "not an ego center" but a "functionary center," one in which all things "must pass through," so that everything can be brought together, "in one line."[11]

The work of this book

What follows this introduction, as the title of this publication describes, is a book of work. It engages, as directly as is possible, with how The Wooster Group make their performances. It does not seek to find thematic or theoretical frameworks in order to contextualize and explain their practice, although theories and contexts inevitably ghost throughout the following pages. Rather, this book's premise is to locate and juxtapose the multiple languages (textual, physical, aural, technological, anecdotal, filmic, televisual and so forth) of The Wooster Group's practice and history in order that the reader might gain some understanding of the diverse and complex ways in which the five performance pieces that make up this book have been put together. Almost all of the documentation has been drawn from the company's archive, from storage boxes and files of gathered and collated material. As well as paper-based documents the archive contains numerous video tapes of rehearsals, works in progress and performances, the earliest of which (in relation to this publication) date back to the initial rehearsals of *Frank Dell's The Temptation of St. Antony*. The archive also houses many beautiful photographs and slides, which are themselves an extraordinary testament to over thirty years of performance practice.

The specific performance works that form the focus of this publication were made between 1985 and 2002, beginning with the documentation of *Frank Dell's The Temptation of St. Antony* and ending with *To You, the Birdie! (Phèdre)*. *Frank Dell's The Temptation of St. Antony* is the final piece in a trilogy entitled *The Road to Immortality*, which also included *Route 1 & 9* (1981) and *L.S.D. (...Just the High Points...)* (1984). The logic for the exclusion of these and earlier Wooster Group works from the documentary sections of this book, apart from issues of page space, is that David Savran's *Breaking the Rules: The Wooster Group* provides an excellent account of the processes involved in the making of these performances in addition to analyzing the individual pieces and the various controversies that some of them accrued. It is also important to note that within the time period covered by this book, The Wooster Group revived *North Atlantic* and performed two Eugene O'Neill plays, *The Emperor Jones* (1993) and *The Hairy Ape* (1995). In the initial planning of this publication, since it was impossible to document every performance, the exclusion of these two O'Neill plays as a body of work felt like the most logical form of omission. The Wooster Group Chronology in the end section of this book gives an excellent account of the dates when these and all the other works dating from 1985 were rehearsed and performed and provides a summary account of the Group's history up until 2006.

As is the case with all Wooster Group pieces, each separate part of *The Road to Immortality* was made in relation to the previous completed work and it is important to contextualize *Frank Dell's The Temptation of St. Antony* by touching briefly on the other two performances that make up the trilogy. While *Route 1 & 9* marked a new direction for the Group in that Gray and his autobiographical narrative and physical presence no longer formed a central thread, it also continued the practice of using a well-known play to form one of the performance's integral structural layers. This had first occurred in *Nayatt School* with its staging of selected scenes from T. S. Eliot's *The Cocktail Party*. *Point Judith (an epilog)* also included a highly condensed version of Eugene O'Neill's *Long Day's Journey into Night* and all the works in this book continue this practice of staging The Wooster Group's encounter with a literary, cinematic or dramatic text. Both *Route 1 & 9* and *L. S. D. (...Just the High Points...)* engaged with "classic" plays (Thornton Wilder's *Our Town* (1938) and Arthur Miller's *The Crucible* (1952), respectively), and placed them in relation to other found material that is performed and presented on the stage. *Route 1 & 9* juxtaposed *Our Town* with Pigmeat Markham's comedy routines, which were performed in blackface and included a lecture demonstration, dance, the presentation of Wilder's text in the style of soap opera on televisions suspended from the lighting rig, task-based actions (the construction of a house) and a pornographic road-movie within its multiple layers. As LeCompte was to acknowledge later, the absence of a central narrative voice, which had been a presence in the pieces made in collaboration with Gray, may have accounted for the some of the angry reactions that *Route 1 & 9* generated in some quarters as a response to the Group's performance in blackface. This reached its negative climax when The New York State Council on the Arts (NYSCA) drastically cut the Group's funding in 1982. Rather than perceiving *Route 1 & 9* as a staged encounter with representational constructions of race (created through the juxtaposition of a solely white version of America in the soap opera framed presentation of *Our Town* with the performance in blackface), members of NYSCA accused it of caricaturing a racial minority.

LeCompte has described how *L.S.D. (...Just the High Points...)* was made in direct response to the fall-out that *Route 1 & 9* created. Drawn to what she identified as the highly moralistic tone in *The Crucible* that dealt with concepts of responsibility and hysteria, LeCompte placed her reworking of the play against sections taken from the life of Timothy Leary, who had been imprisoned for his experiments with LSD and his attempt to establish an alterative community (Millbrook) that renounced the ideologies of a consumer led North American culture. Re-playing the four act structure of Miller's drama, *L.S.D. (...Just the High Points...)* juxtaposed the reading of excerpts from various "authors that might have been at the Leary household, circa 1960" (Act 1), with stagings of *The Crucible* (Act 2), sections taken from a filmed debate between Leary and G. Gordon Liddy that took place in the early 1980s (Act 4) and a performance of a choreographed routine by a dance troupe in Miami (Act 4). Nancy Reilly, who spoke the words of Anne Rower, Leary's babysitter, provided a narrative thread in the work, although the presentational style of the performance, which referenced the McCarthy led judicial hearings of the 1950s, eschewed any overarching fictional framework. Once again, the Group attracted controversy as Arthur Miller took legal action and halted the use of any of his writing in the performance.

In contrast to the two previous works that made up the trilogy, *Frank Dell's The Temptation of St. Antony* marks a return to a more meditative landscape. This is signalled in its source material, which includes Flaubert's *The Temptation of Saint Anthony*, Albert Goldman's biography of Lenny Bruce, Ingmar Bergman's *The Magician* and the spiritualist writings of Geraldine Cummings as some of the piece's many textual references. The structural spine of this performance is "The Monologue" in which Vawter, playing Frank Dell (one of Lenny Bruce's alter-egos), speaks the words of all the characters who appear on a video called "Channel J" ("Channel J" was a late night nude chat show that was shown on cable television in New York in the early 1980s). In the Group's videotaped re-working of "Channel J" Vawter (as the host) along with Kate Valk, Peyton Smith, Willem Dafoe and Anna Köhler (as the guests) improvise a version of the chat show while "riffing" off Nancy Reilly, who is reading Flaubert's text to them (Reilly is only occasionally seen in the video, p. 25). "The Monologue" forms the main focus in the opening documentary section of this book, which includes earlier and final transcripts of "Channel J" (pp. 22–23 and 28–33) and also two pages of Reilly's score that clearly lay out the juxtaposition between Flaubert's writing that she was reading and the particular version of the monologue that was being worked on at the time (pp. 26–27).

"The Monologue" is delivered at the front of the stage by Frank Dell who directs "J.J." to stop, rewind and fast-forward the tape as if it might provide the answer to what appears to be the profound metaphysical crisis that Frank Dell is enduring. LeCompte describes this obsessive replaying of the tape as being driven by the need to find its meaning and alludes to the possibility that all the other figures in the performance are "figments" of Frank Dell's imagination (p. 58). Of course, this attempt to "find the meaning" reflects the autobiographical struggle to create and complete the piece itself—a struggle that always works its way into Wooster Group performances, which in this case was seriously affected by Vawter's hospitalization and subsequent absence for a prolonged period of rehearsal (p. 59). Interrupting the internal meditation of the "The Monologue" are a series of "episodes" that take place on and around a raised platform that dominates the center and rear of the space, which appears to double as a hotel room and a theater (the back wall of the room lowers to create an extended raised playing area). This part of the space is mainly occupied by two women, Onna (Kate Valk) and Phyllis (Peyton Smith), who converse with Frank Dell, rehearse a dance routine, stage a party and help him perform a magic show. Other characters include Sue, Dell's assistant (originally played by Reilly) and two of the hotel's staff, the maid and her boyfriend, who are strapped to doors that swing (loudly) in and out of the space (played by Anna Köhler and Mike Stumm—his performance score is included in the documentation on pages 50–52). Frank Dell's meditation is further disrupted by "visits" from Cubby (Willem Dafoe) performed on video, who as the Devil (a re-working of the figure of Hilarion in Flaubert's text), repeatedly tempts Frank Dell to "follow" him to a more glamorous life in Hollywood (pp. 38–39).

Frank Dell's The Temptation of St. Antony ends with Vawter alone at the front of the stage refusing to acknowledge the urgent request made by Onna to accompany her and the others to stage a show for the "King of Sweden." After the rest of the performers have packed up and left, Vawter puts on a fur coat, switches off the television sets and strikes a final theatrical pose before leaving the stage in darkness. As the concluding action in *The Road to Immortality*, Frank Dell's exit feels like a poignant ending to a specific cycle of The Wooster Group's work. These works had, in their very different ways, created a dense, often humorous and highly nuanced examination of American culture (high and low), while always exploring the potential of performance to express a lived (rather than represented) experience of spiritual and societal crisis.

The brightly lit and open stage of *Brace Up!*, first performed in 1991, marks a striking contrast to the engulfing sense of darkness that concludes *Frank Dell's The Temptation of St. Antony*. The concept of a theater troupe attempting to construct a performance, which had ghosted in the Group's previous work, is brought to the fore in the performed encounter with Chekhov's *Three Sisters* that forms the structural basis for *Brace Up!*. Here, the dramaturgical engagement with Chekhov's text becomes the matter of performance, rather than being relegated to the contextual or background information usually negotiated in rehearsal. The opening page of Marianne Weems's notebook (p. 65) tells us that the idea of a Japanese Theater Troupe staging Chekhov's play came to the Group very early in the rehearsal process (Weems was LeCompte's assistant between 1988 and 1994). As LeCompte explains in the interviews, she was drawn to Japanese performance styles as a means to break up and re-configure the naturalism of Chekhov's dialogue and his hermetically sealed dramatic landscape. The scenic organization of *Brace Up!* is modeled on the Noh stage, with its brightly lit raised performance area, entrances from the sides and rear and table at the back. LeCompte also turns to specific Noh based movement patterns to choreograph the performer's action in and across the space, which she augments by dividing the stage area into sections (p. 83) and inserting a set of rules as to how these areas might be entered and exited (p. 110). The space is also organized so that very little dialogue is spoken directly by one person to another and Chekhov's text is often re-configured as a series of monologues. Conversation takes place between live performer and a close-up on a television monitor or between someone at the back table and another who faces the audience from the center of the stage. The close-ups are often filmed live during the performance via cameras positioned behind screens to the side of the stage (p. 82) and these images are mixed and collaged with other visual material selected from *Godzilla* films, the cinematic work of Yasujiro Ozu and Kenneth Branagh's *Henry V* (pp. 89 and 91).

The Narrator, performed by Valk, acts as the primary facilitator for the on-stage negotiation of Chekhov's text, setting up the scenes, prompting commentaries from Paul Schmidt, the translator of the performed version of *Three Sisters* (Schmidt also plays Chebutykin), filling in for any cut material and explaining the story to the audience (an example of these inserts can be found on page 80). The Narrator, as Valk explains in the interviews, also alluded to the figure of the *benshi*, who would tell the on-screen story live to the audience in the era of Japanese silent cinema. Valk also describes how her performance of the Narrator is a reflection and outcome of her working relationship with LeCompte, how she always has, in some sense, a facilitative connection to the way the work is put together. In this role, she comments, "I'm always creating what I think she (LeCompte) wants to see, keeping track of all the material and finding, as a kind of editor on my feet, a way to put it all together" (p. 158). LeCompte similarly describes the way in which Valk's presence as an on-stage dramaturg, who could always fill in and explain the intricate narrative, allowed her to focus attention on how to organize in the space rather than having to defer to the script as the basis for her compositional process. "The two things—the stage and the page," LeCompte observes, "never meshed in that piece. I always had to be looking at the stage" (p. 110).

LeCompte introduces a further choreographic texture into *Brace Up!* in the form of dance sequences, which are the documentary focus of the last part of this section of the book (pp. 93–103). Clues as to the different sources that informed the construction of these dances can be found in the notes for a presentation that The Wooster Group made at the Whitney Museum of American Art (p. 94). The accompanying photographs beautifully communicate the life-affirming vibrancy and humor that these dances brought to the Group's performed negotiation of Chekhov's text. *Brace Up!* concludes with a condensed version of the final act of *Three Sisters* where the Narrator explains to the audience how the play finishes and everybody sings "The Farewell Song." This underscores the final withdrawal of the military garrison that is the backdrop for the series of sad goodbyes that take place at the end of Chekhov's play (p. 104).

Fish Story, which began preparation almost immediately after *Brace Up!* was completed (although it was not presented in its final form until 1994), picks up the threads of the last act of *Three Sisters* and interweaves it with *Geinin*, a documentary about a Japanese traveling theater troupe who combine popular and traditional forms of performance mainly for tourists and local audiences. In an early rehearsal tape LeCompte proposes that the piece is set in some imagined future, "a flash forward," where the company is attempting to perform a classic play that is now unknown to them. The Wooster Group return to the story of the theater troupe that ghosted in *Brace Up!*, focusing on a playful engagement with its documentary life, which clearly resonated with their own experience as a company. As LeCompte remarks, "I was just thinking and imagining us in the future" (p. 108). In *Fish Story* Chekhov's text is spoken live and also via video monitors. Jeff Webster performs the narrator's voice from selected parts of *Geinin* at a live video station positioned at the back of the space and the on-stage action takes place on a slightly re-organized *Brace Up!* set, reflecting the fact that the Group's original plan was to present the two works together.

Most of the live action in *Fish Story* takes place in the form of highly choreographed dances in which every movement feels saturated with significance. In the interviews LeCompte comments on the way in which she likes to create pictures that are always in the process of transforming, how performers "get in and out of their moves" and this focus on the tension between placement and displacement seems to be one of the central organizing principles at work in *Fish Story* (p. 215). Valk also describes how the piece is sculpted from the paring down of material, what she calls an emptying out of the center, "where there really isn't a play, but just its signs, the props, costumes, articles" (p. 161). While these descriptions capture the work's abstract quality it is important to recognize that *Fish Story* also makes reference to and stages the Group's autobiographical experience. This is evident not only in the highly stylized re-examination of *Three Sisters*, their explicit reconstruction of the "documentary life" of a theater troupe, but also in their performed negotiation of the changes that were talking place at the very creative core of the company. Both LeCompte and Valk describe how Vawter's portrayal of Vershinin's touching farewell to Masha at the end of *Fish Story* doubles as a goodbye to Vawter himself (Vawter died before the piece was finally completed). There is something very moving in the sheer beauty and humor of this scene's composition, which is captured in the video stills and accompanying text in the final pages of the complete score of *Fish Story* that occupies the central section of this book. This score, which is adapted from an original notation by Clay Hapaz, provides a scripted account of the whole work and is organized to reflect the ways in which the piece is constructed out of a finely tuned layering of spoken text, physical action, sound and video. It also gives a sense of the precision that goes into the compositional process and the specific demands (accuracy, timing and so forth) that are made on the performer and technician during the work's performance.

The penultimate section of this book provides a documentary account of *House/Lights*, which the Group began rehearsing in 1996 shortly after their staging of Eugene O'Neill's *The Hairy Ape*. *House/Lights* is structured through a playful interweaving of Gertrude Stein's *Doctor Faustus Lights the Lights* (1938) and Joseph Mawra's B-movie, *Olga's House of Shame* (1964). The choreographic organization of the piece is largely drawn from Mawra's film, which the actors channel and imitate as it is played on video monitors during the performance. LeCompte takes the structural language of the film (the camera moves, the use of close-up and long shot, etc.) and uses it as a template around which to organize the movement in and through the space. For example, a close-up forces the performer to move to the front of the stage, a long shot induces a move to the back. The text of *Doctor Faustus Lights the Lights* is mostly spoken by Valk, who channels Stein's words as she listens to a recording of the text through an in-ear receiver. As Valk explains, the only way to get Stein's text to feel present on the stage was, "to have it recorded and to say it, not ahead, nor behind, but to stay with it" (p. 216). Live action is recorded via a camera placed at the front-center of the space and images are stilled and mixed into sequences of *Olga's House of Shame* as well as other source material drawn from cinema and television (these include *Young Frankenstein* (1974) and *I Love Lucy*), which are shown on TV monitors in the space (pp. 210–212).

Actors' scores make up a large part of this section of the book, often giving a witty and vivid account of what constitutes the main elements and actions of their individual performances. Each score varies in style, detail and content. Some feel organized and definitive, others such as Valk's, with its almost indecipherable writing and crossings out, reflect the way the piece was obsessively reshaped and reworked across the extensive rehearsal process. LeCompte's journals, written during the making of *House/Lights*, give us tantalizing insights into how she thinks through problems and builds the work layer by layer—how, for example, the ideas of pivoting ramps and the overall design of the piece came together relatively early in rehearsals and the ways that different sources, such as Chinese opera and the films of The Marx Brothers, were brought into the mix (pp. 168–171 and 181). In a journal from 1997 she produces a sketch that maps out the way in which the center line in the space (occupied by Faustus/Elaine) forms an axis around which all the action revolves. The diagram and accompanying notes also tell us something about her initial thinking as to the placement of the camera on this line, how it connects to the "eye/I" that is continually moving to, and then dispersing from, the center of the space. This staging of the performer's inability to hold the center adds to the acute sense of identity crisis that haunts *House/Lights*, one that is connected to the experience of always being in the thrall of language and the environment, rather than being their master.

To You, the Birdie! (Phèdre), which the Group began rehearsing in 2000, occupies the final documentary section of this book. This piece is constructed around Paul Schmidt's translation of Racine's *Phèdre* and the design, with its illuminated open stage, marks a return to some of the scenic features of *Brace Up!* and *Fish Story*, although, as LeCompte explains in the interviews, it is also framed by references to American modernist architecture and the Palace of Versailles (p. 264). LeCompte places the dense melodrama of Schmidt/Racine's play within the game structure of badminton. Here, the formal rules of badminton are interwoven with the conventions of the French court, where the referee doubles as Venus, the servants as attendants throw shuttlecocks (birdies) to the players, mop the athlete's brow and clean the court during the match. Developing some of the choreographic approaches explored in *House/Lights*, LeCompte creates the physical score of the piece by having the performers imitate and channel sequences taken from Martha Graham, The Marx Brothers, Merce Cunningham and other sources, which are shown on monitors above, and out of sight, of the audience. The effect of bringing the text of *Phèdre* into play with this choreographic structure is to create a highly formalized sense of disembodiment, where movement and language are rarely allowed to synthesize and the performers move and speak as if possessed by sets of rules that they are never fully in control of.

The documentation focuses on the Group's struggle to construct the piece, which is narrated via the rehearsal logs of Jim Dawson, Richard Kimmel and Judy Tucker. One of the consistent problems that is articulated in these accounts of the rehearsal process is the difficulty of defining a way of being on the stage and of dealing with the play's language without inhabiting it in the style of naturalism. We repeatedly read how the Group return to the badminton in their hunt for an appropriate way to negotiate the text, to find the form in which language and movement can co-exist. However, it is not until LeCompte gives Phèdre's lines to Scott Shepherd that the piece begins to take its final shape (p. 262). Shepherd's role in the performance, as he speaks Phèdre's lines, echoes the *benshi*-like Narrator in *Brace Up!*, and, of course, can be to traced back to the storytelling and dramaturgical figure that LeCompte always seems to have ghosting in the Group's work.

We feel the strain experienced in making this performance in the words of LeCompte's journal where she describes the end of a particular rehearsal period for *To You, the Birdie! (Phèdre)* as being "the worst day of my life" and adds "want to get out. But how?" (p. 229) This journal entry gives us a fleeting insight not only into the struggle that composing such performance work entails, but also a sense of the personal investment that is at stake in this pursuit. Of course, the Group "get out" of the despair caused by this creative impasse by carrying on working, by returning to the every day activity of rehearsing, to those modes of practices that the documents in this book both represent and reflect, until the piece is finally finished. The main documentary body of this book ends with LeCompte's scribbled notes, written to introduce *To You, the Birdie! (Phèdre)* to the audience at a work-in-progress showing of the piece in New York. Her closing words, "Please bear with us, come back, have a good time" capture something of the contingency of The Wooster Group's work, that it is always in some way or another in progress, but most of all, they remind us that it is here to be enjoyed.

Notes

1 See Jacques Derrida, *Archive Fever: A Freudian Impression*, Chicago, The University of Chicago Press, 1996.

2 Carolyn Steedman, *Dust*, Manchester, Manchester University Press, 2001, p. 45.

3 The Wooster Group, *Frank Dell's The Temptation of St. Antony*, in Bonnie Marranca (ed.) *Plays for the End of the Century*, Baltimore, MD, Johns Hopkins University Press, p. 275.

4 For two excellent accounts of the history of the early years of The Wooster Group see David Savran, *Breaking the Rules: The Wooster Group*, New York, Theatre Communications Group, 1988, pp. 2–5 and Arnold Aronson, *American Avant-Garde Theatre: A History*, London, Routledge, 2000, pp. 97–102 and 145–156.

5 In *Breaking the Rules: The Wooster Group*, LeCompte describes how the impact of seeing the work of Robert Wilson, Richard Foreman, Stuart Sherman and Meredith Monk affected her approach to making performance in the early to mid-1970s. See especially p. 4.

6 This attempt to overcome the barriers that separated audience and performer (which was clearly influenced by figures such as Artaud and Grotowski) in order to establish a more equal and potentially democratic and politically transformative form of performance was particularly emphasized in such works as *Dionysus in 69* (1968), *Commune* (1971) and *The Balcony* (1980).

7 Interestingly, the word architectonic not only refers to the attributes of design and structure but also describes an approach to design in which core structural elements are exposed and their function is explicitly expressed. In an interview conducted in 1993, LeCompte comments, "Often I have an architectonic idea of the piece before I even know what text I am using. The text has to come up against my preconceived structure; a certain kind of dialogue goes on between the two and it is usually resolved in one way or another through practical problem solving."

8 See David Savran, *Breaking the Rules: The Wooster Group*, New York, Theatre Communications Group, 1988, p. 45.

9 Lenora Champagne, "Always Starting New: Elizabeth LeCompte," *The Drama Review*, Vol. 25, No. 3, Fall, 1981, p. 19.

10 See David Savran, *Breaking the Rules: The Wooster Group*, New York, Theatre Communications Group, 1988, pp. 133–157 for an excellent account of the making of *Point Judith (an epilog)*.

11 Mindy N. Levine, "An Interview with Elizabeth LeCompte," *Theatre Times*, Vol.3, No. 8, August 1984.

Frank Dell's The Temptation of St. Antony

SCENE ONE: ~~PG 300~~

FANNY
~~PEYTON~~ THINKS SHE'S ~~BEEN~~ IN THE HOTEL ROOM BEFORE — SHE'S LOOKING FOR STASHED DRUGS — CUBBY'S BOTHERING HER.

FIGHT:

KATE'S READING TO RON (ROAD TO IMMORTALITY) DISCUSS BOOK

FANNY
~~PEYTON~~ SHOOTS RON UP AS SHE TRASHES CUBBY. PG 301

PG. 303 MAX VALDEZ ~~SIMPSON~~ ENTERS W/INFO → AND LAWBOOKS ABOUT PASSPORTS (HE TOOK THEM TO BEAUREAU + LEFT THEM) TELLS CUBBY

CUBBY KEEPS DON'S DRUG TIMETABLE (SCHEDULE OF USAGE)

PG 302 FANNY HAS COUGHING FIT

RON — WATERPIPE(?) CAN'T LIGHT IT

VIBRATOR MACHINE ON BED

→ AFTER VALDEZ + PASSPORTS

CUBBY EXITS — COMES BACK IN W/SPEGEL — JIMMY DODD

PHONE CALL FROM DEAD BEFORE

CUBBY EXITS:

1. JACKALS
2. VALDEZ PASSPORTS
3. MORE JACKALS
4. PHONE
5. CUBBY LEAVES

PG 303

CUBBY TELLS DON WHO IS OUT IN THE HALL — JIMMY DODD → HOPPED UP SPEED-FREAK

"I AM AN ACTOR"

"I BELONG TO THE RENOWNED STENBORG GROUP"

FANNY OFFERS JIMMY A DRINK (FLASK)

INFO ABOUT JIMMY ALL THROUGH THIS — CONVERSATION ABOUT HIM.

CUT "LET ME REST FOR A MOMENT"

JUST "NOW TWILIGHT FALLS..."

MAIN QUESTION: HOW DID DODD FIND THEM? (PG 304) WHO IS HE?

THEY BEGIN HERE TO IDENTIFY THEMSELVES AS A TROUPE THAT WAS IN N.Y. — DODD THERE AT SAME TIME.

— ~~VALDEZ BRINGS LAW BOOKS FROM LIBRARY. (THEY HAVE A COURT CASE PENDING)~~

Opposite: *Frank Dell's The Temptation of St. Antony*, "Episode 1: The Monologue" Above: Early *St. Antony* scenario: James ("J.J.") Johnson

SCENE TWO → KATE CALLS ON OTHER PHONE TO ASK ABOUT PASSPORTS

THEY HAVE TO REHEARSE ST. ANTHONY IN ROOM

~~CUBBY ON PHONE TO BRIBE ANYONE TO GET THE ARTISTIC DIRECTOR OF KENNEDY CENTER. THEY KNOW SECLANS MIGHT HELP THEM. SOMEONE (FANNY) TELLS RON WHAT IS GOING ON.~~ CUBBY WRITES LETTER TO N.Y. RON STARTS WRITING LETTERS. (ON BED) OR DICTATE TO KATE. CHURCH BELLS

MAID PEEKS IN. IF DOOR OPENS ALL FREEZE OR FREAK OUT

* CHAIN FOR DOOR. DO NOT DISTURB SIGN
  BLINDS ON WINDOW

THEY BEGIN TO REHEARSE ST. ANTHONY (IN COSTUME) FANNY HAS COUGHING FIT BUT NOBODY NOTICES. CRITIC CALLS (FOR STORY) THEY GET IN NEW (COSTUMES) DISGUISES. THEY ARE (REMINISCING) BAD MEMORIES PARANOID. CUBBY: "KEEP QUIET" HE'LL DO THE TALKING. HE GABS FANNY (COUGHING) & THREATENS HER.

RECAP DISCUSSING ESTABLISH DEL FUEGO STORY — GET IT STRAIGHT

PG. 305 USE OF ACTUAL LINE FROM MAGICIAN ATTRIBUTED TO DODD.

~~KATE~~ ANNETTE GOES BACK TO HER BOOK — DODD ASKS HER ABOUT IT. "BOOK ABOUT AUTOMATIC WRITING" DISCUSSION.

TAKE OUT TUBAL'S LINES ABOUT TRUTH + BEAUTIFUL PASSION. KEEP (306) "TRUTH IS MADE TO ORDER..."

ANATOMY JOKE — DODD LAUGHING FIT (TO DEATH) + PEYTON

KATE DESCRIBES TO RON WHAT SPEZEL IS SAYING (HE'S MUMBLING)

* ASK NORM ABOUT BOOK ABOUT VISIONS BEFORE DEATH.

DODD DIES - WHAT DO THEY DO WITH THE BODY?

TO CLOSE THE SCENE: CUBBY — "RUINED..."

Early *St. Antony* scenario: James ("J.J.") Johnson

SCENARIO #2 LeCompte

SCENE ONE

1. Peyton stashes the drugs.
2. Peyton trashes Will to Ron (why keep him?).
3. Peyton and Will fight about who is most important.
4. Peyton "hears" a scream (hallucinates).
5.
6. Ron meets 'actor'. "Actor's story."
7. Actor and Kate discuss 'truth' and anatomy joke.
8. Actor dies.
9. Will: quote from notes. Talk about their situation with body.

SCENE TWO TRAPPED

1. Phone call informing them that they have to stay. Maybe they can't get rehearsal hall(?); passports taken at airports(?). Character entrance.
2. Reminiscing about the past.
3. They have to rehearse in hotel room.

SCENE THREE

309 1. Critic comes in and troupe pass themselves off as Cubans. 312
2. Critic suspects they are imposters and tries to cross-examine Ron, who pretends either to be mute or speak only Spanish. Critic calls editor--discussion of 'art'--editor has seen the Del Fuegos elsewhere; how could they be in hotel room? comes to interview them
3. Critic tests Ron's powers. Critic demands proof that they are the Del Fuegos. Troupe promises a video tape the next morning.
319 suspects they are not Del Fuegos asks for proof – says he will see them show in 1/2 hr

SCENE FOUR

321 1. Call out for food--real calls to restaurants--no one will deliver.
2. They find a menu + call room service.
3. Anna enters w. food. Pig?
4. Food distributed They Eat.
5. Anna talks w. Antonsson on phone (Antonsson calls (Are they dangerous?) the most scene.)
6. Simpson + Anna scene.
7a. Tobal + Sophia scene (art dealer) – phone
8. grandmother – Anna (proposal of audition)
9. Peyton – Antonsson phone call. Hears voice of a murderer.

SCENE FIVE STORM

NAP TIME – Everyone asleep

1 Peyton & Anna--song & advice. (drugs)
2 A storm begins; thunder & lightning..
3 Peyton sees Spegel move and makes a charm. Spegel exits

SCENE SIX FUCK SCENE

1 ~~Will~~ Jeff & Anna--fuck scene (Comedy routine)
2 Spegel is moving around.

SCENE SEVEN

1. Antonsson enters w/ drinks
1 Spegel rips off the drugs (their livlihood).

SCENE EIGHT

1 They set up for the critic's videotaping.
2 Peyton foreshadows a death.
3 Videotaping
(Seduction scene, ~~Anna~~ ofilia & Ron)? Queen of Sheba
Ron punctures his hands and stigmata appear. on tape
(~~Will overhears and is upset~~)?
4. Spegel returns and says he is a better ghost than a human being, and begs to be used. Then he dies, and ron puts him in the bed. (OD)

SCENE NINE

1. A big party downstairs in arts conference--critic returns to seduce Kate.

SCENE TEN

1. Critic offers Kate assistance to escape her situation--asks her if she ever believed. (She's dropped her disguise).
2. Ron assaults critic. Critic assures Ron of Kate's faithfulness.
3 Critic leaves. Ron removes his disguise.
4. Ron & Kate reflect on the past: 1) Sellars character, 2) run out of NYC. They get into bed. Ron vents his hatred and fear.
5. They blame Will for their downfall. Also Kirby(commercialization). Kate threatens to leave; Ron says she can if she wants. They reconcile.

SCENE TWELVE

1. They overdub the tape
2.
3.
4. Antonsson (~~Mgr~~ bartender/boyfriend) interupts the rehearsal, gets angry, fights with Ron, and thinks he's killed him. He runs out, and the group arranges the body trick.
5. Critic returns, is convinced Ron is dead. He reveals his true intentions (toward Ron & Kate). Ron is angered into attacking him; Kate intervenes. The critic composes himself and leaves (drops money as insult). wants Kate to come with him

SCENE FIFTEEN

3. Antonsson's suicide(?).

SCENE EIGHTEEN

1. Gramma & amanda
1/2 Will announces plans to leave (packing).
Anna decides what to do. She goes for her things.
Ron and Kate wait anxiously. The authorities are coming.
Phone call from Kennedy Center. Money and car on the way.
EXIT

Early *St. Antony* scenario: Elizabeth LeCompte

Channel J—St. Antony September 16, 1985–
Opening Monolog (Transcript)

(Music) Peyton laughing

Liz: Nancy, you have a book, right?

Nancy: Here's the page.

Ron: Are you running, Jeff?

Nancy: Okay.

Peyton: You want Nancy to read to us or what?

Liz: Last time... (inaudible)

Ron: (claps)

Peyton: Our town or something.

New start

Nancy: (reads)

Ron: Before night was over... after that I enjoyed tidying up everything in my cabin. I fixed up my tools... and... at that time my smallest gesture... was a painless thing to perform... It was now dried up...

Kate: (off mic) Did you want me to move anywhere?

Ron: Yeah, come over here... can you sit over here next to me?

Kate: Yeah. (pause)

Ron: ...the one I used to meet everyday ...by the pool... her tunic was open at the hip... go ahead Nancy... okay, you can stop—you can stop now... Nancy can you stop now. First I chose to live in a Pharaoh's tomb. (off mic) So... let's get up.

Kate: Yeah.

Ron: ...and, ah, the pig up here with us. Why don't you come here ...sit right in my lap ...come over. (inaudible)

Kate: You want me to sit anywhere?

Ron: Yeah, yeah. You wanna sit right, right here. Okay, Nancy, go ahead, Nanc... I all of a sudden saw the abominable thing... starting into life... A fff—flock of devils knocked me to the ground... they took me away from them, and so... Didymus... blind though he was, hm, to the scripture... Didymus came, his blind scholar... and, ah, he was rubbed all over with cow dung (dance, pig : oink, oink) ah, ah... we were... the thought crosses my mind... it's hard to pay no attention... It's unnerving (pause) messages were sent to me from everywhere. People came from very far away to see me. Meanwhile... (pause) Two soldiers flogged her with whips... she turned around with her mouth open, and she said... (dance) The two soldiers were, ah, flogging her... where is he now... No one bothers to bring me any news... my disciples have all left me, Hilarion with the rest. He had such a lively mind, and so, he was constantly asking questions, who, I would listen thoughtfully to him, whenever I needed anything he'd always get it for me... is a real funny guy... he was like a son to me... Anthony watches them... how I wish I could follow them... Nancy, do that last sentence again... let's take that slow... I gazed with envy, ah, at the long boats... whose sails... looked like wings... especially when they carried away people who I'd made welcome. Such good times were spent... no one could be more compelling than Ammon... telling me about his journey to Rome... the Coliseum, the piety of eminent women and a thousand things besides... where do I get my offspring? (Let's take a break)... suddenly I lost all thought of what was going on within... they communicate with each other... their discipline is strict... they're short on certain luxuries, but nonetheless they, they bring them eggs and, ah, and gadgets, take the thorns from their feet... around Pittsburgh there are...

Kate: Did you want me to take the thorns from your feet?

Ron: Yeah, yeah, take the thorns from my feet... Ow... ow... ow... ow... no, no, I think, yeah, ow, ow... hm, that's good, that's good... can we get some tablets?... do you have some... a... to take, anything, you got any downs... oh?... hm... what kind of downs can you get? Can you, can you, can you buy secanols... aha... can you buy secanols?

Anna: Buy some what?

Ron: Secanols.

Anna: What is secanols? (general bemusement)

Ron: You know like a... you know like ah... what?

Peyton: You know 14th Street.

Katy: You have just to ask them.

Anna: Oh.

Ron: But... how do you get secanols? Do you have a doctor prescribe them?... you can?... if you know a doctor, do you know any, any kind of cool doctors?

Liz: (instructs)

Ron: Yeah. (coughs) Listen, ah, let's talk this out, (giggles) no. But can you... what, how do people get them? I mean, do they, ah, you know, from, like, ah, loose doctors?

Peyton: Well, I know you can get them, hm, on 14th Street but then you don't know what's in them.

Ron: Aha.

Peyton: But, I guess, if you went to a doctor, but then that's very expensive.

TESTING THE SONY DYNAMIC microphone from 3 feet... testing the sony Dynamic microphone 2 feet
Testing the new psychic dynamophone from 2 feet Tet that phat that - gibberish - Samarod voice
Sucking! Sucking! Sucking — Loud, slurping, sucking sounds

LUST AND DEATH BED SCENE

R: Tortures unspeakable...filled, filled with skies...a building of Hermitage...washening their bodies...curse me for abandonong her...torn, torn my white hair out...Have your corpses left in the middle of the hut...now... between the temple down walls...the hiatus,hernia...nosing forward ...horrible, horrible...no Ammonaria wouldn't have left her...Where is she now? Ammonaria...May be you're in some hot room...One by one the clothes come off...the hot tunic...the necklaces...the nakedness... AHHHH here comes the Haircuts...like a black fleece in spite of itself...in a heated atmosphere...Bodies..she breathes Ammonaria, Ammonaria!...I'm plagued by lust ....three torches at once...I cannot go...I can no longer endure my hard self...leaning into the prepicous preci (stammer,stammer)...I fell forward...Ammonaria come to me, come to me...come to me as an old woman...Ammonaria ...this woman is much older than my sister...where is she? ...the old woman comes to me...her teeth...Ammonaria, is that you?...Your eyes, your eyes are full of darkness. with flames at the center of them ....go on ...What can stop you?

K: Go on . Who can stop you?

R: But I'm afraid of commiting a sin.

K: Think of all the people who have commited suicide, the great people...

R: But An...

K: Antios...Eledea of Elleppo...

R: Who else?

K: Many more saints. The Romans procure it.

R: I am important for death.

K: The virgins of Meletus strangled themselves w ith their girdles.

R: What happened in Syracuse?

K: The patricians of Rome procure it.

R: Yes that love is strong.

K: To do something that makes you god's equal think of that. He created you and you will destroy his work you yourself by your courage freely... the joy of Herostratus was no greater...Besides your body has sufficiently mocked your soul for you to take your revenge...What are you afraid of?

R: Youth. I'm going to take you.

K: Don't be afraid.

\- page two -

R: I'm not afraid.

K: What are you afraid of: a big Black Hole. REPEAT 3 times

R: Hah hah hah hah hah. Ammonar... Are you swimming towards? Come here please...You are she who loves...you are life ...tell me more...

out A: I am she who loves...I am bliss, life...unending happiness...

R: I'll say...But you laugh at the rings of Saturn around my neck. ...there are initiations you can give me...sighs, cries.. tell me about your nakedness...

A: I am she who loves...I am bliss...life...unending happiness.

K: Come to me I am consolation, overlasting peace, restfulness.

R: Well, there are many ways to handle this drunkeness...this wildness of the mind...But you have to be aware of...

K: Aren't you sick of the same monotonous action? The ugly world? The stupid sun?

R: Everything is light and sun.

A: Hermit! Hermit! You find diamonds between the pebbles, fountains under the sand.

R: Every evening I think of you...I hope it will soon...

K: You want it to cover you up.

R: Bless me...Bless me. You're becoming gaunt...tall and gaunt... (whispered) stand up...stand up...You're eyes are rolling. ...You console me...Give me everlasting peace...Your breasts your bliss, your conjugal happiness...I think of you as one...Someone's at the door...A skeleton of death... Theere's a body of lust which blows in my...my hair flies out...she reaches towards me...Death...Death...now or later what does it matter?

K: What does it matter if you take me now or later? You are mine.

R: You gazelle..you crocodile teeth...I remeber when you were my nubis...my dissolve...I accompany every step...death, death come to me.

K: Don't you remember that time behind the pyramid when you felt the piece of skull under your sandal and sifting it thru your fingers, don't tell me you didn't let your mind slip into the black void.

R: Desires, desires...people rush into my mind...where does it come from? These extravagances, these noisy allowances.. death.

K: My irony exceeds all others. There are convulsions of plea-

Opposite and above: **Transcript of early "Channel J" improvisation**

 Top left: ***St. Antony* rehearsal** Top right: **"Episode 4: The Party"** Bottom left: **"Episode 6: The Magic Show"** Bottom right: **"Episode 6: The Magic Show"**

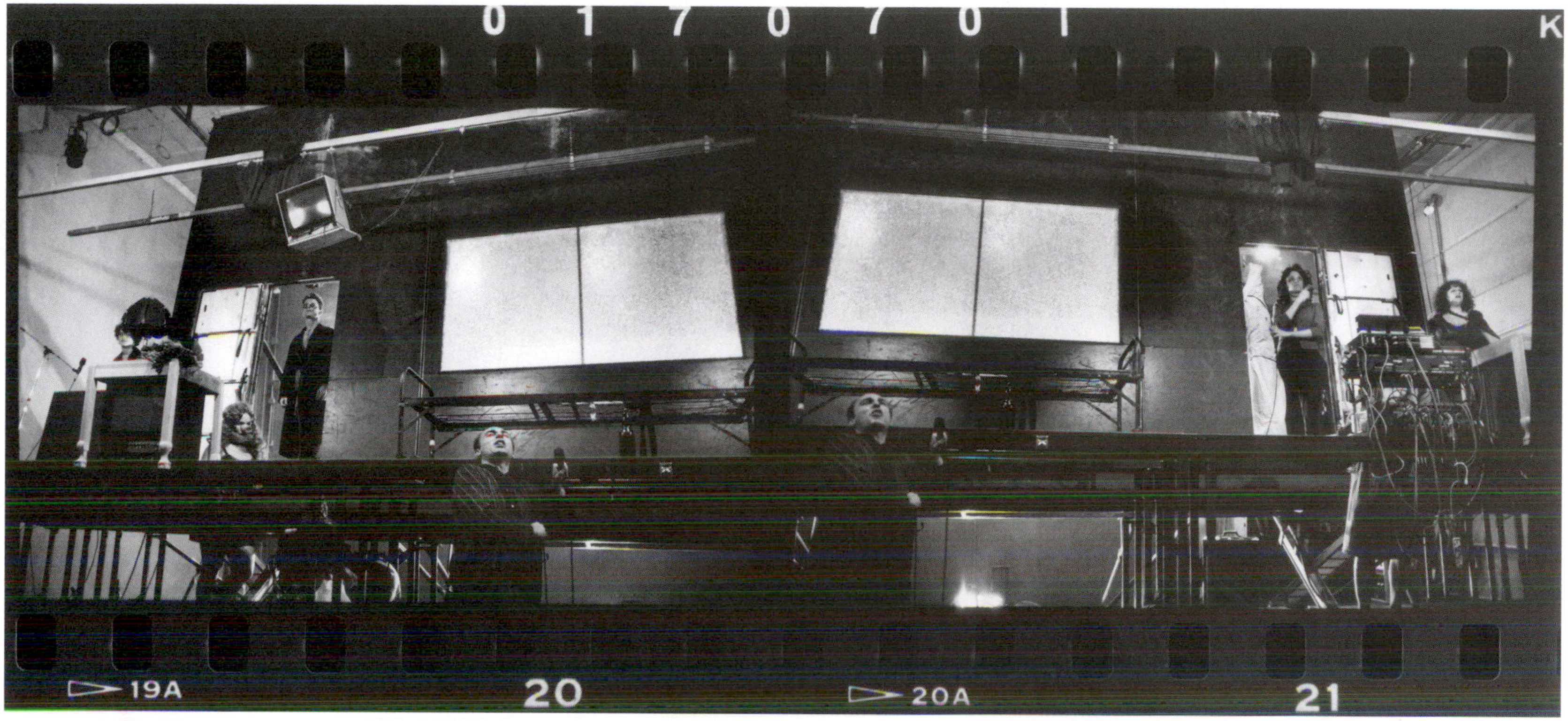

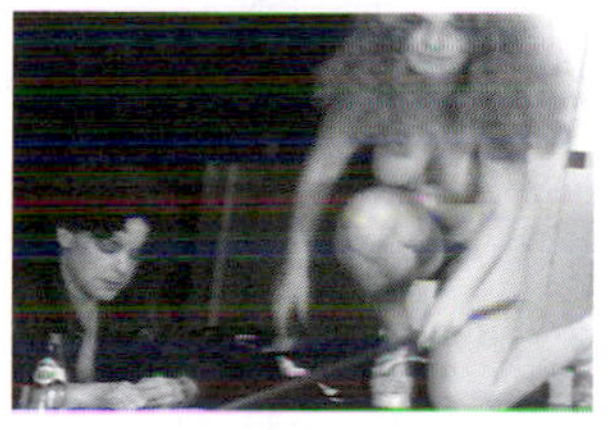
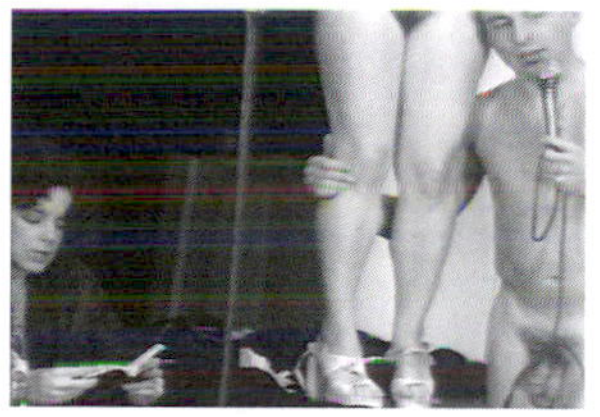
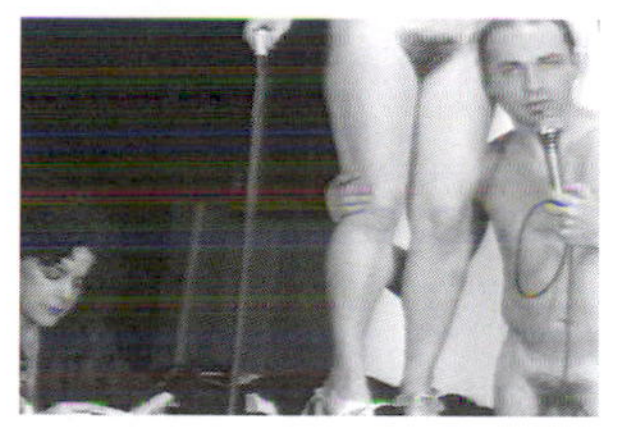

Top: ***St. Antony*** **rehearsal** Bottom: **Nancy Reilly reading Flaubert's** ***The Temptation of Saint Anthony*****: "Channel J" show tape**

4

R: Its necessary to cry. Form is perhaps the error of your
senses and substance an image of your mind.

K: Maybe then appearance is the only reality.

R: Its all is the truth but in one sense are you sure that, uh
seeing...are you sure of even seeing? Are you sure at even
being alive? Worship me and curse the ghost that you call
God. (pause...sound of footsteps then:) THE DEVIL ... HIM
I...Why do I feel so tired today, huh? My bones feel like
they're broken. Is it the dawn or is it a glimmer of the,
uh, moon. I'm tired. Very tired.....(pause) All right,
now where were we where was I with you? Oh yes, I remember
now- you were the local girl made good. I find prayer
intolerable I find...hard as a rock. My heart is as hard
as a rock. I used to be so overflowing with love and now
I don't feel anything. Can you help me?

A: You make me very sad.

R: Have you ever had men come to you eith problems like this? I FEE

A: All the time.

R: They all got problems, huh? I remember a journey I made once
in search of a...a...a..in,in,in distinguishable apple that,
uh, was...uh...side by side to a...to a sing-sing prison,
and when I was there I remember approaching a forest with
many, many processed hens and southerly eastern winds. And
when I was there, there was a pink flush in the sky and it
reminded me when I was a child and, uh, and I watched the
earth revolve, and , it seemed, at the time I thought, the
only word that could come to mind was crispy. It was like
a crispy universe. (soft) Hello...
Ah, Ammonaria, Ammonaria have you come again to see me?

K: Yes.

R: And...

K: I took all my clothes off. THE SECOND LIGHTER ONE

R: I want you to mmet my sister, Ammonaria. She's been away a
long time. She's filled out as you can see. She and I had
a thing going when we were kids and now she's back, uh, and
I'm personally happy to see her. Uh, where have you been all
these years?

K: Um, Ive been away. I've been a lot of places.

R: Met a lot of people?

K: Uh-huh, yeah, lot of people. Lot of beautiful people.

R: Lot of beautiful people out there, we have uh...you can't
uh-forget that the uh- wherever you go, whatever you see,
there's always gonna be people there who are gonna attract
you-and repel you. But they're there! That's the joy of
living.

4A

nor even say that the universe is infinite – for it would first be necessary to know Infinity!

Form is perhaps an error of your senses, and Substance an image in your mind.

Unless – the world being a perpetual flux of things – appearance on the contrary were to be all that is truest, and illusion the one reality.

But are you sure of seeing? Are you even sure of being alive? Perhaps there is nothing!

The Devil has taken Antony; and holding him at arm's length, he surveys him with open jaws, ready to devour him.

Worship me, therefore! and curse the ghost you call God!

In a last movement of hope Antony lifts up his eyes.
The Devil abandons him.

finds himself flat on his back at the edge of the cliff.
The sky is turning white.

I WHY DO I FEEL SO TIRED TODAY

Is it the glimmer of dawn, or a reflection from the moon?

He tries to pull himself up, then sinks back; and with chattering teeth:

I feel so exhausted . . . as if I'd broken every bone!

Why?

Ah! it's the Devil! I remember – he was even repeating to me everything I learnt from old Didymus about the opinions of Xenophanes, Heraclitus, Melissus and Anaxagoras, about infinity, creation, the impossibility of ever knowing anything!

And I'd thought I could be one with God!

Laughing bitterly:

Ah, madness! madness! Is it my fault? I find prayer intolerable. My heart is as dry as rock! It used to overflow with love! . . .

In the morning the sand steamed on the horizon like dusty incense; at sunset fiery flowers bloomed on the cross; and often – in the middle of the night – it seemed as if all creatures and things, absorbed in the same silence, were worshipping the Lord with me. Enchanting orisons, ecstasies of happiness, gifts from heaven, where have you all gone?

I remember a journey I made with Ammon, in search of a

THEY ALL GOT PROBLEMS HUH? I REMEMBER A JOURNEY

wilderness in which to found monasteries. It was the last evening; and we were quickening our pace, murmuring hymns, side by side, without talking. As the sun sank lower, the two shadows cast by our bodies lengthened like two obelisks growing for ever, apparently on the march before us. With pieces of our sticks we planted crosses here and there, to mark each place for a cell. Night was slow to come; black waves were swamping the earth while a great flush of pink still filled the sky.

When I was a child, I played at building hermitages out of pebbles. My mother would watch nearby.

She must have cursed me for abandoning her, must have torn her white hair out by the handful. And her corpse has been left lying in the middle of the hut, under the roof of reeds, between the tumbledown walls. A hyena snuffles through a hole, nosing forward! . . . Horrible! horrible!

He sobs.

No, Ammonaria won't have left her!

Where is she now, Ammonaria?

Perhaps she's in some hot-room taking off her clothes one by one, the cloak first, then the belt, the top tunic, the second lighter one, all her necklaces; and cinnamon vapour wreathes her nakedness. At last she lies down on the warm mosaic. Her hair comes around her hips like a black fleece – and slightly stifled by the overheated atmosphere, arching her body, she breathes, both breasts thrust out. There now! . . . my flesh rebels! In the middle of grief I'm plagued by lust. Two tortures at once, it's too much! I can no longer endure my own self!

He leans forward, looking into the precipice.

Anyone who fell in would be killed. Nothing easier, simply by rolling over to the left; one movement to make! just one.

There now appears

Antony leaps up with a terrified start – thinking he sees his mother come back to life.

But this woman is much older, and unbelievably thin.

K: Uh-huh, but-umm,...ahhh...I'm a little bored.

R: Are you bored? Would you care for a little dance?

K: No, umm...I mean, aren't you bored,too?

R: I am a little bored, but I fight hard to you know keep, you know , not be a you know, sucked into the feeling. I try to, ah, keep mentally alert.

K: Aren't you sick of, uh...

R: ...it all.

K: Yeah.

R: Yeah, its hard not to be. I mean you can get pulled down by all....

K: I mean its, its an ugly world. I mean there's lots of terrible things going on.

R: Yeah, but if you...I think if you, you know if you, if you're, if you just think about those things you're gonna be, you know, pulled into the morass of, you know, just downward thinking and you gotta con...Are you O.K.? Sit down.

A: ...bored with life.

R: You don't think you should be bored with life. Why?

A: I think there are a lot of things going on.

..........(tape cuts out for a few secs)............ ....food, money, going out, dancing.

R: Be a bringer.

K: But, uh, I mean isn't it all, um, it all ends right in the long run. I mean how can, how can you, um, look at a , look at a, look at the cradle without seeing the grave.

R: The grave is always there, looming ahead of us like a door ajar, ah, with a big atrium and water spurts, spurting thru it, you know, and its gonna hit you right in the face if you don't watch out. You gotta laugh at it. You gotta look at it square in the face and take your shoulders and throw them back and lift up your chin and walk thru that door, Right?

A: And before you walk thru that door you have to enjoy your life. Everything that's going on is really nice. If you look at it the right way. It's very important to enjoy your life while you have it.

A shroud knotted around her head hangs with her white hair all the way down her legs, which are lean as two crutches. The brilliance of her ivory-coloured teeth makes her earthy skin duller still. The orbs of her eyes are full of darkness, and in their depths flicker two flames, like grave-lamps.

She says:

Go on. Who can stop you?

ANTONY

stuttering:

I'm frightened of committing a sin!

SHE

rejoins:

But King Saul killed himself! Razis, a just man, killed himself! Saint Pelagia of Antioch killed herself! Domnina of Aleppo and her two daughters – three more saints – killed themselves. And remember all the confessors who outstripped their executioners, impatient for death. To enjoy it the sooner, the virgins of Miletus strangled themselves with their girdles. The philosopher Hegesias, in Syracuse, preached it so effectively that people left the brothels to hang themselves in the fields. The patricians of Rome procure it for their pleasure.

ANTONY

Yes, that love is strong! Many anchorites succumb to it.

THE OLD WOMAN

To do something that makes you God's equal, think of that! He created you and you will destroy his work, you yourself, by your courage, freely. The joy of Herostratus was no greater. And besides, your body has sufficiently mocked your soul for you to take your revenge at last. You won't suffer. It will soon be over. What do you fear? A big black hole? It's empty, maybe?

Antony listens without answering; and on the other side appears:

ANOTHER WOMAN

young and lovely, marvellously so – and he takes her at first for Ammonaria.

But she is taller, blonde as honey, quite plump, with rouge on her cheeks and roses on her head. Her long dress laden with spangles gives out metallic flashes; her fleshy lips are blood-red, and her slightly heavy lids so swimming with languor that she looks blind.

She murmurs:

Flourish, live to the full! Solomon extols pleasure! Go wherever your eyes are drawn and follow your heart's desire!

ANTONY

What pleasure can I find? My heart feels tired, my eyes dim!

SHE

goes on:

Make your way to the district of Racotis, push ajar a blue-painted door; and when you are in the atrium where a water-spout murmurs, a woman will come up to you – in a white silk peplos shot with gold, her hair untied, and with a

laugh like the ring of crotals. She's skilled. In her caress you shall taste the pride of initiation and the stilling of need.

You know nothing, besides, of the thrill of adultery, of the climbs, the abductions, the pleasure of seeing quite naked someone who when clothed was respected.

Have you pressed a virgin in love between your arms? Do you remember her abandoned modesty, and her feelings of remorse slipping away in a flood of gentle tears?

You can see the two of you, can't you, walking in the woods by the light of the moon? The pressure of your joined hands sends a shiver through you both; your eyes meet, pouring into each other as it were immaterial waves, and the heart fills; it bursts; here's a sweet whirlwind, a drunkenness that overflows...

THE OLD WOMAN

One needn't have these joys to be aware of their bitterness! To see them at a distance is enough to put people off. You must be sick of the same monotonous actions, the long-drawn-out days, the ugly world, the stupid sun!

ANTONY

Oh, yes, everything it lights is loathsome!

THE YOUNG WOMAN

Hermit! hermit! you'll find diamonds between the pebbles, fountains under the sand, and a delight in the hazards you despise; the earth is even so beautiful in places that we want to hug it to our hearts.

THE OLD WOMAN

Every evening, as you fall asleep on it, you hope it will soon cover you up!

THE YOUNG WOMAN

Yet you believe in the resurrection of the flesh, which is life's translation into eternity!

The Old Woman, while speaking, has grown even gaunter; and above her skull, which has lost its hair.

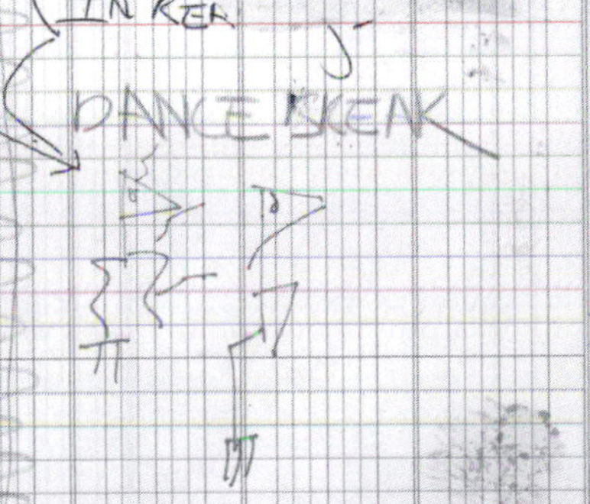

CHANNEL J AUDIO DUB FROM D.C.

R: ...before you start, a little music...any kind. Begin (music) Underneath the apple leaves, down where the sugar patch grows. ..3 dozen joints later..

...a curious thing happened to me there yesterday. I was looking at the uh at the uh electric lights and the uh the spirit came and before you know it I was uh underneath great boulders...Jack, jackin' off and and in the ocean. Two of 3 razor blades later before I lanced the black lace, I looked into the eyes of my betrothed and said...

A: Hey, girl.

R: Hey, girl, what's cookin? There's an echo in my socks.

A: Hey, boy.

R: She said, and I turned around on my tail and went home. Now, this had happened to one about 5 times last week and I was gettin a little bugged. I I I I could barely make out what what I was going to do next - before I knew it a tissue of stars appeared before me. Not even a little eagle but - I was beginning to strain. So, the harmony of the planets gave me a real pain in the old proverbial butt. Now, before spheres started to approach me, I looked towards a little devil of a guy. Here he is...little guy with a mustache... hailing from uh - Cardiff...I'd like to introduce you to - uh him - Mr. Cubby...Cubby what's your last name?

W: Wills

R: Widge?

W: Wills. Wills.

R: Wills, Cubby Wills, Cubby? and you are from...Wales, ah right uh and uh how long you been in this country?

W: Uh, just uh, couple a' years.

R: You like the local girls?

W: They're all right...

R: I'll say. Now you are a local girl aren't you. She's more of a general...anesthesic yeah, now...oh...yeah got little phalanges like ice cubes. You know I'm breathless tonight. There are about 5 stars I'd like to talk to you about...the more you grow, you know, the more you package things. Before you know it you discover that there's a world out there - higher, higher still than...you can possibly multiply.

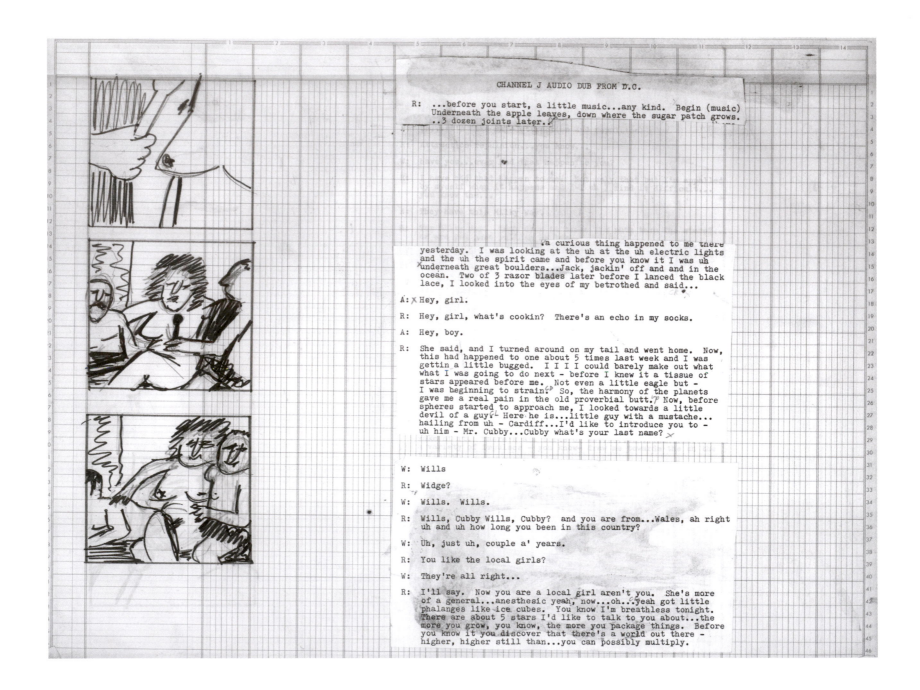

Above and opposite: **Final "Channel J" video storyboard and score: Willem Dafoe**

W: Well, the stars are...

R: The stars are...

W: Multiplied...but at the same time they repell each other.

R: I think that's well taken.

W: Uh...it's like uh - attraction and repulsion.

R: Attraction repulsion...you know...

W: have you...ever had that happen to you?

R: I have had that happen to me. Not only that but I'm appalled by myself when it happens and I-I uh I find it difficult... you know the...

A: They have this Milky Way.

R: The Milky Way. Yeah does it trace the path thru the stars?... or are you just pulling my leg...

A: The Milky Way just happens.

R: It just happened. Was it created or was it molded by the great God Jehovah...

A: No, it just sort of came out.

R: Popped right out,huh?

A: Popped right out.

R: Out of where though?..that seems to be the, uh, the question of the ages. Where? Where did it come from? Do you know?

A: From God.

R: I know that , but I mean, where is...is it he or her? Where is that person?

A: Hisa visa shisa

R: Hisa visa shisa - You know I,I can't think really straight about God and...you know I don't really know what uh to make of it. There's all sorts of so..so..suh...suh..uh... a variety of impulses - you know- draw me towards the uh the infinite

and the universes and one of the big questions I think that we all have uh no matter where we go in life is uh..(a little louder Nancy) you know, you you exist eternally,

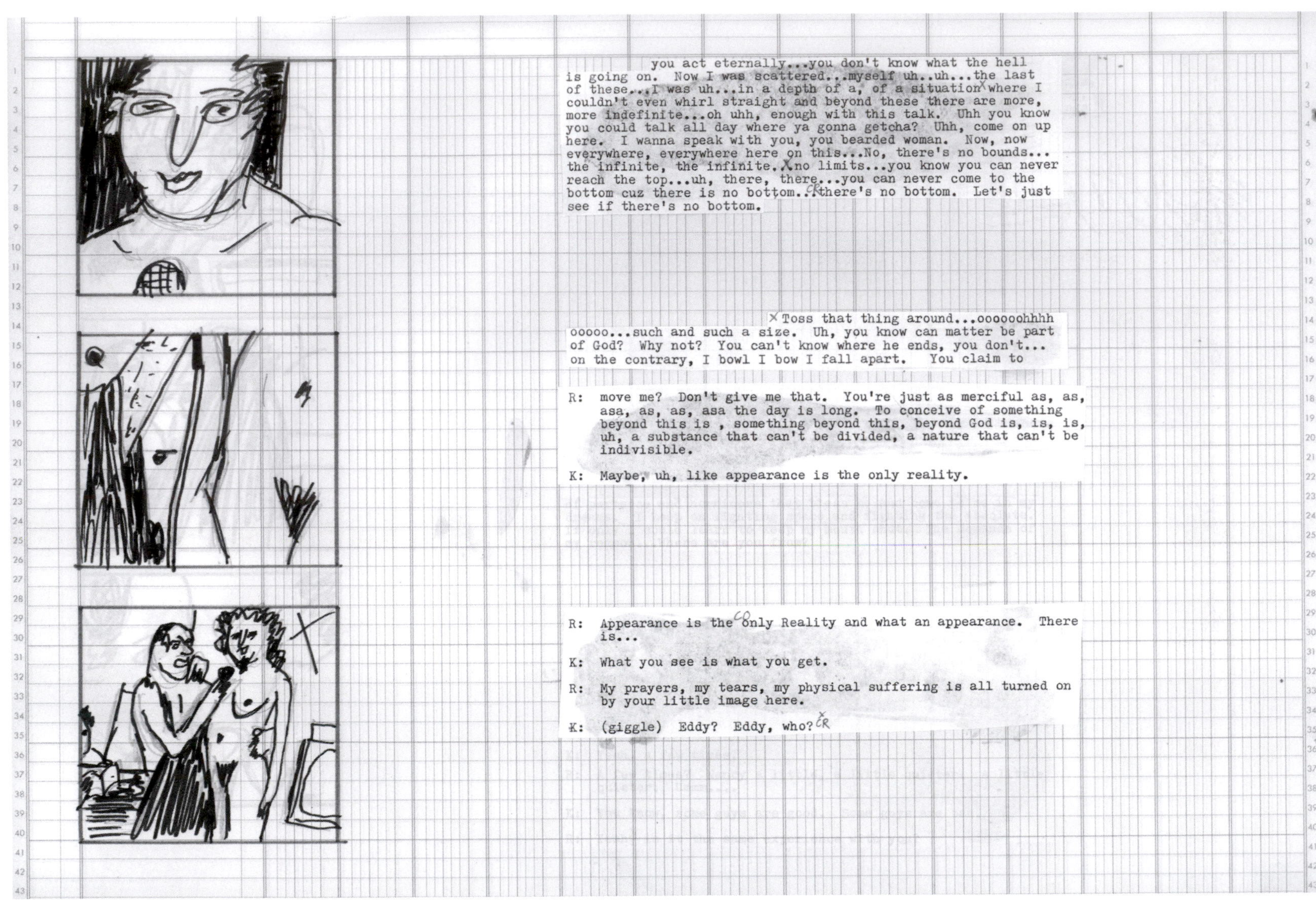

you act eternally...you don't know what the hell is going on. Now I was scattered...myself uh..uh...the last of these...I was uh...in a depth of a, of a situation where I couldn't even whirl straight and beyond these there are more, more indefinite...oh uhh, enough with this talk. Uhh you know you could talk all day where ya gonna getcha? Uhh, come on up here. I wanna speak with you, you bearded woman. Now, now everywhere, everywhere here on this...No, there's no bounds... the infinite, the infinite. no limits...you know you can never reach the top...uh, there, there...you can never come to the bottom cuz there is no bottom.. there's no bottom. Let's just see if there's no bottom.

Toss that thing around...ooooooohhhh ooooo...such and such a size. Uh, you know can matter be part of God? Why not? You can't know where he ends, you don't... on the contrary, I bowl I bow I fall apart. You claim to

R: move me? Don't give me that. You're just as merciful as, as, asa, as, as, asa the day is long. To conceive of something beyond this is , something beyond this, beyond God is, is, is, uh, a substance that can't be divided, a nature that can't be indivisible.

K: Maybe, uh, like appearance is the only reality.

R: Appearance is the only Reality and what an appearance. There is...

K: What you see is what you get.

R: My prayers, my tears, my physical suffering is all turned on by your little image here.

K: (giggle) Eddy? Eddy, who?

Above and opposite: **Final "Channel J" video storyboard and score: Willem Dafoe**

R: !Eddy, who? There must be some...medicines? Medicines! Please, what is it?...OK...if I could feel love or pain, pangs of pity, I could, I wouldn't be able to descend to the , to the feelings of portense and horniness that bless me and come to me in my dreams. I keep on fighting space and fighting the absolute. If only I could learn to keep my mouth shut. The demands of my reason...Where are you from?

K: Baltimore.

R: Baltimore, Maryland. What a town! Umm, I once went impotent in Baltimore. I was with this young woman and uh, things didn't go right you know, that happens. You musta had the same thing happen to you, I mean, with guys that have been with ya.

K: Yeah, a few times.

R: A few times? Nancy a little, a little quieter. A little quieter. Ummm....

K: You know, some guys are good. Some guys are bad.

R: Yeah, is it the same experience with you?

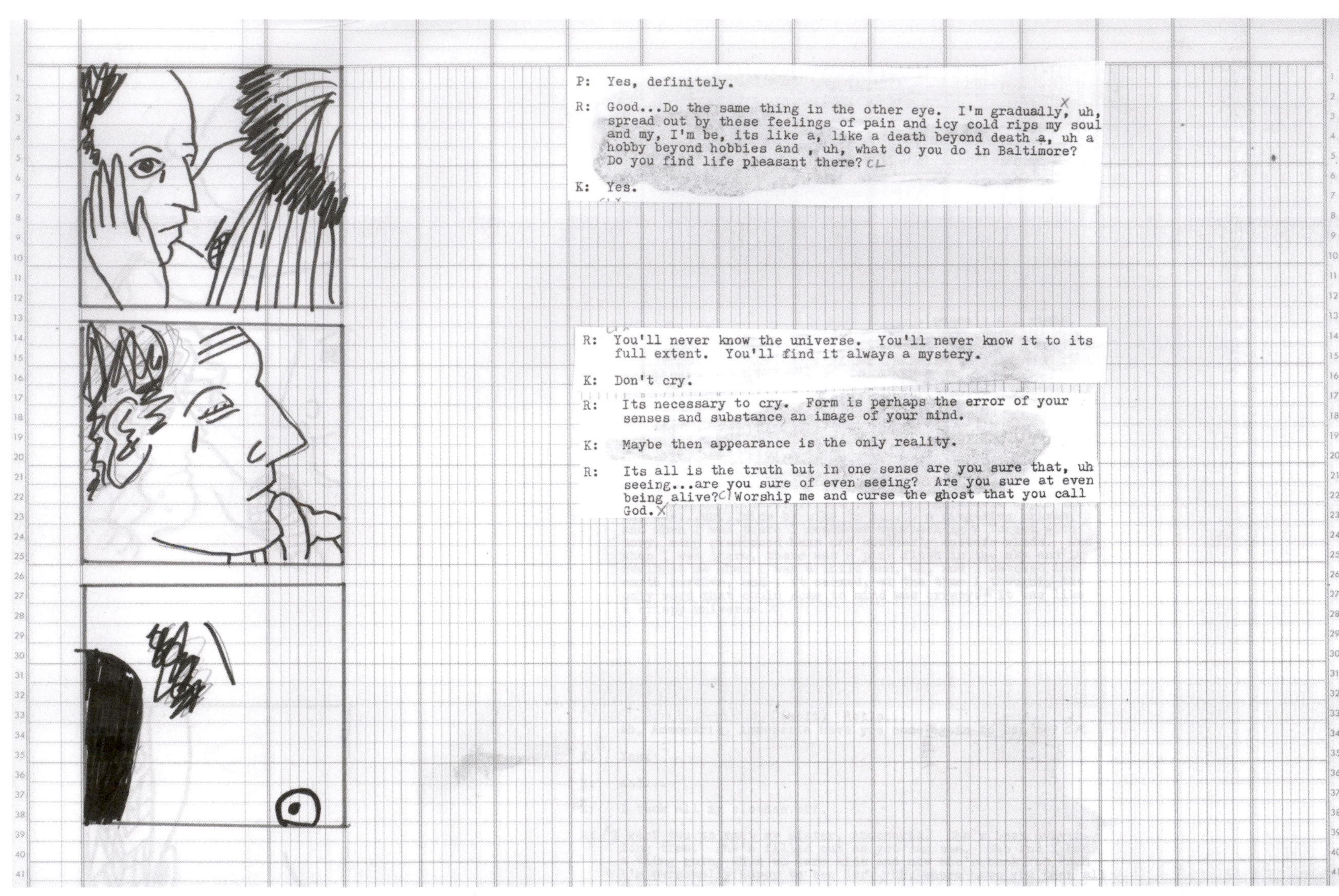

P: Yes, definitely.
R: Good...Do the same thing in the other eye. I'm gradually, uh, spread out by these feelings of pain and icy cold rips my soul and my, I'm be, its like a, like a death beyond death a, uh a hobby beyond hobbies and , uh, what do you do in Baltimore? Do you find life pleasant there?
K: Yes.
R: You'll never know the universe. You'll never know it to its full extent. You'll find it always a mystery.
K: Don't cry.
R: Its necessary to cry. Form is perhaps the error of your senses and substance an image of your mind.
K: Maybe then appearance is the only reality.
R: Its all is the truth but in one sense are you sure that, uh seeing...are you sure of even seeing? Are you sure at even being alive? Worship me and curse the ghost that you call God.

 Final "Channel J" video storyboard and score: Willem Dafoe

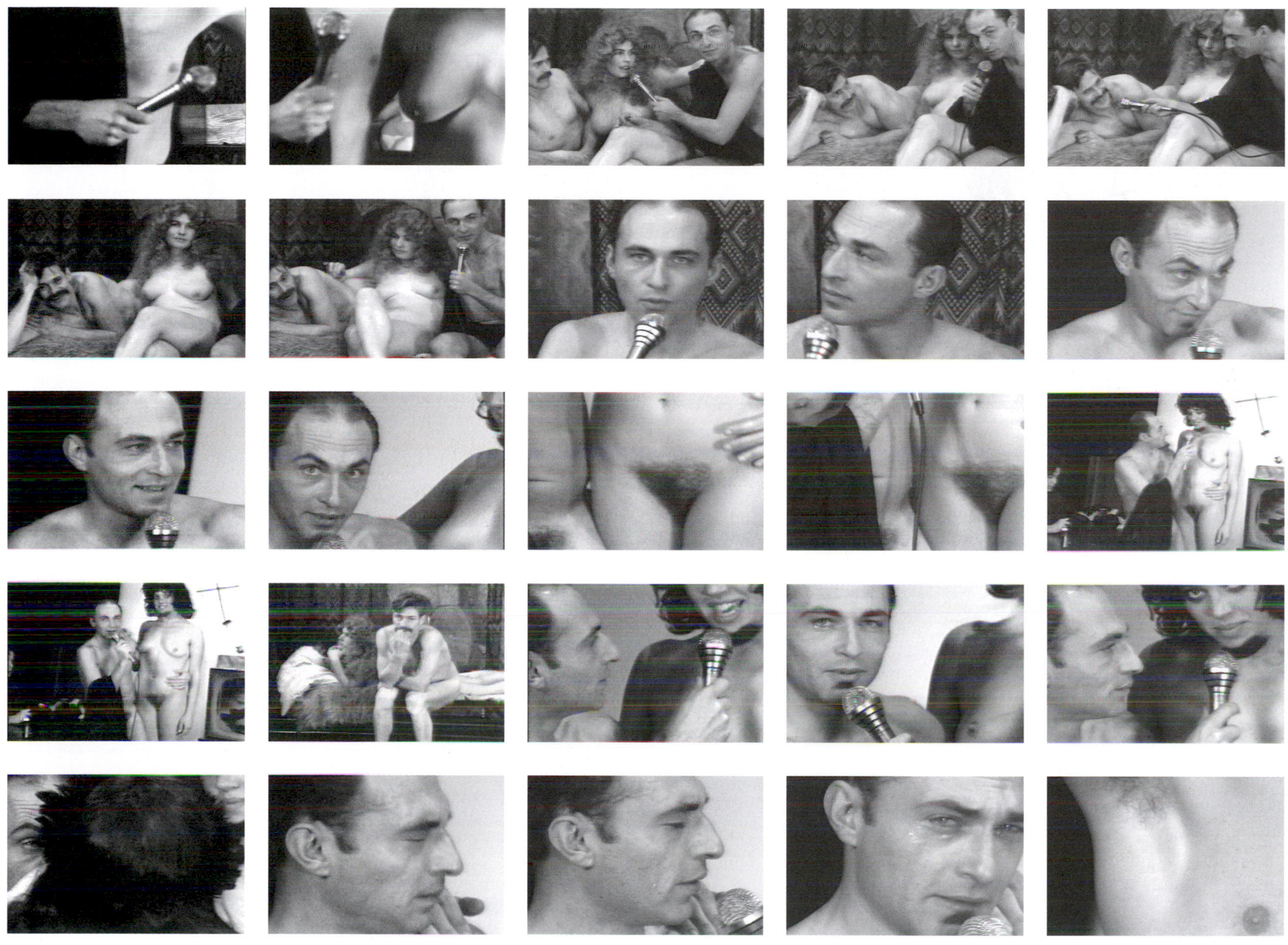

Video stills: "Channel J" show tape

 Frank Dell's The Temptation of St. Antony, "Episode 4: The Party"

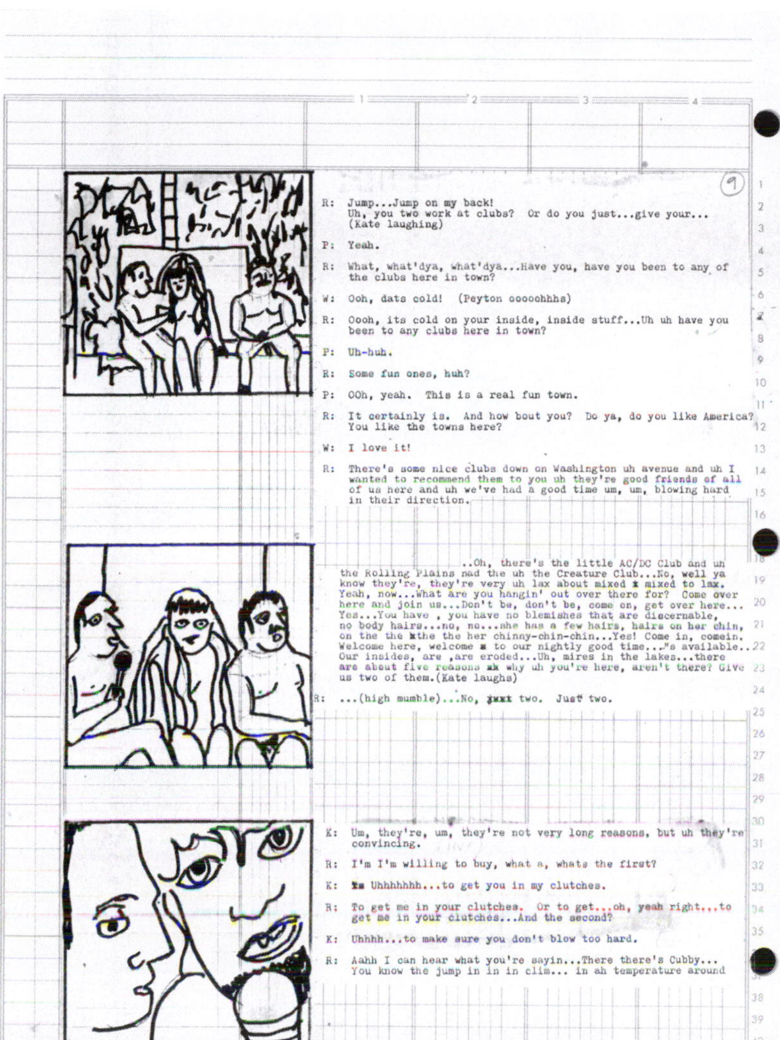

(9)

R: Jump...Jump on my back!
Uh, you two work at clubs? Or do you just...give your...
(Kate laughing)

P: Yeah.

R: What, what'dya, what'dya...Have you, have you been to any of the clubs here in town?

W: Ooh, dats cold! (Peyton ooooohhhs)

R: Oooh, its cold on your inside, inside stuff...Uh uh have you been to any clubs here in town?

P: Uh-huh.

R: Some fun ones, huh?

P: OOh, yeah. This is a real fun town.

R: It certainly is. And how bout you? Do ya, do you like America? You like the towns here?

W: I love it!

R: There's some nice clubs down on Washington uh avenue and uh I wanted to recommend them to you uh they're good friends of all of us here and uh we've had a good time um, um, blowing hard in their direction.

..Oh, there's the little AC/DC Club and uh the Rolling Plains nad the uh the Creature Club...No, well ya know they're, they're very uh lax about mixed x mixed to lax. Yeah, now...What are you hangin' out over there for? Come over here and join us...Don't be, don't be, come on, get over here... Yes...You have , you have no blemishes that are discernable, no body hairs...no, no...she has a few hairs, hairs on her chin, on the the xthe the her chinny-chin-chin...Yes! Come in, comein. Welcome here, welcome x to our nightly good time..."s available.. Our insides, are ,are eroded...Uh, mires in the lakes...there are about five reasons xx why uh you're here, aren't there? Give us two of them.(Kate laughs)

R: ...(high mumble)...No, xxxx two. Just two.

K: Um, they're, um, they're not very long reasons, but uh they're convincing.

R: I'm I'm willing to buy, what a, whats the first?

K: xx Uhhhhhhh...to get you in my clutches.

R: To get me in your clutches. Or to get...oh, yeah right...to get me in your clutches...And the second?

K: Uhhhh...to make sure you don't blow too hard.

R: Aahh I can hear what you're sayin...There there's Cubby... You know the jump in in in clim... in ah temperature around

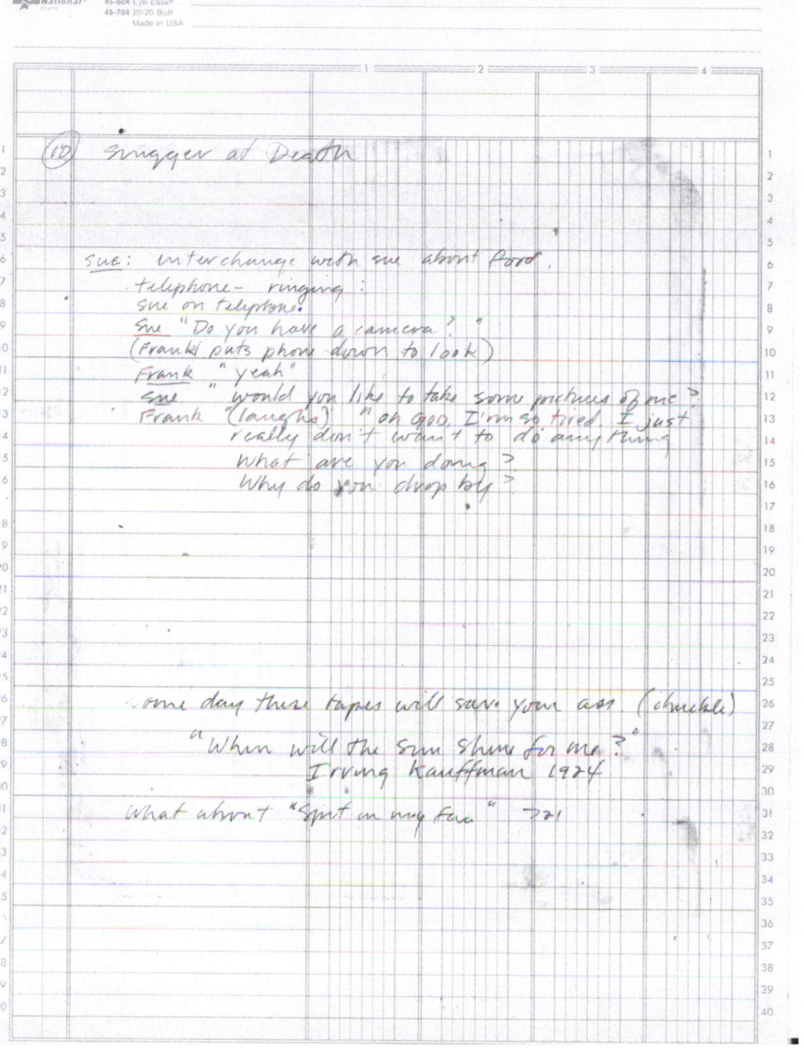

(10) Snigger at Death

Sue: interchange with Sue about food,
telephone – ringing:
Sue on telephone:
Sue "Do you have a camera?"
(Frank puts phone down to look)
Frank "yeah"
Sue "would you like to take some pictures of me?"
Frank (laughs) "oh God, I'm so tired. I just really don't want to do anything
What are you doing?
Why do you drop by?

Some day these tapes will save your ass (chuckle)

"When will the sun shine for me?"
Irving Kauffman 1924

What about "Spit in my Face"

“Channel J” score with Elizabeth LeCompte’s notes

 Video stills: "Channel J" show tape

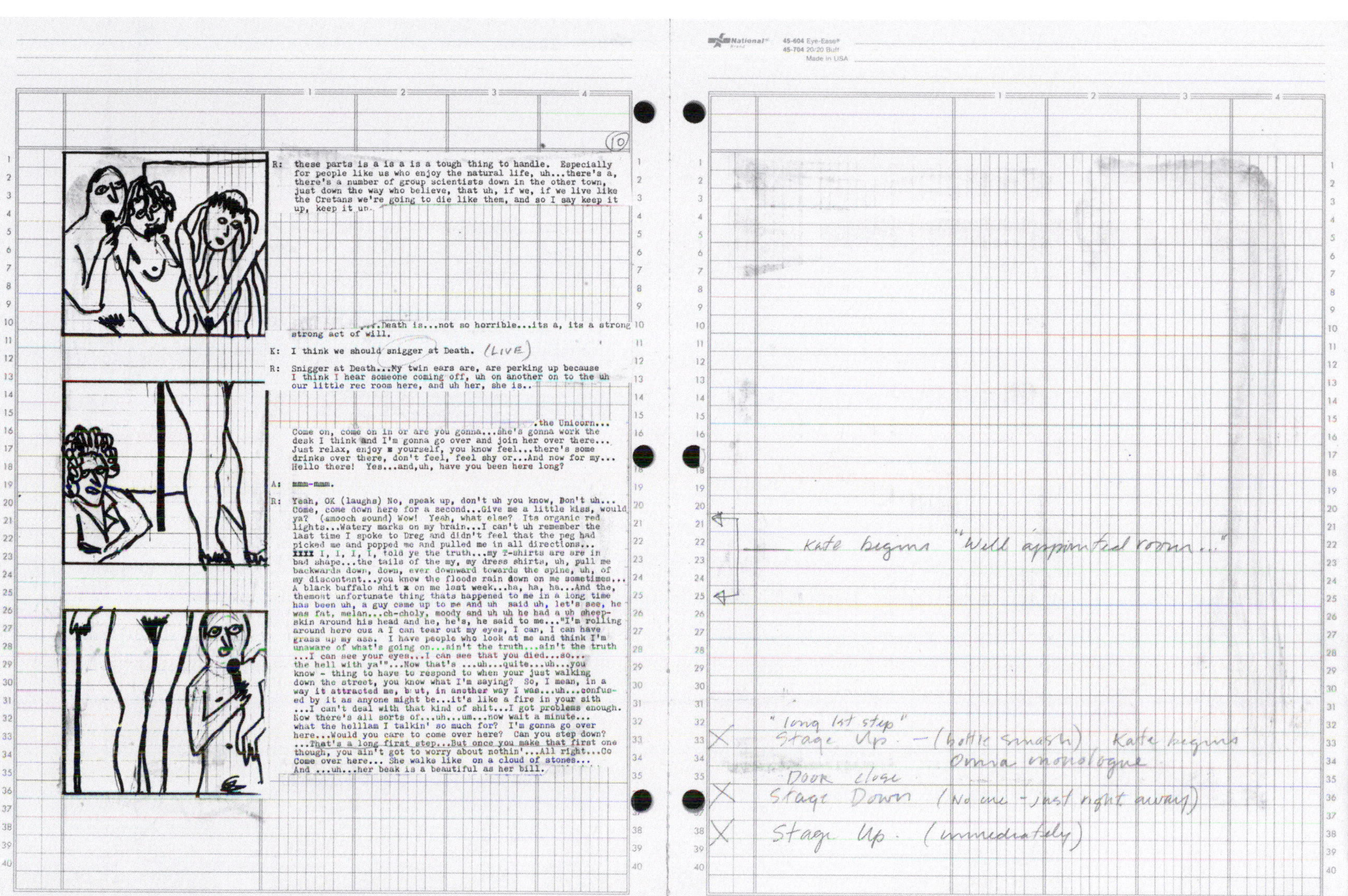

(10)

R: these parts is a is a is a tough thing to handle. Especially for people like us who enjoy the natural life, uh...there's a, there's a number of group scientists down in the other town, just down the way who believe, that uh, if we, if we live like the Cretans we're going to die like them, and so I say keep it up, keep it up.

...Death is...not so horrible...its a, its a strong strong act of will.

K: I think we should snigger at Death. (LIVE)

R: Snigger at Death...My twin ears are, are perking up because I think I hear someone coming off, uh on another on to the uh our little rec room here, and uh her, she is..

.the Unicorn...

Come on, come on in or are you gonna...she's gonna work the desk I think and I'm gonna go over and join her over there... Just relax, enjoy x yourself, you know feel...there's some drinks over there, don't feel, feel shy or...And now for my... Hello there! Yes...and,uh, have you been here long?

A: mmm-mmm.

R: Yeah, OK (laughs) No, speak up, don't uh you know, Don't uh... Come, come down here for a second...Give me a little kiss, would ya? (smooch sound) Wow! Yeah, what else? Its organic red lights...Watery marks on my brain...I can't uh remember the last time I spoke to Dreg and didn't feel that the peg had picked me and popped me and pulled me in all directions... XXXX I, I, I, I, told ye the truth...my T-shirts are are in bad shape...the tails of the my, my dress shirts, uh, pull me backwards down, down, ever downward towards the spine, uh, of my discontent...you know the floods rain down on me sometimes... A black buffalo shit x on me last week...ha, ha, ha...And the, themost unfortunate thing thats happened to me in a long time has been uh, a guy came up to me and uh said uh, let's see, he was fat, melan...ch-choly, moody and uh uh he had a uh sheep-skin around his head and he, he's, he said to me..."I'm rolling around here cuz a I can tear out my eyes, I can, I can have grass up my ass. I have people who look at me and think I'm unaware of what's going on...ain't the truth...ain't the truth ...I can see your eyes...I can see that you died...so... the hell with ya'"...Now that's ...uh...quite...uh...you know - thing to have to respond to when your just walking down the street, you know what I'm saying? So, I mean, in a way it attracted me, b ut, in another way I was...uh...confus-ed by it as anyone might be...it's like a fire in your sith ...I can't deal with that kind of shit...I got problems enough. Now there's all sorts of...uh...um...now wait a minute... what the helllam I talkin' so much for? I'm gonna go over here...Would you care to come over here? Can you step down? ...That's a long first step...But once you make that first one though, you ain't got to worry about nothin'...All right...Co Come over here... She walks like on a cloud of stones... And ...uh...her beak is a beautiful as her bill.

Kate begins "Well appointed room..."

"long 1st step"

X Stage Up. – (bottle smash) Kate begins Omna monologue

Door close

X Stage Down (No one – just right away)

X Stage Up. (immediately)

"Channel J" score with Elizabeth LeCompte's notes

Page 11

Ring Telephone twice (1)

SUE - (2) FRANK, You've got a phone call on line two

Cubby - Frank, Hey Frankie

FRANKIE - ok tune me in to the video ? (3) Am I in the right place?

Cubby - I don't know you go to look in the mirror

Frank - Cubby?, (4)

Cubby - You've got to look in yours eyes and say "WOT Am I doing here"

Frank - (5)

Cubby - Especially after I show you all this

(8) → FRANK - (BUZZ) - what's next

Sue - DANCE BREAK, FRANK

Cubby - I mean come with me.

FRANK - Dieter, music please. Cubby,
I got to work the girls in the dance (music up) Ah, the Queen of Sheba.

Sue - Episode II

Frank - Bats, bats in the air, silk clumpers, my nostrils quiver, my dress shimmer, my purse opens and she's come. BUZZ (6)

Sue - Frank, down forget you've got cubby on hold.

Frank - Fine, tune me back in. what time is it?

Sue - Ah, quarter to Five

Frank - what is that, California time? (7)

Cubby - It's about time to get to the studio

Frank - well, its about 8:30 here, does that make it 5:30 or 11:30 out there. You know, I can never figure out the California New York time differential, I mean it baffles me

Cubby - I'll drop by when I'm in full drag.

(1) x from DL moniter to DR monitor, ring phone twice during pass
(2) swing hips in time to video, then turn to face video to cue sue
(3) x to center spot
(4) look up to video, wave
(6) Ring buzzer
(7) Bounce dance at beginning of song (after intro)
(8) Ring buzzer

 Left: **Early draft of "Episode 2: The Dance Break"** Right: **Video stills from "Cubby Visit One" show tape**

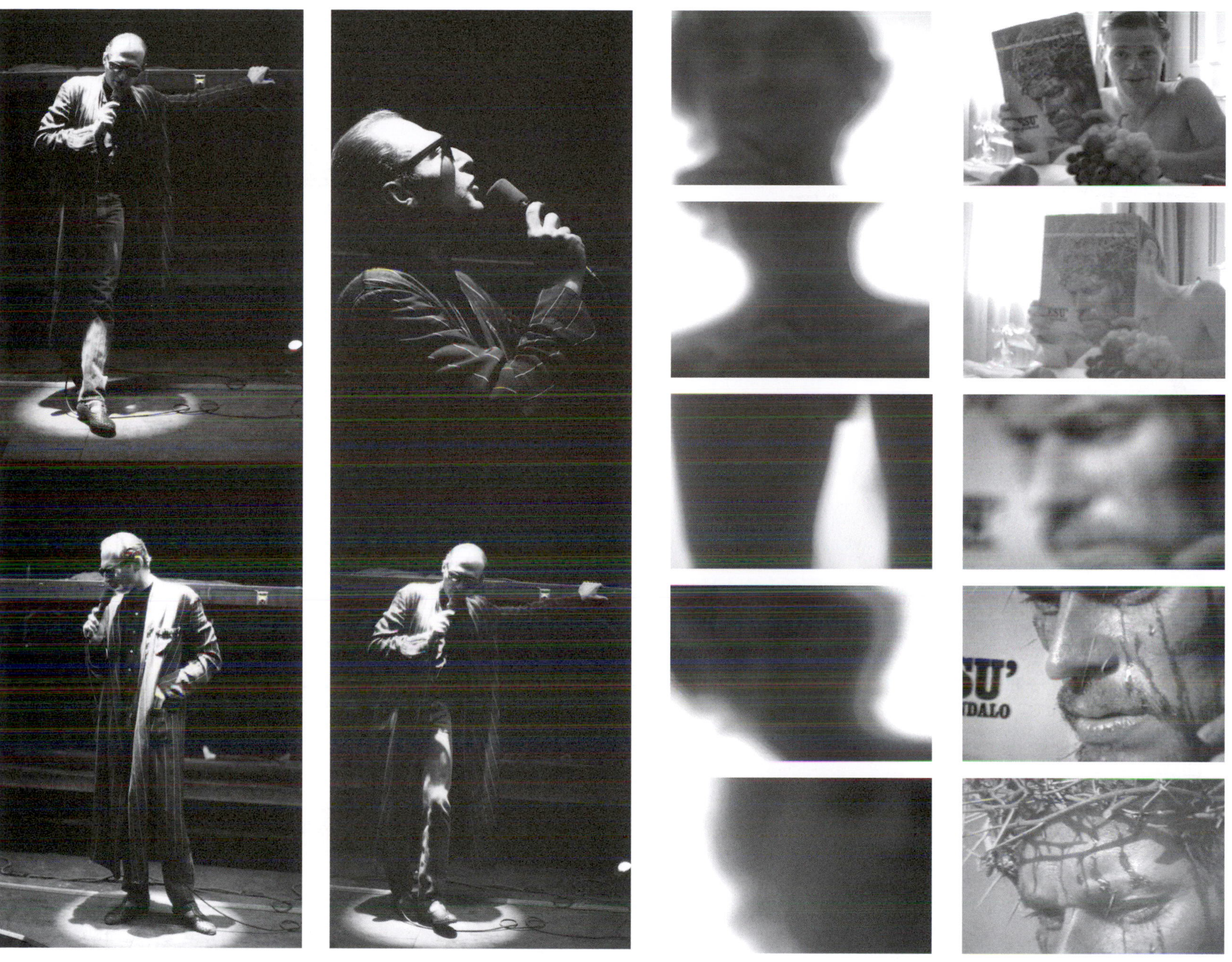

Left: *Frank Dell's The Temptation of St. Antony* Center: **Video stills from "Cubby Visit Two"** Right: **Video stills from "Cubby Visit Three"**

ONNA / Phyllis

I find this a well-appointed room. I see the Hartz mountains out my window. There is my stuffed parrot under glass. My books lie about me, some open to passages. Passages which give me the courage to go on. And I will go on. I think again of dead Pierre, dead in the trench a mortal enemy to my country, he to whom all my love was given. . . .

"watery marks on my brain ... I can't remember the last time I talked to Dreg"

Cue for: "Phyllis, I'm going to begin: now" tie blindfold on and begin

ONNA/ROSE

I find this a well appointed room. I can just see the Heart's Mountains out my window. I can see my parrot under glass. Somewhere I hear an alarm sounding. I'll ignore it for now. I have too much to think about. Too many soughts, deep soughts.

My books lie about me, some open to passages, passages which give me the courage to go on. And I will go on. I think again of dead Pierre, dead in a trench, a mortal enemy to my people, he to whom all my love was given. Over to SL door Bottle Smash

"I want you to keep your mouth shut and I'll do the talking."

I find this a pink-tinged room. The jagged well-appointed peaks of the Transylvanian Alps from out my window. There is my parents under glass. My books lie about me in confusion, some open to passages time has chosen for me. And the dust collected. I feel so sad this morning.

1.

ONNA/ROSE 2

I find this a well-appointed room. I can just see the Heart's Mountains out my window. I can see my parrot under glass. Somewhere I hear an alarm sounding. I'll ignore it for now. I have too much to think about. Too many soughts, deep soughts. Ah! Ah! Oh! Oh! Mon dieu! Mon dieu!

My books lie about me, some open to passages, passages which give me the courage to go on. And I will go on. I think again of dead Pierre, the actor, dead in a trench, or wherever. a mortal enemy to people, all people, he to whom all my love was given. That was very anti-social of me, don't you think? Very selfish to love like that. To love a plague. del Fuego. I have always been his, always been a girl to draw conclusions.

[CROWD APPLAUDS AND SMASHES MUGS ON LONG TABLES. ONNA/ROSE LAYS BACK ON THE BED. HERR DIENST STANDS AND MAKES AN ADDRESS.]

Doors open same time

DIENST

BRAVO! I like this piece and I like this girl. She is contemporary. I have seen her in the streets and I have known her in the drawing rooms.

Cue Phyllis: Does a glance talk? Does a look see something? Who can read other people seeing, what other people say when they see?

Tell Anna to bring drinks. Slam door

2.

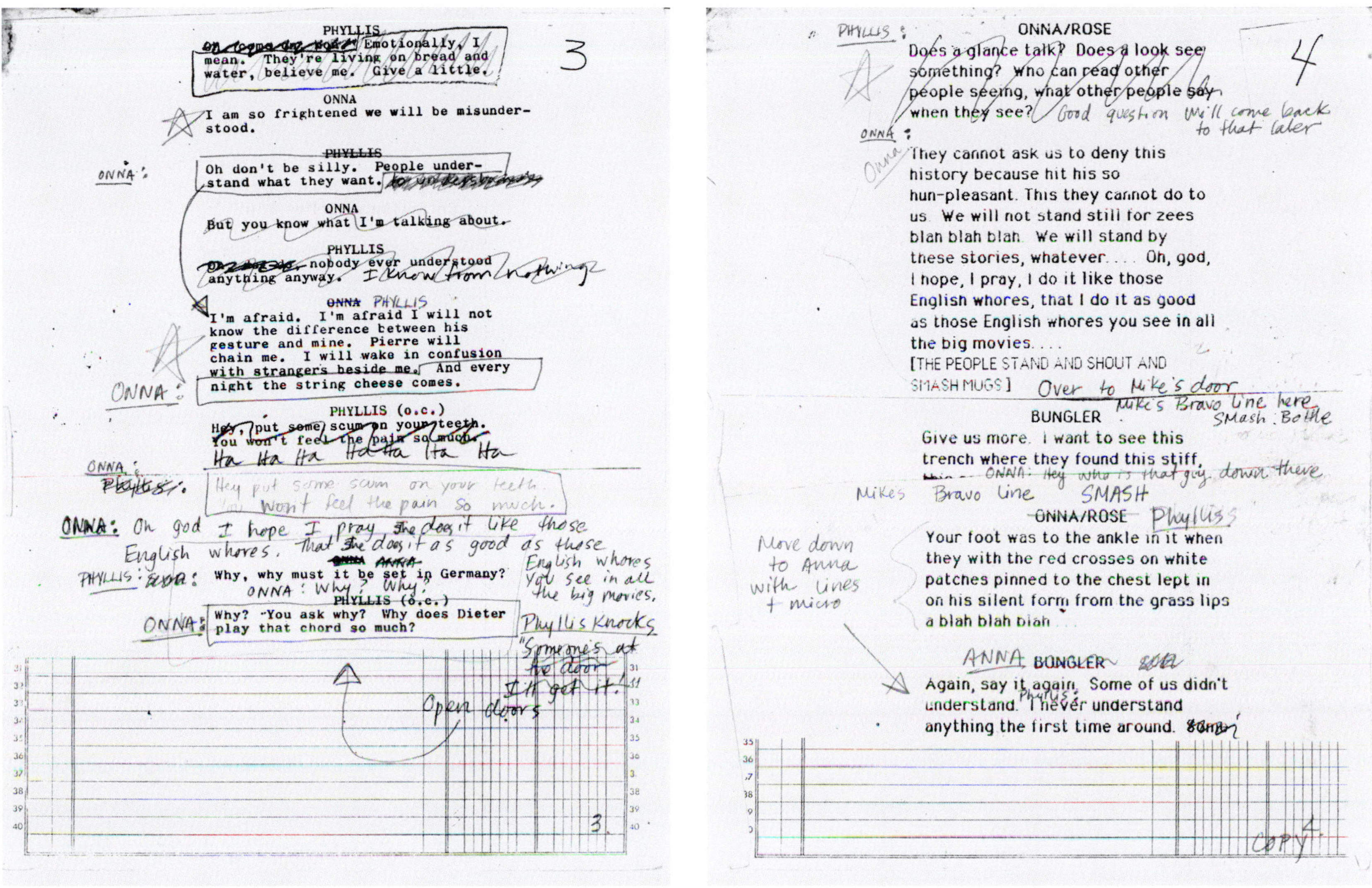

3

PHYLLIS

Emotionally, I mean. They're living on bread and water, believe me. Give a little.

ONNA

I am so frightened we will be misunderstood.

ONNA:

PHYLLIS

Oh don't be silly. People understand what they want.

ONNA

But you know what I'm talking about.

PHYLLIS

nobody ever understood anything anyway. I know from nothing

~~ONNA~~ PHYLLIS

I'm afraid. I'm afraid I will not know the difference between his gesture and mine. Pierre will chain me. I will wake in confusion with strangers beside me. And every night the string cheese comes.

ONNA:

PHYLLIS (o.c.)

Hey, put some scum on your teeth. You won't feel the pain so much.

Ha Ha Ha Ha Ha Ha Ha

ONNA: ~~Phyllis~~: Hey put some scum on your teeth. You won't feel the pain so much.

ONNA: Oh god I hope I pray ~~she~~ does it like those English whores. That ~~she~~ does it as good as those English whores you see in all the big movies.

~~ONNA~~ ~~ANNA~~

PHYLLIS: Why, why must it be set in Germany?

ONNA: Why? Why?

PHYLLIS (o.c.)

ONNA: Why? You ask why? Why does Dieter play that chord so much?

Phyllis Knocks "Someone's at the door" I'll get it!

Open doors

3.

4

PHYLLIS:

ONNA/ROSE

Does a glance talk? Does a look see something? Who can read other people seeing, what other people say when they see? Good question We'll come back to that later

ONNA:

They cannot ask us to deny this history because hit his so hun-pleasant. This they cannot do to us. We will not stand still for zees blah blah blah. We will stand by these stories, whatever. . . . Oh, god, I hope, I pray, I do it like those English whores, that I do it as good as those English whores you see in all the big movies. . . .

[THE PEOPLE STAND AND SHOUT AND SMASH MUGS] Over to Mike's door

Mike's Bravo line here

SMash: Bottle

BUNGLER

Give us more. I want to see this trench where they found this stiff.

ONNA: Hey who is that guy down there

Mikes Bravo line SMASH

~~ONNA/ROSE~~ Phylliss

Move down to Anna with lines + micro

Your foot was to the ankle in it when they with the red crosses on white patches pinned to the chest lept in on his silent form from the grass lips a blah blah blah . . .

ANNA ~~BUNGLER~~

Again, say it again. Some of us didn't understand. PHYLLIS: I never understand anything the first time around.

COPY 4

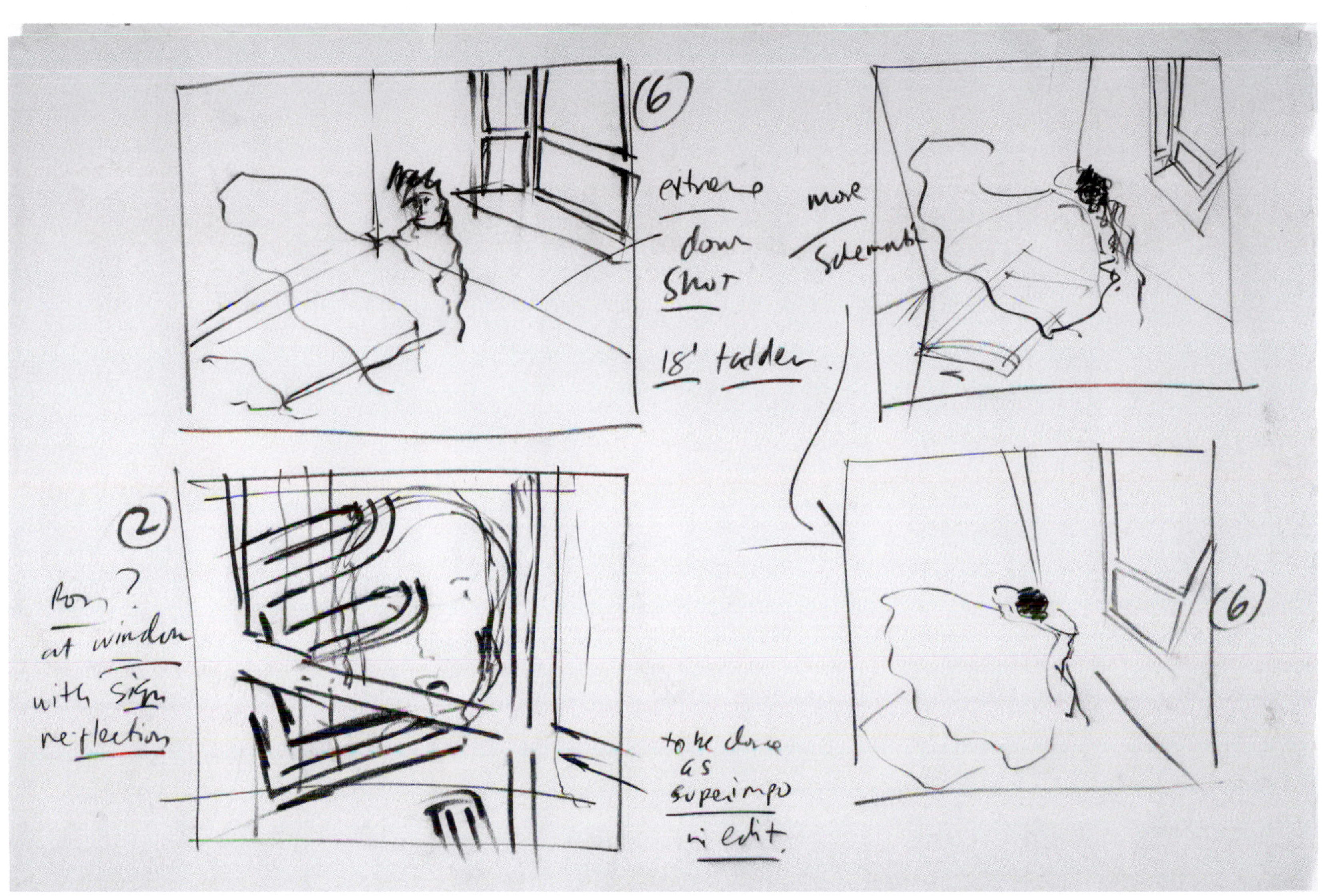

(6)
extreme
down
shot
more
(2)
at window
with sign
reflection
(6)

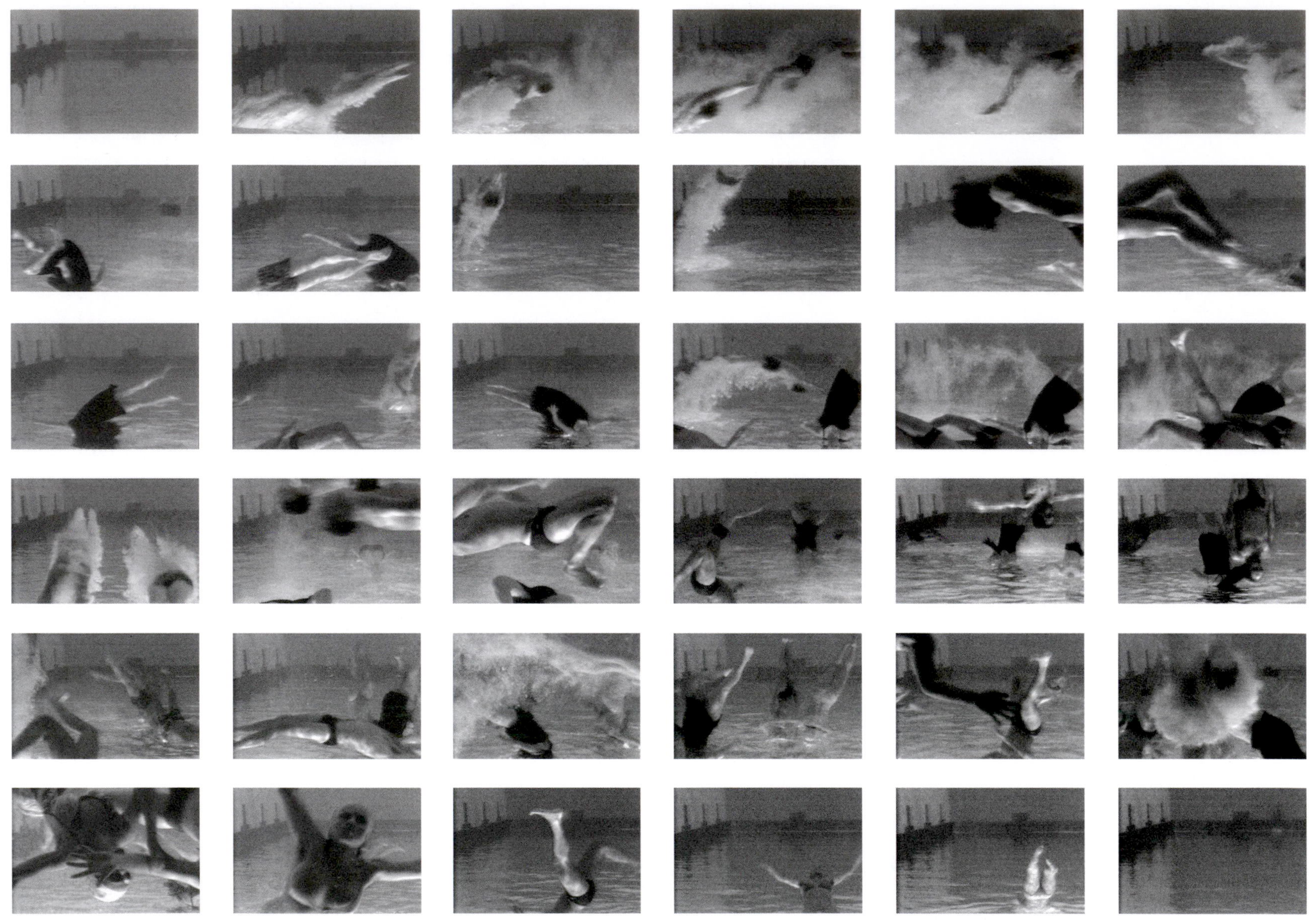

 Above: **Video stills: "Hofstra Pool" show tape** Opposite: **Set drawing: Jim Clayburgh**

NOTES:

Sound and Lighting booth:
2)Tables - 2 at +.90 x .50 x 2.0m
3)2 Music stands
4)4 Tall stools
5)6 worklites
There should be some black fabric available to mask the booth and to surround the tables. Carpet would be wonderful if you have some. It should be possible for the technicians to move without making noise.

Ladders:
We will need a lifts and ladders that allow us to work at all the heights, including both grids, from both the floor and from the stage, all speaker, lighting and rigging positions. There should be enough so that 4 people can be working in the air at the same time.

Front of House Lighting:
The focus on these lights is exact so this pipe must be stiffened. It can not move or roll.

Grid: See the grid drawing for exact placement of pipes. The grid must be secured so that it can not move, shake rattle or roll.

Audience: The audience structure has a different center line than the room. We should try and arrange the seats so that this is not problematic. I have added a row of chairs on the floor.

The chairs should alternate. Carpet makes the structure quieter and lessens the noise as people shift in their seats before walking out.

We Supply:
2 Toa speakers and hanging hardware
Florescent Fixtures

Sound:
We will bring the cable that bridges the Toa SM68 Speakers, but will need the runs of cable from Speaker #9 to the amps and from Speaker #10 to the Amps. The Toa speakers accept a 1/4" phono jack.

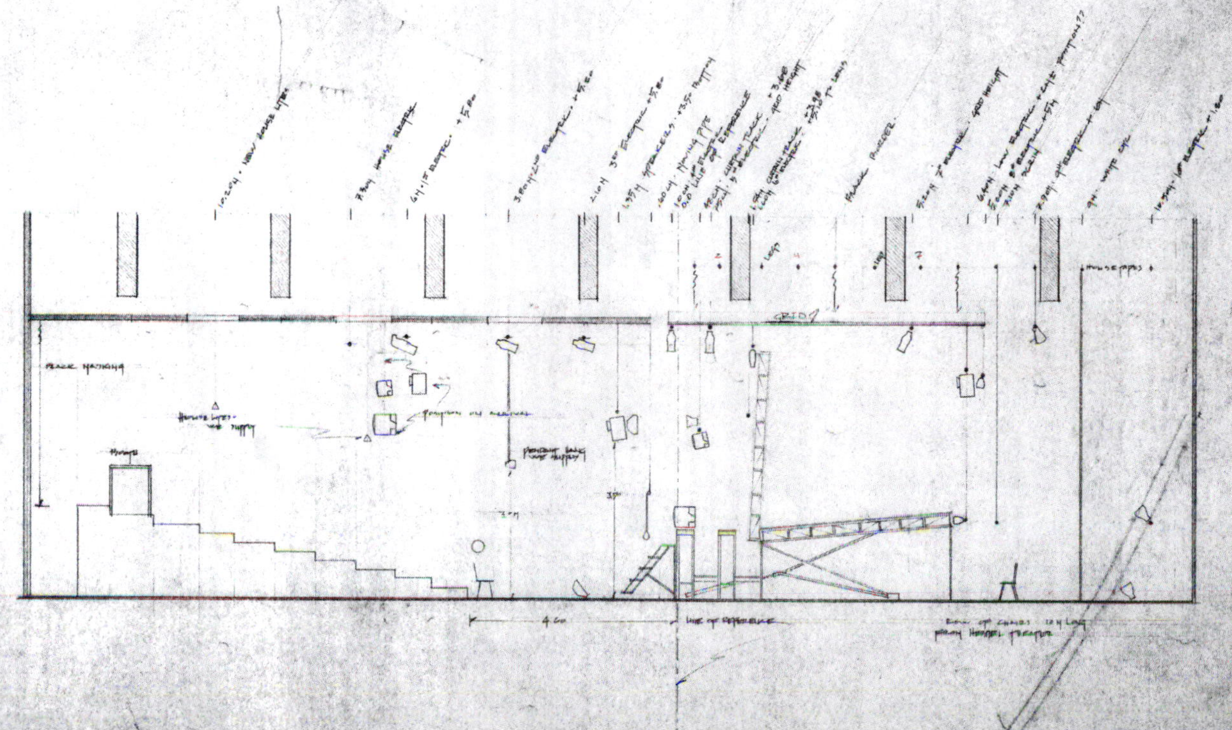

· THE WOOSTER GROUP ·
THE ROAD TO IMMORTALITY - PART 3
FRANK DELL'S
"THE TEMPTATION OF ST. ANTONY"
HEBBEL BERLIN
· SECTION ·

DIRECTOR: LIZ LECOMPTE
SCALE 1:50
DATE: 9/3/94

 Above and opposite: ***Frank Dell's The Temptation of St. Antony***, "Episode 4: The Party"

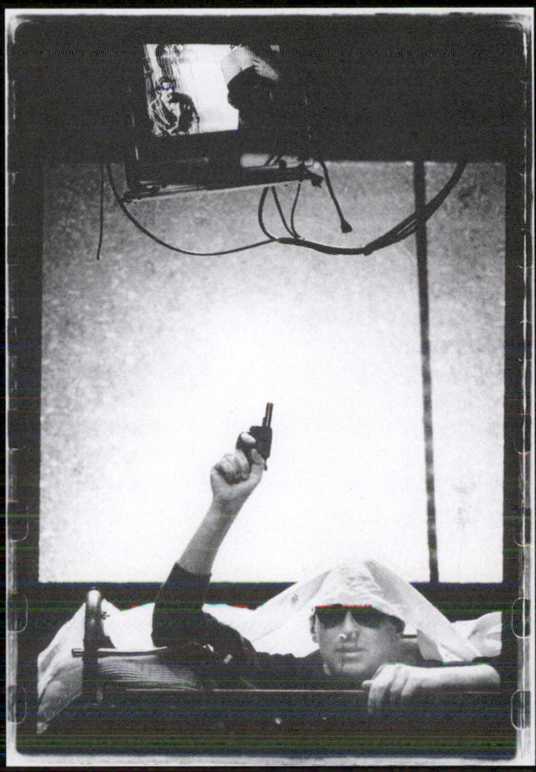

 Frank Dell's The Temptation of St. Antony, "Episode 4: The Party"

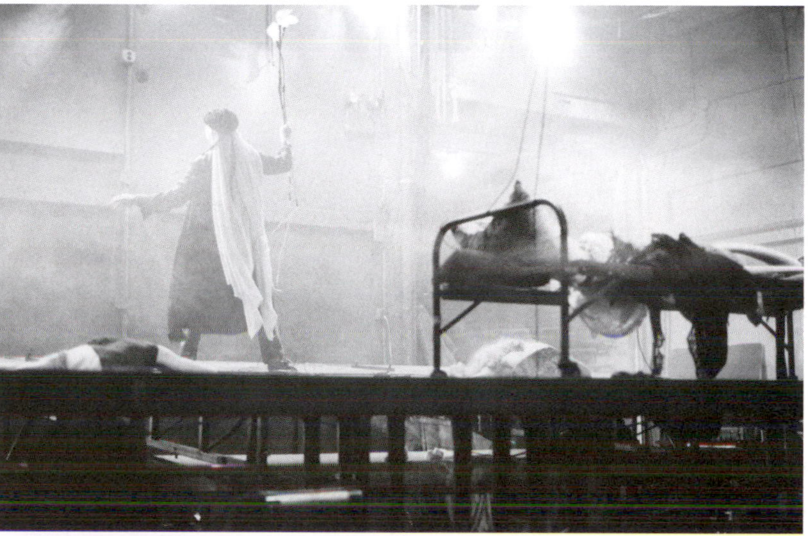
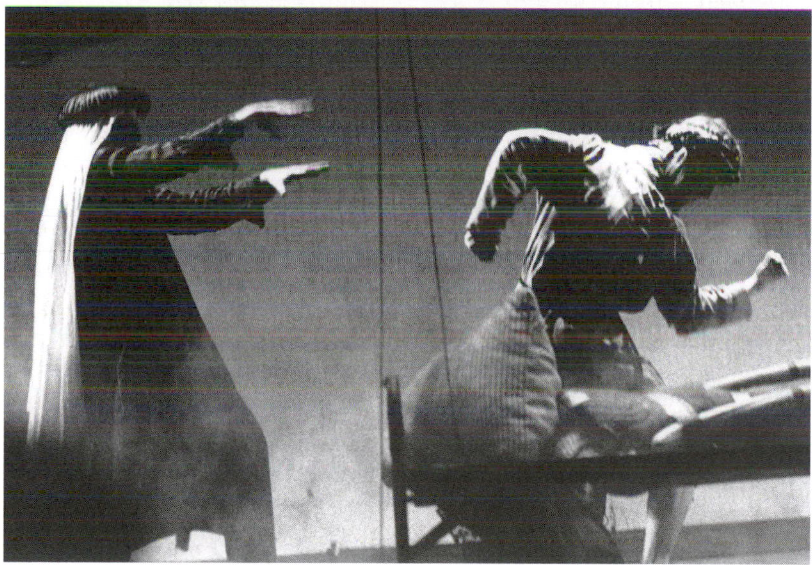

MICHAEL von STUMM

I

MICHAEL'S SCORE

the play starts. i wait backstage, smoke a cigarette, whatever. when the stage rises for the first (1st) time (mary's cue; "dieter, bring the stage up...) i ready myself. when the stage reaches its apex peyton and katexxix climb the ramp and enter from the stage left door. they close the door and i climb the ramp. i climb the stage ribs and hang immediately behind the stage left door. when phyllis reaches "my books lie about me" onna knocks and throws open the door. i hang as long as the door is open. when they close i climb down and buckle myself onto the back of sl door. i wait (calmly) until " ...it's not a parrot it's my parents..." at which point kate knocks and throws open the door once again. a bit of conversation ensues about parties and drinks and kate close the door i reach down and pick up the ice bucket which has been placed to the left of the door and hold it in my ~~left~~ Right arm while x i grasp the Right handle with my left hand which i have crossed over my body to hold myself to the door. door is openedwhen phyllis says "in all the big movies". i grin a bit and hand the bucket to kate. i hang around and mug for a fewmins. until phyllis says (yet again)"...in all the big movies" when i read from a book i have extracted from my left bathrobe pocket: "give us more...stiff".

MICHAEL von STUMM

II

peyton comes over, introduces herself chats, i read onna smashes a bottle, hands me the ice bucket back and shuts the door while peyton holds the mic. the door shuts and the ice spills. i pick up what ice is on peytons skirt so it doesnt fall later on, put kate's wig around my neck &take off moustache. (oh yeah i forgot kate puts moustache on me back there when peyton is chatting with me) i wait until peyton says "morphine" & then start across the back of window with arms outstretched. i wait in this position until i hear kate say"going on and blah blah blah" &then i knock 4 times. i run (not walk) to the stage r doorwhere i strap myself in and pull the wig into beard position, the door opens almost imm. kate hands me the mic. &i recite "i have wired to jacques..." while i do this the stage goes down. when it has reached its nadir i am through. i then perform a dance which consists of hitting my head with my right hand in time to the mucic, as the stage rises. when the stage has risen i stand in the darkness, adjust my glasses, listen to the sounds, wait for kate to come over and pull my beard(wig) into hair(wig) position which she does every nite like clockwork.(go figure) the lights are on bythis t time. i stand for a while and listen to the girls banter until kate says " im hurtin' myself ..." then i remove my book from my left hand pocket and read " im hurtin' myself..." i put the book away

 Above and opposite: **Performance score: Michael Stumm**

MICHAEL von STUMM

III

and remove a blood capsule from my right hand pocket. i wait for kate to say "i got nauseous..." and i say "phil spector" kate gets angry and argues with me she ultimately hits me with a breakaway but not before i put the blood cap into my mouth so that after she hits me i can bite it and spit blood over my hands &face. i brush glass off me until kate slams the doo door which she does after she says "fuk you PH." i unstrap myself and take off the wig which i hand to kate over the stage right ell. i then tiptoe down the s-r ramp and across the back wall to the tunnel where i leave my bookand wipe off blood smoke a cig &wait for the cue in the OTILLIA scenewhich is : kate handing me the phone and saying "here take this and pretend youre talkin' on phone" i pretend to talk and listen on phone until"wee are selling sex just like everybody else"". i whoosh across back ramp to s-r side where i bloody up my face and disarray my clothes, change to breakaway glasses &strap myself in (again) kate opens the door when peyton says"that must be dienst let him in". kate hands me the mic. which i than pretend to hold. she chats to herself ~~ix~~ for a while & then takes it back & proceeds to undress and generally tickle & abuse me until; (frank) "ill make a eunuch..." she rushes offleaving me to say " i dont think i trust you anymore". sue slams door.

MICHAEL von STUMM

IV

i un-buckle &straighten up(tie my robe cahnge glasses comb my hair) grasp my sheet music firmly and crawl to the s-r ell and peer over gradually pulling myself over . i pull the standing mic. close to me. i wait until its my turn &then sing the 2nd verse. when the song ends i pretend to sleep until peyton so rudely opens the doorat which point i push the standing mic. away from me and scurry down the s-r ramp. i grab the megaphone(cap) &and dash across the back wall to the tunnel where i tie the meg. to my robe pick up my book and a cig (which i lite) and dash up the s-left ramp where i grabthe table (over the tv) and proceed back down the ramp depositing the table behind the amp rack. i zip up to the stage-left front trough where i stand smoking until Will:"i think it was the dead sea scrolls..." i then roll the tv to the far farthest edge stage left. i step on my cig. butt and duck down and around jeff over to the bed. i grab the string that raises the dummy and wait for peyton to say"...will float free in the air..." and i pull my string listenin for up and down instructions from anna who is guiding mary and myself. the dummy goes up and the dummy comes down and i duck to the back of the stage to the back trough where i pick up my ST LEFT flower and wait for ron to motion for the flowers to grow. he does and we do. we grow and flop to the left to the right, following rons motions until he picks us starting with me. i hop up and down in time to

MICHAEL von STUMM

musicuntil the big down beat comes when i rise up and begin pounding for all im worth on the stage floor with my knotted fists. i stop when peyton screeches "cut". i wait outstretched on the floor until onna-"not that it hasnt been scary..." & then i crawl behind the stage on the floor to stage right back troughwhere i roll up my left sleeve and wait for kate to say "arnold schwartzenegger" i make a muscle. kate then motions for me to come up i do and gp to the s-r mic. i remove book from pocket and ready myself to read. i untie megaphone and hold it extended in my left hand. kate rushes over and places it on my head. i read while she makes a traverse of the stage, comes back to me (like a boomerang)and cuts me off i plead with her while following her s-left but she is adamant. i leave via s-r ramp. i raise the stupids while the stage is rising. i place my door opening stick behind the s-r door and crawy up the s-r ramp and peek over the s-r ell i pull the standing mic. towards me again and remove my book again and read the telephone convers. with kate. we finish and i push the mic. away & stand behind s-r door. when kate advises dieter to pack the bags and be carefut they are very valuable i push open the door with the stick and go to stand proudly behind the s-r ell. the stage lowers and i go with it down the s-r ramp and behind to take the trunk anna is offering me from the door. i place the trunk on the floor &to the play is over

 Above: **Performance score: Michael Stumm** Right: **"Episode 4: The Party"** Opposite: **Notes to actors: Elizabeth LeCompte**

First Transcript: Actors' notes

Kate Valk: Where was it heavy last night?

Elizabeth LeCompte: From the very beginning. When I say heavy, I mean it isn't wacky; it's not crazed like Gracie Allen. It sounds like you're not dealing with the words as idiocy. It sounds like you're trying to find meaning in it, at least that's how it reads. Instead of she says "I went to the store last night because there were no fruitcakes." She is saying it as though it makes perfect sense. And that's a problem for both of you; though Peyton's got a better handle on it because of where her voice quality is. You more consistently hit that tone when we would play in Europe because somewhere there you knew they did not understand all the idioms; so somewhere deeply you let go a little bit more. Here with everybody, everyone is sitting down on the language in a much heavier way than we ever did on tour and partly that has to do with getting much more familiar and feeling better about it all. Before, we didn't quite like it and so we could throw it away. Here we have to work for that quality because we are getting attached... What's the line when you're on the bed?

KV: "I know he was happy when he died."

EL: Yes, it's not heavy, it's idiocy, it's total idiocy. But it has this tendency to settle into "oh something heavy's going on"—you're saying something heavy. But it should be... you're something light but something heavy is developing, a subtext that slowly comes in and seeps up into "The Devil Dance" so it overtakes it and all of a sudden we're in a world where your psychic world gains a lot more seriousness, becomes a lot more desperate.

KV: Well maybe some day I'll get it all in one show.

EL: It's possible. Then it will be perfect and it's great to have that to work for.

Peyton Smith: It will be a great night in the theater.

Ron Vawter: I hope to be there. (Laughter)

Second Transcript: Actors' notes

EL: Now here's the only thing in general about the performance. You guys have got it now. You have got it now, you've got the flow, you've got the energy on top. What you don't have is... you're not able to drop out. You come very close but you're never really able to stand in this space and say "this is all that is required of me." I feel this. There are very particular places where this comes up where I sense that you either feel the need to rush on to the next line or fill it in some way psychologically with some kind of movement, some way you're just skirting the bottom of it, you know what I mean?

It's like this, right here (Liz stands still for some time in the space, in Ron's position down centre stage).

RV: I don't think we can get away with that.

EL: No, I know, I think you can only get away with it when you need it, if you need it and you use it for real. You can get away with it for the entire performance if you're really thinking. You can't indicate this. You have to be listening to everything in the room. You have to be here. You can't be pretending to be here and that's the trick. It has to be the points where it's most obvious, when you say, "OK freeze frame. Cut" and you come back in before Episode 2. You're filling here. Now, I know that you think I want you to fill there. I don't want you to fill with words there. I want you to fill with presence there. Sustained. Then the other place that this happens is the dance. Whenever you stop in the dance I feel that you are indicating that you're relaxing, rather than you just stopping and listening and then going on. With Katie it comes up in the act with the gunshot. You're still not present. You're making signs that you're now dropping out. But you're not really dropping out. You're not really talking to people. You're making signs.

RV: OK. OK. It's probably, as you know, the hardest thing... it's the hardest thing to do.

EL: Do you remember the Lenny Bruce?

RV: I certainly do. It was electrifying...

EL: For me, he was thinking about the trial and wanting to talk with himself and then realising he was suddenly here and had to perform. For you guys it could be...

RV: ... A physical thing... can you hear the traffic on Broome Street...

EL: ... That's right... Yes. Or who is the fourth person in the second row and can I find out without them knowing? Or, what is Peyton really thinking about right now on stage? Or, what's the loudest sound in the room? Something that is particular, that is real. Actual. Here. And it can be psychological. I'm sure with Lenny Bruce it was a psychological thing where he was really thinking about something that had happened in the past, after WWII. If you're pretending to think about it, it won't work. So Ronnie, you must sustain, without pretending to fill.

FRANK DELL'S THE TEMPTATION OF SAINT ANTONY
--T H E A R G U M E N T--

A HOTEL ROOM IN WASHINGTON D.C.	**SUNSET IN THE DESERT**
EPISODE 1: THE MONOLOGUE IN WHICH **FRANK** RUNS HIS TAPE, AND TAKES A CALL FROM **CUBBY**.	"Enfeebled by prolonged fasting, the hermit finds himself unable to concentrate upon holy things. His thoughts wander; memories evoke regrets that his relaxed will can no longer suppress. His fancy leads him upon dangerous ground."
EPISODE 2: THE DANCE BREAK IN WHICH **FRANK** REHEARSES THE **GIRLS** IN A DANCE.	"The scene shifts. The Queen of Sheba descends to tempt the Saint with the deadliest of all temptations. In fantastic obedience to his fancy, the scene changes again."
EPISODE 3: THE DIGRESSION IN WHICH **ONNA** AND **PHYLLIS** REARRANGE THE HOTEL ROOM FURNITURE AND **FRANK** TALKS INTIMATELY WITH **SUE**.	"Under the guise of a former disciple, Hilarion, the demon endeavors to poison the mind of Antony. He cites texts only to foment doubt, and quotes the evangels only to make confusion. And Hilarion grows taller."
EPISODE 4: THE PARTY IN WHICH **FRANK** TAKES A REST AND **ONNA** AND **PHYLLIS** PRACTICE SOME VERBAL ROUTINES. THEY CONVINCE THE HOTEL MAID AND HER BOYFRIEND TO JOIN IN.	"Hilarion induces Antony to enter with him into a spectral basilica. The hermit is confounded. By this hallucination the tempter would prove to the Saint that martyrdom is not always suffered for the purest motives."
EPISODE 5: OLD TIMES REMEMBERED IN WHICH **DIETER** REVEALS HIMSELF AND THE TROUPE PREPARES TO PERFORM AS **FRANK** TAKES ANOTHER CALL FROM **CUBBY**.	"The tempter assumes the form of a Hindu Brahmin terminating a life of wondrous holiness in self-cremation. Then he seeks to shake Antony's faith in the excellence and evidence of miracles."
EPISODE 6: THE MAGIC SHOW IN WHICH **ONNA** AND **PHYLLIS** RECALL THE COTTON BANDAGE TEST, "THE INVISIBLE CHAINS," AND THE CATALEPSY TEST. THE PERFORMANCE ENDS ABRUPTLY AND THE TROUPE PACKS UP.	"Hilarion reappears, taller than ever, growing more gigantic in proportion to the increasing weakness of the Saint. He evokes deities; phallic and ithyphallic; fantastic or obscene. Venus displays the rounded daintiness of her nudity. Hilarion towers to the stars. Antony is lifted upon mighty wings and borne away above the world."
EPISODE 7: THE MONOLOGUE CONTINUED IN WHICH **PHYLLIS** LEAVES, **ONNA** FINISHES PACKING AND **FRANK** HEARS AGAIN FROM **CUBBY**.	"Antony comes to himself in the desert. The tempter returns as the Spirit of Lust and the Spirit of Destruction. The latter urges him to suicide, the former to indulgence of sense. Antony feels a delirious desire to unite himself with the Spirit of Universal Being. The vision vanishes. The Temptation has passed. The face of Christ is revealed."

--from The Temptation of Saint Antony
Modern Library Edition, 1911

PHYLLIS

Remember, I care very much for each and every one of you. You know that's true because I respect you, I never talk down to you. I don't love you for what you can do to me because you can't.

That's why it is very difficult for me to say this to you: tonight is my last performance. I am leaving the show, I am leaving the theatre. I want to announce that this is my last performance anywhere. For good. And I regret it as much as anyone could regret it.

Well, this probably is easy for somebody else but I'm just not good at this. I never have been. Oh, I see what you're thinking. No, I don't mean I'm not good at this business. It's this life. Originally I got into it to express myself, to dance and sing and feel. But it has gone beyond that now and I feel it as a terrible loss.

And that is something that the Frank Dell organization has never understood and I don't think they can understand, that the people need a good time too. They like a party as much as the dukes and dutchesses and kings and queens who are illegal in this country anyway. Oh, a visit, sure, I've got nothing against that. And I'm sure many of them are more than just charming. But I'm afraid some of them are not very nice

Phyllis "Leaving the Theater" speech: "Episode 6: The Magic Show" (text: Jim Strahs)

Making shadows on the sands:
Frank Dell's The Temptation of St. Antony

An interview with Elizabeth LeCompte and Kate Valk (Oxford, Maine, July 9th, 2005)

Andrew Quick (AQ): How did you first start working on *Frank Dell's The Temptation of St. Antony?*

Elizabeth LeCompte (EL): I think it started with Ron (Vawter) and Peter Sellars. Peter Sellars picked the Flaubert text. He thought we could get some arts funding if we said that we were working on it together, if he co-directed it with me.

AQ: From watching the early rehearsal tapes, you and Peter Sellars were initially working separately on some choreographic sections.

EL: At the time we were in residence at the Kennedy Center in Washington, D.C.. We were there for several months. Some of us would work in an old department store that was being used for artists' studios. That's when we worked on the first monologue and the "Channel J" videotapes and then people would also be working on the set with Peter, doing the dances.

AQ: Did you go to the rehearsals that Peter was running?

EL: I said, "I'll take whatever you make and I'll put it in." It was... like... found material for me.

AQ: When did the other source material, like Lenny Bruce, come into the rehearsals?

EL: It was pretty early, because we had been listening to a lot of different comedians on vinyl. I had a couple of Lenny Bruce records but Jim Strahs had this incredible collection of Lenny Bruce—I think a lot of the Lenny Bruce stuff must have come from him.

Kate Valk (KV): I remember that you were into Lenny Bruce from the beginning, linking his persona to Ron's persona—making it central to St. Antony.

EL: Jim had hours and hours of Lenny Bruce's routines and we just started playing these at certain points, for Ron's persona. It was an odd mix because Ron wasn't anything like Lenny Bruce.

AQ: And did he like Lenny Bruce, as a persona?

EL: I don't think he ever noticed. He was ill at the time and I think he was having trouble concentrating. He would sleep a lot during early readings of the Flaubert. I mean, have you ever sat down and tried to read Flaubert's *The Temptation of Saint Anthony*? We read two versions, the earliest and then the last one; we probably did more reading of that text than anything before or since. A lot of this was taking place outside the rehearsal space, maybe because we were performing something else downstairs in the Garage. We would read the Flaubert one at a time.

KV: But remember when we went up to Boston and did the science fair projects? That was very funny. Everybody had to take one part of Flaubert's The Temptation of Saint Anthony *and explain it like a science fair project at school.*

AQ: These were presentations?

KV: Yes. I remember staging The Patrician Women *with Peyton (Smith) and Willem (Dafoe). It was fun. We did a lot of crazy things to try and get familiar with the Flaubert text. A little after this, I remember Liz and I meeting in the hotel room in Washington and underlining certain sections of the Flaubert. We would read the sections that she had underlined and then we'd meet again and something else would get underlined until finally, the whole book was underlined.*

EL: That was how we doggedly tried to understand what the hell was going on. The Flaubert was such a long text. It was such dense imagery in a kind of closet drama. You could hardly imagine it in your head, let alone stage it. Then we got into Flaubert's letters from Egypt and somewhere around that time I just realized that I couldn't stage this play without some other language. That is when I started making up things. I had Ron riffing off stuff and then I brought in Jim Strahs to do some writing and gave him all the Flaubert material we had been working on and asked him to come to rehearsals. By that time I think I was tossing bean bags at the performers on the stage. I didn't know what else to do.

KV: That was later—you threw the bean bags at us when we had come back to the Garage. Before that we were in Washington, where we were developing the "Channel J," which we had started to work on upstairs in the Garage right at the start. Liz had come up with the idea of Ron as a naked talk-show host, which she put alongside Nancy Reilly, a kind of vocal scribe, who relentlessly read out Flaubert's text. Ron riffed off the text and interacted with a few of us as we bounced in and out of the scene as different characters. So, we developed this and we actually got somewhere, because the videotape we eventually used was one of the last passes of the text that we did in Washington. We used the beginning bit of this tape for Ron's monologue in the finished show. Meanwhile, back at the Kennedy Center, Peter Sellars was staging these huge death numbers with all of us. I remember he had an apple hung from the ceiling and Ron, with his hands tied behind his back, would be trying to grab the apple. As this was happening, we were on set being sea anemones or flowers and Peter would be shouting, "Grow, grow, grow" (laughs).

But this persona, Peter directing us, became an important part of the choreography that we used in making St. Antony. *It became integrated in that thing of Ron trying to get the show together, trying to make the act work, which we ended up with in the final piece. A lot of this came out of Peter's attempt to summon up magic to make a big dance number out of the Flaubert. I remember Matthew (Hansell) had the words from Flaubert for the dance: "The two arms of the cross make a shadow on the sand."*

AQ: What was your response when you saw these dances?

EL: I thought, "I can use some of this."

KV: Two other things happened in addition to Peter doing the dance numbers. Liz was also working on the set and trying to make a story; because there wasn't really any story in Flaubert's Saint Anthony*—well, there is a story: it's a single day and there's this guy who has wild hallucinations and he comes to terms with himself alone in a cave. I don't know how we got to Bergman's film,* The Magician *(1958), but it was based on the story of a theater troupe. This gave us a more literal story of trying to make this act work, trying to carry on, trying to survive, trying to get out of a small room—it was like Flaubert, but different.*

EL: The hotel room became a metaphor for the stage and we were in a hotel room making the piece.

AQ: Didn't Lenny Bruce finally end up alone in a hotel room?

EL: No, it was his house, in a small room—the bathroom—it's the same idea. We were taking the stage directions from the screenplay of *The Magician* and inserting them. We were trying to create a stage-world with these stage directions and deal with the text from *Saint Anthony*, so people wouldn't just be standing and delivering prose.

AQ: I understand—*The Magician* provided you with a more tangible framework for you to stage the Flaubert.

KV: And there were great personas for all of us in that film: Ron as Dr. Vogler or St. Antony or Lenny Bruce. They all stacked up. And then, everybody in the troupe: Tubal and Fanny; Aman, the world-weary wife of Dr. Vogler, who has to dress as a man; the strongman in the invisible chains. These were all fun personas for us to take on. These people could be in Saint Anthony *as The Show they were trying to invoke—back to Peter directing us, "Grow, grow, grow."*

AQ: Does the set re-work the stage designs of earlier Wooster Group works?

EL: Yes, it was the same set for *North Atlantic* (1984) and *L.S.D. (...Just the High Points...)* (1984).

AQ: The set seems higher than the one used in *L.S.D.*, with the back wall coming up as a ramp.

EL: Yes, but we'd used the ramp in *North Atlantic*. No, it was exactly the same stage. We just took the table from *North Atlantic* and *L.S.D.* and put in two doors and a window—that was the only difference.

AQ: I recall thinking, "Am I behind the set or am I in front of the set—is this the backstage that I'm looking through?"

EL: I remember Peter coming to see the design while he was working on the dances, when Jim Clayburgh got the set up in the space. He said, "That's the ugliest set I have ever seen." I guess it was brutal and ugly and it didn't have any sense of quietness either.

AQ: It was clunky, but it really worked.

EL: Like the whole piece—it had a clunkiness to it.

AQ: I wanted to ask about the monologue that dominates the first part of *St. Antony* that's based on Ron doing all the voices of the "Channel J" video that you made in Washington. Was the "Channel J" based on a real TV show?

EL: Yes. At the time there was this nude interviewer and he would have porn actresses come on and he'd interview them naked. They'd sit on couches and they would be totally comfortable. It was called "Channel J" and it was on early cable TV.

AQ: Did it ever get serious or philosophical?

EL: No, it was all about the porn thing: "What's your next film? Are you still called Foxy Boxy?" I can't remember who the interviewer was, but he was so serious—he was a little intellectual and he was a little uncomfortable. Being naked was a statement for him: nothing but a microphone. It felt a little like something that Lenny Bruce might have been involved in had he done anything naked. There was something a bit self-aware about this man, whereas all the performers were really comfortable. They were all exhibitionists. Well, he was an exhibitionist, but he was different—he was sleazier. He was more like Lenny Bruce.

AQ: Did you feel there was something in its tone, in its dealing with sexuality, which connected to Flaubert's *Saint Anthony*?

EL: Oh, no. I just felt like, "God we need nakedness in this piece, because how are we going to keep anybody awake?" Basically, this was the impulse—the only way to get through this mess is to keep everybody awake.

KV: I love it though, because it reminds me of that thing in cinema when certain directors want to do something serious and they bring out the nudity. It's like, "I've got some heavy stuff to get through out here. Get the naked girl out and get the cameras rolling, 'cos I've got some philosophy." I mean, I don't think we considered it like this at the time, but it's part of that wonderful tradition—that was the fun part of it.

AQ: The juxtaposition of this philosophical meditative language with the nudity certainly makes you watch.

KV: Now I've got your attention—drag out the heavy stuff.

AQ: Was the "Channel J" created with the idea that Ron would perform all the voices? There's something hallucinatory about the fact that he does this, like he's watching the TV and fantasizing that he's in it.

EL: Well, it had to be a monologue, so he had to do all the voices. I thought of it like one of Lenny Bruce's comic monologues, where he'd do all the voices. It was like that obsession Lenny Bruce had when he went through all those tapes of his trial again and again. Here, Ron is obsessed with the video operator. That's his live relationship with a real person. When he's listening to the other people on the stage, they're all figments in his mind. It's the tape that's the only real person in the room. It's his obsession with the tape—going over the tapes and having the conversations with the Devil.

AQ: What's the impulse that makes Ron go over the tape again and again?

EL: The meaning; let's find the meaning in this. That's the obsession in it—the drive. The conflict is internal—Saint Anthony with the Devil.

AQ: And the idea of the theater troupe...

EL: That had come up in *L.S.D.*.

AQ: I remember there was a dance at the end of the performance by...

KV: Donna Sierra and the Del Fuegos.

AQ: Was this idea of the troupe ghosting around in earlier Wooster Group pieces?

EL: Yes, there was a little of this idea in *Point Judith* (1979), with the people stuck on an oil rig and entertaining themselves by making up party pieces.

AQ: It's there, rather opaquely, in *Brace Up!* (1991) and then you actually announce it very clearly in *Fish Story* (1993).

EL: I think there's always this ghosting of the troupe in different guises—the troupe trying to make the piece at the same time that we're making the piece in the space.

AQ: Is this a reflection of the process that The Wooster Group goes through?

EL: Well, it's always those two stories together. One story might be more submerged at any one time, because, somewhere, this is where we make work from.
KV: Liz isn't getting a play and casting it, and then collecting a production team together to make it. It's in the room. So, in one sense it's always autobiographical. Sometimes this autobiographical element is much more evident because it's way out front and other times it's submerged in a mask or some sort of vehicle or frame—a story that we can feel ourselves in.

AQ: I watched the *Geinin* film that you drew such inspiration from for the making of *Fish Story* and I saw your unfinished video project which directly works off this material. I found both the original documentary of the Geinin troupe and your own video version of this Japanese theater troupe very touching, this story of a group who could no longer make the work they really liked doing, who had to perform to tourists and who claimed TV was destroying the theater tradition that they came from. It was very autobiographical and you were clearly connecting this story to your own history as a company.

EL: When we saw the *Geinin* film it was just too good. It was very like us in our upstairs room at the Garage, watching television all the time and only doing a play every once in a while—unlike the Broadway people who were performing every day of the week. We barely had people coming to see our work. This was back in the days when we had trouble getting audiences at all. So, we were happy to see a troupe that actually had to leave the theater and go to a hotel or spa to perform. It was like... God, it was like looking into the future. And this is echoed in *Poor Theater* (2004), when Scott Shepherd says, "We bring our little cultural dances to the tourists."

AQ: You worked with a writer, Jim Strahs, on *St. Antony*. Did he produce text with you, which you then wove into the piece?

EL: No, we ordered the text. I would give him the material that we were working on and he would come to a couple of rehearsals and then he would go back and write what he wanted. Then, Katie and I would edit what he produced.

AQ: There are so many strange references in *St. Antony*, like the reference to Dunkirk...

EL: That's about a Lenny Bruce piece that he does about performing at The London Palladium, where he really bombs—it's a great piece. And then we took Flaubert's letters, which he wrote while traveling down the Nile.

AQ: You also make reference to a spiritualist as well...

EL: Yes, Geraldine Cummings—and Lenny Bruce's secretary, Sue, used to read some of Cummings' writing to him.

AQ: Hilarion, the Devil, played by Willem (Dafoe) as Cubby on the video, claims to come from Cardiff and yet he has this terrible Cockney accent. I wondered if this accent had something to do with the Hollywood tradition of using the English accent to portray evil...

EL: The only reason for this is that it's the only accent we all knew. I'm not sure how Cubby came about. It's in the "Channel J" tape, so it must have been early. All I remember is that Willem could do a bad Cockney accent. That's why I thought of him as Smithers in *The Emperor Jones* (1993).

AQ: There's a key tonal shift in *St. Antony*, when Ron suddenly stops. He sort of backs away from the main action. He lies on the bed.

EL: That's when he was ill. He was in hospital for a while and couldn't come to rehearsals. He had a seizure when we were doing a retrospective at The Kitchen in New York (December, 1986). It was during that time when the AIDS tests were not conclusive, but I think everyone, well maybe not me so much, was beginning to face what might be happening—Ron dealing with his own mortality. He wasn't there a lot of the time and we had to imagine that he was in the bed on the stage.

KV: Then Dennis Dermody gave me a book called Learned Pigs and Fireproof Women *(1986), by Ricky Jay, for my birthday. Liz picked it up at the party and had one of those moments.*

AQ: Is it about strange theater acts?

KV: Yes, it's about this particular circuit in Europe where freaks would perform to the crown heads of Europe: a woman with a pig's head who was very intelligent; a man who could write and play the violin with his feet; somebody who could feign death on the stage—there was a whole section on death in show business. I think we came across this book right at the time when Ron was ill and so Liz saw a rich connection.

EL: We actually used a bit of dialogue from that particular man who could feign death—it's used when Kate and Peyton are on the upper level and Ron is running around at the end of one of the episodes.

AQ: I think I remember the scene—when the women are cranking up the energy, they're vamping, filling the time.

EL: Vamping is a good term. It's exactly what I would say: "Look, you're just vamping."

AQ: There's a really frenetic tempo to it.

EL: It's like that thing with women, when the main guy in the household is dying, and they're all running around trying to do something and they can't. There is nothing they can do. They are just talking—yammer, yammer, yammer.

AQ: Then Ron comes back, doesn't he? He returns and attempts to do the show, which sort of falls apart and fails?

EL: Well, they just have to do the show and it totally fails. He has a seizure on the stage. His pants are down round his ankles and he falls down dead into the pit.

AQ: Once again, this is informed by pragmatics, about what was happening to Ron?

EL: Yes, it's about what is happening to the company. Trying to find a way of dealing with it, a way of talking about it without it being literal.

KV: It was the same with Willem as Cubby, as the guy in Hollywood, as the Devil who tempts Ron. Liz made these videotapes of Willem driving around, being in LA and speaking about how wild it was to be there.

EL: Saint Anthony is tempted by the Devil and in this case the Devil comes to him as a guy who has just got a big Hollywood gig, which is what Ron wanted more than anything else. He wasn't so successful in film, because of the way he looked. Willem was in Hollywood at the same time that Ron was trying to get film work and we worked this in.

AQ: It was very funny having the Devil come from Hollywood. Some of the video appears to be shot in the desert and there's this whole road movie feel to it.

KV: Well, Willem's on the road. He makes these video-calls back, "Hey, I'm here in this great hotel room. My life is fantastic. Come on out." And he was playing Jesus in The Last Temptation of Christ *(1988) and this happens in Flaubert's* Saint Anthony, *when the Devil tricks Saint Anthony with a vision of Christ, but it's really the Devil.*

EL: Yes, isn't that just perfect?

KV: You filmed the poster for the film and Cubby says, "Hey, look at this," and it's a picture of Cubby as Christ.

EL: How funny that that should have happened at exactly the same time. He was with us in Washington, but after that he couldn't be there because of the film work he was involved in.

AQ: Yes, he's in some of the earliest recordings of rehearsals.

EL: Yes, the rehearsals in Washington. He was in and out, but basically I had him painting. I put him slightly to one side, because I knew he wasn't going to be there and I didn't want him to build a character. So, he was upstairs painting while we worked on the piece.

AQ: Did you use the paintings at all?

EL: We used one of the paintings as the backdrop in the "Channel J." The paintings were inspired by images of the play.

AQ: I wanted to ask about the film *Flaubert Dreams of Travel but the Illness of His Mother Prevents It* (1986), which you made with Ken Kobland. It appears in the later episodes of the piece, it has a beautiful texture to it…

EL: Yes, and he made a very beautiful soundtrack to the film. I used that soundtrack with our soundtrack. *St. Antony* has so many threads—it's like a tapestry. I remember someone once saying after they'd seen it, "Oh it's like Islamic art," where you might just see the pattern or the strand or something and then as you looked closer you could discern the bigger images that made the story.

AQ: I saw the piece in Antwerp and I remember finding it very moving at the end. I hadn't really seen such an affecting meditation on mortality.

EL: That's because the person at the center of the piece is deeply living it.

AQ: Then, there was that other dynamic in *St. Antony*, which was such a contrast—the women grabbing hold of life, keeping it going like those people who spin plates in variety acts. I loved that, not wanting the energy to drop away. It reminded me how fragile theater is, how it's so close to failure or has failure built into it somehow. That sense of, "keep going, keep going." Mind you, I suppose by the time I saw it you'd performed the piece many times. How was it received when you first staged it?

EL: Oh, not very well. People loved Ron in the opening monologue—that was funny and moving and fine. But they were mystified by the rest of the piece.

AQ: Did that mean you had to rework it extensively, or did you just keep going with what you'd made?

EL: No, we just kept playing it.

KV: Also, I think there was a problem about taking the energy we had in rehearsal and translating it into performance.

EL: Not only you, it was everyone.

AQ: Was this because you couldn't make that bridge between rehearsal and performance?

KV: Yes. So, it felt really flat because there wasn't a lot to hang on to. Every now and again inspiration would arrive and give the piece the right energy, which would be enough to keep us all going. Then it would fall flat again.

EL: Yes, maybe it was because you became so focused. But you learned a lot in *North Atlantic*. But, somewhere, *St. Antony* was sound enough, structurally. It's funny you said that thing about theater as failure.

AQ: But isn't it? Isn't that its glory as well—that theater can't be perfect?

EL: Yes, it's a lot about that too. That seems like a good point to end on.

AQ: Yes, thank you.

Brace Up!

35
KODAK 5063 TX
35
35A

– Buy Make up book – Asian How to make people look Asian.
for FILM (or theater) – Aging

Call Bobby – ONTBABA

– Geriatric vests, booties, wristcuffs, chairs w/trays

1/2/90

Kodygin: Liz: Call Steve B. – will he be here in Feb.
Liz: call Ruth
Vershinin: Paul Schmidt

Part 1 Chekhov – company run by Jap. ♀ who've hired in Western men. Men have a kind of humorous effeteness. "Where are all my men?"

Part 2 Geinin – Troupe is performing in a hotel room for bussed-in tourists in New York waiting for their performance. NY has become a dilapidated city run almost by computer from the outside. Like the stagehands in 1+9. Geinin troupe is doing 3 Sisters, a Western play.
– Uses script from Geinin film. "Everyone usually gets up about 1½ hrs. 'til the perf. But one wonders what time they would sleep to if there was no work scheduled." "Laziness" – an apathy. Searching for a psychic motivation to go on.
– "American Beckett"
– Just a small group (Jeff, Mike, Kate, Peyton, JJ, Jim, Anne, Mary H.)

SET
Two monitors
Two sound systems – on table in back + lots of props (extension of Nayatt School)

Videos
– Hotel rooms w/ reporters – reporting on Panama, Tienen Square, etc. reporting only from a great distance.
– Slow-moving, unspecific imagery
– New porn films. Much more casual + naturalistic. "Gang of 9 with 8 off to the side." from Robyn Byrd show.

2/7/90

PART 3 This takes place in a nursing home. The head nurse (Jamaican) is Kate, Mike is the orderly. The 3 Sisters are being chased by the men who are trying to marry them + kill them.

Opposite: **Rehearsal: *Brace Up!*** Above: **Early rehearsal notebook: Marianne Weems**

ICHIKAWA HOUSEHOLD / PROZOROV HOUSEHOLD

These two servants are demon gods (à la Noh) but are also the fools – dropping, breaking, etc.

2/12 Problem w/use of t.v. Wants to use it as a "visual aid", + a "teaching aid" – not another character. But it also has to collude with soap operas from ... – i.e. Andrei/Natasha's early love scenes.

Go to Benshi to get away from Chekov's naturalism. What remains are speeches + occasional interchanges that are almost schematic. The rhythm of the play can be kept but will be abstracted (+ collaged with the other material.) And the naturalistic "plot" will be dropped

"Islands of speeches" which come up.

4/19 Chekhov being divided into 2 plays 1) The men on video as Thirty-Something style soap opera 2) Simple Noh play with three sisters who live together with their maid. Natasha comes in + attacks the maid with her crassness, the story is resolved when one of the sisters takes the old maid away with her.

2 stories, Noh story should be built on anger, the women's anger (as in New Yorker article on Russian women.) The men will be sensitive, effeminate, tearful – the women are hard, frustrated + angry.

STORYBOARD VIDEOS FOR MEN

 Above and opposite: **Early rehearsal notebook: Marianne Weems**

1/90 - Watched porn films (looking for Candy — new porn) and watched Geinin film. (Especially notable; The Woman In The Window.)

2/5 - 2/22
- Marked through 3 Sisters 2 times w/ full cast.
- Watched Ozu's "Floating Weeds" + Geinin film
- Rehearsed ♂ + ♀ Polynesian dances.
- Added props from other pieces to BRACE UP set.

2/25 Marked beats for Act I w/ Kate + Liz

2/26 Norin Seito brought in several Japanese TV dramas plus a cartoon - AKIRA

2/27 Act 2 - Marked beats + sketched out summary for 1st 1/2.

2/28 Work on video shots for the next month and a half. The shots will not have any literal rel. to the play. Not cutting the play but finding a way to work each moment through:
1) psychology/ pacing - each scene will be distinct + marked
2) actions not decorative - real, Pouring tea, playing a game. Not dramatic.

"Morality" play of the 3 ♀ pulled wrongly out of Chekhov. A Noh story out of badly-interpreted Chekhov.

3/2 Worked through 3 + 4. Marked beats + video scripts.

3/4 Worked on Masha's crying scene in Act 4 (pp. 120) Acting style btwn. Stanislavsky (natural) + Meierhold (symbolic) so that her waving the handkerchief crying etc. is like a Japanese-formal-actor trying to act naturalistically.

3/20 Game based on "Go" + House bldg. from "1+9" for Act 4. 3 SKs are blind (Ron's idea.)

3/24, 3/25, 3/26 Act Four In-Process showings for Guggenheim.

3/27 Reconnoiter after Guggenheim. Edges taken off like Chekhov – upbeat but very nostalgic. Breaks should be taking out the overlying "landscape" (music) + letting everything continue.

New Age – "blocked, protected + "blinded" from violence in the world. Hammacher. Schlemmer catalogue – Stress Relieving Dream Medium glasses

Wim Wender's Peter Carey script – futuristic "dream" which acknowledges the creative side + Not the "blocked" side.

 Above and opposite: **Early rehearsal notebook: Marianne Weems**

11/20/09

Liz has always used 'naturalism' as a formal, decorative device, incorporating it convincingly into a melange of many styles which comment upon themselves through their juxtaposition.

The error of almost all critical writing in rel. to H/work is the <u>identification</u> of the bearer of the narrative (i.e. Spalding in the first trilogy, Ann Rower, Ron, etc.) with the "story".

Her history and many other elements are lain over the tops of these story lines but the naturalistic elements are done very convincingly which throws people.

3A
4

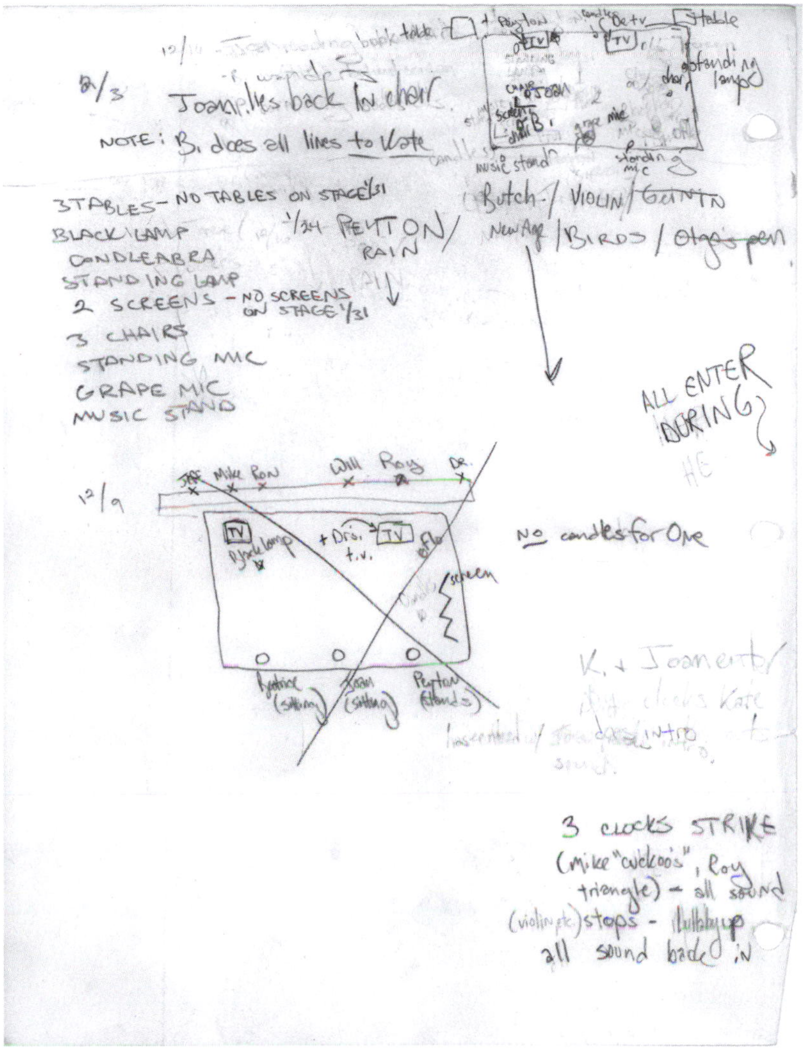

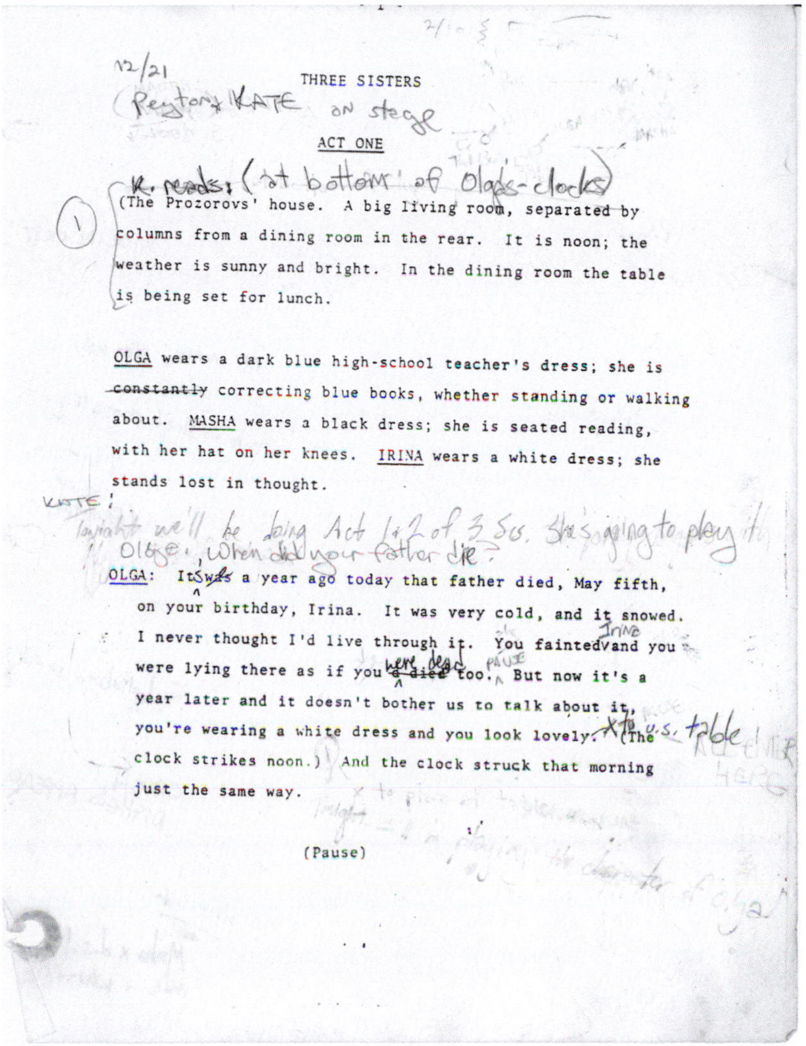

THREE SISTERS

ACT ONE

(The Prozorovs' house. A big living room, separated by columns from a dining room in the rear. It is noon; the weather is sunny and bright. In the dining room the table is being set for lunch.

OLGA wears a dark blue high-school teacher's dress; she is ~~constantly~~ correcting blue books, whether standing or walking about. MASHA wears a black dress; she is seated reading, with her hat on her knees. IRINA wears a white dress; she stands lost in thought.

OLGA: It ~~was~~ a year ago today that father died, May fifth, on your birthday, Irina. It was very cold, and it snowed. I never thought I'd live through it. You fainted and you were lying there as if you ~~a died~~ too. But now it's a year later and it doesn't bother us to talk about it, you're wearing a white dress and you look lovely. (The clock strikes noon.) And the clock struck that morning just the same way.

(Pause)

Opposite: **Rehearsal: *Brace Up!*** Above: ***Brace Up!* early score: Marianne Weems**

10A
11
11

- 2 -

I remember when they carried father's coffin out there was a band playing, it was a military funeral, and at the cemetery they fired rifles over the grave. He was a general, a brigade commander. I thought there should have been more people, ~~at the funeral~~, but it was raining, raining hard, and then it started to snow.

WALKS AROUND STAGE ONCE

IRINA: Let's not think about it.

BEAT

(Baron Tusenbach, Chebutykin and Solyony appear in the dining room.)

OLGA: Today it's warm enough to leave the windows wide open, even though the birch trees haven't put out any leaves yet. Father got his command eleven years ago and we left Moscow and came here, it was the beginning of May too, I remember exactly, Moscow was already full of flowers, it was warm and there was sunshine everywhere. That was eleven years ago, and I remember it all exactly, just as if we'd only left Moscow yesterday. Oh, my! This morning I woke up and realized it was springtime, everything was so bright, I felt such a wave of happiness inside me, and I wanted so much to go back home.

CHEBUTYKIN: ~~No, goddam it~~ The hell you say!

TUSENBACH: You're right, it ~~[illegible]~~ doesn't make sense. ALL ALOT OF NONSENSE.

(Masha looks up absently, and whistles under her breath.)

13

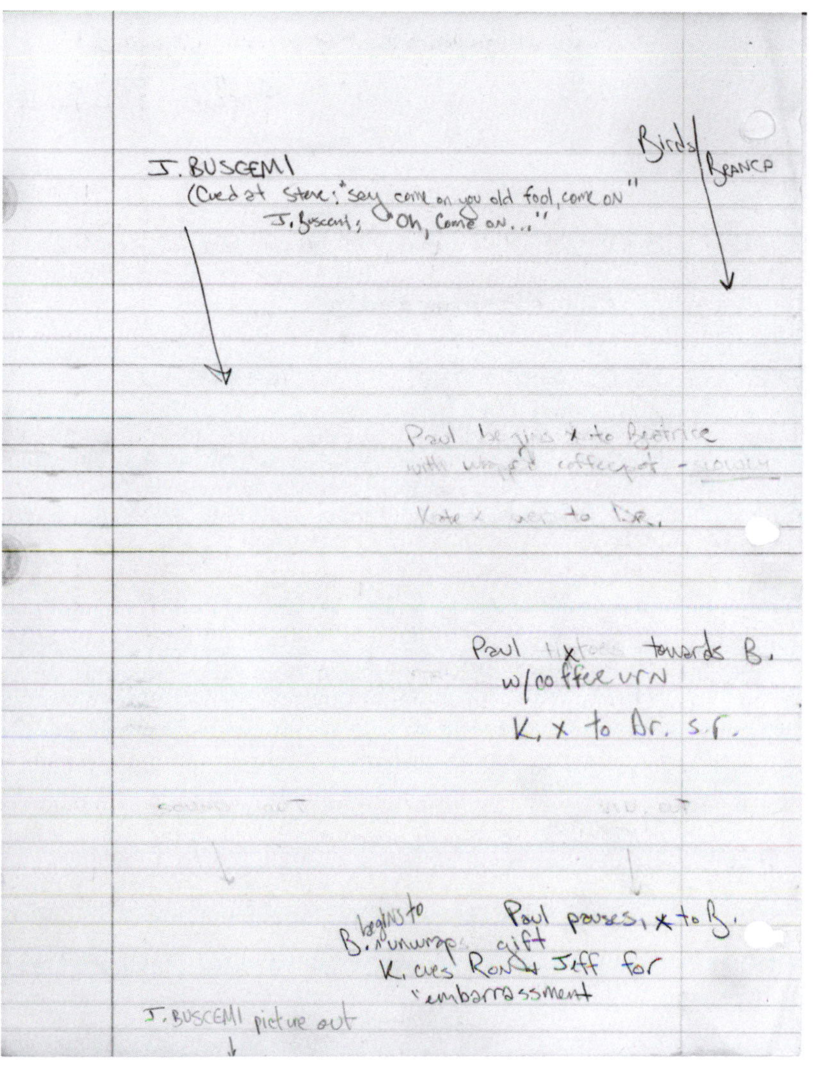

J. BUSCEMI
(Cued at Steve: "say come on you old fool, come on"
J. Buscemi: "Oh, Come on..."
Birds
Paul tiptoes towards B.
w/coffee urn
K, x to Dr. s.r.
Paul pauses, x to B.
B. begins to unwrap gift
K. cues Ron & Jeff for "embarrassment
J. BUSCEMI picture out

K: Oh, Anfisa's in the back room w/Ferapont with

ANFISA: Come on in. Come on, come on, it's all right, your feet are clean. (To Irina.) ~~It's from the council office, It's a birthday cake.~~ From Protopópov.

"IT'S A B-DAY CAKE. A PRESENT FROM PROTOPOPOV OVER AT THE COUNCIL OFFICE."

IRINA: Thank you. (She takes the cake.) Tell him thank you.

K: He can't hear you.

~~FERAPONT: What?~~

IRINA: (Louder.) ~~Tell him thank you.~~ Thank you, Ferapont

OLGA: Nana, give him something to eat. (LOUDER) Ferapónt, go on, she'll give you something to eat.

K: "I don't think either of them can hear you."

~~FERAPONT: What?~~ (to Nana) Did you hear that? Did you?

ANFISA: "Oh" Come on, you old fool, come on, come on.

(She goes out with Ferapont.)

MASHA: I don't like that Protopopov, or whatever his name is. You shouldn't have invited him.

IRINA: I didn't.

MASHA: Good.

(Chebutykin comes in; he is followed by a soldier carrying a huge silver tea service. There is a general reaction of suprise and embarrassment.)

"UH OHH" → RON & JEFF → KATE cues THEM

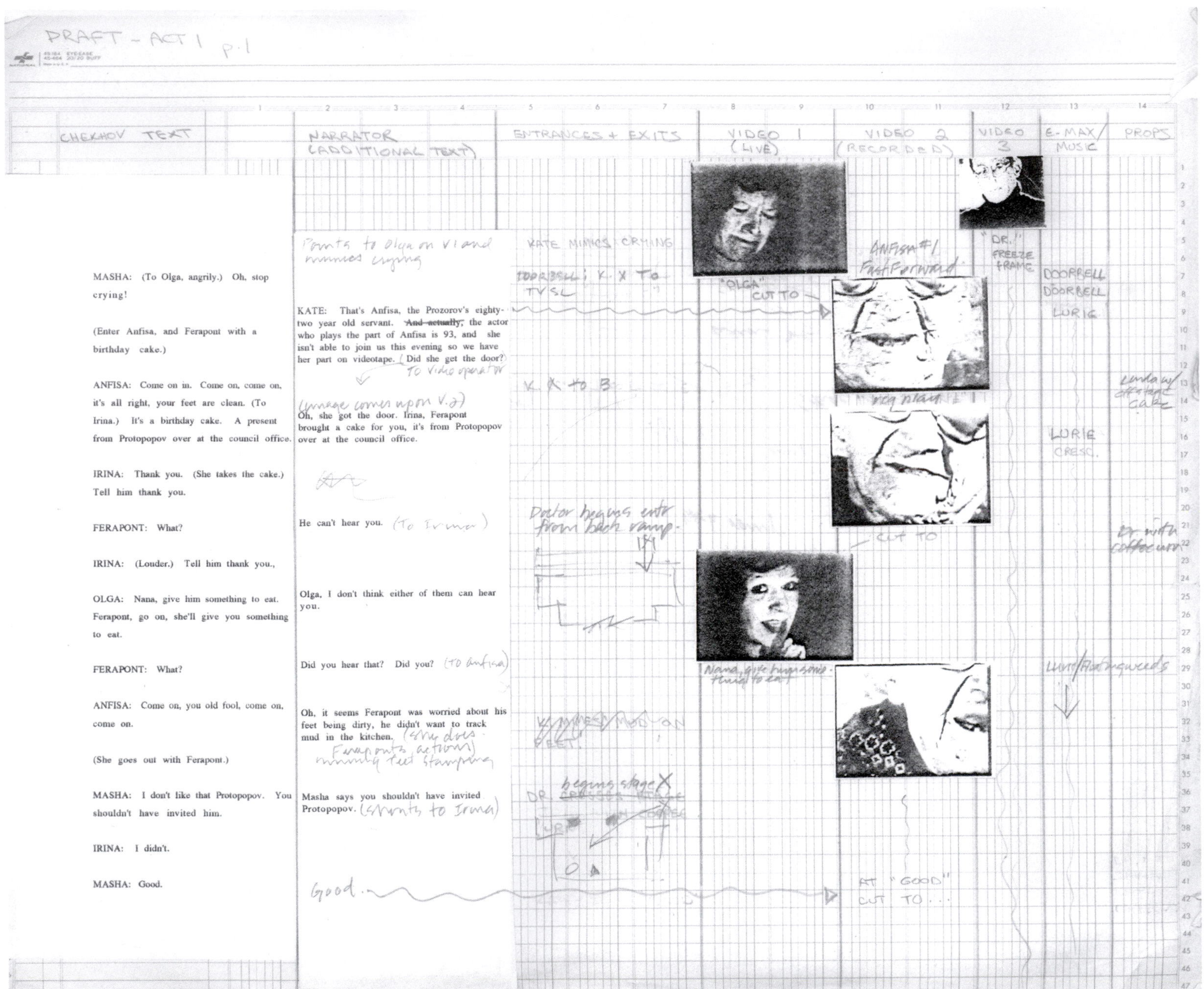

DRAFT – ACT I p.1

CHEKHOV TEXT | NARRATOR (ADDITIONAL TEXT) | ENTRANCES + EXITS | VIDEO 1 (LIVE) | VIDEO 2 (RECORDED) | VIDEO 3 | E-MAX/ MUSIC | PROPS

MASHA: (To Olga, angrily.) Oh, stop crying!

(Enter Anfisa, and Ferapont with a birthday cake.)

ANFISA: Come on in. Come on, come on, it's all right, your feet are clean. (To Irina.) It's a birthday cake. A present from Protopopov over at the council office.

IRINA: Thank you. (She takes the cake.) Tell him thank you.

FERAPONT: What?

IRINA: (Louder.) Tell him thank you.,

OLGA: Nana, give him something to eat. Ferapont, go on, she'll give you something to eat.

FERAPONT: What?

ANFISA: Come on, you old fool, come on, come on.

(She goes out with Ferapont.)

MASHA: I don't like that Protopopov. You shouldn't have invited him.

IRINA: I didn't.

MASHA: Good.

KATE: That's Anfisa, the Prozorov's eighty-two year old servant. ~~And actually,~~ the actor who plays the part of Anfisa is 93, and she isn't able to join us this evening so we have her part on videotape. Did she get the door?

Oh, she got the door. Irina, Ferapont brought a cake for you, it's from Protopopov over at the council office.

He can't hear you.

Olga, I don't think either of them can hear you.

Did you hear that? Did you?

Oh, it seems Ferapont was worried about his feet being dirty, he didn't want to track mud in the kitchen.

Masha says you shouldn't have invited Protopopov.

Above and opposite: ***Brace Up!* early score: Elizabeth LeCompte**

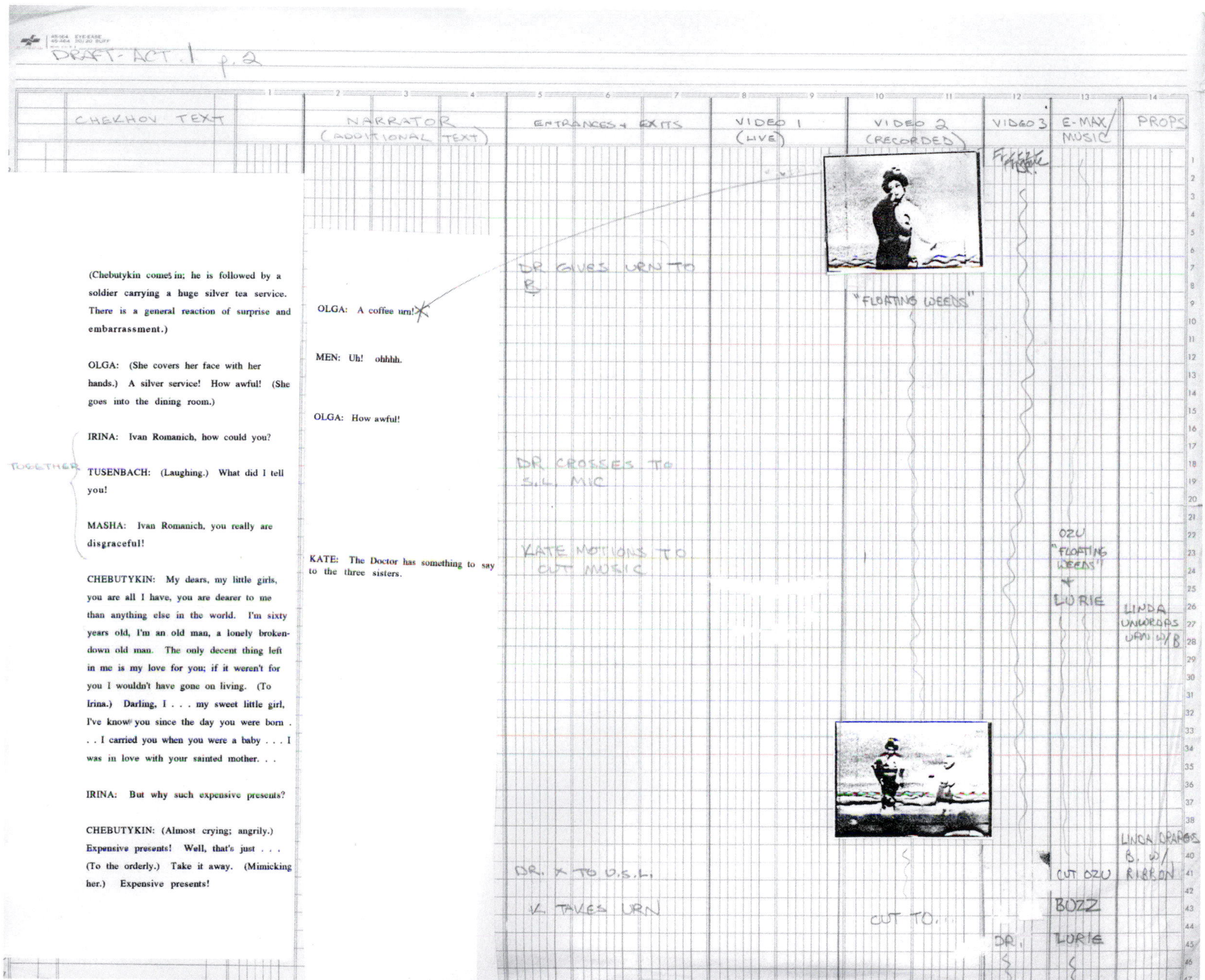

DRAFT - ACT. I p. 2

CHEKHOV TEXT | NARRATOR (ADDITIONAL TEXT) | ENTRANCES + EXITS | VIDEO 1 (LIVE) | VIDEO 2 (RECORDED) | VIDEO 3 | E-MAX/ MUSIC | PROPS

(Chebutykin comes in; he is followed by a soldier carrying a huge silver tea service. There is a general reaction of surprise and embarrassment.)

OLGA: (She covers her face with her hands.) A silver service! How awful! (She goes into the dining room.)

IRINA: Ivan Romanich, how could you?

TUSENBACH: (Laughing.) What did I tell you!

MASHA: Ivan Romanich, you really are disgraceful!

TOGETHER

CHEBUTYKIN: My dears, my little girls, you are all I have, you are dearer to me than anything else in the world. I'm sixty years old, I'm an old man, a lonely broken-down old man. The only decent thing left in me is my love for you; if it weren't for you I wouldn't have gone on living. (To Irina.) Darling, I . . . my sweet little girl, I've know you since the day you were born . . . I carried you when you were a baby . . . I was in love with your sainted mother. . .

IRINA: But why such expensive presents?

CHEBUTYKIN: (Almost crying; angrily.) Expensive presents! Well, that's just . . . (To the orderly.) Take it away. (Mimicking her.) Expensive presents!

OLGA: A coffee urn!

MEN: Uh! ohhhh.

OLGA: How awful!

KATE: The Doctor has something to say to the three sisters.

DR. GIVES URN TO B.

DR. CROSSES TO S.L. MIC

KATE MOTIONS TO CUT MUSIC

DR. X TO U.S.L.

K. TAKES URN

"FLOATING WEEDS"

CUT TO. . .

FREEZE

DR.

OZU "FLOATING WEEDS"

LURIE

CUT OZU

BUZZ

LURIE

LINDA UNWRAPS URN W/B

LINDA DRAPES B. W/ RIBBON

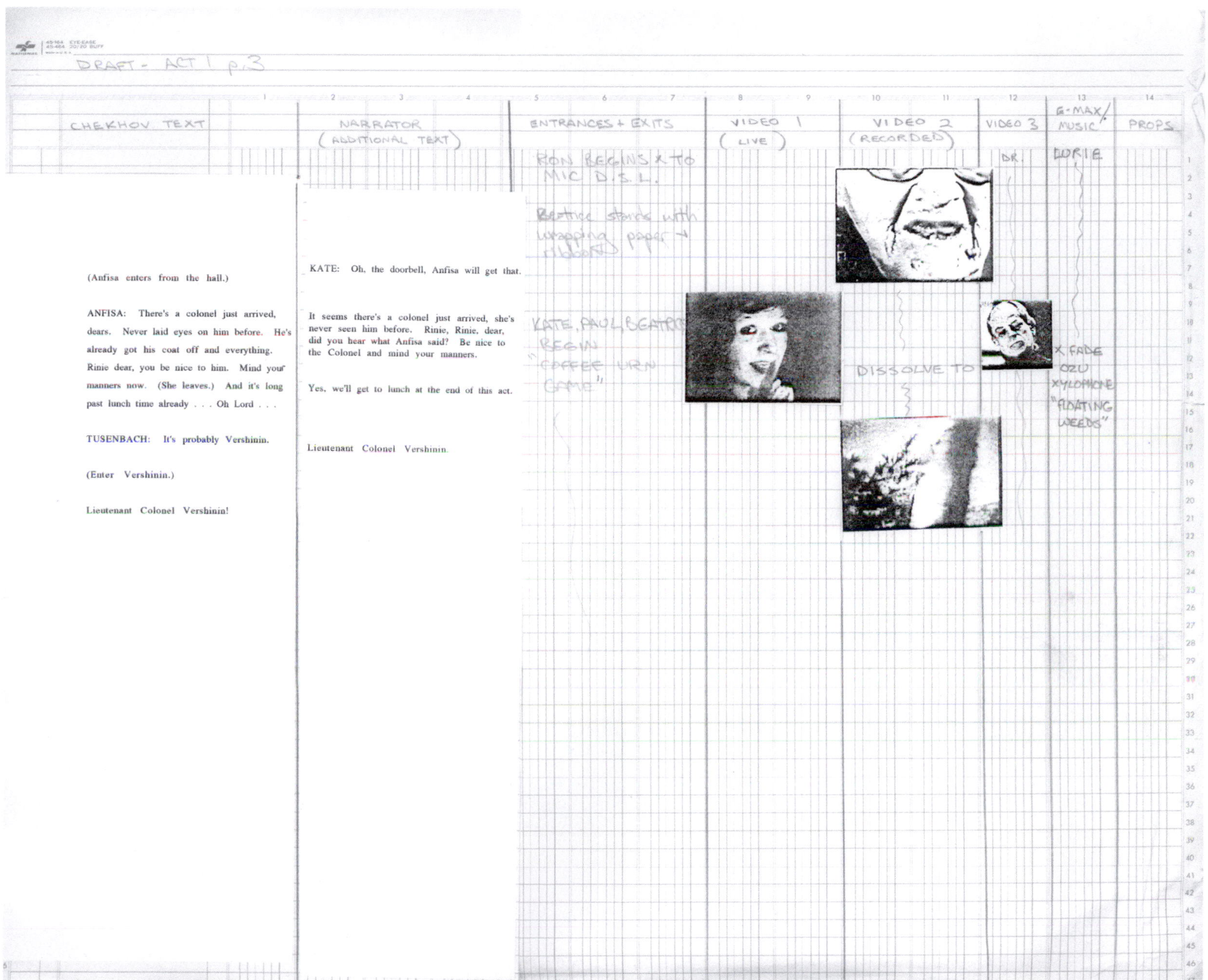

DRAFT - ACT I p. 3

CHEKHOV TEXT | NARRATOR (ADDITIONAL TEXT) | ENTRANCES + EXITS | VIDEO 1 (LIVE) | VIDEO 2 (RECORDED) | VIDEO 3 | G-MAX/ MUSIC | PROPS

RON BEGINS X TO MIC D.S.L.

Beatrice stands with wrapping paper + ribbons

(Anfisa enters from the hall.)

KATE: Oh, the doorbell, Anfisa will get that.

ANFISA: There's a colonel just arrived, dears. Never laid eyes on him before. He's already got his coat off and everything. Rinie dear, you be nice to him. Mind your manners now. (She leaves.) And it's long past lunch time already . . . Oh Lord . . .

It seems there's a colonel just arrived, she's never seen him before. Rinie, Rinie, dear, did you hear what Anfisa said? Be nice to the Colonel and mind your manners.

Yes, we'll get to lunch at the end of this act.

TUSENBACH: It's probably Vershinin.

(Enter Vershinin.)

Lieutenant Colonel Vershinin!

Lieutenant Colonel Vershinin.

KATE, PAUL, BEATRICE BEGIN "COFFEE URN GAME"

DISSOLVE TO

DR.

LURIE

X FADE OZU XYLOPHONE "FLOATING WEEDS"

ACT I

- He just hangs on and complains about her
  BLAST!
  the doctor reads from the newspaper

- I won't... I won't
  BLAST
  this is where the Baron talks about how he understands the desire to work –
  And Doctor what about you?

- JOKE
  Short Blast/ wave it off
  Mike could you take Solyony's line here

- perhaps even sinful
  Mike could you read the Baron's Lines here

- Will you let it alone its not funny anymore

- Shorter cigarette thing with Ron

- If I were you I just wouldn't go
  Its very simple, why not?

- That'll do Vassilly Vassilich let it alone.

- Irina ~~[illegible]~~ talks privately to the Baron
  the Baron asks Irina what she's thinking about.

- STICK DANCE w/ SCOTT
  Now's the time for ~~This is~~ Roday's big scene. ~~[illegible]~~
  So come on up here
  Now You've just taken some of the high school boys out for a walk
  You're the gymnastics coach

ACT II

- That'll give me plenty of time
  So Mike could you read the Baron's lines here.

ACT III

Give it to who?

Ferapont.

We don't have anybody playing Ferapont tonight.

what a nightmare all of this is. And how tired of it all I am.

What happened?

Wave off Fedotik music
"Beatrice, could you cover for me while I rearrange things."

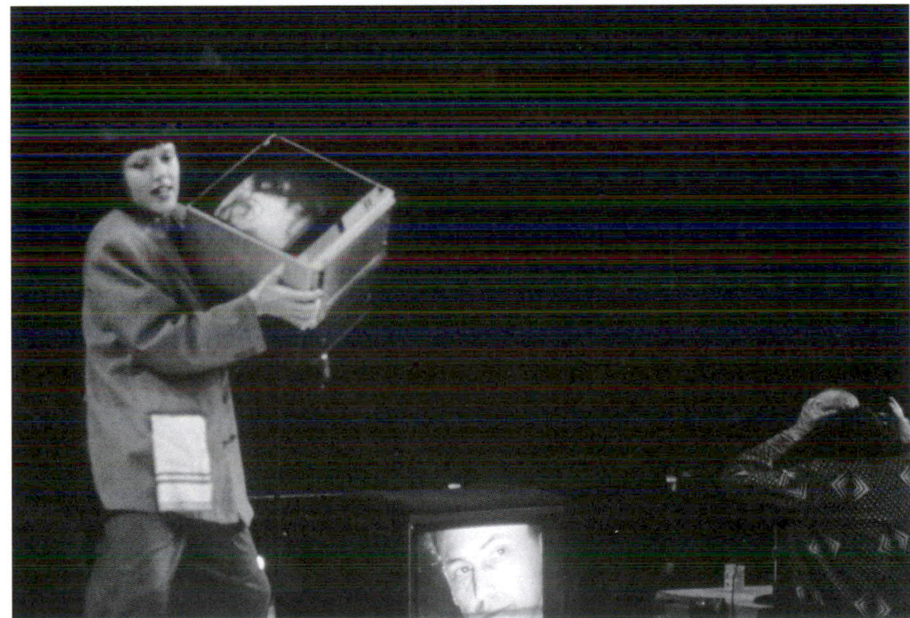

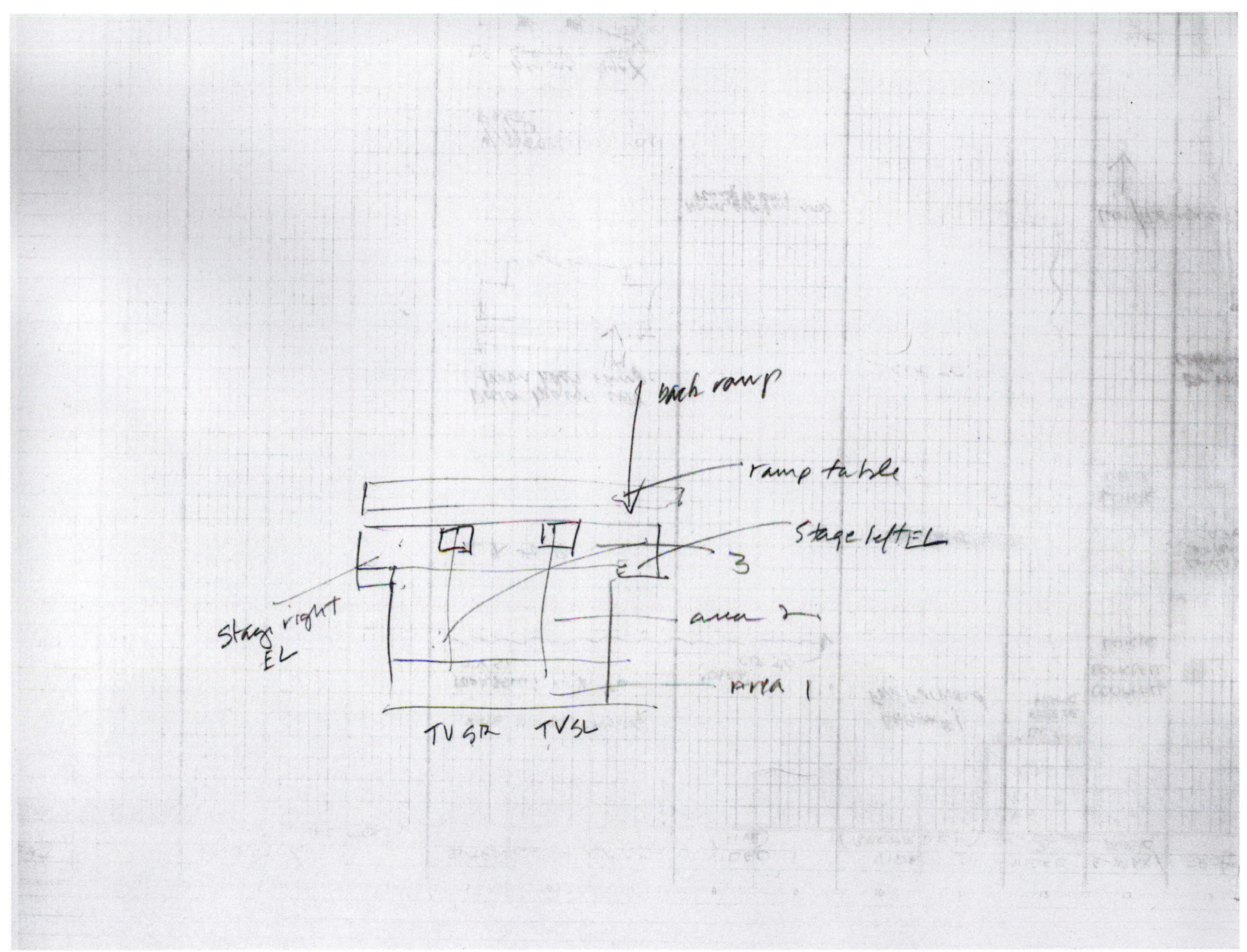

Opposite: ***Brace Up!*** **live camera position, stage left** Above: **Early sketch of set design: Elizabeth LeCompte**

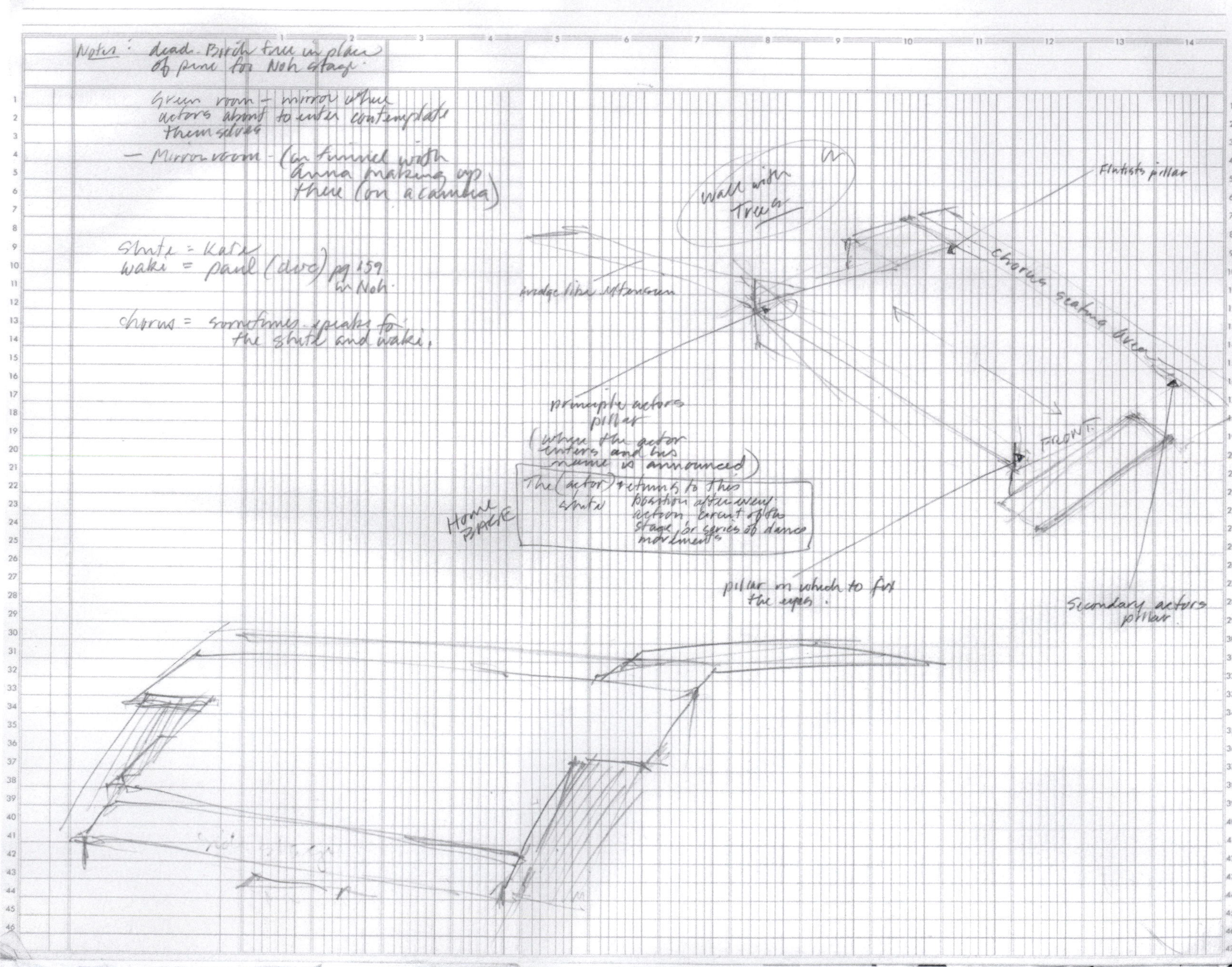
Notes: dead. Birch tree in place
of pine for Noh stage.
Green room – mirror where
actors about to enter contemplate
themselves
— Mirror room – (on tunnel with
making up
there (on a camera)
Shite = Kate
waki = paul pg 159
in Noh.
chorus = sometimes speaks for
the shite and waki.
Wall with
Trees
Flutists pillar
Chorus seating area
bridge like extension
principle actors
pillar
(where the actor
enters and his
name is announced)
The (actor) returns to this
shite
position after every
stage or series of dance
movements
FRONT
pillar on which to fix
the eyes.
Secondary actors
pillar

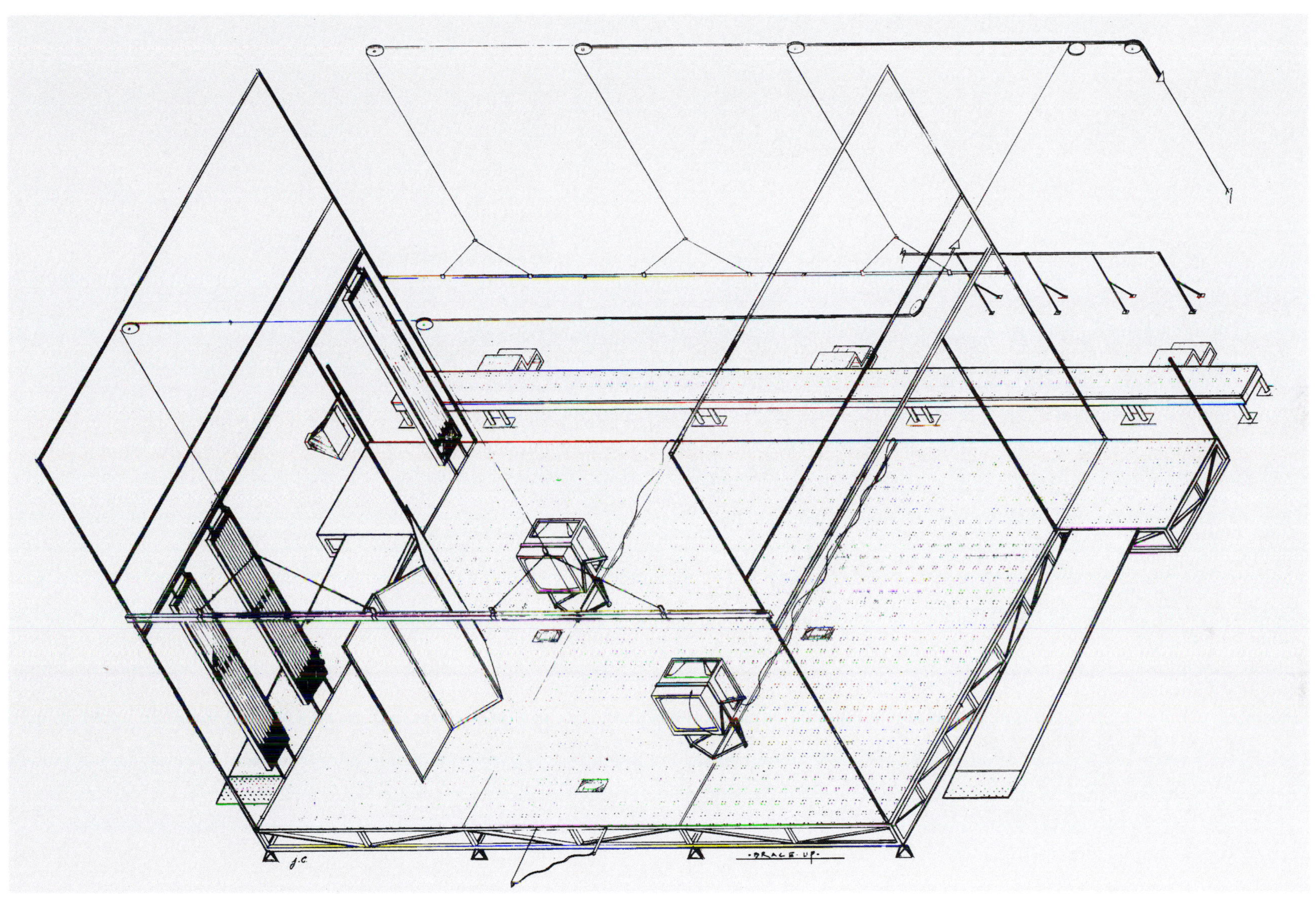

Opposite: **Early sketch of set design with notes: Elizabeth LeCompte** Above: **Final set drawing: Jim Clayburgh**

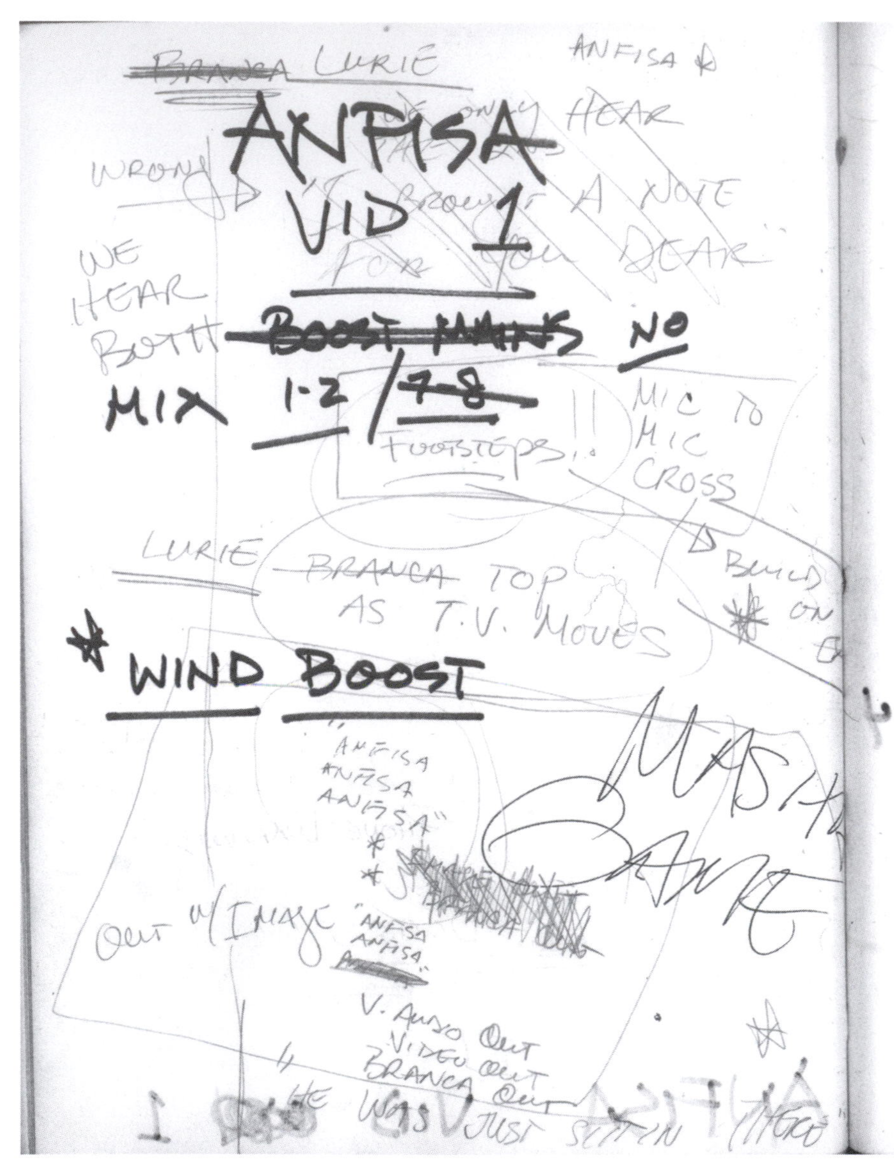

ANFISA: (Handing a cup of tea.) Somebody brought a note for you, dear.

VERSHININ: For me? (He takes it.) It's from my daughter. (He reads it.) Oh god, wouldn't you know ... Excuse me, Maria Sergéevna, I have to go. I'll just slip out quietly. I can't stay for tea. (He stands up, he's upset.) It's the same old story ...

MASHA: What's the matter? I hope it's not a secret.

VERSHININ: (Quietly.) My wife has taken too many pills again. I have to go. I'll go out this way. It's all very unpleasant. (He kisses Masha's hand.) My dearest, you wonderful woman ... I'll just go out quietly ... (He leaves.)

ANFISA: Now where's he going? I just gave him his tea! Really, I never saw the likes ...

MASHA: (She flares up.) Go away! You just stand there bothering me all the time ... (She goes with her tea-cup to the table.) I'm sick and tired of that old woman ...

ANFISA: Now what's gotten into her? My lord!

ANDREI'S VOICE: Anfisa!

ANFISA: (She mimics him.) Anfisa! He just sits there ... (She goes out.)

Early technical score: James ("J.J.") Johnson

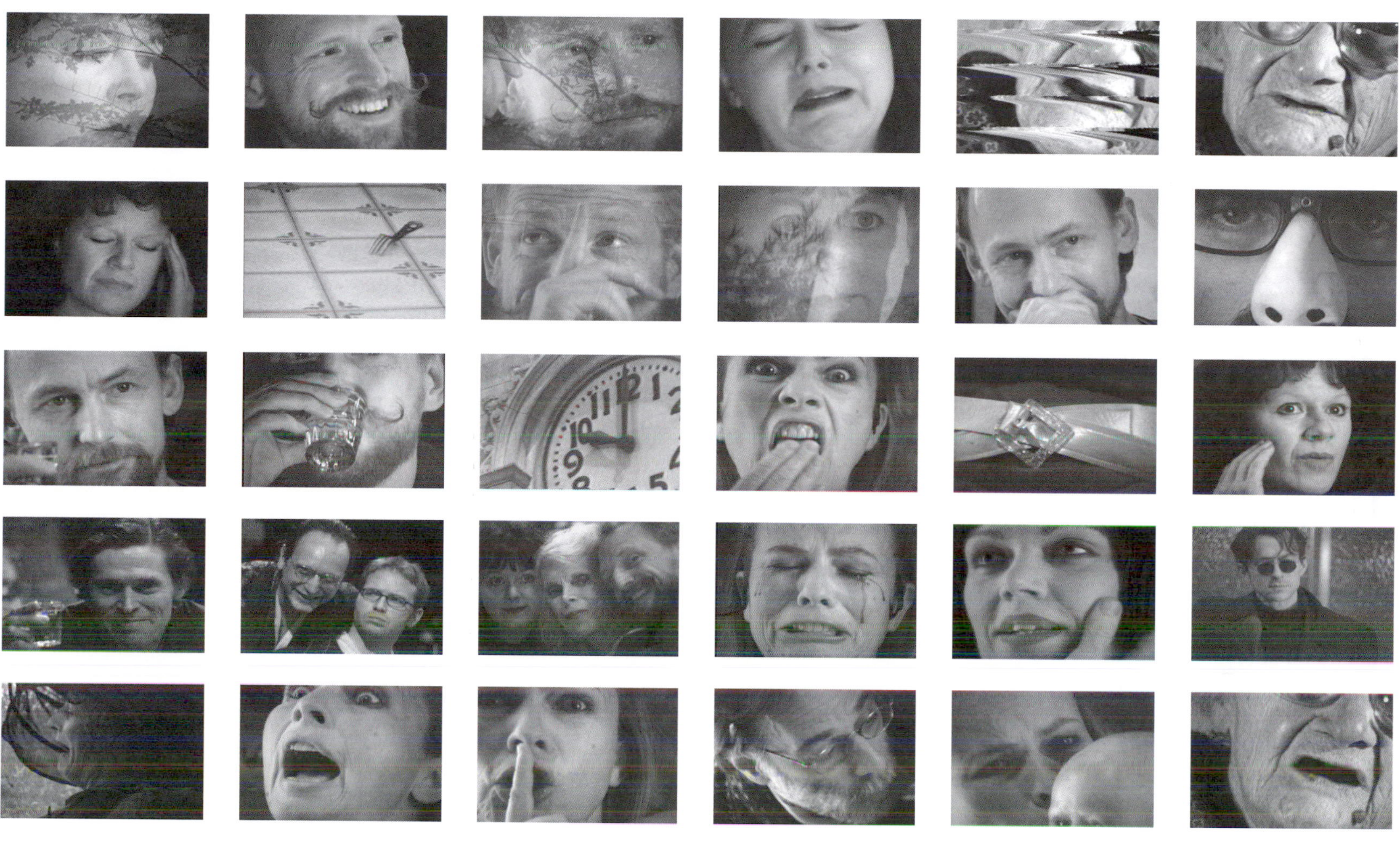

Video stills: *Brace Up!*

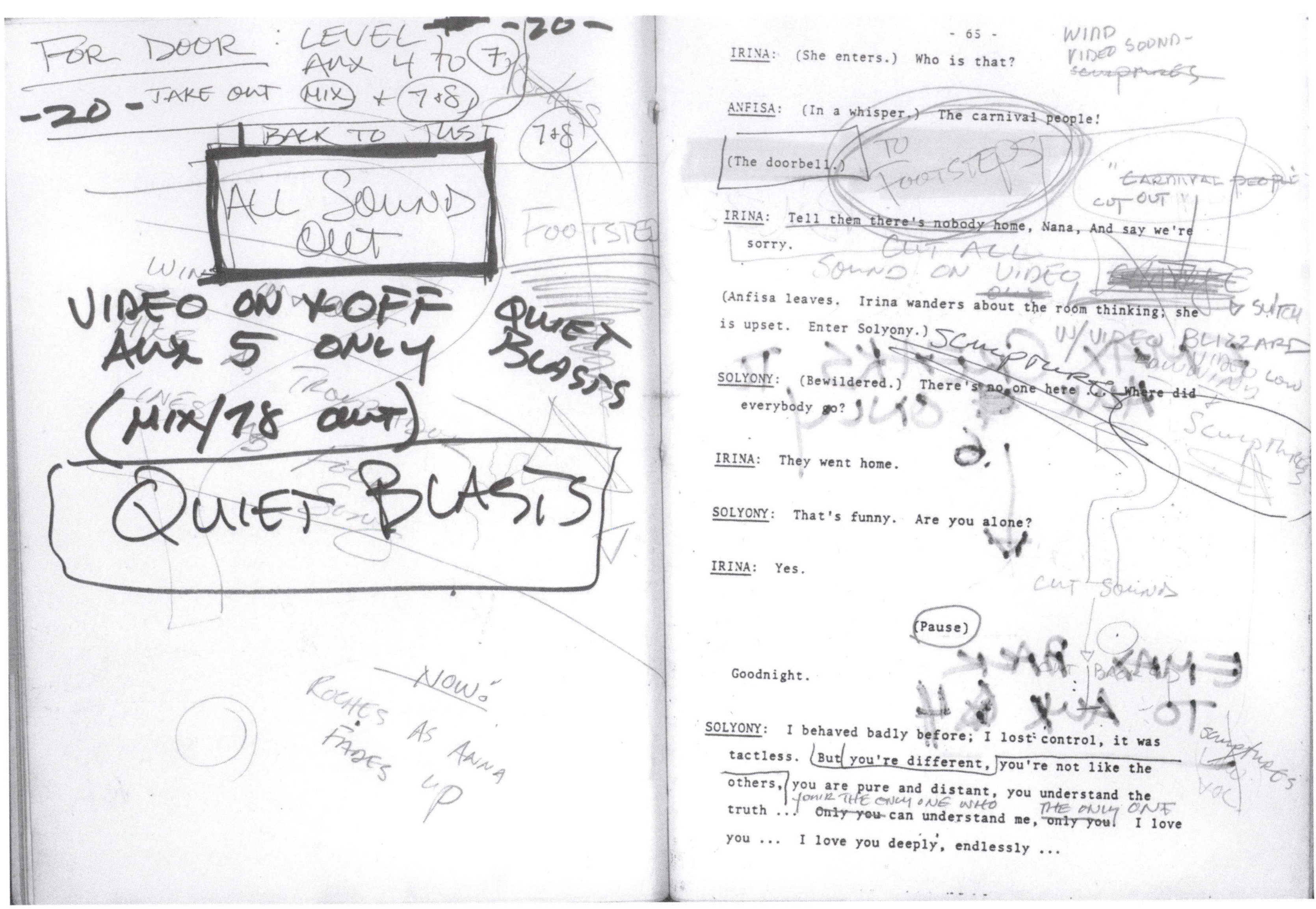

\- 65 -

IRINA: (She enters.) Who is that?

ANFISA: (In a whisper.) The carnival people!

(The doorbell.)

IRINA: Tell them there's nobody home, Nana, And say we're sorry.

(Anfisa leaves. Irina wanders about the room thinking; she is upset. Enter Solyony.)

SOLYONY: (Bewildered.) There's no one here ... Where did everybody go?

IRINA: They went home.

SOLYONY: That's funny. Are you alone?

IRINA: Yes.

(Pause)

Goodnight.

SOLYONY: I behaved badly before; I lost control, it was tactless. But you're different, you're not like the others, you are pure and distant, you understand the truth ... ~~Only you~~ YOU'RE THE ONLY ONE WHO can understand me, ~~only you~~ THE ONLY ONE. I love you ... I love you deeply, endlessly ...

 Early technical score: James ("J.J.") Johnson

Video stills: *Brace Up!*

PROP LIST BRACE UP

shotglasses
fans
round fans
glycerin bottles
menthol cigarettes
matches
~~pill bottles~~
black trays
silver trays
~~strawhat~~
~~black hat~~
multi - coloured duck tape
~~japanese wine glasses~~
brown bottles
~~pepper vodka~~
seethrough bottles
Peyton's note books
samovar
~~silver decanter~~
golden slippers
telephone earpieces
~~purses for sisters~~
ankle weights
ash trays
samurai swords
board games - GO
~~gift wraps~~
candles
pink high heels
Kate's sneakers
Kate's belt (mic)
perfume bottle (Mike Stumm)
blank guns
flasks
deck of cards
little red book
very little red book
pen knife
old woman masks
handkerchieves
eye pads
jap glasses
sun glasses
silverware
wooden sticks
black umbrella
black walking stick
hand mirrors
two screens
2 ~~X~~ floor lamps - 1 lamp, 1 candelabra
music stand

~~baby carriage~~
baby doll
3 belts
2 trunks
3 shower chairs
picture frames - Wilhelm w/ dogs
pillows
coat rack
standing ashtray
japanese wigs
~~breakaway bottles~~
~~spray bottle~~
~~small chair~~
~~seats for the backtable~~
screens

Route 1 + 9 clock

 Left: **Props list:** ***Brace Up!*** Right: **Screen and standing ashtray** Opposite: **"Fast Dance," Act 2:** ***Brace Up!***

Under the alias we use for dance engagements ,"Rae Whitfield and the Johnsons", we'd like to give a lecture/demonstration about how we develop dances and integrate them into our work. And to do this we've assembled a video tape, which includes some of the source material for the music and choreography that went into the making of our current piece BRACE UP! which is based on Chekhov's Three Sisters. We'll be alternating between showing you source tapes and the demonstrating our dances.
The first tape is of a dance from the Cook Islands, which I made at the 1988 Pacific Arts Festival in Townsville, Australia. Following that is the title sequence from a documentary about the gypsy-like world of a Japanese theater troupe, the Geinin.

COOK ISLAND TAPE
GEININ TAPE

And now an excerpt from the men's dance.

MEN'S DANCE

The next tape is also from the Pacific Arts Festival, a dance from Naura, a Melanesian Island.

NAURU TAPE

And now these elements comingled with Act Two of Three Sisters in which the Baron gets drunk and plays the piano. The waltz is by Evan Lurie.

Jeff: "Alright ladies and gentlemen here we go . . ."
WALTZ/FAST DANCE
Anna: "Ivan Romanich!"
Kate: That's Natasha--she's upset because the part woke the baby.

Next is a dance from the Melanesian Island, Fiji. And a section from Ozu's film A Story of Floating Weeds. Followed by a snippet of Godzilla from Monster Zero.

FIJI TAPE
FLOATING WEEDS TAPE (BOAT)

Now these elements comingled with Act Three of Three Sisters, in which there's a big fire in town. Fedotik, a minor character, enters and does a little dance. The dance is interrupted by Solyony.

FEDOTIK DANCE

KATE: That was Solyony.
Next on the video is another brief section of Ozu's film A Story of Floating Weeds. And a dance from Hiroshi Inagaki's film, Duel at Ichijoji Temple in which Toshiro Mifune watches a courtesan perform the "Tassel Dance." And "Bedtime for Sniffles" from Warner Bros.

FLOATING WEEDS TAPE (WOMAN AND BOY DANCING)
TASSEL DANCE TAPE
SNIFFLES TAPE

And now these elements comingled with Chekov's Act Four, a group of street musicians appears in the garden.

BEAUTIFUL DREAMER

Anfisa, the old nurse gives them money, and they leave.
Another dance from the Pacific Arts Festival, this one is from Hawaii.

HAWAIIN TAPE

(CANYON LANDS MUSIC STARTS) We'd like to present a dance which we are developing for our new piece, Fish Story or Today I Must Sincerely Congratulate You. Music by David Lanz and Paul Speer, "Canyon Lands."

CANYONS LANDS DANCE

We'll close with the Farewell Song we perform in BRACE UP! which is running at the Performing Garage through the end of April. It's from Act Four, of Three Sisters, the brigade is leaving town. The music is a tarantella by John and Evan Lurie, lyrics by our translator, Paul Schmidt.

And you guys have the lyrics to this right? Why don't you hop in on this?
TARANTELLA

 Above: Notes for presentation on *Brace Up!* and other dances (Whitney Museum of American Art) Opposite: "Stick Dance," Act 1: *Brace Up!*

STICK DANCE

2 GROUPS OF

1) • ON FLOOR 4 KNEEL + CROSS STICKS
x 6 TIMES RISING – ANNA CALLS "GIVE ME A BANANA"
HIT HIT HIT

2) – ALL TURN AND FACE CIRCLE, HIT STICKS,
– COUNT TWO BEATS SILENT
– PULSE WHACK – START TO THE RIGHT • 3 SETS OF 8
(MICHAEL COUNTS OUT EACH 8)
– ANNA YELLS LAST 4 BEATS OF LAST 8
– ALL HOLD AND COUNT SILENT 4

3) ALL TURN TO THEIR SQUARE AND HIT ON 1

4 SETS OF 4 (4th COUNT HOLD, JUMP ON AND 1)
Man Woman
Woman Men

1) ① TOP R, ② TOP L, TURN STICK ③ BOTTOM R, ④ HOLD

2) ① TOP R, ② BOTTOM L, ③ ♀ STICKS OVER LOW R
♂ HIGH R ④ HOLD

HORIZONTAL 3) ① ♀ STICK OVER BOTTOM L (HIT TOP OF STICK)
♂ BOTTOM L (DON'T TURN OVER)
HORIZONTAL ② ♀ TOP L
♂ TOP L
VERTICAL ③ ♀ HIT TOP R
♂ TOP R
④ HOLD (+ JUMP)
Men jump to inside (outside?) left
Women jump to inside (outside?) r

5th CYCLE – ANNA COUNTS LAST 2 OF CYCLE 4
– ALL TURN + FACE BIG CIRCLE
⟶ GO TO SETS OF 4
– (ON + 1) ALL JUMP TO R, 2 ON ENDS
MAKE FULL CIRCLE JUMP

– WHEN BACK TO ORIGINAL SPACE, TURN TO
ORIGINAL SQUARE POSITION
– DO SET OF 4 THEN:
♂ JUMP TO INSIDE LEFT OF SQUARE
♀ JUMP TO INSIDE RIGHT OF SQUARE
– DO SET OF 4
– JUMP ACROSS (FACE OUT) ON 1, 2
TURN AND CROSS STICKS ON 3, 4
PULSE WHACK 2 SETS OF 8 ^(ANNA YELLS LAST 4) PLUS ONE
GO DOWN TO KNEELING ON FLOOR X 6

END – POUND STICKS VERTICALLY ONCE

 "Stick Dance" notation: Jo Andres

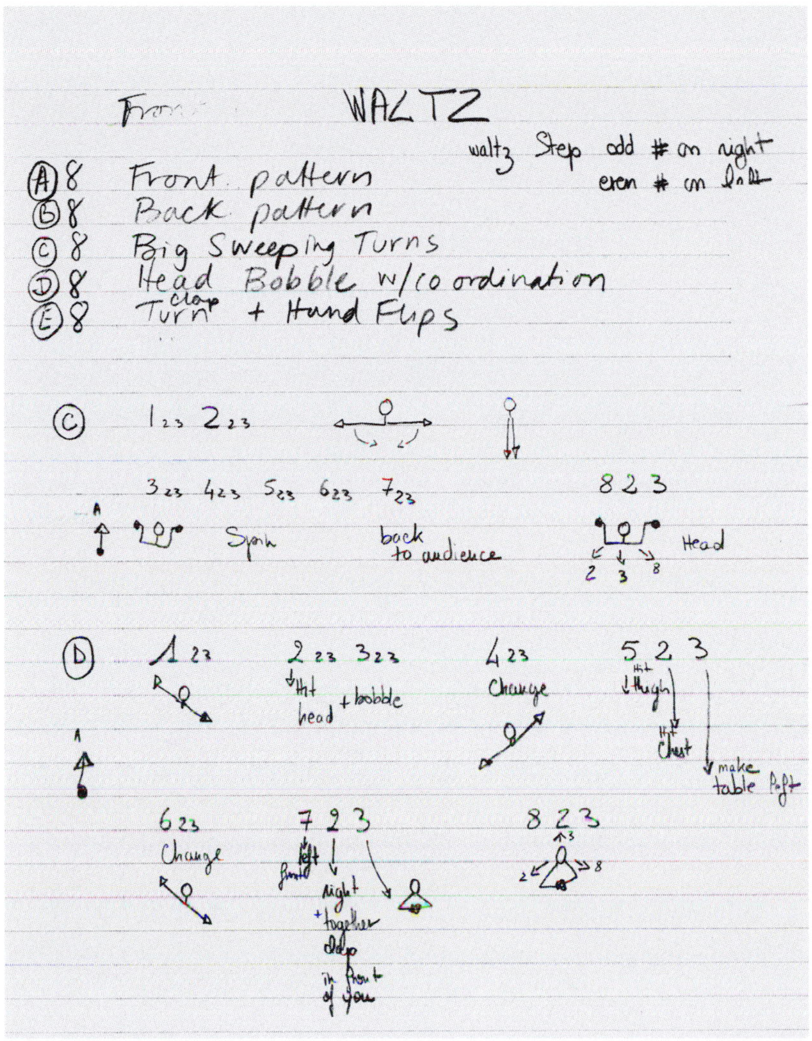

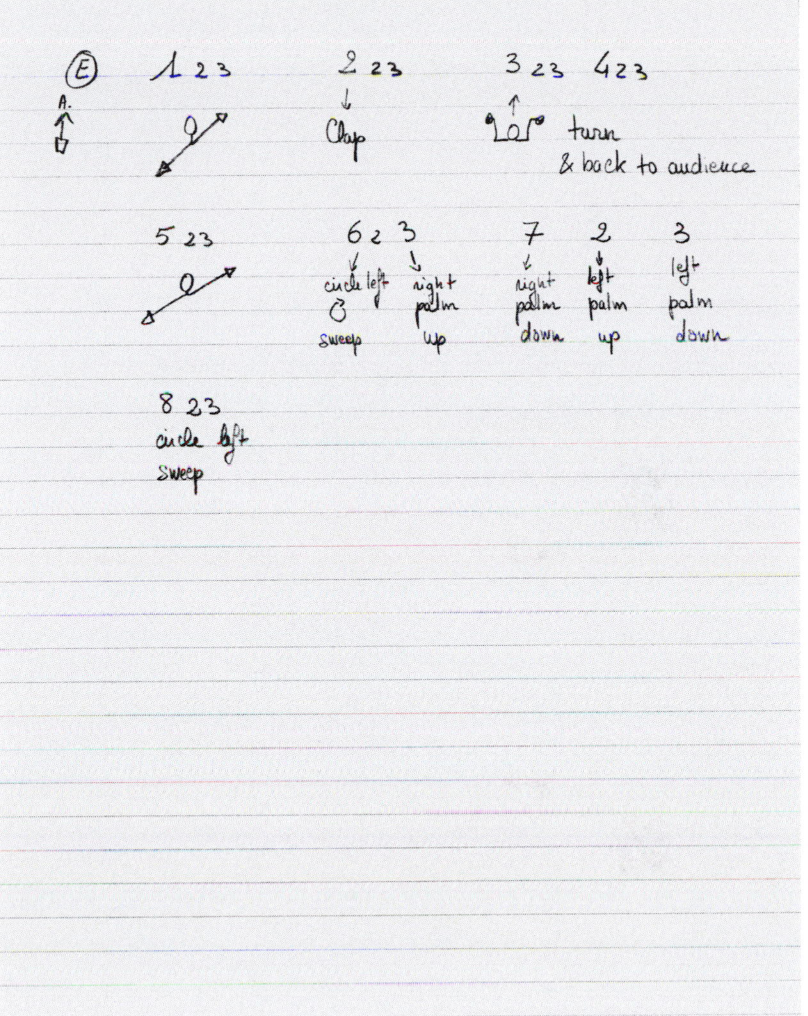

"Waltz" notation: Jo Andres

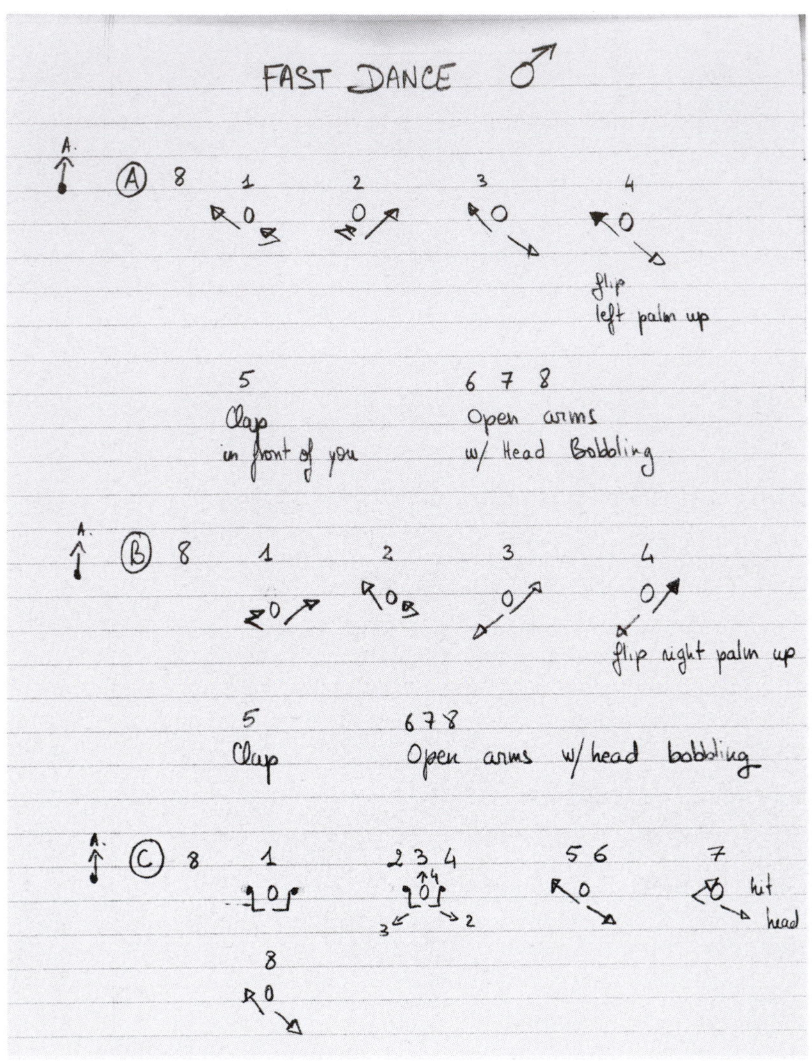

FAST DANCE ♂

A. (A) 8

1 2 3 4

flip
left palm up

5
Clap
in front of you

6 7 8
Open arms
w/ Head Bobbling

A. (B) 8

1 2 3 4

flip right palm up

5
Clap

6 7 8
Open arms w/ head bobbling

A. (C) 8

1 2 3 4 5 6 7

hit
head

8

A. (D) 12

1 2
Change arms
through center
horizontal in front
of you

3
Hit left
thigh

4
Hit chest
w/ left hand

5
left hand table

6
circle
sweep
left hand

7 8
flip right palm
up & down

1 2
flip left palm
up & down

3 4
circle
sweep left hand.

"Fast Dance" notation: Jo Andres

Top: **"Fast Dance," Act 2: *Brace Up!*** Bottom: **Dance from video: *Geinin (Today I Must Sincerely Congratulate You)***

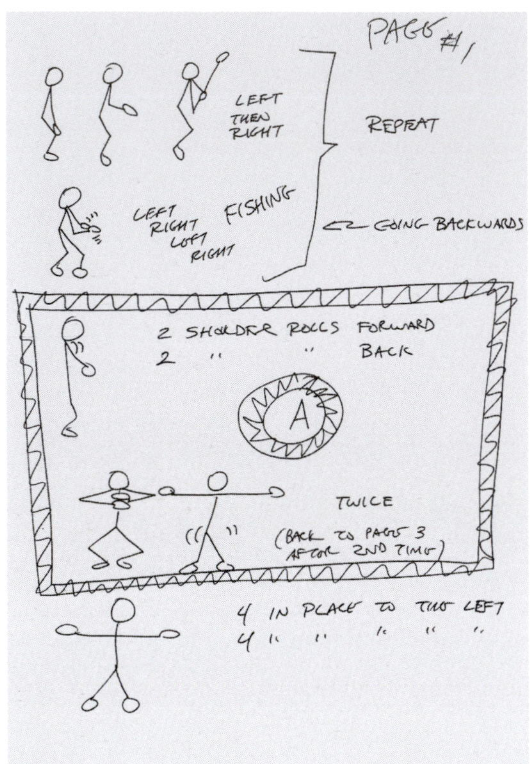
PAGE #1
LEFT THEN RIGHT
REPEAT
LEFT RIGHT LEFT RIGHT
FISHING
GOING BACKWARDS
2 SHOULDER ROLLS FORWARD
2 " " BACK
A
TWICE
(BACK TO PAGE 3 AFTER 2ND TIME)
4 IN PLACE TO THE LEFT
4 " " " " "

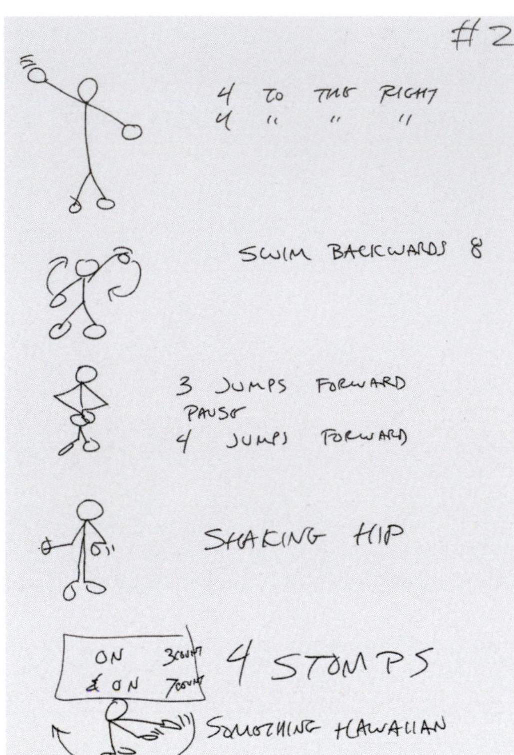
#2
4 TO THE RIGHT
4 " " "
SWIM BACKWARDS 8
3 JUMPS FORWARD
PAUSE
4 JUMPS FORWARD
SHAKING HIP
ON 3 COUNT & ON 7 COUNT
4 STOMPS
SOMETHING HAWAIIAN

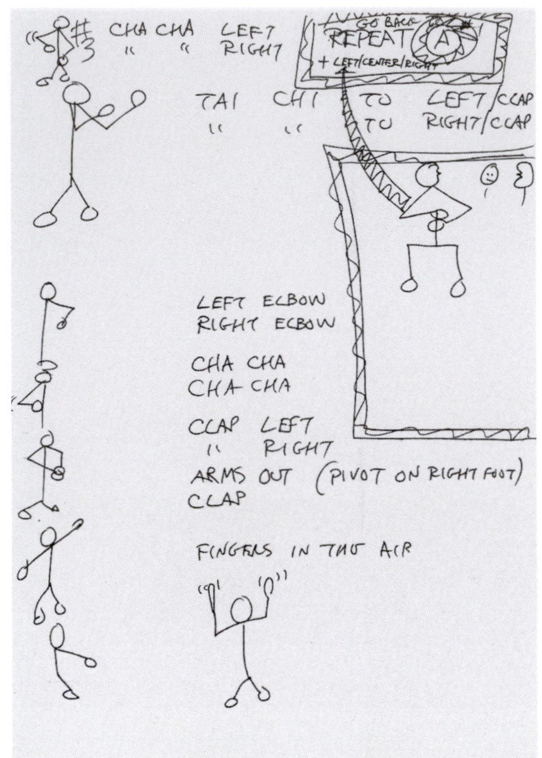
#3
CHA CHA LEFT
" " RIGHT
GO BACK
REPEAT A
+ LEFT/CENTER/RIGHT
TAI CHI TO LEFT/CLAP
" " TO RIGHT/CLAP
LEFT ELBOW
RIGHT ELBOW
CHA CHA
CHA CHA
CLAP LEFT
" RIGHT
ARMS OUT (PIVOT ON RIGHT FOOT)
CLAP
FINGERS IN THE AIR

Brace Up! dance notation: Roy Faudree

HP5
2 6 5 7
ILFORD
29A
30
30A

ACT IV
"Beautiful Dreamer"
Jeff's Dance

Clap front –
bend – Punch
~
Clap front – back – front – under (L) Knee
~ Clap front – back – front – under (R) Knee
~
Clap front – bend – Punch
~
Swing Step Left
~
Swing Step Right
~
Push left ~ Again (Right leg + arm long)
~
Push right ~ Again (left leg + arm long)
~
Clap – bend – Punch
~
Left hand flourish
Right hand flourish
Left hand flourish
Right hand flourish
~
Clap – bend – punch
~
Stir motion w/hands counter clockwise
to right

 "Beautiful Dreamer" notation: Kate Valk

FAREWELL SONG

ACT 4

It's time to say goodby forever now,
we'll never see each other here again.
The things we said won't matter anyhow,
and we'll forget the things we did back then . . .

Take another picture . . .

[KULYGIN: (speaks quickly) Who knows? Maybe if you're lucky you'll get yourself a Polish wife, they kiss you all the time and call you Kohany.]

Who wants to meet again in fifteen years?
I'll hardly know you , and you won't know me.
Who wants to reawaken long lost tears?
We won't remember how it used to be . . .

Just another picture

[RHODE: (speaks quickly) Where's Maria Sergeyevna?
KULYGIN: (speaks quickly) Masha's somewhere out here in the garden.]

Solyony and the barge are in the rear,
and all the rest of us go with the men.
In half an hour we'll be leaving here,
and peace and quiet will return again . . .

Just another picture . . .

Wait a minute now, half a minute now,
wait a minute now, just a minute now,
wait a minute now, take a minute now,

Goodbye

 Above: "Farewell Song," Act 4: *Brace Up!* Opposite: Irina's birthday party photographs: Act 1: *Brace Up!*

Top left: **"Cockroach juice."**

Bottom left: **"Well, we only live once, by God, and sometimes you win, sometimes you lose."**

Top right: **"Irina dearest, here's hoping you find yourself a suitable fiancée."**

Bottom right: **"The weather is just wonderful today. Really beautiful."**

Rehearsing goodbyes in *Brace Up!* and *Fish Story*

An interview with Elizabeth LeCompte (New York, July 12th, 2006)

Andrew Quick (AQ): What drew you to Chekhov's *Three Sisters* for the performance of *Brace Up!*?

Elizabeth LeCompte (EL): Oh, Ron. First of all, I think Ron (Vawter) knew that he was very sick and, in his way, he was kind of preparing the group. I wasn't very focused at that time because I was concentrating on the piece we'd just made. But he was always thinking ahead, even though he was so ill. And he wanted to do a piece where he wasn't the central focus, so that he could leave—first of all, because he was working on *Roy Cohn/Jack Smith* (1992) and also because he wanted a piece that had more women in it. We had more women in the company at that time, because Katie (Kate Valk) and Peyton (Smith) were the heart of the Group. So, as I recall, he suggested reading Chekhov. I'd never read any Chekhov. I had seen a couple of plays, but I don't think I had ever seen a production of *Three Sisters*, except in Dutch.

AQ: And did you know about Paul Schmidt's translation?

EL: No. Nobody did. Even Ronnie didn't know about it. We started reading as many translations as we could get hold of. I think we read four or five. We looked at the standard one and it was kind of icky. It was the first time I had to deal with a translation of a play. It had an awkward tone, a bit like Flaubert's writing in *St. Antony* (1987). But, the Chekhov also felt very English, very afternoon tea. Around this time I met Paul Schmidt—he'd come to a couple of shows. He was a friend of Ron. Ron spoke to him and he said, "I have something I've been working on." He hadn't published it yet. So, he came in and read his translation with us. He said it wasn't quite finished, but I loved it.

AQ: Why did you like it so much?

EL: It just seemed to flow very naturally. It just felt very easy. There wasn't a place that I didn't think someone from the cast couldn't say the words. Unlike something by Shakespeare, they all felt sayable.

AQ: How did you deal with the Chekhov text in the early rehearsals?

EL: I used a video camera. I had different people either reading the text or passing the reading on to somebody else. They could choose any parts. I think Katie and Ron chose up to four parts and then I would watch and tape them in close-up as they moved around in the room.

AQ: In the earliest rehearsal tapes I found you had older women playing the sisters, with Kate and Peyton sort of acting as their assistants.

EL: That's what I did. I went there very quickly. I went to Beatrice (Roth) playing Irina pretty much right away, because I knew her. She'd been in several pieces and I knew her tone and I knew Joan Jonas would be Masha because I had worked with her and also knew her tone. I was thinking in terms of what was right spiritually and emotionally, rather than age.

AQ: Oh, so it had nothing to do with the performers' ages at all?

EL: No, it was more that these people could handle the language. They could handle the emotion. Originally, I had thought of Ruth Maleczech as Olga and Peyton and Katie were both going to play the maids and serving people, moving around the main characters, taking some of the lines. But Peyton didn't want to do this. So, I put her in Olga's spot.

AQ: Was it because she identified with the character?

EL: No, no. She wanted a part that she didn't have to develop. She wanted something that was already written and that was what was great about Peyton. She didn't like rehearsals. It was more a pragmatic thing for her. Peyton didn't like to improvise at all. So, it all kind of fell into place that way. And she was brilliant in the role.

AQ: In the early rehearsals the sisters were seated in wheelchairs covered by large hooped skirts. Was this so you could move them around to create some sense of mobility in the space?

EL: Yes. I had problems with performers moving on a big stage. I hadn't really worked with performers moving on a big stage before. In all the other pieces I'd made, the performers were attached to the stage or attached to the doors or they were on a very narrow plane that would define their movements in terms of depth. Their movements were all defined by the physical world of the space. Their choices were limited and this was easier for me with performers who were comfortable in naturalism, who were at ease on the stage. Many of them would have been comfortable on film. I had so many different styles of performer that I tended to have to unify them by creating very strong exterior ways of containing them, or framing or holding them. Here, I just had a big open space, which was modeled for me on the Noh Theater stage: the flat platform with an entrance on the back and to the side, where the musicians and chorus sat. It was all arranged around this idea. I knew I had to find some structure that they could move in, that would give them a solid base for movement, that wasn't improvised or wasn't natural. I didn't have any naturalistic props or anything they could use on the stage. I found the solution lay between the chairs that they would have to sit in and Katie, who could move on the stage so well, being able to move the chairs as if they were props. It was like the doors in *St. Antony*—if someone didn't need to move, I tied them to the door, so they couldn't move. This was a development of that idea. It was a little more open than just tying someone down to a piece of furniture. I looked into finding chairs that could be moved easily, so you could get things going quickly, things that could move across the stage, have interesting patterns and be fun to watch.

AQ: Did you have to make the chairs?

EL: I found the chairs in a medical catalogue. I was looking for something with very good casters on them. Those particular chairs are shower chairs. They have to be able to be moved into a shower and then turned around in a tight circle, so all four casters are movable and all four casters can be locked. This meant I could spend a great deal of time arranging the motion and emotion that could come out of the relationship between the performers and the chairs.

AQ: What drew you to the form of Noh Theater? It seems a big leap in style from *St. Antony*.

EL: Yes, it was a big leap. I had taken a trip to Japan on the way back from Australia, sometime in 1986. I don't think any Noh Theater was running at the time, but Katie and I went to see some Kabuki. I can't remember whether that was what set me off or whether we went to Japan because we had started watching Japanese silent films...

AQ: But you hadn't seen *Geinin* (1977), the documentary about the Sentaro Ichikawa Troupe, the traveling Japanese theater company?

EL: No, it was a little later, at the end of the 80s, when I was thinking of making a film like the *Geinin* documentary instead of making a theater piece. And then we used it directly in *Fish Story* (1994).

AQ: So, you were watching early Japanese cinema?

EL: Yes. After we had been watching the Japanese silent films I guess we got into (Yasujiro) Ozu's work. I think I got interested in Ozu's style because the dialogue in his films was Chekhovian to me.

AQ: Did this impression of Japanese culture as seen through film create some resonance with an idea of Russia?

EL: Maybe it had to do with repression and a certain kind of Victorianism. I also saw a fully developed physical style in the Noh Theater and in these films that was not naturalistic. It had a structure outside naturalism. This was great for me. Whenever I didn't know what to do, I could always go back to a pattern from the Noh, because I had the books that had diagrams of the movements. So, I would follow these patterns, depending on the Noh play, and completely superimpose them on the Chekhov. If I didn't know what to do, or a character didn't know what to do—if there wasn't a window to go up to, or there wasn't a tablecloth to ruffle, or something like that—I would have them complete the pattern of movement in some way, as something else was going on. It gave me a way of moving people on the stage without worrying about creating something literal. I guess it was a device to get away from any literalness on the stage, which really wasn't interesting to me.

AQ: And I presume the Japanese Noh tradition also gave you a way of thinking about the costumes and the overall look of the piece.

EL: At the time I remember there were several designers around who were also interested in Japanese culture and we would go and look at their things and then we would recreate our own version of what we saw, or we would buy second-hand pieces. We got several items that we cut up and we made, or we copied things that we had seen by adapting already tailored clothing. It was something that was around in the fashion industry at the time. We were just cutting and pasting and making our own kind of rough copy of these costumes.

AQ: You didn't have a specific costume designer then? It was all done in-house, as it were.

EL: Not at first. It was really between me and Katie. Then, Elizabeth (Jenyon) arrived in the middle of this process. She made some of the pieces for the final show. For instance, there was a coat of mine that I cut up and gave to Beatrice and then Elizabeth made a beautiful organza top, like a white pinafore, which went over her head. She made it to accompany the coat. After that she came in and made several beautiful and really important pieces. She also came at the end and made all of Anna Köhler's costumes—the crazy ones—creating them from stuff we had upstairs in the Garage. We started out ourselves, but Elizabeth came in pretty early on and definitely put her stamp on it.

AQ: One of the consistent things about your staging is the types of props you use—this is especially true of *Brace Up!* and *Fish Story*—they're very beautiful and often have an antique or nostalgic feel to them. They're from a time when craftsmanship was still respected. I'm thinking here of the lamps and tables that you put on your stages. I remember when I first saw *Brace Up!* that the clash of culture, the clash between the American and the Eastern, seemed significant, as if the economic shift between East and West that was going on in the early 90s was somehow reflected in the use of props. You know, an old world meeting a new one. Seeing it in 2003 was very different, as Japan had recently gone through its own economic crisis. But in the 90s Japan felt like the future. It felt like the new world.

EL: That's right—like China is now. I hadn't thought of that.

AQ: It's interesting that in Chekhov's play Vershinin is so concerned with the future and something about your staging appears to be set in the future—an imagined future. I know this idea of the future was something that directly informed *Fish Story*. In one of the early rehearsal tapes you jokingly say it's set in 2020.

EL: That's true. I wasn't even thinking so much of the Japanese; I was just thinking and imagining us in the future.

AQ: You were imagining the idea of The Wooster Group?

EL: Actually, we are there now.

AQ: This notion of the future was vividly brought to life in the 2003 revival of *Brace Up!*. I think it was obvious to everyone, even those that hadn't seen the original production, that the concept of change, of people getting older, of people dying, was being negotiated. Take the video of Paul Schmidt, for example. His absence, his death, was movingly and wittily acknowledged. Yet, despite all the ghosts that seemed to haunt the stage there was definitely an air of "We move on, we move forward and things change and we get on with it." A bit like the people in Chekhov's play, really.

EL: Definitely.

AQ: The televisions in *Brace Up!* seem to have a slightly different function compared with their use and placement within the space in previous works, such as *Route 1 & 9* and *St. Antony*.

EL: Well, I always intended to use the televisions. The use of television in the pieces has evolved as the ability to quickly edit videotape in-house changed. I think this was the first piece where Chris (Kondek) could edit something upstairs in the Garage that night and come back with it into the rehearsal the next day. Before, we had to go over to a place on Rivington Street before midnight to get the cheap editing set-up.

AQ: It must have been slow and expensive to edit the material that way.

EL: Yes, it was really hard. And that dominated how we had made all the previous pieces. This was the first time we could control the editing. Plus, I think this was the first piece where we used video live on the stage.

AQ: In *St. Antony* you create the sense of live video—for example, when Ron asks the sound operator to rewind the tapes.

EL: Yes, but it was all pre-made. Ron had to stay with the video. It's the reverse now, the video has to stay with the performer—catch up with them. *Brace Up!* was also the first time where we had a technical person looking after all the video material. Before, we'd all done it. Kenny (Kobland) would help a lot. I would do some. Sometimes it would fall to somebody else. Chris came in and became the designated video person. He just took it over, which made this part much easier for me because I didn't have to worry about the video side of things. Chris just went off on his own. Plus, Roy (Faudree) joined us for *Brace Up!* and he really enjoyed working with the live video. He works with a lot of video in his own pieces. He went to the corner of the set where he used the camera to do the live recording of Paul (Schmidt) as Chebutykin. So, I had two people who really enjoyed the camera, who enjoyed being there, and that made a big difference.

AQ: And there's a sense of video effects being used in *Brace Up!*.

EL: Yes. But, there aren't really any effects—maybe they were considered effects back then.

AQ: You could use cross fades and create certain textures or particular bold colors.

EL: We started to play around. There were only very simple video effects at that point. Yet, they were wonderful and they were perfectly Japanese as well. The images that we could create had a simple child-like quality that Japanese toys have. There's a strong element of animation, of cartoons in Japanese culture, so these early effects were perfect.

AQ: Isn't this the first time that you create the sense that the TVs are also windows? You literally put a frame on them.

EL: Yes, when Natasha yells out of the window on the TV, that was the first time.

AQ: I remember I found the use of TVs as windows very funny when I first saw *Brace Up!*. I suppose it had something to do with the fact that in Stanislavski's original production the set had these huge windows, which dominated the back and the side of the stage. And you had reduced those windows to these small black boxes. I remember thinking how appropriate this seemed—that today televisions are our windows onto the world.

EL: These old televisions are also boxes and it's a beautiful thing that there is something inside this box. You always have that freedom with a TV, even if it's a flat screen. If you take away the light producing front and put in a neutral density filter on the screen, it's more like you have to go into the TV rather than have the image coming at you. And for me that was very pleasing. You seem to think that these things are actually happening in the box. Like when you were a child—you probably didn't do this—but when I was a child, I would take the boxes my parents had no use for and I would cut the bottom out and cut a hole in it and pretend I was on the television.

AQ: And you had that amazing sound effect, as well, when the televisions came forward — a sort of rumble.

EL: This was the first time, besides the rewind sound in *St. Antony*, that I really began using sound from the video-track. To make the sound score, we took the sound from the films that we were using, or a Noh Theater videotape, or the sounds from the Japanese films — like *Godzilla*. When we took the sounds of instruments from the Noh and the Kyogen, I just electronified them a little bit.

AQ: The sound score is very important in *Brace Up!*. How do you select the different sounds, what was informing your decisions?

EL: The sound score grew as I developed the piece. If something didn't work, I would bring in the sound. Or, if something didn't work on the stage and I needed some kind of punctuation or something else, I would bring in that one sound. I also used it throughout *Fish Story*. I can't describe it, but it's from one of the Noh tapes — a kind of "keee." I used it a lot for punctuation, the same way I used the crash sound in *House/Lights* — to put an end to something, to say "ha hah," to be like a door slamming shut. So, I think the sound score comes out of a combination of things. If I think I need something, I just tell the sound people and Chris to turn up the sound on whatever is running through their systems. Chris always had something going on several tracks and if it worked I would say, "Yes, take that out and keep it." If it didn't work, we would try something else.

AQ: Did you work that way with *Fish Story*?

EL: Yes, Chris took the sound track from what I had on tape. It was the same process. All of the sounds are from the videos or films that were involved in the piece. Sometimes we took the visual away but we kept all the sounds. As I recall, there might be one or two things that are anomalies, taken from another piece, but all the sound in *Fish Story* is from Japanese tapes.

AQ: In *Brace Up!* you supplement the excerpts from Japanese film with brief glimpses of Kenneth Branagh's *Henry V* (1989). How did Shakespeare get in the mix?

EL: That's a good question. I don't know how that got in. It was probably Chris.

AQ: It's so appropriate, all that military machismo.

EL: Chris was so good at that — he and Katie. They both brought a lot of great material into the rehearsals. Chris had no fear of interfering with anything I was doing. He would just come in with anything at any time and it wasn't intellectual, he was an intuitive guy that way. It was very easy making a piece with the video because Chris and Katie were completely on my wavelength with it. Katie loved certain parts of the language and stories in some films, so she would bring in something appropriate to that story. Chris liked visual images and the sound, so he would work on that side of things — we made a great threesome (laughs).

AQ: It's clear that Chris has an understanding of film, of the language of it, as an aesthetic, as a history.

EL: Kenny (Kobland) has that too. Now, people working with video seem much more intellectual, they're much more technology driven. Now, it's more about finding what's appropriate and using video more as an adjunct, rather than as something that is absolutely integral, without any logical meaning. Maybe there's too much logic with video now.

AQ: You use a videotape of *Godzilla* to take over the character of Solyony. Was this a pragmatic way to solve the problem that the actor wasn't available for rehearsals?

EL: Yes, it was pragmatic. We just happened to have the *Godzilla* material there because we were using it as a soundtrack and so when Mike (Stumm, who played the part of Solyony) didn't show up we just turned it up. And this happens because Chris is right there in rehearsal. I would say, "We need the television up," and he brought in the *Godzilla* at a loud level.

AQ: So, he was bringing in ideas and responses into the process for you?

EL: Yes. I had to rely a lot on the technical people doing great things in that piece. The big idea might be mine, but how they implemented it was theirs. They could do whatever they wanted and I don't always work like that. It just depends on the person and there was a good combination of people to work in that way in *Brace Up!*.

AQ: I want to ask you about Kate's role as the interlocutor in *Brace Up!*. She's mentioned to me that she's been a facilitator on stage for you — a link between you and the audience. Did you have this function in mind early on or did it evolve in rehearsal?

EL: No. I always knew she would have that kind of function.

AQ: Because she is so pivotal, isn't she, to how the piece moves?

EL: Well, I didn't think we could do the piece without Kate having that role. The play had so many characters that I didn't really think we could do the piece without someone who loved the language and could follow it and could come in and out of the parts that might be missing; because from the very beginning we weren't even sure who was going to be able to be there every day. We sometimes had rehearsals where a large number of people would be missing, because we couldn't afford to pay everybody. So, she would always fill in. I needed someone who had a really good memory and who loved all the parts and didn't identify with any of them like a conventional actress. She identified with everything.

AQ: So, she became a vital link between you and the stage in rehearsals. It's almost a dramaturgical role, isn't it? In *House/Lights* she was your dramaturg.

EL: Katie knew the play so well. When I'd say, "We need something more here, what's happening here?," because I wouldn't remember where we were in the text, she would be able to say, "Oh, we're here," and then she would be able to run the scene out for me. So, I never had to rely on the script. I didn't have to look at it. I could hear it in the space.

AQ: This meant your attention was always on the stage.

EL: Yes, rather than looking down. As soon as I looked down I would say, "Oh, this is perfect" and then I would look up and it wouldn't work. The two things —the stage and the page—never meshed in that piece. In rehearsal I always had to be looking at the stage.

AQ: I wanted to ask you about Ron Vawter. Did you always know that he was going to play the role of Vershinin? His performance seems so placed in *Brace Up!*.

EL: No, at the start I didn't know what part he was going to play. I don't know if he knew. Maybe he did, but he would never have said to me, "I want to play this part." He just never would have done that. You see, I didn't know the play. I didn't know that Masha was considered such a big part in it. I had no idea. I saw all three women as integral. When I started to hear people going "Oh, she's playing Masha," I didn't understand why they were saying this because all the sisters seemed equally important to me. Masha didn't seem any more special than the other two. I still don't think she is, unless I'm misreading the play. Masha is as wonderful and crazy and as silly as the others are and she doesn't seem any more romantic than Olga.

AQ: Yes, the play seems deliberately structured in order for us not to focus on a central character. In Ron's case...

EL: ...With Ronnie, I just remember being aware of the number of the male roles and I remember saying, "Oh, you should play Vershinin." He must have known he was going to play Vershinin, but he didn't say anything. Of course, after I read the play I realized Vershinin was a military person, he was a military officer, and so Ron was perfect for this. But at the beginning I didn't know what happened to Vershinin in the play, I didn't know he left or that he said goodbye at the end. This was before I really understood all the ramifications of the casting.

AQ: Did you know from the beginning that you were going to frame Vershinin in the way that you ended up doing in the performance, with that sense of stillness, that beautiful sense of placing him in the space?

EL: Well, the thing about Ronnie was he didn't move comfortably on the stage. That's why he has extremely abstract movement patterns running through all of the pieces. You don't see Ronnie being natural in any of them. Whenever he would improvise—he would improvise in all his roles—for example, I would say "You have to cross over here," or "You have to get to there" and he would make up how he got there and it would always be something that was totally abstract. So, what I would do was then make use of that abstract movement, because there was always something that I could see that he needed to do and wanted to do with this movement. He wasn't one of those performers who made it up to get attention. He had an idea in his brain, and I don't think it was a psychological idea so much, I don't know what it was, but when he moved you believed it. You believed that movement was the only way that he could have done it.

AQ: So, in a way, this abstraction was natural to him?

EL: Yes. The way he holds his head—he just picked up things and took them and did them with such authority. I think some of this came from his military training. You know, you just have to run over a big embankment, climb a wall, come down, pick up your rifle—and there is no reason for it, except you have to do it and you have to commit yourself to it without thinking. And that's how he performed. He would just head out onto the stage and do what needed to be done with some kind of wild abstract pattern that usually occurred in the middle. Something that only Ronnie could do. So, I kind of put everything around that. When he came across the stage, if he did something abstract, then I would set something off against it. So, I would frame it. His whole first scene is defined in this way. I would say, "You have to stay in the middle section here, you can't move out of that section" and, "When you're in the middle section you have to keep moving." I would say this because I divided the space into background, middle ground and foreground. Middle ground had certain kinds of movement you could do and background had certain kinds of movement and foreground had other kinds of movement. He had these rules in mind and he worked off them.

AQ: Did these rules affect all performers; did they have to work within these rules as well?

EL: Yes. Now, every once in a while someone could take a big risk and go through all three spaces and do whatever they wanted. But it had to be for a purpose, like they had to get somewhere fast. You could only override the system if it was imperative, if it was for some other bigger purpose. It always remained pretty solid, although some people did change things by the end. Ronnie would take the rules totally literally and he never forgot when he passed into the middle ground. And when he went to the back, you would see him change again. He understood that kind of patterning. He understood that way of structuring.

AQ: I remember he would drop his posture at precise times on the stage, almost like crossing a line, he would change position.

EL: I don't know whether this came with his training in the military, or whether it was just me taking him to this point. He had this ability in the early pieces as well; he had it in *Nayatt School* (1978). I think he was drawn to me because of my interest in this... in this sense of abstraction as well. I don't think we developed him. You know how things work; we just gave him the chance to let it come out.

AQ: When you came to revive *Brace Up!* in 2003 without him, was this a consideration?

EL: It was really difficult because I thought I'll just have someone repeat his pattern of movement and then from that pattern make it new—and this was one of the first times that I tried this. But it was hard work because Ronnie's patterns were so individual that I had to make changes. I began with the pattern as it had so dominated everything that I'd done in the first section. Whoever came in had to follow that pattern at first and then I adjusted, depending on the person's ability to work with it. If someone couldn't hold the pattern for fifteen seconds without caving in, I would have to add a sound that would help them to hold it or have a second person moving in relation to the moment to make it hold. I would have to amplify whoever came into the part, to help them. So, the whole thing would change because of this problem and the role of Vershinin altered immensely, depending on who was doing it. You can see from the rehearsals that Ronnie was so dominant and I was never able to really fix or get back what I originally had in Act 1 without him—it was built on his incredible energy and ability to bring the audience to him. I didn't have to worry about what other people were doing while he was on the stage.

AQ: Yes, in fact, when he appears it's almost like everyone else relaxes at the edges of the space.

EL: Exactly.

AQ: Was *Brace Up!* an easy rehearsal process for you?

EL: No, it wasn't easy. I remember it being hard to keep everyone together. There were so many different kinds of performances going on.

AQ: I remember in one rehearsal tape you talk about the problem of getting the right movement language for *Brace Up!*.

EL: It was about getting on and off the stage.

AQ: "Entrances and exits." I remember you using this phrase in one of the rehearsal tapes.

EL: Yes, and where the kind of naturalism of Chekhov's world would intersect with the crazy kind of Noh Japanese Victorian world. That meeting place was very hard. It was hard because some performers understood the way of moving right away and would just do it and other people needed to know why they were crossing the stage or why were they moving to a particular place. I would have to say, "You're moving there because musically you have to move there." They wouldn't always understand this because the next moment I would say, "You have to raise your hand here because someone who's in trouble would raise her hand here." So, the performers would reply, "Well, how can you have both?" Or, "How can I do both?" That was hard, but I think once everyone understood that it could be both of these things then it was just a matter of choosing which was right for which moment and we finally got it.

AQ: This dynamic seems to inform *Fish Story* as well. In one of the early rehearsal tapes you say to the performers that you don't want them to fall back on an easy form of naturalism. You say something like you're attempting naturalism but within a new frame. You're always asking them to somehow go through the process of doing something for the first time. So, even when the performers learn the dances, or there are movements that you like, you go, "No, no—you are doing it as if you are performing it. You have fixed it. I don't want that. I want something that is changing; that you are doing something in the moment."

EL: This is what I'm always trying to get in every performance—where the audience thinks that what's happening on stage has never been done before, that they're seeing it for the first time, even if it's something that we've obviously rehearsed millions and millions of times. I'm probably still hunting for this, no matter what style I go through. I'm still searching for this in the second part of *Poor Theater* (2004), which we're working on now. It's a major part of this piece. I tell the performers, "Well, it looks like you know what you are going to do, or what you are going to say" and I can't have that. Yet, at the same time, there's a structure that they have to know. I think this is everybody's problem now. It comes from film, where we want to see everything as if it's for the first time. This is the difference between older films, where it's highly structured and staged, often for the laughs, like in Noel Coward. Now, it's all about the first take, the camera catching it for the first time. You don't repeat it, because that was the real thing. I think this is how film has changed our idea of the theater, why it is so hard to do, because people don't suspend disbelief in the same way.

AQ: When I watched *Poor Theater* I saw a connection with *Fish Story*. In the original Japanese *Geinin* documentary, and you re-work this in *Fish Story*, you see a performance tradition reduced to entertainment for tourists. The performers seem out of time, from a different era, they hang around to do shows

for the tourists who arrive late. In the second part of *Poor Theater*, Scott (Shepherd) says, through his portrayal of William Forsythe, "We're doing cultural tourism; dances for the tourists." It made me think about the sense of farewell in *Fish Story*, not just because of it being Ron's last piece with the Group, or about his role as Vershinin, but also as a kind of beautiful and allegorical goodbye to theater itself.

EL: Sure, it comes back to me again and again.

AQ: Does it then become a question of how to carry on?

EL: Yes—how do you go on? There was definitely something of this in these pieces. Yet, even though Willem had left by the time we were finishing *Poor Theater*, this was a secondary thing when it came to being about us as a company. It was more a response to the fact that Bill Forsythe's company was going. Then, there's Ronnie's death and Ryszard Cieslak's (one of Grotowski's major collaborators) death: the disappearing tradition.

AQ: What was the impetus for doing *Fish Story* so soon after *Brace Up!*?

EL: I was having so much trouble trying to figure out the style for *Brace Up!* and the text was so huge; it was the first time we had taken on a full-length play. So, we didn't really do the last act. When it came to *Fish Story*, Ronnie tried to get me back to what I had done before, which was to take either the last act, or a section, and make a little thing around it. He didn't see any reason why we should be doing the whole of *Three Sisters*, but for some reason I wanted to do the full play. So, I think that I just had the energy to return to where we had got to with *Three Sisters* and then I thought why don't I just do what Ronnie said—I'll make another piece that's just the last act that could be attached to *Brace Up!*. And if it didn't work with *Brace Up!*, it wouldn't matter.

AQ: Did the two pieces perform alongside each other?

EL: Yes, in a couple of places in Europe we did the two next to each other. In fact, if we do *Brace Up!* again I'm hoping to add *Fish Story*. Mind you, it wasn't a big money maker. I think it ruined us until we made *The Hairy Ape* (1995). It ruined us for touring; we didn't tour for two years.

AQ: Did people find it too abstract?

EL: Yes, I remember people in Vienna walking out saying, "What?" They were totally mystified by it and everywhere we went people would roll their eyes in response. I think this was because, before *Fish Story*, our pieces always had a person standing at the front of the table speaking to the audience, letting them in, and audiences liked that kind of thing. They liked the direct address and *Fish Story* had a sort of barrier in front of it, a distancing quality to it. In Europe they liked us Americans to do rough stuff and this was the complete opposite. I mean, it was rough in some ways, but at the same time it was really controlled. This isn't what they expected and I think it changed how people thought of us.

AQ: *Fish Story* feels like one of the most tightly choreographed pieces, or at least marks its choreography very explicitly.

EL: Well, I think they all do. It's just that *Fish Story* had more position. You know what I mean? In *St. Antony* Katie had some leeway before she went to touch the bed—she had three or four seconds of free time to do whatever she wanted there. Whereas with *Fish Story*, because of what was being negotiated, no one moved without knowing exactly what they were doing. Every moment of the dance was choreographed. It's true that the other pieces aren't as tightly choreographed as this, but they are all choreographed, even the earlier ones like *Route 1 & 9* (1981)—every single move was choreographed.

AQ: What's really interesting watching the rehearsal tapes is how you construct the choreography around the way each individual performer moves...

EL: Yes.

AQ: You don't submit them to working in an absolutely pre-determined pattern. It emerges from improvisation, in trying things out. This is so clear, say with the performance of Jeff Webster, where you work completely in relation to how he moves, how he dances...

EL: Yes, because he loved dance and he's great on video.

AQ: Did you know that Ron was always going to be on the video, that he wasn't going to perform live?

EL: Well, Ron could have performed in *Fish Story*. But, I wanted it to be like *Point Judith* (1979)—that was a goodbye piece as well. I knew during *Point Judith* that Spalding wasn't going to be in the work in the same way again and it was the same with Ron in *Fish Story*. This was a similar goodbye to Ron.

AQ: Something had changed?

EL: Something had changed. First of all, he was making his own work outside of the Group and he was very ill.

AQ: Did he like the piece?

EL: Yes, I think he did. Actually, he came to see it on New Year's Eve 1993/94 when we were performing open rehearsals and we went out afterwards to Lucky Strike and spent New Year's Eve there and sang *Auld Lang Syne* together. I remember talking with him about it, but he died just a few months or so later. I don't think he saw it properly open.

AQ: I think the piece is very moving whether or not you know the explicit biographical details. There's something very sad in the last section, it's a sadness that percolates throughout *Fish Story*. I think it's to do with the rhythm, its slow sense of winding down.

EL: It is interesting for me because that piece was so much about Ron and so many other people. We're such a tiny company and everybody knew Ron, so I didn't worry about what it meant in relation to what was happening to him and the company. If I ever revive *Fish Story,* I don't know whether we'll have to make a reference to this. I think I might have to, because we've been working on a DVD of *Brace Up!* and we're putting Ron back into the DVD as a ghost. So, I think people will understand this reference and there are so many references to the deaths of people. It's full of ghosts.

AQ: This sense of ghostliness is very present in the video material in *Fish Story*. I'm thinking here of Karen Lashinsky's constant weeping as Masha. There's something ghost-like in the texture of that video, like it's the remnant of some other lost performance, like it's breaking up in the very act of communication —like a really old film, where it still amazes us, but we've lost any real sense of what it originally meant. This comes up in the rehearsals when you discuss how the piece is set in a future where there are traces of a theater tradition that have, in the main, been forgotten. Maybe it's a bit like the idea that people will do slapstick routines in a hundred years, but they won't know where they came from.

EL: I still have that when I watch old Vaudeville films (laughs). Do you know that routine with the powder puff? Where did calling "Make up!" and throwing powder in the face come from? I only did it once and it got incorporated into all of our routines (laughs).

AQ: (laughs) That seems a great place to end: thank you.

Fish Story

A Documentary about Theatre Life in Eight Dances

 Left: **Sensaburo/Tusenbach: Jeff Webster** Center: **Yukio/Andrei: Scott Renderer** Right: **Sentaro/Rohde: Dave Shelley**

Left: **Sensha/Olga: Peyton Smith** Center: **Hiroko/Kulygin: Roy Faudree** Right: **Taro: Chris Kondek**

Left: **Asako: Kate Valk** Right: **Eiji/Irina: Beatrice Roth**

From left to right: **Natasha: Anna Köhler; Ferapont: Elion Sacker; Masha: Karen Lashinsky; Vershinin: Ron Vawter**

 ***Fish Story* set**

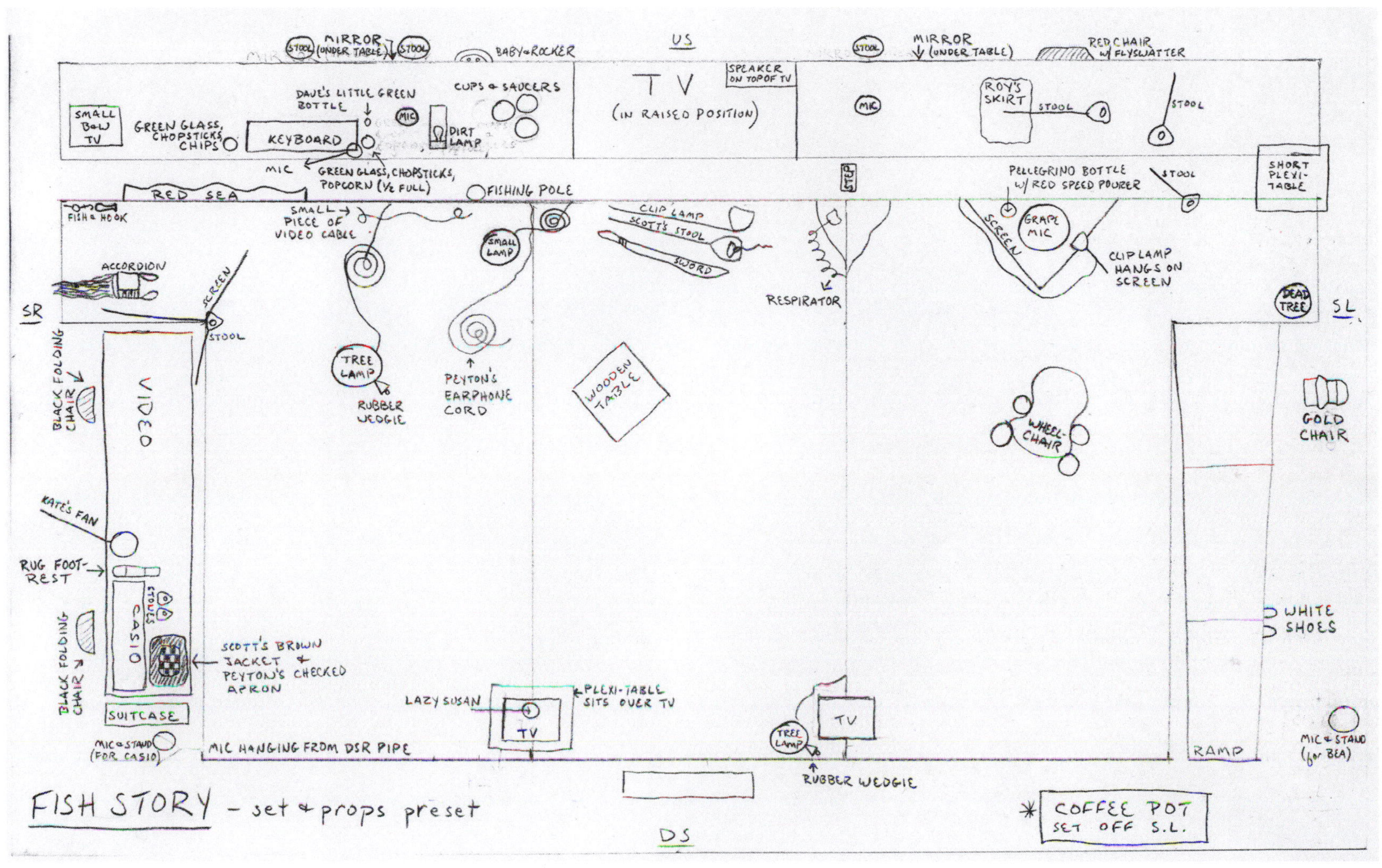

Set and props preset drawing: Clay Hapaz

Score

Cast

Hiroko/Kulygin	Roy Faudree
Stage Assistant	Cynthia Hedstrom/Jack Frank/Ari Fliakos
Taro	Christopher Kondek
Masha	Karen Lashinsky
Eiji/Irina	Beatrice Roth
Yukio/Andrei	Scott Renderer/Willem Dafoe
Sentaro/Rohde	Dave Shelley
Sensha/Olga	Peyton Smith
Asako	Kate Valk
Sensaburo/Tusenbach	Jeff Webster

On Video

Masha	Karen Lashinsky
Vershinin	Ron Vawter
Natasha	Anna Köhler
Ferapont	Elion Sacker

Score adapted for this publication from a notation by Clay Hapaz

Text	Stage	Sound	Video
	The Ichikawa Sentaro Troupe take the stage		
			PRE – SET
	TARO & ASSISTANT sit at video table, SR. SENSABURO sits on back table, USL, facing audience with mic. YUKIO sits at back table, SL of TV and puts on mirror and holds mic. SENTARO sits at back table, SR of TV and puts on mirror and holds mic. HIROKO is at USL live camera station. SENSHA sits on edge of stage, DSR. ASAKO stands at top of ramp, SL. MASHA sits behind keyboard, USR.		DS – Still White Burlap US – No image
PROLOG In which Anfisa goes off into the garden calling for Masha.			
	SENSHA – nods to Asako to begin	*Bee sound/Buzz*	
	ASAKO – walks down ramp and onto stage.		
	Swatting the Fly Dance		
	FIRST STAMP		
Masha! Masha!		*Masha, Masha*	
	SENTARO & YUKIO – begin to shave ASAKO – spins and pulls flyswatter out of her sleeve/ performs ritual holding flyswatter in front of her face		
	SECOND STAMP		
Sentaro: This razor only makes noise. Yukio: It's quite old, isn't it?	ASAKO – circles clockwise around table, shaking flyswatter		
	THIRD STAMP		
	SENSABURO – 4 snaps		
	ASAKO – moves to DSR TV plexi-table/on 4th snap swats fly	*SPLAT* *Bees/Buzz out*	DS – Fast Dissolve to Flyswatter & Fly
Narrator: Asako, the maid, wanted very much to express her feelings about the troupe. She says, "Everyone agrees Sentaro's troupe is the best of them all. I've seen everything they have done. The performers work perfectly together. I owe very much to this troupe."	ASAKO – holds hankie in front of her mouth		
	ASAKO – lifts flyswatter		
	ASAKO – wipes up fly with hankie/puts flyswatter in tree		DS – Fly wipe/dissolve to still white burlap

DANCE 0 In which Olga has a conversation with Vershinin who has come to say good-bye to Masha.	**Sensha prepares for her entrance and Asako, the maid, discreetly arranges the stage**		
	SENSHA – moves to DSC floor, sits on edge of stage		US – Olga tape
Olga: Do you think we'll ever see each other again? (pause)	ASAKO – brings earplug cord to Sensha/gets hanging mic/takes fan from Assistant/places mic and fan in back holster/goes to DSC tree	*Beep-Beep* *Beep-Beep*	
Yes, yes. Of course. Don't worry. (pause)	HIROKO – sits on back table, SL of TV, facing DS YUKIO – sits on stage, SR of USL screen, facing US SENTARO – to behind USR screen SENSABURO – sits on stage, SL of USL screen, facing US	*Beep-Beep* *Beep-Beep*	
Tomorrow there won't be a single military man left in town, it will all be a memory. And of course for us it will be the beginning of a new life... (pause)		*Beep-Beep* *Beep-Beep*	
Things never work out the way we want them to. I didn't want to be headmistress, but here I am. Headmistress. And of course I'll never get to Moscow... (she sniffs and wipes her eyes) Why doesn't that Masha hurry up...	SENSHA – sniffs & wipes her eyes/stands & faces US ASAKO – cues tech	*Geinin soundtrack* *Geinin sword dance with snap track*	
DANCE 1 BACKSTAGE In which Masha sobs violently.	**Asako assists Sensha onto the stage**		
	SENTARO – moves to USR tree SENSHA – raises left hand ASAKO – holds flypaper/takes Sensha's trembling hand/helps Sensha onto stage		
	Sensha Dances, shadowed by Asako, punctuated by Zen whacks		
	SENSHA – dances DSC ASAKO – shadows		DS – Ron / Vershinin with yellow frame US – Masha crying – fast tape (volume up & out & freeze frame for whacks)
Vershinin: Write me... don't forget. Let me go, I've got to go...	SENSHA – whacks Asako/lip synchs to moaning HIROKO, YUKIO, SENSABURO – head whack in time with whack ASAKO – careens doing "pain" gestures HIROKO – at USL screen/holds cable YUKIO & SENSABURO – stand on stage, leaning on "stupid"	*crying* *WHACK* *Dave moans into USR tree mic*	
	SENSHA & ASAKO – resume their dance, DSC	*crying*	

Sensha Dances, shadowed by Asako

 Video stills: Top 3 rows: **Masha crying (fast tape)** 4th row: **Vershinin/Ron** 5th row: **Fork dropping**

Vershinin: Olga Sergeyevna, take her, I've got to go… I'm late…

SENSHA – whacks Asako
YUKIO & SENSABURO – head whack in time with whack
HIROKO – drops cable & hides behind USL screen
ASAKO – careens doing "pain" gestures
TARO – takes place in trough, SL of TV

WHACK
Dave – moans

Three rounds of "Go-Go-Go" & "Hit-Hit-Hit" & "Knee Drops"

Each round:
SENTARO – facing US, conducts the beat
SENSABURO – snaps time

Sentaro: Go, go, go… Hit, hit, hit… 1, 2, 3, 4, 5, 6, 7…

Y, H, T & S'BURO – do arm & hand gestures in response to Sentaro's beat
SENTARO & S'BURO – on 1–7 count do "samurai" knee-drop
ASAKO – follows with a knee drop

Whistle (with all knee drops)
Crying up (on knee drops)
Add "Tangerine Dream" with clicks (at first "hit" of third round)
Roy – "whoosh"
Moaning

DS – Fork dropping (around first knee drop)/ returns to Ron / Vershinin

Samurai Sword Dance with Table and Chair

ASSISTANT – taps stones in time to "Tangerine Dream"
SENSABURO – tosses sword to Sentaro/jumps table
SENTARO – does "samurai" gestures with sword/stabs
Sensaburo pulls out sword
SENSABURO & ASAKO – drop to knees
SENTARO – crosses to join dance
YUKIO – looks over USL screen/turns/plays air guitar on green stool/waits
ASAKO – picks up DSL tree/stamps & snaps cord
SENSABURO & YUKIO – jump cord
SENSABURO – crosses to dances with Sentaro
ASAKO – moves tree to wheelchair/dances in unison with Sensaburo & Sentaro
YUKIO – two steps, full turn, six drag steps to DSL corner
SENTARO – after turn moves to DSR
SENSABURO – after turn moves back to USR tree
ASAKO – dances in unison with Sensha
SENTARO – calls "Yukio"
SENTARO & YUKIO – 16 count slide step
SENSHA – whacks Asako
HIROKO – drops cables & hides behind screen
ASAKO – careens in "pain"/picks up plexi-table /carries above head

WHACK
Jeff moans into USR tree mic

	ASAKO & SENSABURO – do "circle" move, DSR	*MUSIC CHANGE to "click track"*	DS – Masha crying
	YUKIO & SENTARO – move in a clumsy circle/stamp/slide with right leg		
	S'BURO – 3 stamps to US/into trough/to USL video station		
	ASAKO – struggles with table		
	HIROKO – back on stage, works with cables & plugs/goes back into trough after Sensaburo crosses		
	SENTARO – stamps		
Sentaro: Yukio... cross now... the tree...	YUKIO – hesitates to cross		
	SENSHA – whacks Yukio	*WHACK*	
	YUKIO – spins around, shakes head, crosses to SR	*Masha's crying fades down*	
	ASAKO – as Yukio passes her, spins in a circle		
	SENTARO & YUKIO – play "guitars"	*Casio/"guitar"*	
	YUKIO – spins and knocks over USR tree lamp with guitar		
	TARO – dives & catches tree		
	HIROKO – hides behind USL screen		
	YUKIO – spins again		
	TARO – pulls away tree lamp		
	ASAKO – places plexi-table next to wooden table		
	ALL – do sinking "knee drops"/lights dim	*Whistle* *music OUT* *Casio OUT*	
	Yukio's Introduction		
	SENSHA – lies down on table		
	ASAKO – takes fan from back holster and holds it out in front of her, waiting for followspot		
	FOLLOWSPOT		
	ASAKO – with followspot on her fan, crosses SR to illuminate Yukio's face		
	YUKIO – plays one chord	*Guitar chord*	DS – Jeff's mouth
Narrator: Yukio, who joined the troupe four years ago, is a relatively good guitarist, being the only member other than Sensha who can read and write music...	YUKIO – plays one note	*Guitar note*	DS – Freeze Jeff's mouth
	ASAKO – wave off/lights up	*ALL OUT*	DS – Wipe to "blue" Jeff ("blue" = hand-held flashlight)
INTERLUDE In which a muffled shot is heard in the distance.	**The Troupe rearranges itself for the next dance**		US – No image
... In fact, most Geinin groups are not known as the best of musicians, the Ichikawa Sentaro troupe being no exception. But what they lack in profes-	YUKIO – puts down his guitar and gets his respirator		
	TARO – returns to video table		
	HIROKO – puts on skirt/moves screen		

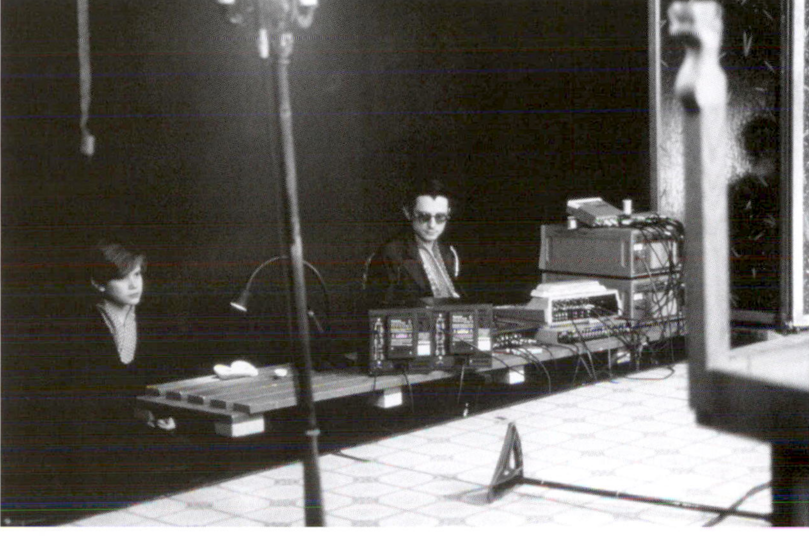

Top left: **The Troupe relaxes** Top right: **The Stage Assistant and Taro** Bottom left: **Olga has a conversation with Vershinin** Bottom right: **Yukio/Andrei**

sionalism, they often make up by offering warm and spirited performances.	ASAKO – stands, moves mic and checks the cable SENTARO – hands sword to Hiroko SENSHA – cues Eiji's entrance/sits on front of stage	 *Geinin soundtrack*	
Kulygin: (humming) ... She's not going to cry anymore, that's good. (makes kissing sound)		*Footsteps* *Kiss*	US – Masha & Kulygin (bubble)
	YUKIO – drops respirator MASHA – revolves a "45" on record player ASAKO – moves small lamp to DSC/checks cables	*Gunshot* *"Beside the Sea"*	DS – Tusenbach's head being dragged US – No image
	SENTARO, YUKIO, SENSABURO – lean on US "stupid" and tap morse code messages through it SENTARO – gets his fishing pole YUKIO – SL of TV, with 2 forks SENSABURO – taps stool with chopstick	 *Masha crying*	 DS – Dissolve to Masha crying
DANCE 2 IN THE DRESSING ROOM In which Kulygin wears a fake beard and moustache.	**Asako assists Sensha onto the stage**		
	ASAKO – mimes crying/goes to SL tree & rustles leaves/back to DSC/cues J.J.	 *Storm*	
	SENSHA – stands & faces US/raises left hand ASAKO – holds flypaper/takes Sensha's trembling hand ASAKO – helps Sensha up 1 step/gives Sensha pill bottle	*Gosha Dance/* *Geinin soundtrack*	 US – "surging crowd" / cut to Kulygin with "Groucho" glasses
Kulygin: (clears throat & "uh-hums") Yesterday I took this away from one of the boys at school. (covers face & "whoops"/"yoo-hoos") It looks just like the German teacher, doesn't it? (laughs & "yoo-hoos") Those boys are so funny.	SENSHA – slowly crosses the stage ASAKO – fingers stick to the flypaper **Table and Chair Placing Dance**		DS – Dissolve to white burlap
	SENTARO, YUKIO & S'BURO – take a few steps backwards SENSHA – cues Sensaburo SENSABURO – taps stool with chopstick 5 times EIJI – enters up ramp and stands at top SENSHA – takes a pill ASAKO – moves backwards to center 2 STAMPS ASAKO – picks up plexi-table 2 STAMPS ASAKO – puts down table		
	ALL – do "knee-drops"	*Whistle*	

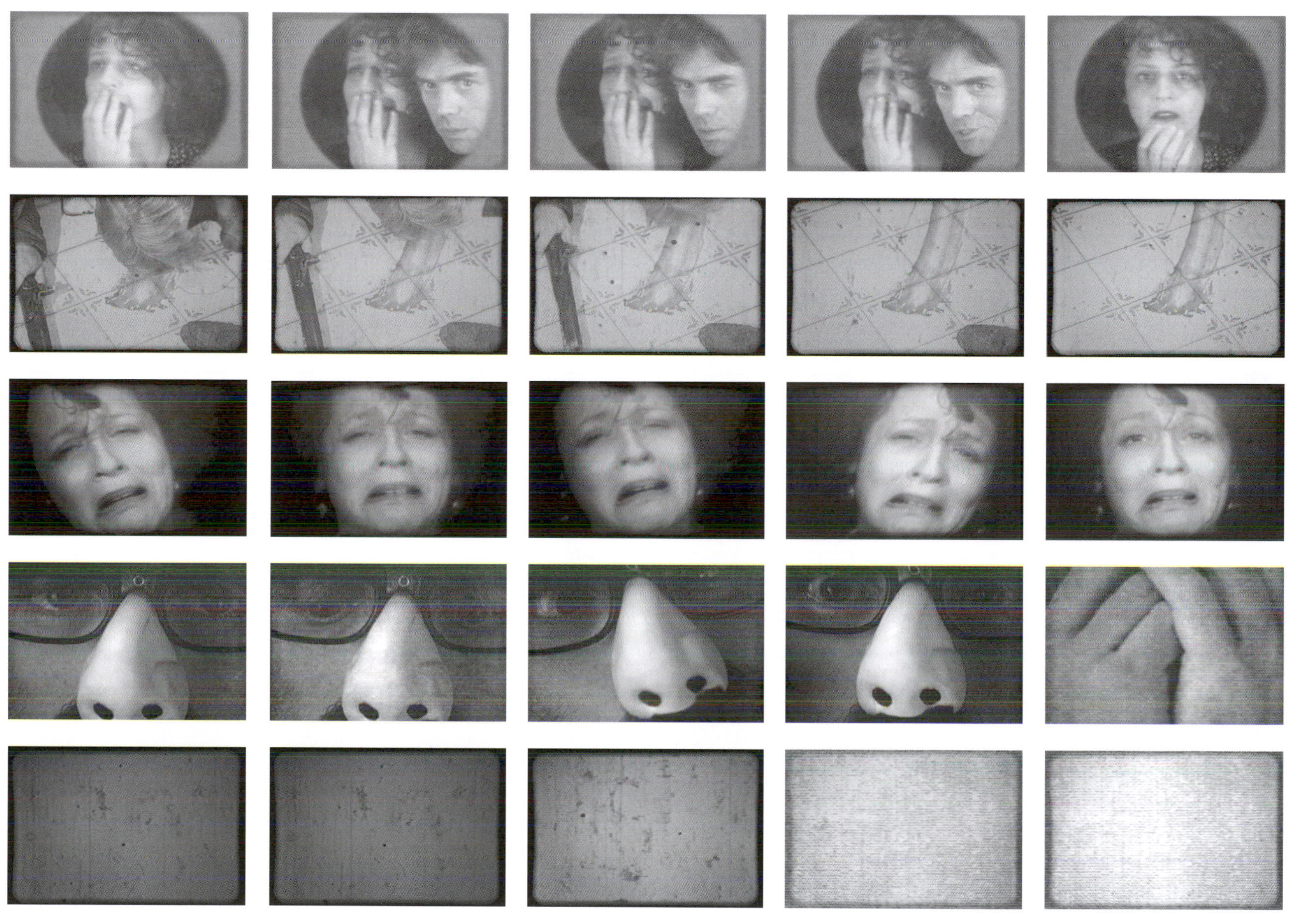

Video stills: Top row: **Masha & Kulygin (bubble)** 2nd row: **Tusenbach's head being dragged** 3rd row: **Masha crying** 4th row: **Kulygin with "Groucho" glasses** 5th row: **Dissolve to white burlap**

 Top: *Fish Story* **rehearsal** Bottom: **Hiroko steps on to stage**

	HIROKO – Steps on to stage, USC, raises "Groucho" glasses	*Music Down*	
Yukio: Pssst. I got lost completely. Did you notice?	YUKIO – speaks into the mic on Asako's back		DS – Dissolve back to Masha
Sentaro: The third part I did very well.			
	HIROKO – crosses to DSC and sits on stool	*Music Up*	
	ASAKO – sets mic for Hiroko		
	EIJI – crosses to behind SL tree		
	YUKIO – dances with Asako		
	SENTARO – dances with fishing pole		
Masha: (on tape) It really does look like he's German.	SENSHA – peers over SR tree light		
Olga: It really does.	SENSABURO – crosses DSL/taps stool with chopstick 5 times		US – Masha, then back to Kulygin (repeat a few times)
(Olga & Kulygin laugh)	2 STAMPS		
	ASAKO – picks up plexi-table/hops twice		
	YUKIO – follows Asako/tiny steps backwards to USC		
	YUKIO & ASAKO – do "in & out" with table		
	1 STAMP		
Irina: Masha, don't.	ASAKO – stamps twice/lifts table over head/falls to knees DSL/pushes table under Sensaburo, who sits on it		US – Wipe to clock
	ALL – do sinking "knee-drops"	*Whistle*	
Kulygin: Exactly like him.		*Music DOWN*	US – Woman crying
	YUKIO – "race-car" spin		
	SENSABURO – taps stool with chopstick 5 times	*Music UP*	DS – Masha fades to white
	SENSHA & YUKIO – do "Geisha" dance		
	EIJI – exits down ramp		
	ASAKO – moves wheelchair forward & back		
	SENTARO – 2 Stamps		
	ASAKO – spins around/Asako & chair land behind Hiroko		
	HIROKO – drops stool/sits in chair		
	ASAKO – dusts off Hiroko's shoulders/swings chair around/chair knocks into Yukio		
	YUKIO – falls down		
	ASAKO – 4 stamps over to DSL/pushes S'buro off table/picks up table		
	SENSABURO – stamps		
	ASAKO – stamps & moves to center/spins in frantic circles		
	SENSABURO – "face-off" with Asako/both move back		
	ASAKO & SENSABURO – "in & out" with table		
	YUKIO – drops forks/down onto his hands & knees to pick them up		
	ASAKO – spins around with table, over Yukio's head		
	YUKIO – looks up, then down		
	ASAKO – repeats spin		
	YUKIO – stands up		

	ASAKO – spins around for the third time & whacks Yukio with table	*WHACK*	
	YUKIO – waves arms in "pain," walks backwards & sits in wheelchair		
	HIROKO – holds wheelchair for Yukio, then places bottle in Yukio's left hand		
	ASAKO – crosses to front/puts table down		
	ALL – do sinking "knee-drops"/lights dim	*Whistle* *Music OUT*	
	The Troupe relaxes		
	SENSHA – sits on table		
	ASAKO – places two tables next to each other	*Train*	US – Train
	ASSISTANT – hands rug-roll to Sensha/takes pill bottle	*Geinin OUT*	
	SENSHA – takes rug-roll from Assistant/lies down on table	*Roy snores*	
Narrator: (translates song) "Even though I wear night time make-up, You say my heart is purer than anyone else. Your gentle words almost make me cry. If you love a woman like me, I will dedicate my life to you, only you."	ASAKO – crosses to SL tree	*Mandarin song*	US – Dissolve from train into radio
	YUKIO – asleep and snoring		
	SENTARO – fishes/taps foot to cue Yukio		DS – Jeff's mouth
	YUKIO – shakes leg in time with line pull		
	ASAKO – smokes a cigarette		
	FOLLOWSPOT Full on Yukio	*Song OUT*	US – Foot hits radio – first time
	YUKIO – wakes up & is blinded by the light	*Static IN*	
	ASAKO – with followspot on her fan crosses the stage		
	YUKIO – drops bottle		
	when the sound of bottle rolling finishes		
	ASAKO – brings "fan" to illuminate Sensha's face	*Static OUT* *Geinin sndtrck. IN*	US – Foot hits radio – second time
	Sensha's introduction		
Narrator: Sensha, as the oldest brother and former star, is the group's boss. He is responsible for most of the group's material…	ASAKO – Wave off /lights up	*ALL OUT* *(Geinin OUT)*	DS – wipe to "blue Jeff"
INTERLUDE In which Natasha enters.	**The Troupe rearranges itself and prepares the next dance. Eiji takes the stage**		US – No image
…Because their repertoire changes every ten days, he is constantly searching for new song, dance and drama ideas, often browsing through record stores looking for new releases. Sensha is a true Geinin, skilled in all aspects of performing, he only admits to a slight weakness at singing.	SENSHA – adjusts eyes to light/gets up from table/faces US		
	ASAKO – puts wooden table upside down on TV/puts apron on Sensha/helps Sensha sit on stool & cues tech		
	HIROKO – blows nose as Sensha sits on stool		
	YUKIO – waves to Eiji to enter/moves wheelchair		
	EIJI – enters up ramp & sits in wheelchair/sleeps/holds bundle		

	YUKIO – sets armrest, footrest, Eiji's hand, etc. SENTARO – moves plexi-table to center/places fork on table	*Beep - Beep*	**DS** – Freeze Jeff Dissolve to live fork with blood **US** – Natasha, in bubble, with blossoms, add fork
Natasha: Who left this fork out here? I want to know who – left – this – fork – out – here! Do you here me? Shut up when I'm talking to you! Kulygin: She does get mad.	HIROKO – crosses to "grape" mic YUKIO – peeks over top of SL screen	*Gosha music (for Dance 3)*	**DS** – Jeff taps fork in sync with "who-left-this-fork-out-here!", then smears it off **DS** – Dissolve to flowers
DANCE 3 IN THE DRESSING ROOM In which Irina learns that the Baron has been shot.			
Masha: Our men. They're going away. Well... I hope they have a pleasant trip. Let's go home. Where's my hat and my coat? Kulygin: I took them inside... I'll get them right away.	SENSABURO – sits at USL live camera station ASAKO – rustles leaves	*Fast tape of Masha*	**US** – Masha-soft focus
Olga: (breath) The music sounds so happy, so positive, it makes you want to live. Oh, dear God. (sniff) The day will come when we'll go away forever too, people will forget all about us, they'll forget what we looked like and what our voices sounded like and how many of us there were, but our suffering will turn to joy for the people who live after us, their lives will be happy and peaceful, and (breath) they'll remember us kindly and bless us. My dears, my dear sisters, life isn't over yet. We'll go on living. The music sounds so happy, so joyful, it almost seems as if a minute more, and we'd know (breath) why we live, why we suffer. (huh... breath) If only we knew. If only we knew!	SENSHA – holds hankie, breathes along & lipsynchs tape MASHA – at back table, eats potato chips	*Slow tape of Peyton*	**US** – Masha putting on make-up
	Stool/Stick/Stamp Dance		
Olga: If only we knew! If only we knew!	TARO – hits wood block ASAKO – to center table, sits on edge/swings flyswatter like a pendulum SENSABURO – sits on edge of stage, USC HIROKO – sitting on back table/peeps from behind stool in "Groucho" glasses SENTARO, S'BURO & YUKIO – 4 stamps		

 Top: **Dance 3** Bottom: **Kulygin & Masha giggling and kissing in the cherry blossoms**

Dialogue	Action	Sound	Stage
	ASAKO – drops flyswatter/picks it up		
	STAMP		
	SENTARO, S'BURO & YUKIO – do "toe" dance/spin/hip swing	*Gosha Geisha*	
	YUKIO – after "hip swing" in pause cues Eiji's line		
	STAMP		
Irina: What? What is it? For godssakes, tell me!	ASAKO – whacks Eiji with fan/sits back down on table	*WHACK*	US – Kulygin & Masha, giggling & kissing in the cherry blossoms
	SENTARO, S'BURO & YUKIO – to "stupid"		
	HIROKO – goes to Eiji, whispers in his ear		
	SENSHA – claps		
	STAMP		
Irina: I knew it! I knew it!	ASAKO – whacks Eiji with fan/sits back down on table	*WHACK*	
	STAMP		
Irina: Someday everyone will know what this was all about, all this suffering, it won't be a mystery anymore...	SENSABURO – sits on table		
	ASAKO & SENSABURO – lean into each other back to back		
	YUKIO – wipes brow with hankie		
	SENTARO – slow-motion gesture with left arm		
	SENSHA – claps		
	ASAKO – plucks leg bungee	*BOING*	
Sensaburo: It's here, difficult.	SENSABURO – crouches down & speaks into Asako's mic		
	ASSISTANT – puts skirt over Eiji	*Add Crows*	
	2 STAMPS		
Irina: ...but until then we have to go on living... and working, just keep on working.	1 STAMP – during Eiji's lines		
	STAMP		
	SENTARO & SENSABURO – cross to US		
	HIROKO – goes to Eiji & puts his hand on her shoulder		
Yukio: Oh my gosh, they're filming. They're every-where.	YUKIO – DSC/holds "dummy" & fans himself with stool/speaks into mic on Asako's back		
	SENSHA – spins table		
	YUKIO – scampers to USL		
	HIROKO – to trough		
Irina: I'll go away tomorrow, by myself. I'll teach school, and devote my whole life to people who need it... who may need it. It's autumn, winter will come, the snow will fall, and I will go on working and working.	SENTARO, SENSABURO & YUKIO – do "sinking" steps		US – Mix fish with blossoms
	SENSHA – drops stool/holds onto table/steps off stage		
	SENTARO – "fishes" USR		
	SENSABURO – gets into trough/does swimming feet		
	HIROKO – shines clamp light on his feet	*Begin Music Fade*	US – Freeze Fish
	ASAKO – on "working and working," spins table		DS – Blossoms
Olga: If only we knew! If only we knew!	SENSHA – on floor, lipsynchs tape/spins table		

 Yukio cues Eiji

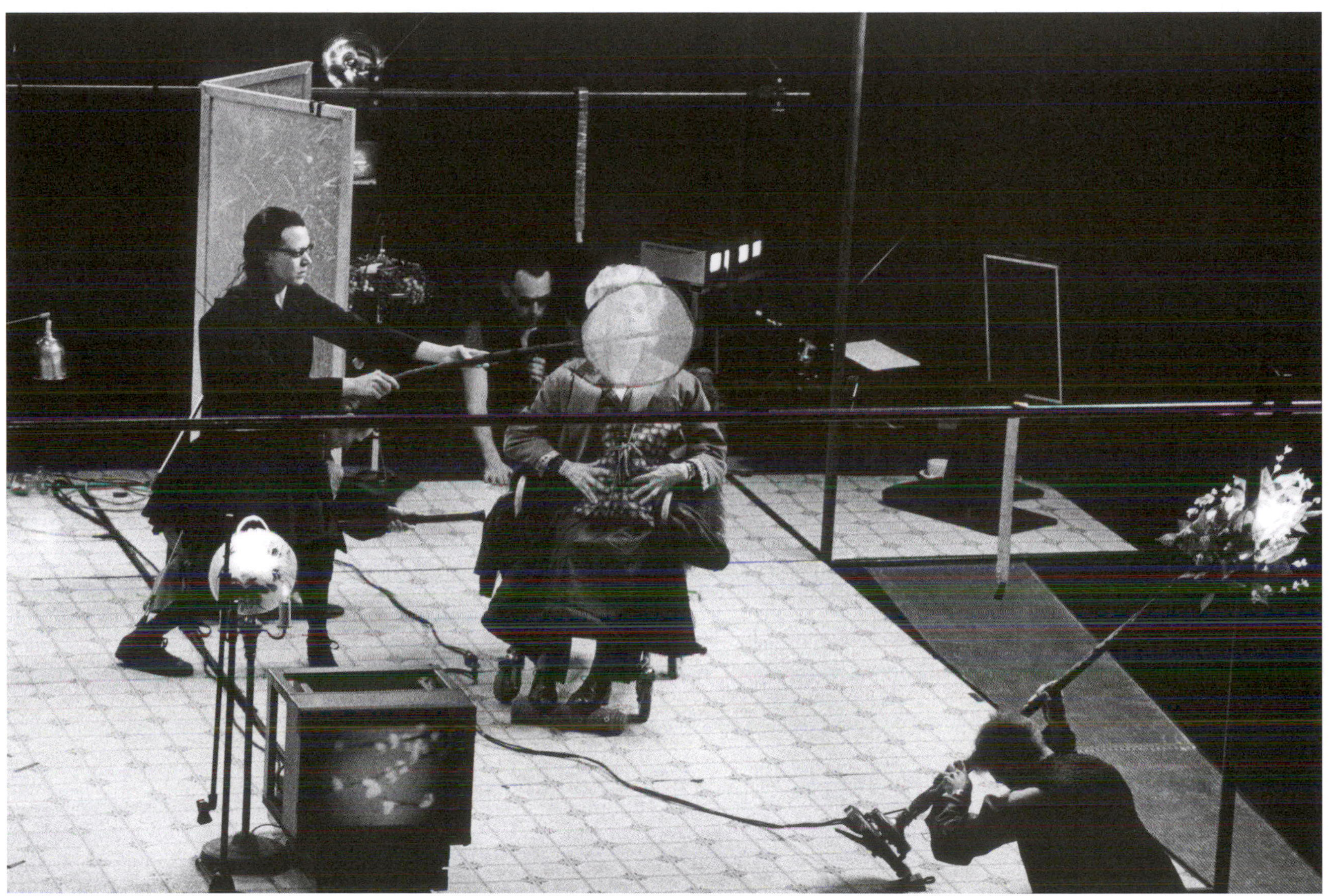

	Eiji's introduction		
	Asako holds fan in front of Eiji		
	FOLLOWSPOT on Eiji		
	ASSISTANT – holds SL tree at angle		DS – Jeff's mouth
Narrator: Eiji, a newly recruited member of the troupe, must learn a new part. Although he usually plays drums, in this number he must learn the role of an old woman. This difficult performance will require several years of training.	ASAKO – Wave off	*ALL OUT*	US & DS – Blossoms
INTERLUDE In which Irina stands thinking for a moment, then wanders into the garden and sits in a swing.	**The Troupe rearrange themselves and prepare for the next number and then have coffee**		
	ASAKO – puts fan down/picks up plexi-table/exits down ramp		
	SENSHA – walks around stage to trough/dusts off US TV & picks up a cup & saucer		
	HIROKO – moves screen & places stool for S'buro/crosses carrying Eiji's blue chair/walks down ramp/sets chair & mic stand under DSL tree		
	EIJI – follows Asako and Hiroko/sits in blue chair under tree		
	YUKIO – costume change into Andrei outfit		
	SENSABURO – to USL live camera station		DS – Jeff's mouth
	SENTARO – climbs down to back table		
Narrator: Still the busload of tourists is delayed. No problem, there's time for another cup of coffee.	ASAKO – brings on percolator	*Footsteps*	US – screen
	SENSHA – gestures/snaps fingers for Asako to put the percolator on top of US TV		
	ASAKO – places percolator/stands in trough		
	SENSHA – hands Asako a cup & saucer		
	ASAKO – holds cup & saucer at the bottom edge of the TV		
	SENSHA – pours Asako a cup of coffee	*Coffee pouring*	US – coffee pouring
	ASAKO – crosses to Eiji	*Footsteps*	
	HIROKO – turns on DSL treelight		
	ASAKO & EIJI – do "handing cup" routine		
	HIROKO – to DSR, sits at sewing machine		
	SENSHA – pours a cup of coffee	*Coffee pouring*	US – coffee pouring
	HIROKO – sews at machine	*Footsteps*	US – on 3rd "sewer" pass Tusenbach/S'buro (frozen)
	ASAKO – cleans up		
	ASAKO & HIROKO – hear the arrival of the bus	*Bus – coming out of 3rd pass of sewing machine*	
Narrator: The bus arrives. The show must go on.			
	HIROKO – takes coffee from Sensha/sits at the back table		
	YUKIO – sits at back table		

	Sensaburo's introduction		
Narrator: Sensaburo, the middle brother, suffered stage fright at a early age when his father forced him to take part in the troupe. Not wanting to perform, he ran away from home at the age of seven. Upon the urging of Sensha, he returned to the troupe.	ASAKO – takes fan over to the front of US TV screen	*Footsteps*	US – change to 'bubble' image of T'bach/S'buro
	ASAKO – removes fan from TV		US – to full image of Tusenbach/Sensaburo (unfrozen)
DANCE 4 ON STAGE In which the brigade prepares to leave.	**The Troupe sings the "Farewell Song"**	*Beep-Beep* *"Tarantela"*	
Tusenbach: (speaks in sync with video) You're a good friend...			
	ASAKO – goes to Eiji/puts fan down		
Rohde: Yoo-hoo...			
Tusenbach: ...we had good times together.			
Rohde: Hey-hey...			
Tusenbach: Once more... Goodbye, Rohde!	ASAKO – cues Eiji with flyswatter tap		
Irina: Till we meet again!			
Fedotik: No, this time it's goodbye forever, we'll never see each other again!			
Kulygin: Who knows? Even I'm starting to cry.	ASAKO – cues Eiji with flyswatter tap		
Irina: We may meet again sometime.			
Fedotik: What, in ten or fifteen years? But we won't hardly recognize each other, and we'll be very nervous and embarrassed.			
Rohde: No, we'll never see each other again... Thank you for everything, thank you so much!			

Tusenbach: I hope we do meet again.

Rohde: Yoo-hoo...

Tusenbach: But you be sure and write us...

Rohde: Hey...

Tusenbach: ...don't forget.

Rohde: Goodbye, trees!

Tusenbach: What beautiful trees they are!

Rohde: Hey! Hey! Goodbye, echo!

Tusenbach: And how beautiful the life around them ought to be.

SENTARO – cues music

"Farewell Song"

Rohde, Kulygin, Fedotik, Tusenbach: (singing...)

ASAKO – kneels by Eiji/plays flyswatter "guitar"

DS – Jeff's mouth dissolves to "Henry V" breakdown tape

It's time to say goodbye forever now,
We'll never see each other here again.
The things we said won't matter anyhow,
And we'll forget the things we did back then...

Take another picture...

Kulygin: (speaking) Who knows? Maybe if you're lucky you'll get yourself a Polish wife, they kiss you all the time and call you Kohany.

Who wants to meet again in fifteen years?
I'll hardly know you and you won't know me.
Who wants to reawaken long lost tears?
We won't remember how it used to be...

Just another picture...

Rohde: Where's Maria Sergeyevna?
Kulygin: Masha's somewhere out here in the garden.

Solyony and the barge are here in the rear, and all the rest of us go with the men…			
Sentaro: My shoes. Get my white shoes.	ASAKO – gets white shoes from under ramp/runs them over to Sentaro/returns to DSL tree		
In half an hour we'll be leaving here, and peace and quiet will return again…		*"Farewell Song" – fade out*	
Just another picture…	YUKIO – breathes into respirator	*Roy – breathing*	**DS** – dissolve to Jeff's mouth
Narrator: Yukio's sister recently died of a kidney disease. Unfortunately, he is suffering from the same illness…	ASAKO – Wave off	*Breathing OUT*	**DS** – Freeze Frame Jeff / wipe to live, "blue" Jeff at light change
In fact, he has lost both of his kidneys. Still, he tries to join as many performances as possible even though he currently must spend five or six days a week at the hospital.	ASAKO – hands mic to Yukio/hides behind SL tree YUKIO – crosses to DSC SENSHA – switches to front of table YUKIO – leans on "dummy" holding respirator ASSISTANT – crosses stage with suitcase in circling movements avoiding cables/puts suitcase down by screen/takes Eiji's chair & flyswatter/returns to the video table EIJI – walks up ramp and sits in wheelchair		
Tusenbach: …happy. it's almost as if I were seeing these trees for the first time in my life, they all seem to be looking at me and waiting for something.	HIROKO – moves "grape mic" & prepares to rock baby SENTARO – hands baby & rocking chair to Sensha SENSHA – sets baby & rocker on stage ASAKO – turns on tree light cueing video and lights	*Beep-Beep* *"Desert Rain"*	**US & DS** – Tree light – live (freeze after light comes on)
Tusenbach: Irina!… Irina!			
Irina: What? What?			
Tusenbach: I didn't have any coffee this morning. Ask them to fix me some, will you?			
DANCE 5 ON STAGE CONTINUED In which Andrei talks with old Ferapont who has come with some papers. Ferapont can't hear him.	**Yukio/Andrei's agitated dialogue**	*"Desert Rain"* *Baby cries*	
Andrei: Oh, whatever happened to the past…	YUKIO – DSC, holding respirator		**DS & US** – Ferapont
Ferapont: I can't remember. I can't hear too well.	SENSHA – pours a cup of coffee & brings it to Masha/exits to behind USR screen	*Coffee pouring*	**US** – coffee pour over Ferapont

Andrei: ...when I was young and happy and intelligent, when I dreamed wonderful dreams and thought great thoughts, when my life and my future were shining with hope? What happened to it?

HIROKO – rocks baby

ASAKO – hangs fan on US "stupid," in front of Hiroko

Add rocking

Ferapont: I don't know. I don't know. This fella was telling us...

US – Tree light (freeze frame)

Andrei: We barely begin to live and all of a sudden we're old and boring and lazy and useless and unhappy. This town has a hundred thousand people in it.

Ferapont: I can't hear too well.

Sentaro: And not one of them...

Andrei: And not one of them...

Ferapont: I really can't hear too well.

Andrei: And not one of them has ever amounted to a thing. Each one is just like all the others, they eat, drink, sleep and then they die...

Ferapont: What?

Andrei: They die. More of them are born...

Ferapont: Papers. Papers.

Andrei: ...and they eat, drink and sleep too...

Ferapont: Papers. I don't know.

Andrei: ...and then because they're bored they gossip...

Ferapont: I can't hear too well.

Andrei: They gossip, they drink, they gamble, they sue each other, the wives cheat on the husbands

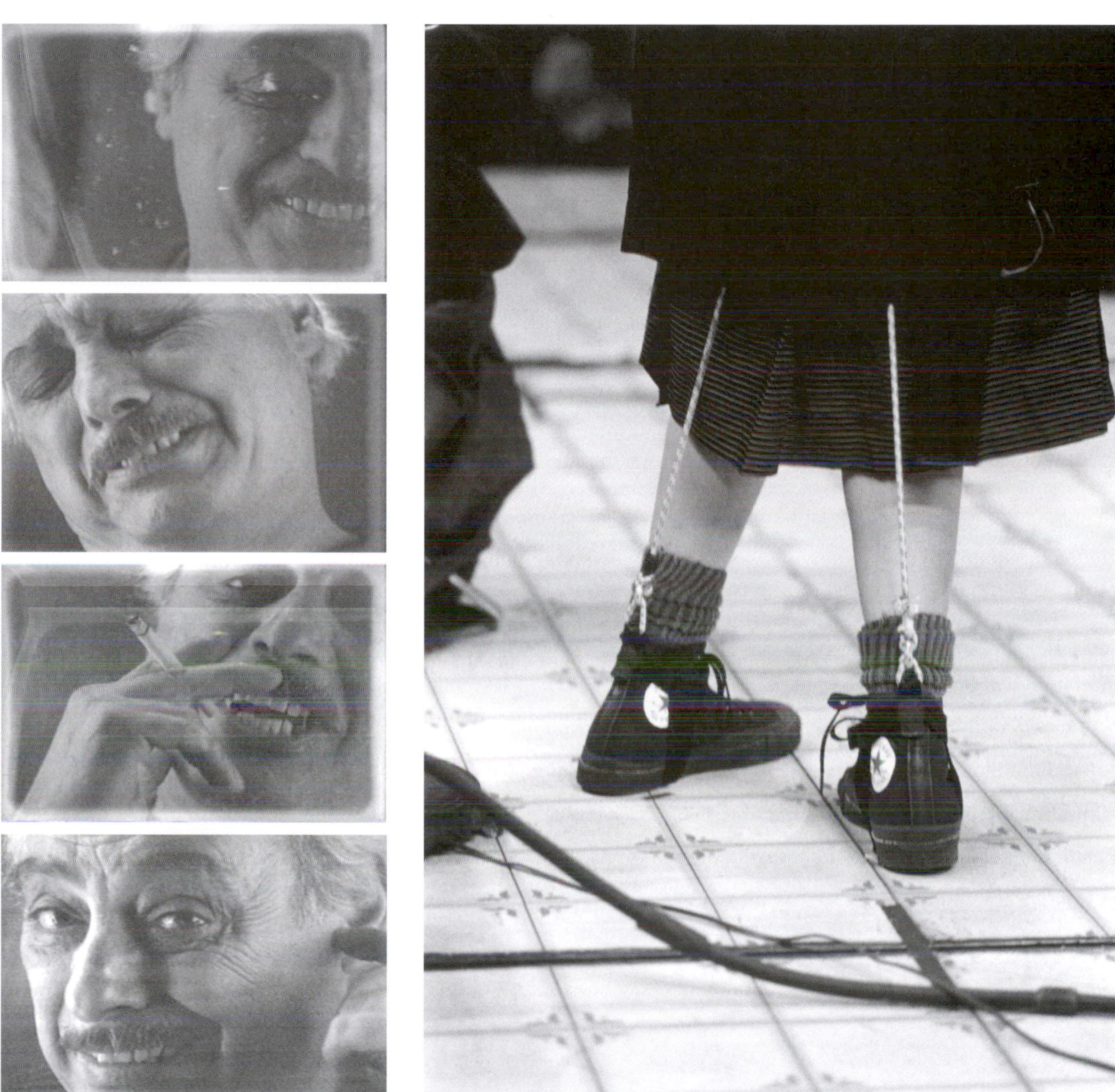

Left: **Ferapont: video stills** Right: **Asako's feet**

and the husbands lie...

Sentaro: They pretend...

Andrei: ...they pretend they don't see anything or hear anything...

Ferapont: What?

Andrei: See anything or hear anything.

Ferapont: Papers. Papers.

Andrei: And the children end up just as aimless and dead as their parents... What do you want? I'm sick and tired of you.

Ferapont: What's the other line?

Andrei: The present is awful...

Kulygin: Has the head-mistress gotten home yet?

Ferapont: Nope. Things just didn't work out that way. You know what I mean?

Andrei: ...but when I think of the future, I feel better; in the distance a light begins to break. I can see freedom; my children...

Ferapont: I can't hear too well.

Andrei: I can see freedom; my children and I will be free from laziness...

Ferapont: I really can't hear too well.

Andrei: ...from drinking too much, from eating too much every Sunday, from too many naps after dinner, from living like insects...

Top: **Dance 1** Bottom: **Dance 3**

(underneath Andrei and Ferapont's dialogue, Tusenbach has occasionally gently punched through with lines from his final scene with Irina, such as: "This tree is dead, but it still moves in the wind with the others." and "Those papers you gave me are on my desk...")

Sentaro: He calls to his sisters.
Andrei: My dear sisters, my wonderful sisters!

Masha... dear Masha...
Masha...
Masha... Masha...
Masha...

Sensha takes center stage as Yukio clatters off

SENSHA – enters from behind USR screen, with accordian, waits by SR tree
YUKIO – strikes a pose each time he calls "Masha"/clatters off
ASAKO – crosses to center & places a fork on the floor
SENSHA – on third "Masha" crosses diagonally to DSC
YUKIO – bends down to pick up the fork
SENSHA – on sixth "Masha" gestures with left hand to introduce Hiroko/whacks Yukio on the cheek as he stands back up
YUKIO – moves backwards/jumps cord/stops near baby
ASAKO – with pain gesture moves in time with Yukio
YUKIO – stamps foot/turns/lets go of respirator
ASAKO – turns around/gestures toward Hiroko

Cross-fade – up
"Beautiful Dreamer"
out – "Desert Rain"
WHACK
Rocking out
Dave – moans

US – Masha running

DS – fork on red cloth

DS – Jeff picks up fork, in sync with Yukio

US – Tree light
DS – Jeff's mouth at slight angle

Narrator: Prior to her marriage, Sensha's wife, Hiroko, had never been on a stage. When asked her feelings about performing, she only smiles.

Hiroko's introduction

FOLLOWSPOT full on Hiroko

ASAKO – Wave off

Music OUT

DS – Freeze Frame Jeff's mouth

The Troupe assembles for the finale

EIJI – stands behind DSL tree/peers over light
MASHA – enters from behind screen & goes to USR tree/stands behind tree on point
ASSISTANT – positions to shadow Asako
SENTARO – crosses to DSR
SENSABURO – crosses to DSL

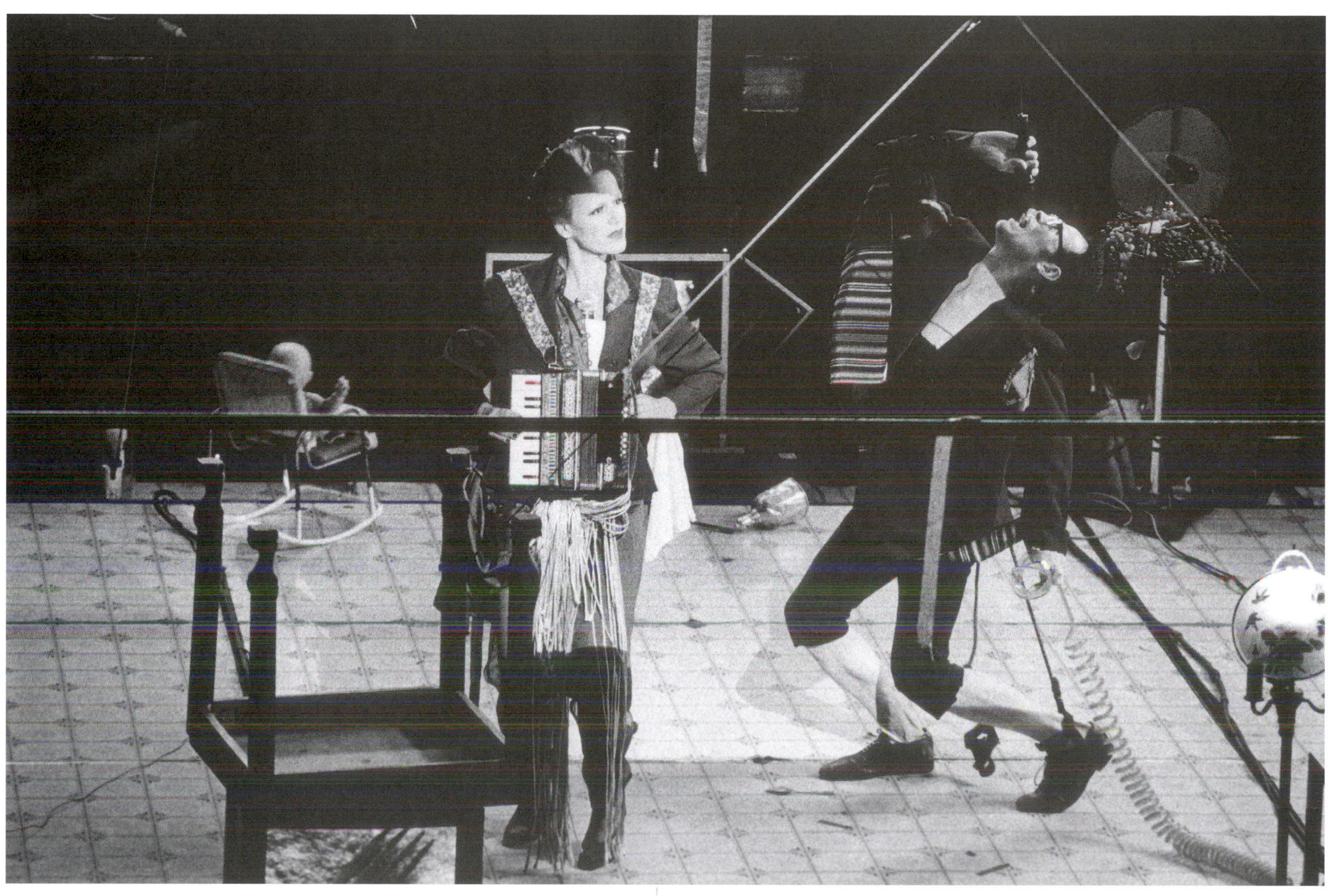

Sensha takes center stage as Yukio/Andrei calls to his sisters

DANCE 6 FINALE In which street musicians come into the yard.	**"Beautiful Dreamer" Dance**		
Sensha: Hiroko, try singing this. Hiroko: (singing) "Beautiful Dreamer, wake unto..." (speaking) It's too slow.	SENSABURO – 1st stamp (after "Dreamer") MASHA & EIJI – shake trees	*"Beautiful Dreamer" (with lyrics)*	
Sensha: No, it's not.			
Hiroko & Sensha: (singing) "Starlight and dewdrops are waiting for thee..."	HIROKO – rocks baby SENSABURO – 2nd stamp (after "thee") MASHA & EIJI – shake trees	*Rocking*	DS – Dissolve to white burlap
Hiroko: (sings alone) "Sounds of the rude world..."			
Olga: (speaking) Our yard is like a parade ground. People are always coming and going.			
Hiroko & Sensha: (singing) "...heard in the day, lulled by the moonlight have all passed away... Beautiful dreamer, queen of my song..."	SENSABURO – 3rd stamp (after "day") MASHA & EIJI – shake trees SENSABURO – 4th STAMP (after "moonlight") MASHA & EIJI – shake trees with extra vigor SENSABURO – crosses SR, dances with Sentaro	*UP – Static, Thunder, Applause*	DS – Static
	ASAKO – Wave off	*ALL OUT* *Rocking continues*	DS – Dots
INTERLUDE In which Andrei is embarrassed.	**The Troupe rearranges the space and Sentaro sets up his fishing line**		
	SENSHA – turns & gives Yukio a look		
Andrei: I'll be quiet.	YUKIO – stops the rocking chair with his foot/assists Sentaro with costume change MASHA – exits SENSHA – is assisted off the stage HIROKO – removes baby & rocker/sits on the back table SL of TV ASAKO – removes fan from "stupid"/crosses to sit in wheelchair, SL	*Rocking out*	US – Tree light fades out

 Sentaro catches a fish: "First it went one way, then another."

Sentaro catches a fish

Narration	Action	Sound	Video
Narrator: Sentaro is an avid fisherman. Tonight he has had good luck. He hooked it at about 9:40 and finally pulled it out at 10:05, a 25-minute battle. First it went one way, then another. One mistake and the line would break. When the waves came, he wound in his line. As they went out, he let it swim. Every time he gained a little more. It took 25 long minutes. When it came within reach he got nervous. He called Yukio for help...	SENTARO – stamps foot to cue Yukio & tech.	*"Mothra" & Lurie*	**DS** – Dissolve from "dots" to "blue" Jeff **US** – Fish (done live by Scott) at USR live camera station
Sentaro: Yukio! Yukio!	HIROKO – raises US TV		
Narrator: He picked it up by the gills. He was surprised! People began to gather around. They even came into the water. The villagers were surprised. They had never seen such a big fish.	FOLLOWSPOT on Sentaro		**US** – Dissolve to Blossoms **DS** – Fish on plate

Sentaro's introduction

Narration	Action	Sound	Video
Sentaro is a bachelor. He enjoys a relatively free lifestyle and will continue to do so as long as his popularity with the fans remains high.	ASAKO – wave off	*ALL OUT*	
	ASAKO – crosses to pick up fan	*BUZZ*	
	HIROKO – removes flypaper from "stupid"/exits		
	SENTARO – moves fishing pole to back wall/exits		
	YUKIO – exits		
	ASAKO – looks for fly with fan in hand	*BUZZ*	
	FOLLOWSPOT up on screen	*Footsteps*	**US** – Jeff's mouth (in **B&W**)
	TARO – moves head into light on screen		
	ASAKO – swats fan into the light	*BUZZ OUT*	

Taro's introduction

Narration	Action	Sound	Video
Narrator: When he was a baby, Taro was adopted by Sensha who is training him to be the group's next star. Although he has never been to school, Taro is quick-witted and a fast learner, being particularly knowledgeable about all aspects of the stage and performing.	ASAKO – Wave off/crosses to small lamp & unplugs it/exits	*Footsteps*	
	SENSHA – remains seated at the back table/eats popcorn with chopsticks		

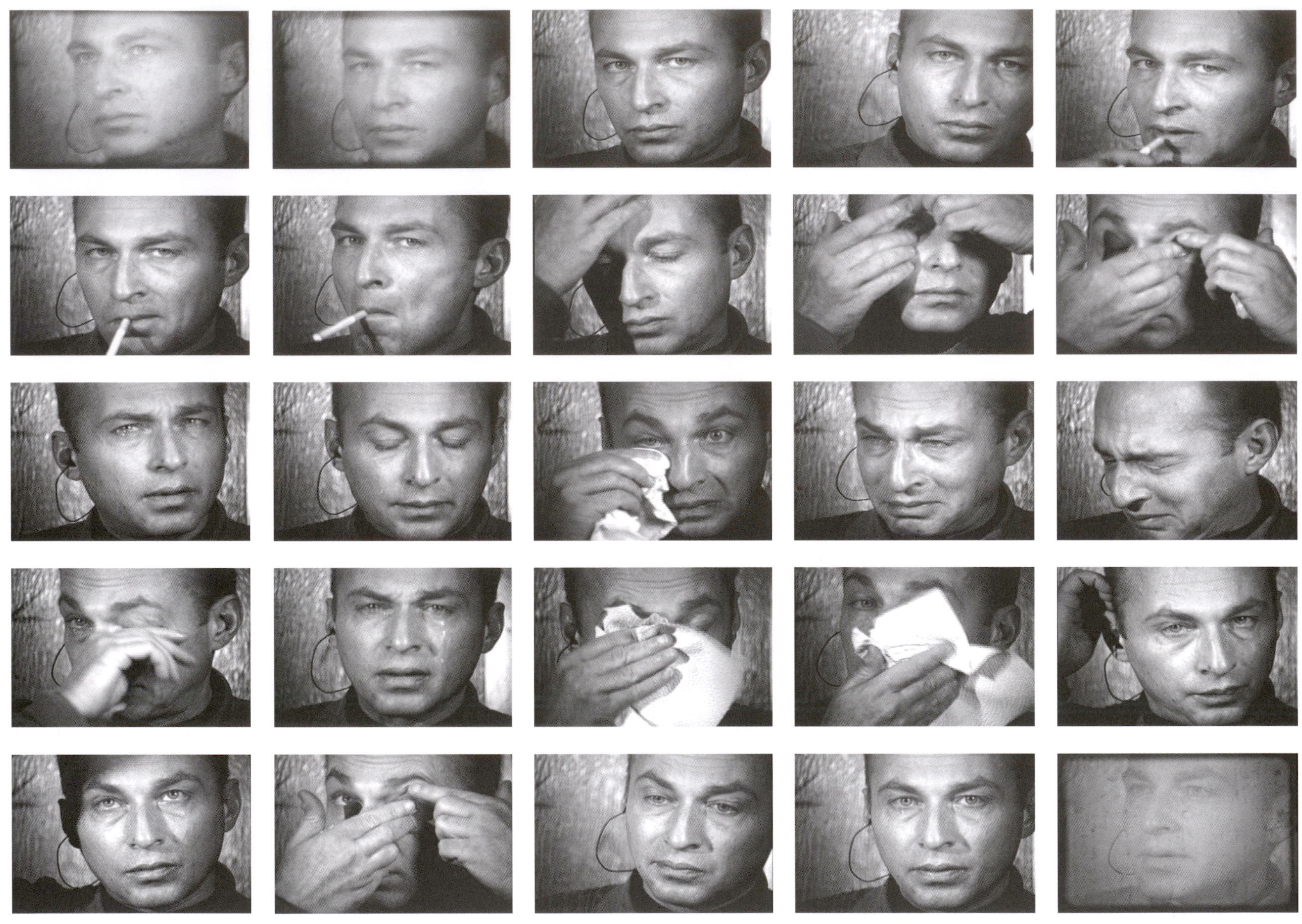

 Vershinin speaks to Olga: video stills

DANCE 0 REVERSE In which Vershinin speaks to Olga. Masha finally enters.

The Troupe begins to leave the stage

Vershinin: Olga Sergeyevna, we're leaving right away. I have to go.

Beep-beep

US – Ron / Vershinin
DS – floor

I think it's time for a cigarette. Would... right... thank you.

"1 to 5"
Beep-beep

I wish you all the best... Where's Maria Sergeyevna? Please. I have to hurry. Well, everything comes to an end. Now it's time to say goodbye. The town gave us sort of a farewell lunch, champagne, the mayor made a speech, and I ate and listened, but my heart was here. I kept thinking of you. I'm going to miss this place... Probably not.

Beep-beep

Let's try, uh, some, uh, glycerine. Oh shit... oooh-aaah... Yeah – all set. You, uh, you... I was what?... Oh, I see. OK.

Beep-beep

My wife and my two little girls will stay on another month or so; if they need any help, do you think you could...

Beep-beep

I think I put too much glycerine in. Would you hand me... good... thanks. Too much in one eye and none in the other... really... alright... yeah, here we go.

Beep-beep

Do you have any Kleenex?

Beep-beep
"1 to 5"

Oh... Uh – yeah – like.

Beep-beep

Well... Thank you for everything. Forgive me if things were... I talked a lot, I know. Forgive me for that too...

Is this a pause? What's that? Yeah.

"1 to 5"

And don't think badly of me. What else can I tell you by way of farewell? Shall we talk a little more? Life isn't easy. Sometimes it must seem stupid and hopeless, but we have to remember that it is getting constantly brighter, and better, and I don't think the time is far off when it will be completly bright. I've really got to go. Mankind is passionately seeking something, and eventually, we'll find it. I hope we find it soon.

Beep-beep

Let me have a little more glycerine. Yeah, no, this is fine. Am I moving in and out too much? Yeah... yeah... yeah... yeah, I'll try that... like, like that, alright...

TARO – throws cable toward US TV, crosses to USC in trough, gives headphones with cord to Sensha

Beep-beep

We must find a way to join love of work to love of higher things, mustn't we? Well, now I must go... I came to say goodbye.

TARO – standing in trough, coils cable in synch with image on DS TVs/returns to video table

US – Ron / Vershinin & Masha have their prolonged "farewell kiss"

THE END In which Olga interrupts Vershinin and Masha's prolonged kiss.

Olga: Now, now, that's enough.

SENSHA – 4 counts into Masha's look at the camera – "Now"

US – Dissolve into floor

2 counts – "now"
1 count – "that's enough"

Lights up & out

US & DS – floor Fade out

Music

THE END

US – 'THE END'

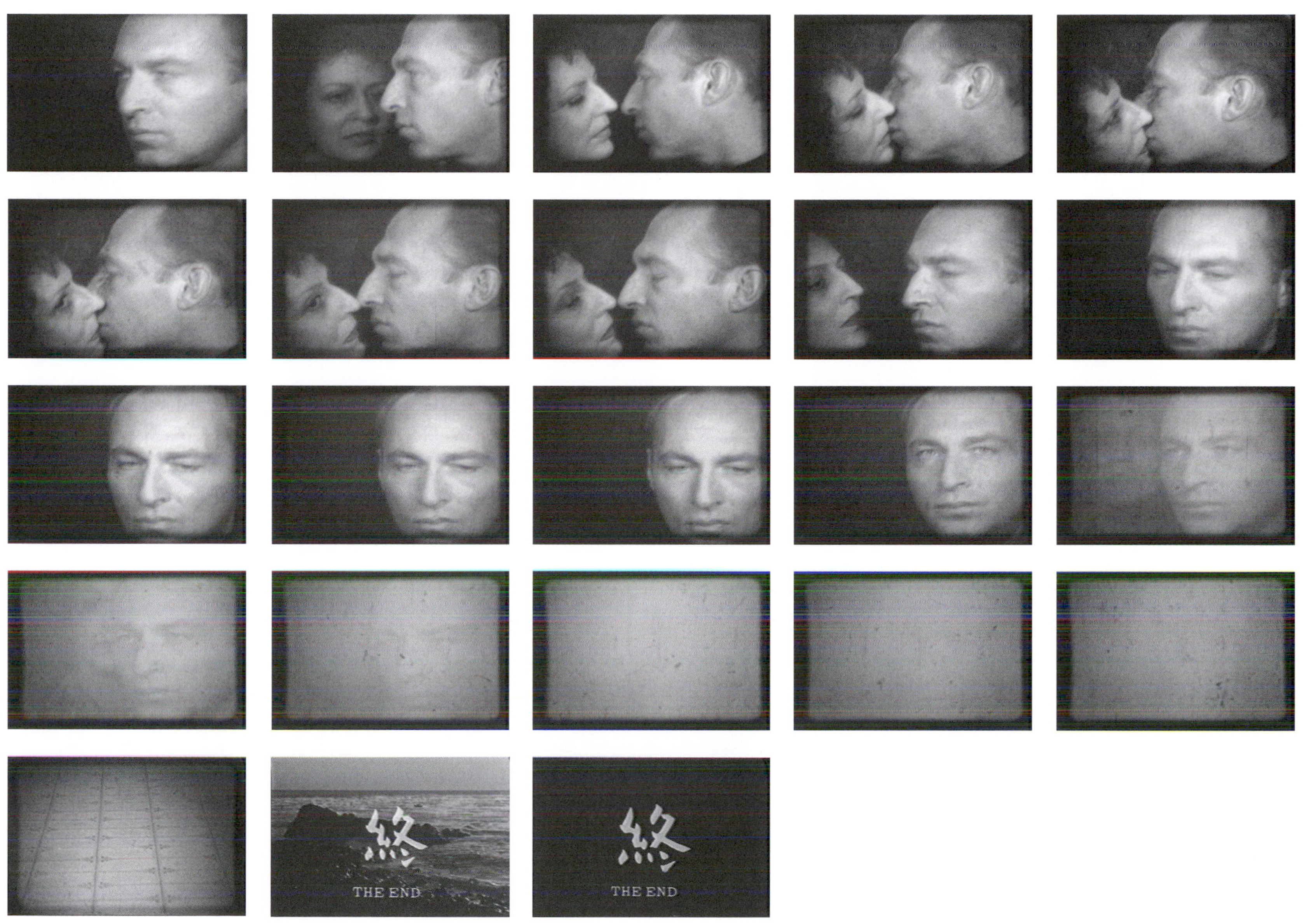

Vershinin & Masha have their prolonged farewell kiss: video stills

On listening to rooms

An interview with Kate Valk (New York, December 5th, 2005)

Andrew Quick (AQ): How did you become involved in The Wooster Group?

Kate Valk (KV): I had gone to NYU in the Department of Drama and had studied in the Studio Program, and as part of my studies I went to the Stella Adler Conservatory of Acting. I had a good time—Stella Adler was still alive and I was working with a great group of people. I was there for just two years because I was a transfer student. When it came close to leaving I got really concerned and I thought, "Am I going to have to get a photograph and a résumé and be an actor?" I just couldn't imagine it. I was looking for a way to live my life and I had to do an extra semester as a transfer student. NYU had this new program and The Wooster Group was teaching the semester. So, I met Liz and Ron and Spalding and had a fantastic time with them. They were mounting their trilogy, *Three Places in Rhode Island* (1978). So, I went to The Performing Garage and I saw *Sakonnet Point* (1975), *Rumstick Road* (1977), and *Nayatt School* (1978). Everything just spoke to me on a deep level. It wasn't even a choice; I just wanted to be there.

AQ: You knew there was a right place, then?

KV: I just wanted to be there. I wanted to work with them and make work like they were making and so I volunteered my services to Liz and she said, "Well, what can you do?" I was working as a seamstress at the time, so I started making things for her.

AQ: The costumes?

KV: Yes. The first thing she had me do was re-create a gown and make a lampshade. Then her stage manager quit, so I took over as stage manager. I ran the fog machine for *Point Judith* (1979) and then I ran the lights with Ken Kobland. The next piece she was working on became *Route 1 & 9* (1981). She wanted these Pigmeat Markham routines transcribed, so I did that and we got very familiar with the routines and that was the first piece that I performed in.

AQ: Why were you so taken with The Wooster Group's work?

KV: They were deeply interested in every aspect of the theatrical event. They were questioning what the frame was for the theater and that was terribly exciting to me.

AQ: In the rehearsal tapes of *Frank Dell's The Temptation of St. Antony* (1987), Liz often talks about the relationship with the audience, saying things like, "They're alongside us," "Don't reach out to them in a particular way" and "I don't want you to love them but I don't want you to hate them." I've never heard a director speak about the relationship to the audience in this way. It's respectful to the audience, but it's also very mindful of the performer's relationship to the audience. I thought this must be quite difficult for actors, the letting go of a particular and intimate relationship with the audience, where you're always tempted to work in response to them, to get them onside as it were.

KV: I was so young when I came into the company and, outside of school, I hadn't worked with any other director. I think that Liz doesn't like the actor's ego to dominate and all her energy's tuned toward integrating all the elements at play in the theater. I don't want to say that the performer is subservient to the piece as a whole, but, in a way, there is a system that is larger than any single ego. In the Noh Theater they speak of the performers, the musicians and singers performing with the intensity of one mind and I think this is very much what Liz is interested in. So, there is no place or need for a singular ego.

AQ: I'm interested in how you approach these works as a performer, how a role develops across a rehearsal process. When watching the rehearsal tapes for *St. Antony*, I was struck by the extraordinary detail in Liz's notes, how the demand on you was always to add something new to the performance, even well into the run.

KV: What is interesting about Liz is that she is always there; she's at every performance. And the show's not finished when it opens. It's her work of art, so she gets her hands in there, tweaking and tuning and changing and manipulating whatever she needs, until it is realized for her. *St. Antony* was a very interesting piece, because Liz built my role, and I can only speak for me, around my rehearsal energy, which had been very much determined by my role as facilitator. In this facilitory role I'm always creating what I think she wants to see, keeping track of all the material and finding, as a kind of editor on my feet, a way to put it all together. I had an intimate relationship with the material, literally all the pages of the different scripts on the stage, and my drive in the rehearsals was to put this all together. What was very shocking for me as a performer was that I did not protect myself enough going into the actual performance of the piece. Performances aren't rehearsals and I wasn't experienced enough to make the jump from who I was in rehearsal to what was demanded of me in the performance. I was stunned when I got into the performances, I wasn't able to hang on to that kind of dropped out energy I had in rehearsals—that you can just pick something up, drop it, go on to the next thing. Try this, drop it; try that, cut it; try that, go back and do it again, with the kind of real presence and sense of drop-out that I had in rehearsal. It got very brittle. When I went into performance it was almost like I wasn't breathing—it was, "Oh my God, what was I doing?"—I didn't know. As a performer, in all the pieces up until *St. Antony*, I had performed in blackface. I'd always had a huge mask. So, here I was, maskless and not experienced or aware enough to be able to play myself as a person in front of the audience, taking on and dropping all these different personas for the sake of getting the show up. I panicked. I choked, I really did. Then, it was the long slow journey of building up the score, the structure, gaining the confidence to be able to make it work.

AQ: What informs the building of the score and the production of that confidence?

KV: I think that if we did the show now, it would be very, very different because over the years we have developed all sorts of tricks or techniques for keeping the actor/the performer in the present. If we did it again I might be following a tape, which would completely liberate me.

AQ: It's interesting that you should say this because Ron Vawter follows the "Channel J" video tape recording through the opening sections of *St. Antony* and it clearly liberates him. In her rehearsal notes Liz sometimes points out that he's struggling when he doesn't have the tape to refer to. And even with the tape, I remember that Liz often warns him against learning the video too well, that he always has to have a present and real relationship with the recording as he works through it.

KV: He was so beautiful in that role. I think I was really good in rehearsal and on some nights I could get it to work through sheer inspiration—but I wasn't able to sustain it. But if the inspiration wasn't there it was just terribly flat. What was amazing was the way Liz stuck with it.

AQ: I remember Liz saying that the struggle for all of you was about being alive with the material, having the confidence to throw it away and to always avoid any pretending. I recall her advising Ron to be alive to all the elements in the room and him replying that it could be a physical thing, like listening to the traffic on Broome Street.

KV: (Laughs) She was saying that for me. That was learning how to be present on stage without a big mask and learning how to breathe and take the space.

AQ: Things were very different in *Brace Up!*.

KV: Yes, I'm not a character in the play. That's why I totally took on the role of facilitator. I don't think I was allowed to act after *St. Antony* (laughs).

AQ: So, what's the mask in *Brace Up!*?

KV: I am the narrator and I have the wig and I have a kind of mystery built into an androgynous persona.

AQ: When you went back to using this mask was it a kind of relief to you or did it feel like a direct progression from the piece you had just made? Do you actively discuss what has and hasn't worked previously or does it evolve out of early rehearsals? When I watched the first rehearsal tapes of *Brace Up!* it seems that at this stage both you and Peyton were taking on facilitator roles.

KV: Yes, Liz always starts off with who we are, following all of us through all the pieces. She takes on all the possibilities, the different mutations, from one show to the next. So, she imagined that Peyton and I, as the two women from *St. Antony*, the facilitators, would also, in some new incarnation, be the two people who are facilitating this other play, *Three Sisters*. Then Peyton wasn't comfortable with this, she was much happier playing one of the sisters. So, I became the sole facilitator. I am always good at moving furniture around.

AQ: In *St. Antony* you and Peyton sort of facilitate the whole play's energy. You keep it all going when the performance appears to break down, which is beautiful, moving and very funny: theater's magic, as it were. In *Brace Up!* you have a different function because the internal dramatic structure of Chekhov's play has its own momentum that you are guiding us through, very subtly, which seems to require a different type of performance. And this is framed by the traces of Japanese theater, specifically Noh Theater, that ghost through this staging. Whereas *St. Antony* feels so American.

KV: Yes, maybe taken from Vaudeville.

AQ: There's something so strange and desperate in your sections of *St. Antony*, there's something showgirl about it...

KV: "I'm just a crummy showgirl and I want a place in the country real bad" (laughs)...

AQ: ...whereas in *Brace Up!* your performance is placed and delicate—even when you are moving furniture around, getting people in exactly the right spot, moving things a little here and a little there.

KV: Well, the performance has the feeling of a game board and the audience is looking down on the floor. The floor is light and it's like a game of *Go*, where if you move one piece, the whole perception of the game board shifts. *Brace Up!* has got that subtle play, like a game on a *Go* board. The linoleum on the floor we used actually has the same grid pattern as a *Go* board.

AQ: And there is a real game of *Go* being played on the stage, isn't there?

KV: Yes. I don't know if they knew what they were playing. The rules of *Go* are easy to learn, but they take a lifetime to master.

AQ: How important was Japanese theater to *Brace Up!*? Did you have to do a lot of research?

KV: Actually, for *Brace Up!* we did start watching a lot of Noh and Kyogen performances, so this must have been infecting our work in the space. But we didn't try and recreate or imitate Noh Theater. It would be ridiculous to think that we, as Americans, could actually, in such a short time, take on thousands of years of performance history. There was certainly some synthesis with the aesthetics of Noh Theater: the Noh props, the Noh stage, the Noh space, the Noh sense of time. The grammar of the feet—very important. And the light stage and the audience looking down at the floor, so that when Ron picked his foot up and put it on the footrest it would be a huge gesture. How people walked across the stage and how they sat in the chair, it spoke everything.

AQ: *Brace Up!* seems such a shift from *St. Antony*, a shift in performance style, with its formal relationship to the audience. The audience looks down whereas in *St. Antony* they had to look up at the action.

KV: In *St. Antony* the audience is looking up and through. The floor becomes the wall, the wall becomes the floor. Very dark, a lot to do with heaven and hell, earth and spirit, top and bottom, real and imagined.

AQ: And the sense of Frank Dell's breakdown, of dying and theater somehow helping to keep all of this at bay.

KV: Yes, perhaps Frank's alone and the whole thing is happening in his head. Whereas, in *Brace Up!* it's all inclusive; someone is speaking directly to the audience. In both pieces there's a person up front who's at the center point between the audience and the show. In *St. Antony* it could all be happening inside the head. In *Brace Up!* it's lighter, it's talking directly to the audience, telling them a story.

AQ: So, it wasn't a difficult transition, returning to this role as facilitator in *Brace Up!*?

KV: No, not really. I was always good at moving props and furniture and I loved it. I have a feel for the placement of things and moving on that stage, and it was almost a relief not to be a character in *Three Sisters*. I was in it in college, and so I knew the play really well. My role as narrator came very naturally because of this. I had sat next to Liz during a four-hour Dutch production where I told her the whole story as it was going on. It was a very natural extension of my relationship to the play and my relationship to Liz too.

AQ: Turning to *House/Lights* for a moment—is there a mask in this performance?

KV: Yes, definitely and it's as strong as the blackface. It's the televised face. It's the TV screen itself.

AQ: I wanted to ask you about the in-ear recording of the Gertrude Stein text that you worked from during the performance.

KV: I was the channel for the text. I would try to just let the words pass through me, not be ahead of them or behind them. My task was to speak as I heard it, although I had learned it.

AQ: Yes, I remember seeing one of the early performances in Copenhagen, where you gestured to the sound booth for the tape to be rewound, so you could find your place in the text. Turning back to *Brace Up!* for a moment, the mask doesn't seem so obvious. You're not working that often from a pre-recorded tape; you don't have an in-ear device. I suppose you are at the beck and call of the other performers, of Chekhov's text.

KV: Yes. It's like the Master of Ceremonies, or the *benshi* narrator who told the story live in Japanese silent cinema. They would stand next to the silent film and tell you what was going on; even put in the dialogue for the characters and maybe even just comment on the action.

AQ: Did *benshi* narrators take liberties with the material?

KV: I think if they got powerful enough, they could do whatever they wanted. And you know with *Brace Up!*, since I am not following a pre-recorded track, it was more or less successful on different nights.

AQ: What made it successful for you?

KV: When I could really respond. Like Ron said, when to really listen to the traffic on Broome Street, to really listen and respond—not ahead or behind the impulse.

AQ: And in many ways the play's energy was channeled through your role as facilitator.

KV: Well, this is what Liz had set up. It was a device based on having somebody on stage that could set up each of the different scenes, who could set up each of the different characters, so the play could be driven. Somehow, the play could have somebody driving it who didn't have to be in the play itself.

AQ: It's interesting isn't it, thinking back to your description of creating an environment in which no ego dominates, how Chekhov's text seems to embody this sense of an egoless place. I mean, there's no singular story that we follow, is there? There's a kind of entwining of stories, where no singular narrative or character is allowed to dominate.

KV: Yes.

AQ: Coming back to *House/Lights*, you're sort of facilitating Stein's text through the in-ear device, aren't you? Was this task difficult? It must have put you under severe pressure in the performances.

KV: To channel the text we had recorded? No, it was liberating. At the time I had a very good memory and Stein's text was very hard to memorize because of the repetitions, because of the plasticity of each word. So, I was having to rewind the tape, fast forward it, play it back and the sequences were very difficult to memorize. So when we did it from memory the text was laborious. Then, when we started using the in-ear and I worked directly off the tape it was more like channeling it, and the words... started to percolate.

AQ: How did you arrive at the idea of the in-ear device?

KV: I would say from the very beginning Liz has used the idea of re-creation as a seminal idea in her work. I'm thinking of the troupe in *Three Places in Rhode Island*—bits of that—lip-synching to those original tapes. I'm thinking of *L.S.D.* when *The Crucible* (1952) section was presented as a re-creation of a play that Timothy Leary's babysitter said she took the kids to see. This doesn't happen to the women in *St. Antony*, but Ronnie's re-creating the "Channel J," so the idea of re-creation is pretty central.

AQ: In *St. Antony* there's a sense of re-creating a show, isn't there, a magic act?

KV: Yes, there is.

AQ: In *House/Lights* you have to respond to and channel a film as well as Stein's text?

KV: Yes, *Olga's House of Shame* (1964) and Gertrude Stein's *Doctor Faustus Lights the Lights* (1938).

AQ: I presume the task of having to move between these two texts creates the set-up that allows you to drop in and out of different energies, to move between the demands of Stein's words and the film?

KV: Yes, the two different texts run concurrently. Sometimes they merge and sometimes one surfaces while the other is submerged and then they merge again. But they are always running concurrently, which I love, because the whole thing is so much about electricity.

AQ: The charge between the two?

KV: Yes, channeling and currents running and all of that.

AQ: It's fascinating how Liz works to keep actors' energies moving. From looking at the rehearsal tapes I get the sense that she really doesn't like it when things get too rigid. She's always working to break things up, bringing in another level of complexity to keep it alive. I suppose one could see *Fish Story* (1994) as one such response to *Brace Up!*. I mean, *Fish Story* has such a different tone to *Brace Up!*, even though it builds directly on the last act of *Three Sisters*, which wasn't completed in *Brace Up!*. How did you start working on *Fish Story*, what was the impulse?

KV: When we finished *Brace Up!* there were still eight pages left of Chekhov's *Three Sisters*. We did do the beginning of Act IV and we summed up what happened to all the characters, but we didn't actually do the last eight pages. We'd watched this Japanese film, which was a documentary about a geinin troupe and Liz was so taken with it. It seemed such a good vehicle for our story—you know, a thinly veiled tale of a theater troupe that was forced to reinvent itself in a modern world, where they didn't have access to the big theaters, where they weren't able to do the long shows they had once done, where they had to perform at hotels and tourist hot spots. There was just something sad and funny about the film and it allowed us to have a vehicle in which to tell our story. It was a lot of fun to take, to assume, the characters in that documentary and they were all sad and moving and this was coupled with Ron's illness and his goodbye as Vershinin. The tape of Ron that plays at the end of *Fish Story* was a kind of fetishization of Ron's goodbye. We had thought of *Fish Story* as a sort of flash forward and Liz always imagined what would happen if a troupe in the future, after the great days of theater were long gone, found the last eight pages of Chekhov's *Three Sisters* and recreated a performance of the play from video tapes.

AQ: Remnants of videotapes of The Wooster Group's performance of the play?

KV: Yes, The Wooster Group's. But in *Brace Up!* Liz always had the idea that somewhere there was the story of the troupe, which was doing the play. In *Brace Up!* the idea of the troupe is hidden and so she wasn't finished with this possibility. She still wanted to tell the story of the troupe that did *Brace Up!*, that was trying to bring back to life remnants of this theater troupe and their pieces.

AQ: I recall you discussing in one of the first rehearsal tapes the notion of the piece being about the future, the company's future. I think Liz even gives it a precise date like 2020.

KV: *Fish Story*—a flash forward—epilogue. You have to remember that the piece was made very quickly; from proposal to performance took a short time for us.

AQ: *Fish Story* brings to the fore the dance structure that was one of the layers of *Brace Up!*.

KV: Well, it's a documentary of theater life in eight dances, very much inspired by the *Geinin* documentary. Here we really fetishize the play's words. The idea of putting on a play is ritualized and fetishized to the point where you only need eight pages, because each thing, each move, sound, word, is so potent. With *Fish Story* I also think there's something of our idea of the Japanese theater aesthetic, of Japanese art, where there's an empty center, where there really isn't a play, but just its signs, the props, costumes, articles.

AQ: Your character is based on the maid and you move stuff around and get things ready for people. Sometimes you get in the way and interfere with the

action. In fact, there's something threatening about you at times—with the black costume and the giant fly swatter on your back—almost like a weird Samurai warrior.

KV: You're right; there is something demon-like about that character.

AQ: You say it was a quick process. Was it an easy rehearsal period for you?

KV: I loved it, yes. And we had just made *The Emperor Jones* (1993), so I almost felt that I didn't want to be in the show. I felt like I wanted to step back and I chose to be mute. But, I loved moving the props and spinning that energy around.

AQ: We're back to facilitating again.

KV: Yes, making everything happen but quite delicately—back, not the center of the attention.

AQ: It's not subservience, is it?

KV: No, there's a lot of power in being a maid or the servant. There's a tradition in literature and film of power residing in the servant. I think I was more the servant in the early part of my work with Liz. Yes, first, the servant. Later, I probably changed into the medium.

AQ: So, is this partly about your relationship with Liz?

KV: Well, as facilitator. I think everybody is her on stage, but I could be really close because of being a woman and having the freedom in the subservience.

AQ: Which brings me neatly onto *To You, the Birdie! (Phèdre)* (2002), because in this performance you are the queen, aren't you?

KV: The queen, but the puppet queen.

AQ: You make use of the in-ear again in this performance, don't you?

KV: Well, let me tell you the story of the in-ear, because it really sums up the whole metaphor of the puppet. When we were first starting to work on *To You, the Birdie!*—the *Phèdre* text—I had a difficult time saying the words. I could be very big on stage physically, but unable to say the words naturally. Then, sometimes I got close to saying the words, but I couldn't get it to work physically on the stage. The size of the theatrical gesture had to be so huge to make the story interesting, to stop it being boring melodrama. I had a very hard time with the words.

AQ: The actual Racine text?

KV: The Paul Schmidt translation/adaptation. His version was very naturalistic and I couldn't get a feel for the language. It wasn't until we separated the words from the action by Liz saying, "OK Scott, you go and sit over there and do all the text; Kate and Ari, you move on stage." It wasn't until we worked out this way to separate the words and action that things started to happen and out of this emerged the character of the queen. The business of making the queen took a lot of effort. I remember we had tried so many different things with the in-ear where I would be listening to Monica Vitti for a modern cinematic tone. We were looking for a kind of cinematic naturalism with the dialogue. I was listening to Italian cinema actresses, I was listening to Bugs Bunny, I was listening to so many things coming through the in-ear. When Liz took the words away from me—and thank God she did, because I was ready to relinquish the crown at that point anyway—I still wore the in-ear, even though there was nothing coming through it. I just thought, "Let me keep wearing this, just in case."

AQ: It was like a crutch?

KV: No, I wanted to have that channel open and available if something interesting came along. I didn't need a crutch. I had several canes all over the stage and my elbows were tied to my waist. I had a lot of limitations to work against physically. I remember a couple of days before we were going to do our first open rehearsal, I went back to a bit of rehearsal video tape to work out some blocking. Liz was calling out directions and orders from the back of the room on the bit of tape I was watching, and I thought to myself, "The most interesting thing in the room is Liz." So, I asked Geoff Abbas, our sound man, "Can you put Liz on microphone and get her to come through on the in-ear," and he said, "Yes." I had learned my lesson from *St. Antony*, that you had better find out what is really vital and make damn sure you have that when you go into performance. This is what I meant when I said wasn't experienced enough in *St. Antony* to ask for what I needed. With Liz on the in-ear and calling instructions, it was a ball. It started to happen—it was the opposite of *St. Antony*. That was the reality that *To You, the Birdie!* was built on, that was the reality from which the piece was made. I was not the queen in the room. We know who the queen is, and I needed her power.

AQ: You needed that voice, that energy?

KV: It was the whispering in my head that became the liberating thing for me in that piece. A lot of sports coaches use the in-ear to speak to the athletes. It also made us able to respond to a sharp command as a group. All the performers wore them. It just worked perfectly and we use this device again in Part Two of *Poor Theater* (2004), when Natalie (Thomas, the movement coach) calls out some of the instructions, the modalities, for us to make specific movements. Coming back to *To You, the Birdie!*, I was very happy to at least have a modicum of awareness, through experience, to be able to ask for what was necessary. To watch that rehearsal tape and see what was really happening in the room. It gets tight if we lose sight of what's happening in the room. Finding it made us free.

House/Lights

DAK 400TMY
29
KODAK 400TMY
30
28A
29
29A
30

Frank Henenlotter's Sexy Shockers

BODIES RACKED BY UNSPEAKABLE TORTURES!
OLGA'S HOUSE OF SHAME
Only a woman could do what Olga did to twelve young girls!
THERE WAS NOTHING THEY WOULDN'T DO!
AN UNSPEAKABLE NIGHTMARE OF EROTICISM!

Olga's House of Shame

Volume 33, #5108
1964, b&w

The third in the infamous OLGA series and arguably the best.

Olga, the ultimate sadist, moves her headquarters from Chinatown to a deserted ore mine in upstate New York. There, with the help of her malignant brother Nick and numerous semi-clad gals in push-up bras, she controls a crime syndicate involving narcotics, prostitution, and jewel smuggling. But what the film is really about, of course, is scene after scene of gals being tortured, whipped and beaten: Stacey has a soldering iron stuck into her cleavage; Paula is scrubbed with a wire brush; Christine has her fingers shredded; Holly is juiced in an electric chair that reduces its victims "to the moronic stages of life"; and Nadja is given "horse discipline." As narrator Joel Holt, (the same guy who narrates THE CREEPING TERROR), grimly informs us "Olga felt great excitement in tormenting her victims." Eventually one of Olga's victims, the sweet-faced Elaine, (Alice Davis from SIN IN THE SUBURBS), abruptly switches sides, becomes Olga's "protege," and helps Olga with the torturing. She also gets it on with creepy Nick ... sort of. She makes Nick get on his knees and beg for her. Then she slaps him.

Sick, sick, sick. And, thankfully, there isn't a politically correct moment in it.

Frank Henenlotter

With Audrey Campbell, Alice Davis, W.B. Parker. Directed by Joseph P. Mawra.

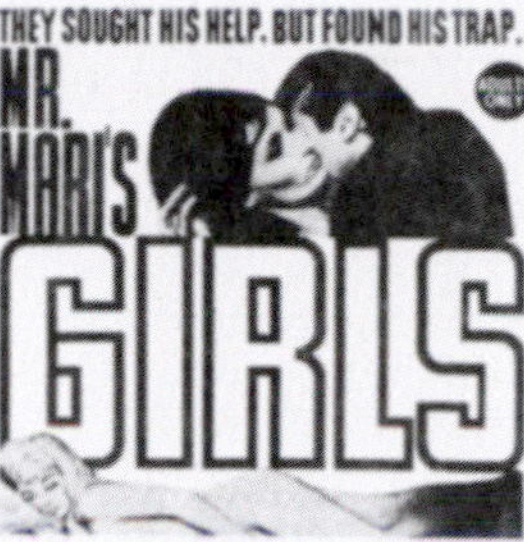

THEY SOUGHT HIS HELP. BUT FOUND HIS TRAP...
MR. MARI'S GIRLS
ADULTS ONLY

Mister Mari's Girls

Volume 34, #5111
1967, b&w

"Women, as you know, are complex animals ..." Especially Mister Mari's Girls, a bunch of diverse women in trouble who come to millionaire Mari for help. And good-hearted Mari calmly finds a sensible solution to their problem's ...

Like, among others, Stella, a junkie in desperate need of a fix who gets raped by a black drug dealer instead. Mari graciously gives her some dope, (which Stella shoots up while sitting on the toilet,) then sits there smiling as she dances nude for him. Or underage Diana, a "smart little girl" who ends up getting pregnant by the English teacher tutoring her. Mister Mari happily pays for an abortion. And then there's "hard as nails" Dirk, a dyke in love with blind artist Barbara, who's afraid Barbara will leave her after she has an operation to restore her eyesight. Mari's elegant solution? He marries them!

And Mari does all this without ever asking for anything in return. Punchline: He then invites all the girls he's helped over to his place at the exact same time and is quite amused as they jealously fight and kill each other until they all wind up dead in a pile on the floor while Mari cackles and sprinkles money on the bodies, saying, "Thank you, girls, thank you very much ..." Go figure.

Another one of those twisted ones that could only have been made in the sick, sick sixties ...

Frank Henenlotter

Directed by William K. Hennigar.

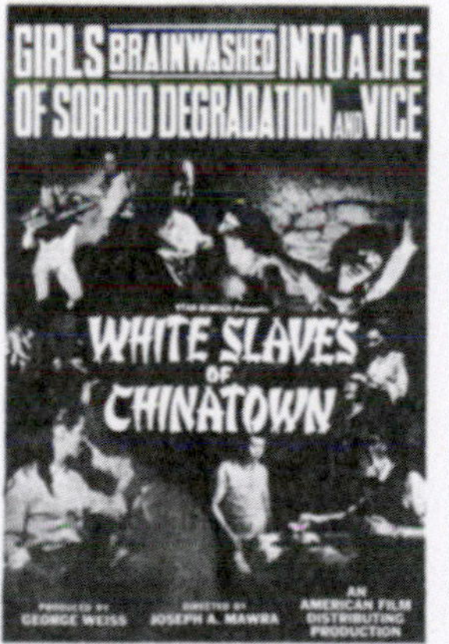

GIRLS BRAINWASHED INTO A LIFE OF SORDID DEGRADATION AND VICE
WHITE SLAVES OF CHINATOWN

The Girl and the Geek

aka Passion in the Sun
Volume 35, #4351
1964, b&w

A deranged, utterly hilarious, forgotten nudie-horror that's a real jaw-dropper!

A crazy looking carnival geek - specifically, "a poor twisted mind running wild in a body that has slipped from the lowest rung of the ladder" - escapes from a small-time amusement park. Meanwhile, stripper Josette, on route to the Sans Souci strip club, is held hostage by gangsters Raul and Ernesto. After Josette and Ernesto tour the Texas highway by clobbering the hell out of each other in the back seat of a convertible, Josette escapes with the gangsters' briefcase and charges naked across the countryside, followed by Raul, the geek, and two deputies (one of whom is director Dale Berry). Yet despite the intensity of the pursuit, busy Josette still finds time to bathe in a stream, clean her clothes, and even take a nap (!) until the geek drowns Raul and hops aboard a pickup truck Josette comandeers. With the slobbering geek hanging onto the driver's side and going nuts, Josette just happens to turn into the very same amusement park the geek escaped from and, not being a rocket scientist, tries to elude him by riding "The Wild Mouse ..." All of which is periodically interrupted by strip acts!

Quite incredible. Originally released as the innocuous sounding PASSION IN THE SUN, this was briefly rereleased under the far more descriptive GIRL AND THE GEEK moniker. Either way, it's a bona fide Sexy Shocker cult *classick* ... and a milestone in geek cinema.

Frank Henenlotter

With Josette Valague, Dale Berry, Mike Butts, and the Sans Sousi Girls. Directed by Dale Berry.

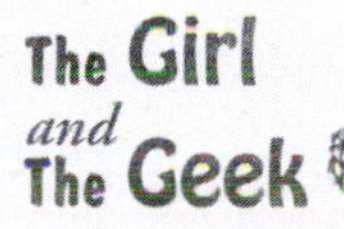

White Slaves of Chinatown

Volume 36, #5110
1964, b&w

The first of the incredible OLGA films!

After a montage of headlines lifted from the beginning of THE DEVIL'S SLEEP, Olga, a woman who "possessed a mind so warped that she made sadism a full-time business," picks up Lola from the women's house of detention and scurries her directly to her headquarters in New York's Chinatown. More specifically, she takes Lola to her "torture chambers" where, for the next 60 minutes, she keeps Lola and a half dozen other gals in various forms of bondage. As the narrator helpfully explains, "The disease called Olga cannot be fought. Sooner or later you become a white slave." She also holds drug parties for her girls that feature opium, heroin, and marijuana "or, as it's more commonly known, pot." After all, "Olga was an animal who wouldn't think twice of selling pot to young school children. Anything for a buck." And when one of her gals gets pregnant, who does Olga call? Yup! Producer George Weiss (!) who performs an abortion "in his usual filthy manner. Chalk up another one for this old butcher!"

Quite depraved. And, of course, successful enough that two more OLGA films were released the same year. If you really want to toy with your head, watch this back to back with OLGA'S HOUSE OF SHAME. And bring plenty of rope.

Frank Henenlotter

With Audrey Campbell, Marlaina Abbie, and Miss Chinatown. Directed by Joseph P. Mawra.

35

Opposite: **Rehearsal: *House/Lights*** Above: ***Olga's House of Shame*: "Something Weird" catalog**

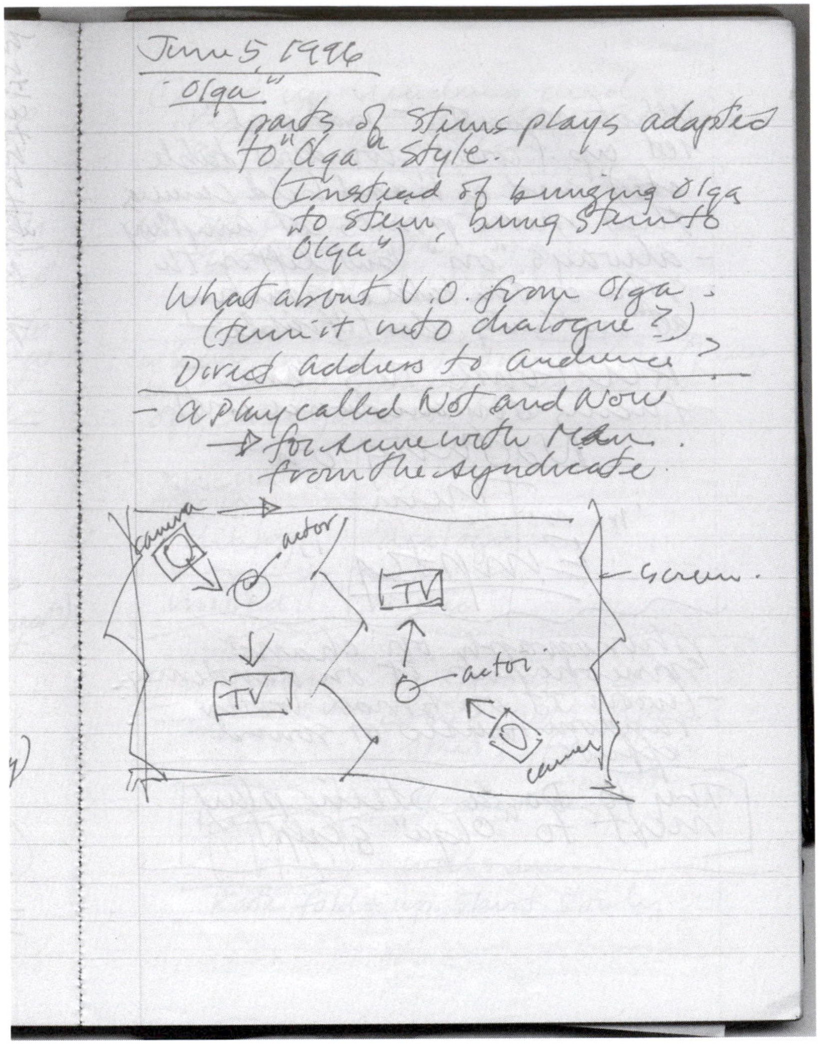

June 5, 1996

"Olga"

parts of Steins plays adapted to "Olga" style.

(Instead of bringing Olga to Stein, bring Stein to Olga")

What about V.O. from Olga. (turn it into dialogue?)

Direct address to audience?

– a play called Not and Now

→ for scene with Medu. from the syndicate.

camera → actor TV screen. TV actor camera

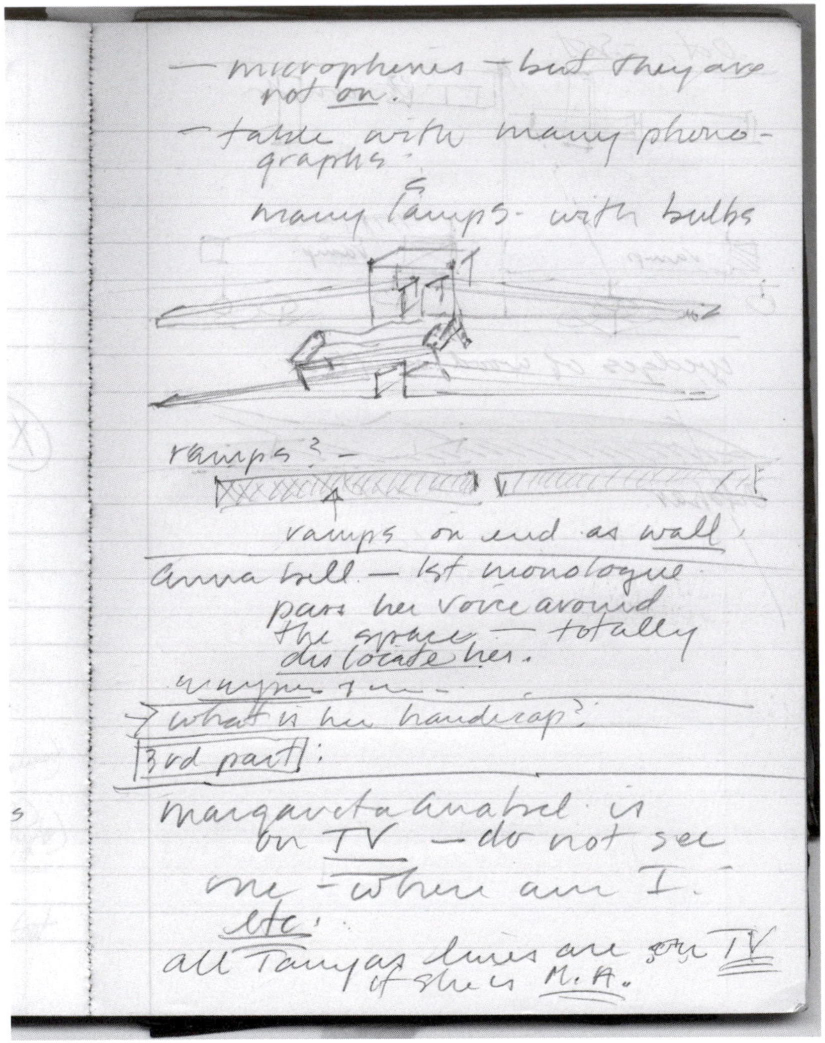

– microphones – but they are not on.

– table with many phonographs

many lamps – with bulbs

ramps? –

ramps on end as wall.

Anna bell – 1st monologue. pass her voice around the space – totally dislocate her.

→ what is her handicap?

[3rd part]:

Margaretta Anabel is on TV – do not see me – where am I. etc.

all Tanya's lines are on TV if she is M.A.

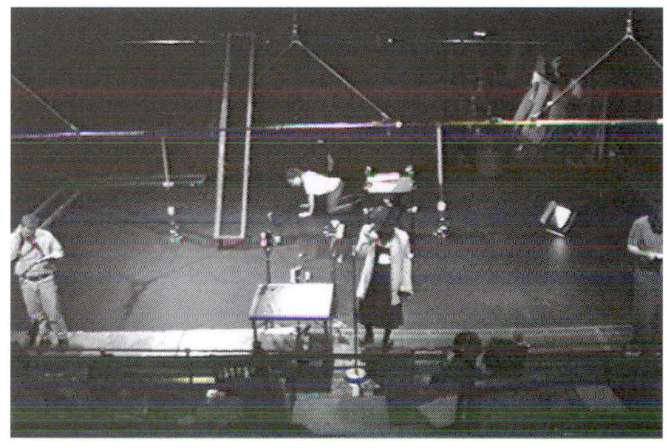

Laying out the set: *House/Lights* rehearsal video stills (October 1996)

Oct 26 – Horsefeathers
– movement across furniture
– talking to audience
– musical interlude
– exits and entrances.
– Knocking on doors which makes everyone scatter from stage.
– "straight men" are really straight
No reaction at all to Groucho. Just waiting for next line
– returning phrase from "I love you"

Costumes
To change costume. – web. like macrame out fits OVER Prada (Net-macrame-etc)
With fur-collars? (Victorian)

Nov 3, 1996 – LANDSCAPE?

see/saw only for props
– sound of see/saw landing – always PROP on table that bounces up. (Bottle/lamp – from Olga)

~~Worry about failure~~ failure to make it happen.

Props for golf ball scene →

hang-mics & cameras on stand pipe – from Olga – (torture devices hanging on wall)

sieth scythe mic

panasonic camera

[illegible]

Dec 21, 1996 – Olga.
Kate/Faust's voice is "echoed" (2 frames) Doubling. OR "Syncopated Time"
"your emotion is either behind or ahead of the play at which you are looking" (Stein)

Performers watch video & react to moves – always a little behind the move OR anticipating the coming move.

Syncopation – contraction of a word by omission of one or more syllables or letters in the middle.

The action of beginning a note on a normally unaccented part of the bar and sustaining it into the normally accented part. Produces the effect of shifting back or anticipating the accent.

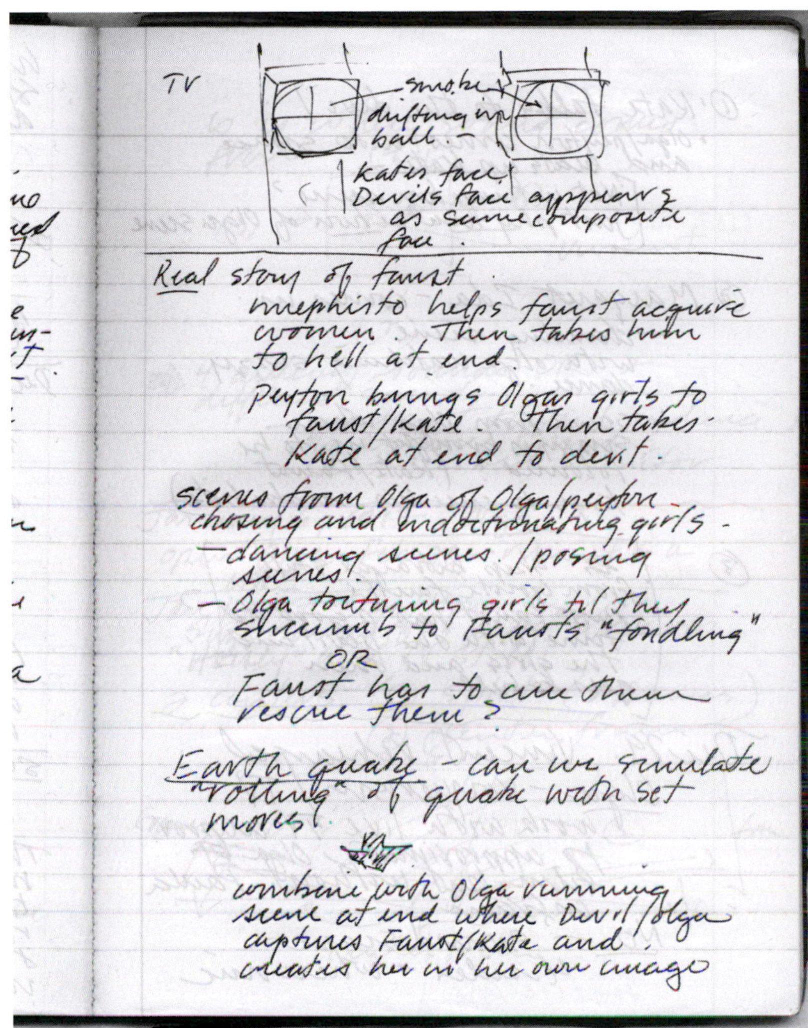
TV

smoke drifting in ball.

Kate's face
Devil's face appears as same composite face

Real story of Faust.

mephisto helps faust acquire women. Then takes him to hell at end.

Peyton brings Olga's girls to Faust/Kate. Then takes Kate at end to devil.

scenes from Olga of Olga/peyton choosing and indoctrinating girls -

— dancing scenes. / posing scenes.

— Olga torturing girls til they succumb to Faust's "fondling"

OR

Faust has to cure them rescue them?

Earth quake - can we simulate "rolling" of quake with set moves.

combine with Olga running scene at end where Devil/Olga captures Faust/Kate and creates her in her own image

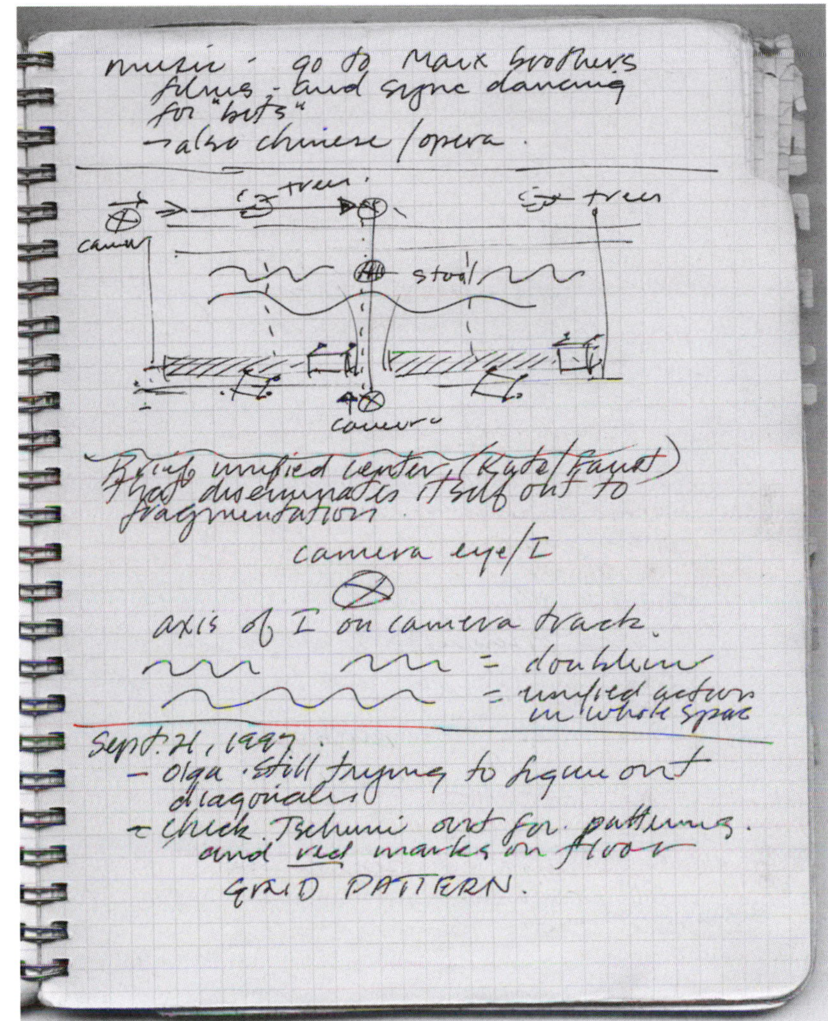
music - go to Marx brothers films - and sync dancing for "bits"

→ also chinese / opera.

trees

trees

camera

stool

camera

Brief unified center (Kate/Faust) that disseminates itself out to fragmentation

camera eye/I

axis of I on camera track.

= doubling

= unified action in whole space

Sept. 21, 1997

- Olga still trying to figure out diagonals

- check Tschumi out for patterns. and red marks on floor

GRID PATTERN.

Begin "Car Ballet"
Stool 1 foot in front of Ramp
front mic in center front video position
– Kt turn in car ballet move to L head lead as in [illegible]

Move front when car door opens

1st Faust break when Olga goes to black up front in car ballet section one from beginning to

Slide [illegible] to reveal yellow [illegible] and to last Olga shot

Right before is Elaine blood drip
At 2nd FF start TV to black
Set up for Nadja begin right there w/ VD

2nd Car ballet / after / 2nd Elaine beating
2nd Faustus section
Rewind w/ hysteria

DOCTOR FAUSTUS LIGHTS THE LIGHTS — Kate

Space set for Running (Boom mic in rear hole)

• 1938 •

except stool in place for Car ballet (foot or so away from

(1) Car Ballet

(2) ACT I Running

Faust standing at the door of his room, with his arms up at the door lintel looking out, behind him a blaze of electric light. Just then Mephisto approaches and appears at the door.

Faustus growls out.—The devil what the devil what do I care if the devil is there.

Mephisto says. But Doctor Faustus dear yes I am here.

Doctor Faustus. What do I care there is no here nor there. What am I. I am Doctor Faustus who knows everything can do everything and you say it was through you but not at all, if I had not been in a hurry and if I had taken my time I would have known how to make white electric light and day-light and night light and what did I do I saw you miserable devil I saw you and I was deceived and I believed miserable devil I thought I needed you, and I thought I was tempted by the devil and I know no temptation is tempting unless the devil tells you so. And you wanted my soul what the hell did you want my soul for, how do you know I have a soul, who says so nobody says so but you the devil and everybody knows the devil is all lies, so how do you know how do I know that I have a soul to sell how do you know Mr. Devil oh Mr. Devil how can you tell you can not tell anything and I I who know everything I keep on having so much light that light is not bright and what after

89

Faust intro

1st Faust break up front

2nd Faust break straddling back ramps

Above and opposite: ***Doctor Faustus Lights the Lights*** script with notes: Kate Valk all is the use of light, you can see just as well without it, you can go around just as well without it you can get up and go to bed just as well without it, and I I wanted to make it and the devil take it yes you devil you do not even want it and I sold my soul to make it. I have made it but have I a soul to pay for it.

Mephisto coming nearer and trying to pat his arm.

Yes dear Doctor Faustus yes of course you have a soul of course you have, do not believe them when they say the devil lies, you know the devil never lies, he deceives oh yes he deceives but that is not lying no dear please dear Doctor Faustus do not say the devil lies.

Doctor Faustus. Who cares if you lie if you steal, there is no snake to grind under one's heel, there is no hope there is no death there is no life there is no breath, there just is every day all day and when there is no day there is no day, and anyway of what use is a devil unless he goes away, go away old devil go away, there is no use in a devil unless he goes away, how can you remember a devil unless he goes away, oh devil there is no use in your coming to stay and now you are red at night which is not a delight and you are red in the morning which is not a warning go away devil go away or stay after all what can a devil say.

Mephisto. A devil can smile a devil can while away whatever there is to give away, and now are you not proud Doctor Faustus yes you are you know you are you are the only one who knows what you know and it is I the devil who tells you so.

Faustus. You fool you devil how can you know, how can you tell me so, if I am the only one who can know what I know then no devil can know what I know and no devil can tell me so and

I could know without any soul to sell, without there being anything in hell. What I know I know, I know how I do what I do when I see the way through and always any day I will see another day and you old devil you know very well you never see any other way than just the way to hell, you only know one way. You only know one thing, you are never ready for anything, and I everything is always now and now and now perhaps through you I begin to know that it is all just so, that light however bright will never be other than light, and any light is just a light and now there is nothing more either by day or by night but just a light. Oh you devil go to hell, that is all you know to tell, and who is interested in hell just a devil is interested in hell because that is all he can tell, whether I stamp or whether I cry whether I live or whether I die, I can know that all a devil can say is just about going to hell the same way, get out of here devil, it does not interest me whether you can buy or I can sell, get out of here devil just you go to hell.

Faustus gives him an awful kick, and Mephisto moves away and the electric lights just then begin to get very gay.

The Ballet

Doctor Faustus sitting alone surrounded by electric lights.

His dog comes in and says

Thank you.

One of the electric lights goes out and again the dog says

Thank you.

The electric light that went out is replaced by a glow.

The dog murmurs.

My my what a sky.

And then he says

Thank you.

GO TO LATER IN BOOK

"THANK YOU" by T. (end of RUNNING)
INTO
SWIM —— stu ↓

H – to SR RACK – get cuffed
KR – to SL RACK – " "

K – to DSC (@ RAMPS) – BRING ROPE CUFFS
SR RAMP to HOME
HOOK CUFFS – ANGLE towards DSR

A – to SL TABLE – RAMP to HOME
RIGHT LEG ON TABLE –
FOLLOW R's CROTCH TAPE

R – to STOOL – MSC
ROLL STOOL to DSC – SIT
SET MIC – LIGHT CIG.

P – to DSL – LEAN ON BAR

Stu – ↑ – AFTER K. IS 'HOOKED'
Dummy – ↑ – AFTER H & KR ARE 'HOOKED' –

CLAY – STUPID HOOK to #ONE – ORANGE

CAR BALLET

WINDOWS w/CROSSHAIRS	TVs
~~START 'WHITE'~~ ~~CHANGE to~~ GLITCHES & 'LEAVES' w/ K's ~~ACTION~~ to – 'LEAVES' BECOMES 'PEYTON & LEAVES' ~~for~~ ~~CAR BALLET~~	~~'WHITE'~~ DISSOLVE to: LEAVES & GLITCHES then to CAR BALLET (OLGA) ↓ ~~@ END~~ SUZ DRIVING into CAR BALLET
SOUND HPK – ATMOSPHERE O SNOTRK – LOW ↑+↓ TANYA – 'KLINK' & 'BLIP' SOUNDS 'CROW' for OLGA BONG / QUACK JC – LIP SMACKS for K	K – ENTER from USR – WALK OVER USC PLATFORM to MSC STOOL T – ENTER from USR – ANGLE DOWN to COMP – OVER RAMP to COMP Sh – USL – to CNCH

Above and opposite: **Assistant director score: Clay Hapaz ("Car Ballet," Act 1)**

CAR BALLET
Q101 K ENTERS
K- SLOW TURN - toward SL - END FACING USR
- COUNTER CLOCKWISE
0 SNDTRK.
LOW
K- SLOW TURN - toward SR - 2 TIMES - END FACING USL
- CLOCKWISE
STUPID
3 CONT.

National Brand 45-682 Eye-Ease 45-382 2-Pack Made in USA

Prepared By | Approved By | Initials | Date

<u>TVs</u> to BLACK then to K on LIVE CAM. / CUP LIGHT

<u>WINDOWS</u> – (to CUP LIGHT – – – ?)
– LEAVES + ~~PEYTON~~ SUZZY

K – PLACES HANDS (~~w/cuffs~~) ON STUPID

~~ACT I~~

Faust standing at the door of his room, with his arms up at the door lintel looking out, behind him a blaze of electric light. Just then Mephisto approaches and appears at the door.

T. – 'BONG'
("BUZZ" of ELECTRIC . . . ?)

Faustus growls out.–The devil what the devil what do I care if the devil is there.

Mephisto says. But Doctor Faustus dear yes I am here.

Doctor Faustus. What do I care there is no here nor there. What am I. I am Doctor Faustus who knows everything can do everything and you say it was through you but not at all, if I had not been in a hurry and if I had taken my time I would have known how to make white electric light and day-light and night light and what did I do I saw you miserable devil I saw you and I was deceived and I believed miserable devil I thought I needed you, and I thought I was tempted by the devil and I know no temptation is tempting unless the devil tells you so.

T. – 'QUACK'

~~SOUND~~

① FADES OUT
HPK – ATMOS. REMAINS
(~~HPK goes out for a second~~)

<u>TVs</u> – RETURN to CAR BALLET / OLGA

Stupid ↗

K – ROLL BACK to SR TABLE / RAMP

LQ-103 – AS K ROLLS US/BACK

HPK ATMOS.

Assistant director score: Clay Hapaz ("Car Ballet," Act 1)

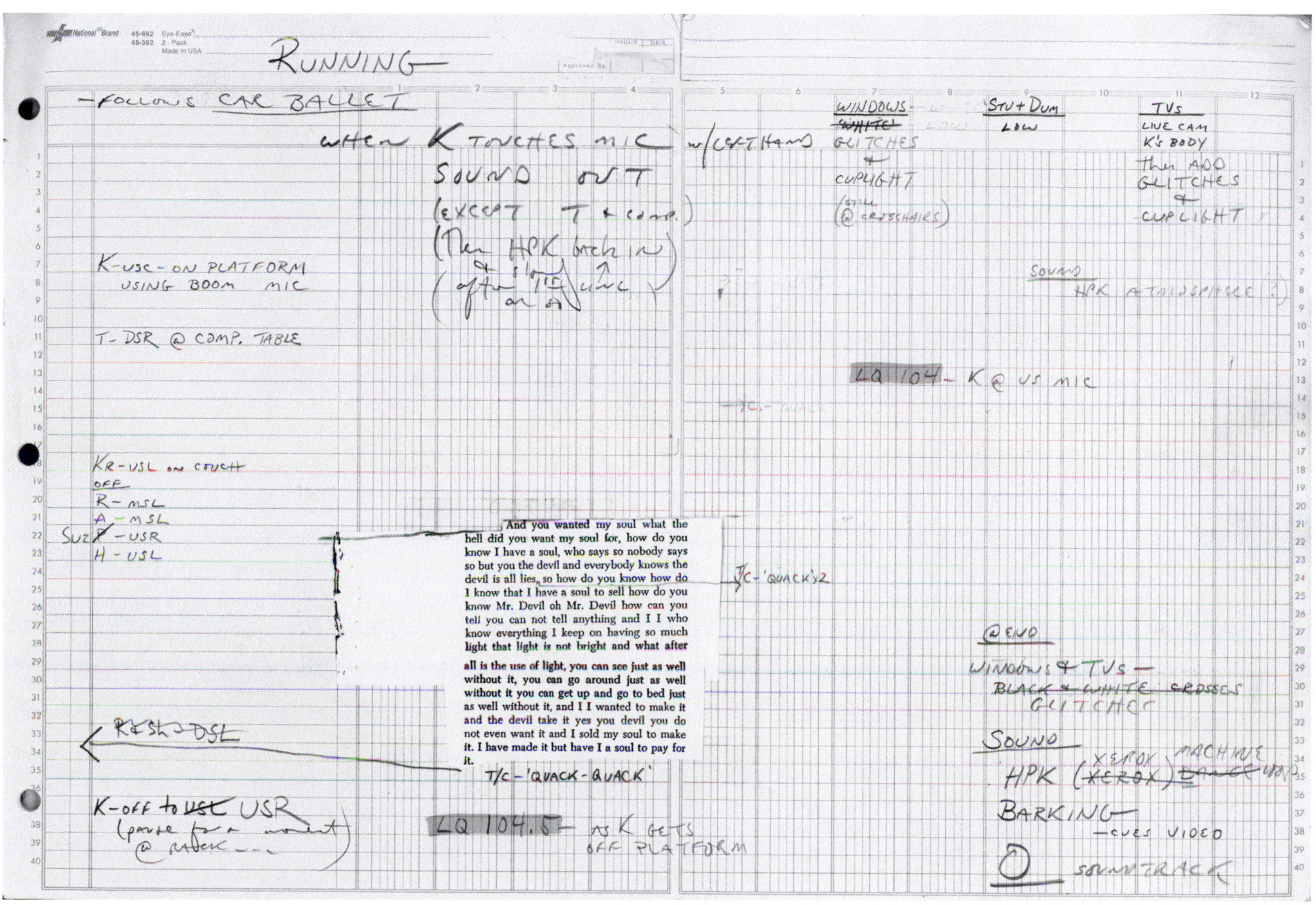

RUNNING

—FOLLOWS CAR BALLET

WHEN K TOUCHES MIC w/LEFT HAND

SOUND OUT (EXCEPT T + COMP.) (THEN HPK back in) (after 1st line)

WINDOWS — GLITCHES + CUPLIGHT (@ CROSSHAIRS)

STU + DUM — LOW

TVs — LIVE CAM K's BODY then ADD GLITCHES + CUPLIGHT

K-USC - ON PLATFORM USING BOOM MIC

T - DSR @ COMP. TABLE

LQ 104 - K @ US MIC

KR - USL on couch

R - MSL

A - MSL

SUZ - USR

H - USL

And you wanted my soul what the hell did you want my soul for, how do you know I have a soul, who says so nobody says so but you the devil and everybody knows the devil is all lies, so how do you know how do I know that I have a soul to sell how do you know Mr. Devil oh Mr. Devil how can you tell you can not tell anything and I I who know everything I keep on having so much light that light is not bright and what after all is the use of light, you can see just as well without it, you can go around just as well without it you can get up and go to bed just as well without it, and I I wanted to make it and the devil take it yes you devil you do not even want it and I sold my soul to make it. I have made it but have I a soul to pay for it.

T/C - 'QUACK' x2

T/C - 'QUACK-QUACK'

K-OFF to USR (pause for a moment @ rack ...)

LQ 104.5 — as K GETS OFF PLATFORM

@ END

WINDOWS + TVs — GLITCHES

SOUND

HPK (XEROX MACHINE)

BARKING — cues VIDEO

SOUNDTRACK

Assistant director score: Clay Hapaz ("Running," Act 1)

 Above and opposite: **"Running,"** ***House/Lights*****, Act 1**

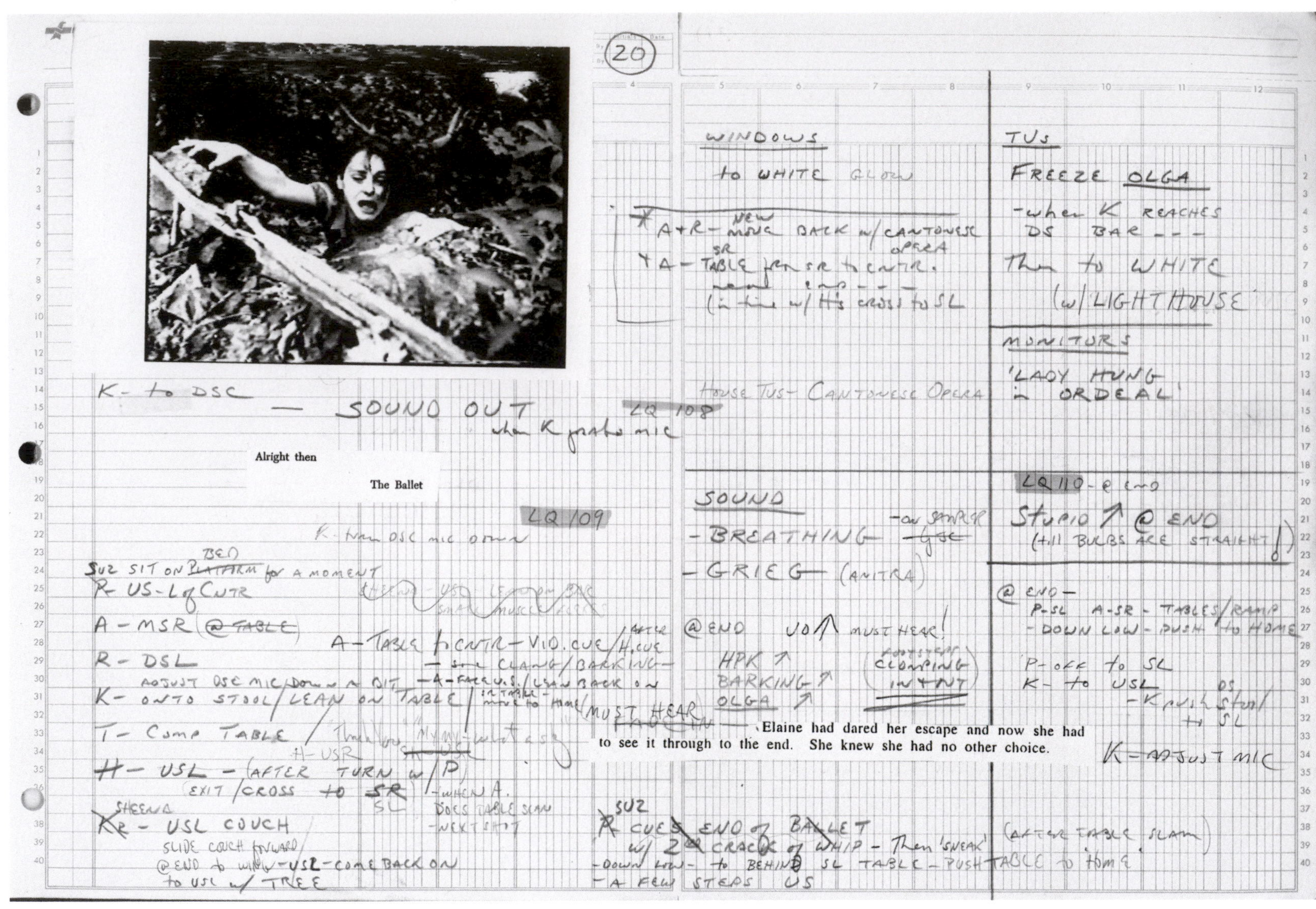

Above: **Assistant director score: Clay Hapaz ("The Ballet," Act 1)** Opposite: **Elizabeth LeCompte: journal entry (1996)**

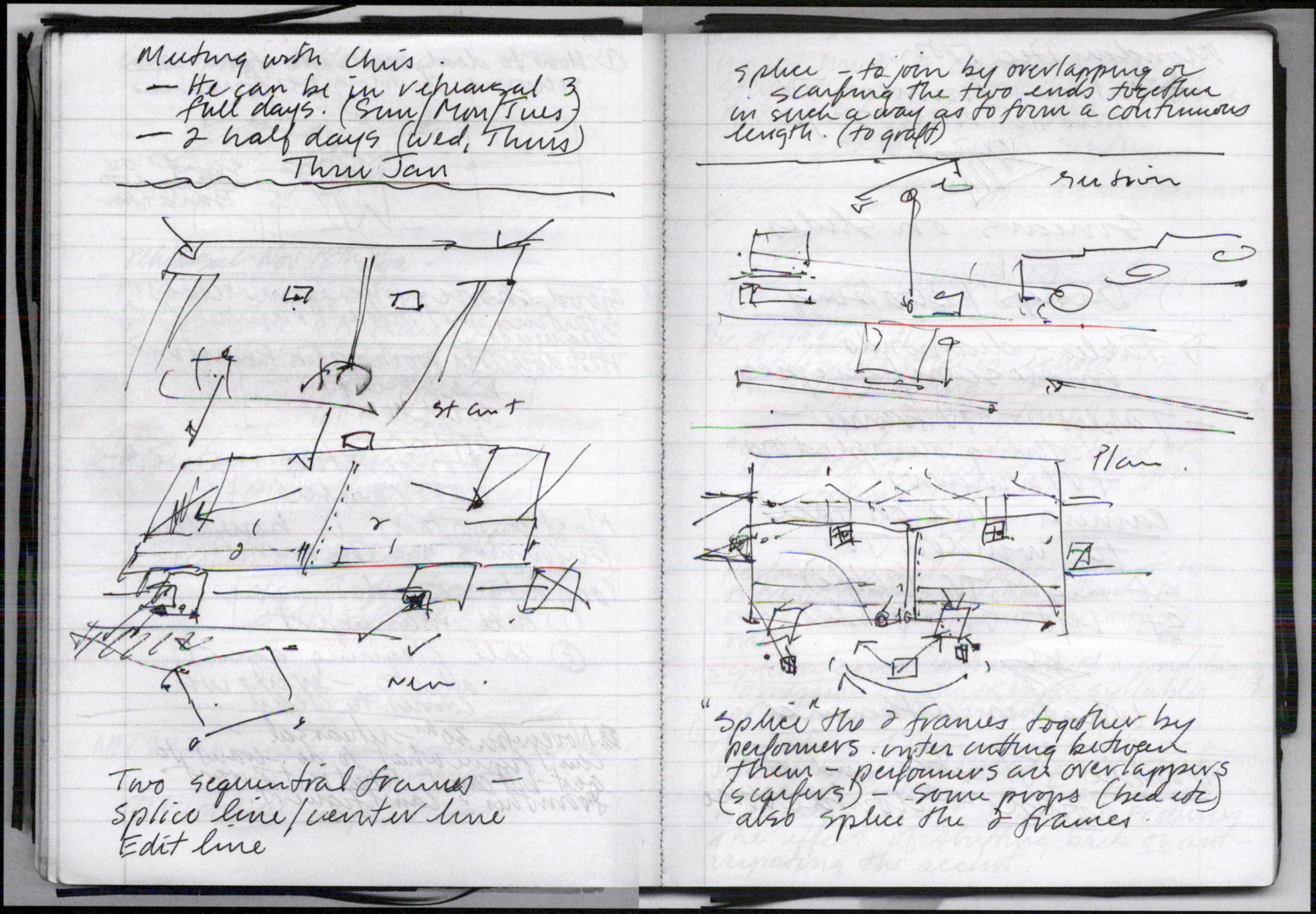

Meeting with Chris
— He can be in rehearsal 3 full days. (Sun/Mon/Tues)
— 2 half days (Wed, Thurs)
Thru Jan

St cut

New

Two sequential frames —
Splice line/center line
Edit line

splice — to join by overlapping or scarfing the two ends together in such a way as to form a continuous length. (to graft)

Section

Plan

"Splice" the 2 frames together by performers. inter cutting between them — performers are overlappers (scarfers) — some props (bed etc) also splice the 2 frames.

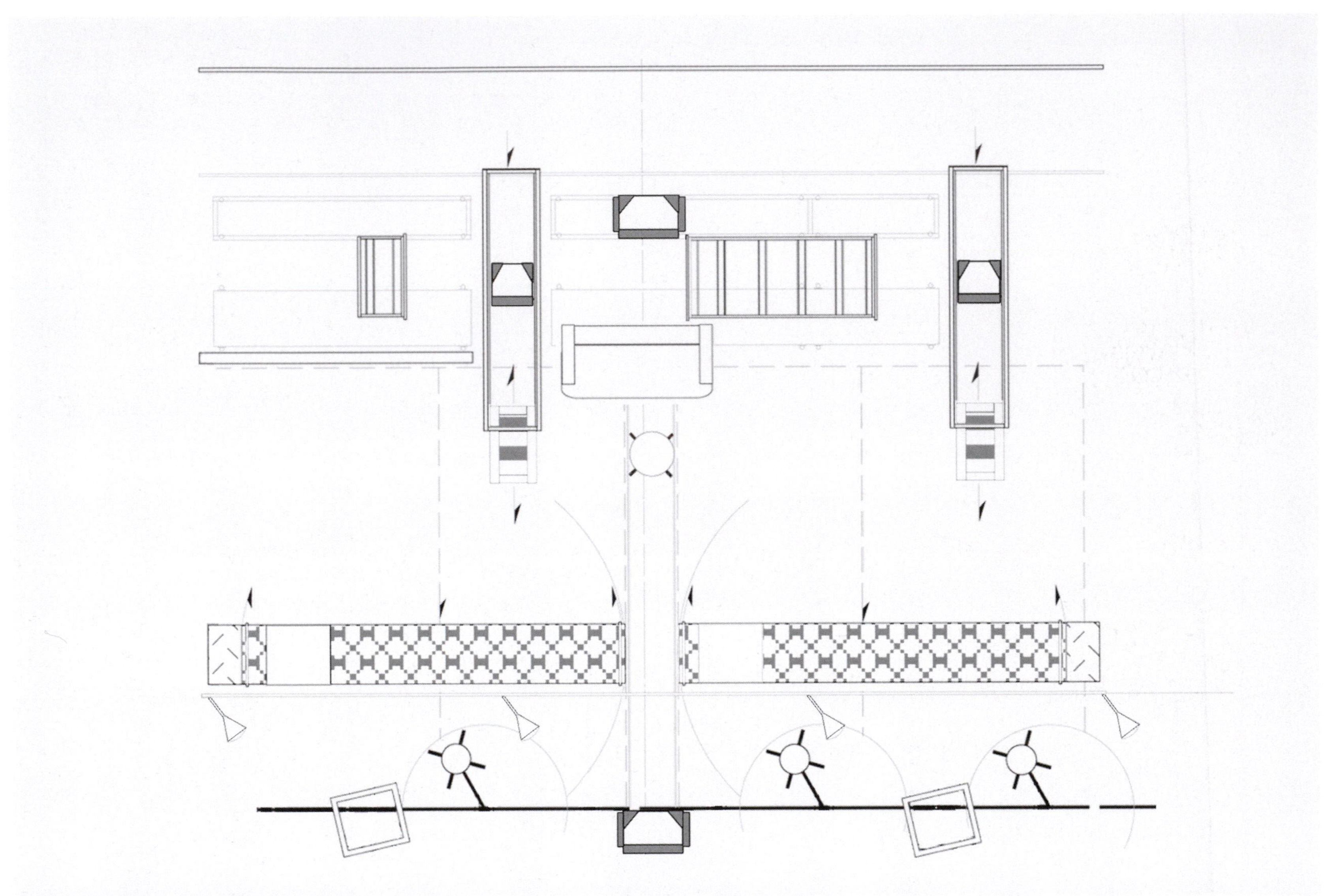

 House/Lights, set drawing: Jim Findlay

Above: ***House/Lights* set** Overleaf: **Basic sound lines: Hans Peter Kuhn**

4 BASIC SOUND LINES:

① BEGINNING (NEW START)
- SCRATCHING METALS (RATHER SOFT, LOW)
- DOG'S PANTING
- TEMPLE BLOCK (TAC TAKE TAKE TAC...)
- DOG'S BARKING
- SCREAMS (HIGH PITCH)
- RATS (HIGH PITCH PEEPING)

② ACT 1 SC 1+2
- BOATSWAIN WHISTLE
- POLICEMAN'S WHISTLE
- TRAINS: SCREAMING SOUNDS
- BASS DRUM (TYMPANI)
- GERMAN NUMBERS

③ ACT II
- OXYGEN MASK
- COKE CAN'S (SOUNDS JAPANESE)
- ALTO FLUTE
- SCRATCHING CERAMIQUES

④ LOW BASS RUMBLE
- BASS SOUND OF PASSING TRAIN
- SOUND OF SCRATCHY VINYL RECORD
- RATS
- HPK + DAVID MOSS SINGING "HEAVEN I'M IN HEAVEN

⑥ OTHER THINGS
- FOTO COPIER (SINGS HIGH PITCHES)
- KIDS PLAYING
- ELECTRO WELDING
- BEND METAL BALANCING ON TABLE

- PIZZICATO "I SIT AND SIT WITH MY BACK TO THE SUN..."

Performance

olga...and the devil

wig
horns
two clips
hair band
cream colored slip
olive dress
brown socks
brown boots
rope/belt for ear plug and monitor
lipstick and mirror (stuffed in sock for touch ups)

....
enter from upstage right with whip at tunnel shot of olga in running
stand on upstage right iron things to pointing shot
exit middle stage right
enter when elaine is running with ari and roy
face downstage left tv with olga running
switch to downstage right tv when olga changes direction
switch again to downstage left tv
then to front center tv and then to green line with kate at head turn
exit middle stage right

enter when tape starts again to catch
olga running downstage right tv
switch to downstage left tv
switch to downstage right tv
duck to table
come to downstage center for close up (right)
then switch to closeup (left)
push table down ramp
go to downstage right microphone - breath
tickle tanya's throat
cross ramp to middle stage center with olga cut
turn around and sweep across center to exit over upstage right iron things
come around and enter with olga to center stage - abrupt change of feet direction -
go to downstage right microhone - breath
tickle tanya' throat
cross over ramp with olga shot
get caught by ari grabbing leash
head for upstage left iron things (sit on bed)

ballet
start looking at downstage left tv
switch to right when roy and ari jump back
stand on turn - turn around
do dance with tv

go to center left ramp when olga comes back on
stoop there and rise with nick's head
look around
follow kate down center with tv
go over ramp and come back to center right ramp for foot stomps
exit middle stage right
emerge with nick's footsteps
catch shot of olga at center ramp with hand on table looking out
go around ramp and off upstage right

re-enter on "a pause no words"
go back to helen who has tree upstage center
she moves, take tree across to upstage left, stepping high (still on stage)
peek from behind tree
double kate when she sits on stool and dances to downstage center
go back behind tree
follow elaine's cross and sit down on bed when she sits on tv
wait for kate to cross to stool
cross over ramp with olga on tv to downstage right center
come up through ramps to shot with elaine and olga at water
split with kate and sit on bed
cross to center stool when nick has close up with breathing
fight with kate
go to ramp for slaps
let ari lead ramp to downstage microphone for kate's"nobody knows what i know"
when ramp drops go to middle stage right
let roy cross
go back to downstage left ramp and pull kate to downstage left table
give two breaths
when kate moves push ramp to middle stage left
bend into v with tv
sit on floor (with tv) and pull offstage left (middle stall)
....
nick and elaine

enter to downstage left stool (scene two in ear piece is the cue) with purse and rubber thing
look to nick and elaine during voice over and then back to downstage left tv through nick and elaine until "I'll go get olga"
cross to center stool - set up for elaine and olga scene

 Previous: "Act 1 Special Dance (to *Young Frankenstein*)," *House/Lights* Above: Mephistopheles/Olga score: Suzzy Roche

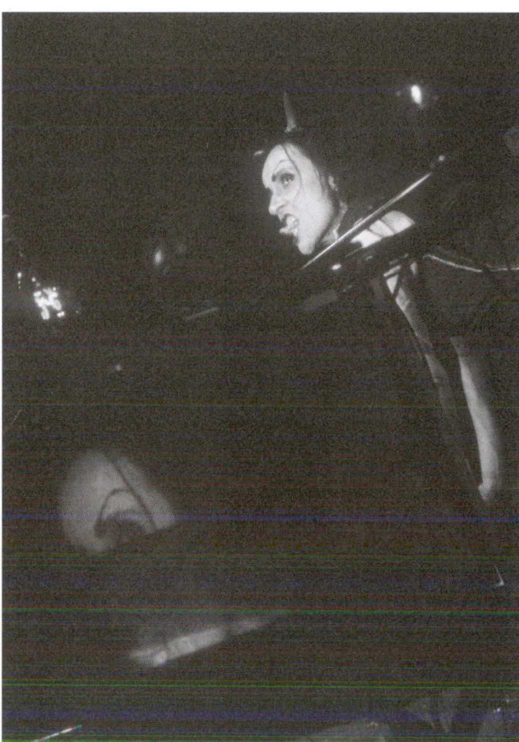

Left: **"Olga/Elaine Interrogation,"** ***House/Lights*****, Act 1** Center: **"Running Reprise #2," Act 1** Right: **"Clumping," Act 1**

follow center tv for open and closing legs with hand, etc.
follow olga on center tv for head shake and face rub
on "i'd rather be the hunter..." look to tanya, stand left of stool, breath to booth,
get kicked in the ass by kate - go to middle center stage - dance with ari and roy
exit to upstage right past helen
...
clumping

enter on breast shaking when roy and ari bring in couch
climb over couch , get sniffed by ari, hold ties with arm and foot
let go of ties on hand shaking shot
follow tv
when ari and roy are holding kate up - remove stool to left
look down kate's dress to audience
go back down behind her, come up again, looking down her dress, then bite -
go back to couch, slump over until kate gets up
put on shirt
follow tv through dancing sequence
after "i am not here" when kate spins
go to center microphone - telling roy to turn off music on the way
do "i couldn't help hearing the music" with mic in center position
then put it into downstage center left position
finish speech with tanya ending with "i'll call you later and we'll play"
cross to middle stage left green line to join with kate and stool
cross over ramp to downstage left (center) tree with kate as she moves ramp
"but and she lets out a shriek"
shake tree on "in the distance there is daylight near to there is none"
turn on "quick turn" shake tree again
turn on "quick turn" cross to helen downstage left stool
hug her until light comes down, bite on "perhaps it was one"
then turn to downstage left mic and say
"you just listen to me honey and everything will be allright
believe it or not ellie i do really like you
so behave from now on"
on "sits thinking"
get record player off center left ramp, bring it to stage left middle stall
go immediately to tie up tanya with helen
shake tree, play with tanya - exit to stage right
reapply lipstick
...
ring of fire

put on jacket
enter as ari exits and gets to stage left green line
pull ramp down to center right, go to center mic - kate says hi -
start intro

'well, well this is the dr. faustus
he has the pretty lights
he has not gone to hell
over there is a dog
he says thank you
there's a little boy
in the back is margerite ida and helena annabel
she did get bit by a viper and she wants dr. faustus to cure her"

sing song
say off mic "take it away boys"
go to center stool - sit
take steering wheel and drive
fit into camera and screen switching when kate switches
when she comes up and schreech happens throw steering wheel
collapse onto stage left ramp
come up - let kate guide face into frame -
fall slowly back onto stage left table
come up twice with cross eyed looks to audience
go back down on table until "we will take a one minute pause"
exit to upstage left stall
take off jacket
put stool on for water ballet

act two

put on inner tube
enter when sheena indicates after kate goes underwater
stay upstage left until bubbles on tv
then go onto upstage left stool in tandem with tanya
dance with ari
swing around on ramp when roy gets kicked on tv
sit on ramp until ari and roy lift kate - then rush in to "sea monster" shot on tv
with undulating arms and then bite!
quickly offstage left
phone rings
grab phone go to downstage left mic, sit on stool
wait for dialogue, exit after 2nd "what" to stage left stall (middle)

scene change

pull bed to stage right position
carry off stage right stool to downstage right stall
exit to upstage right stall
put on collar, reapply lipstick

 Above and opposite: **Mephistopheles/Olga score: Suzzy Roche**

enter on "they all leave" after "kissing"

take microphone out of upstage center position
go sit on bed
rise to middle center stage when kate says "very excited and sings"
sing song

which of you can dare to deceive me
which of you he or she can dare
i who have a will of iron
i who can make what will happen
i who can win men or women
i who can be wherever i am
which of you have been deceiving
which of you he or she
which of you have been deceiving me

if there is a light who has the right
i say i gave it to him
she says he gave it to her
or she does not say anything
i say i am mephisto
and what i have i do not give
no not to anyone
who's been in her
who's been in him
i will win

turn to face upstage center tv
look in 'the mirror"
finish da da da (singing under kate)
put mic in center stage position
climb on railings facing stage right (center stall) hand on hip
"come one my little fillies"

pony...

tanya comes from stage right (center stall)
hands me whip and rope
go in between red and green line
cut to center stage dance with tanya facing upstage tv
whip tanya, she crosses over ramp
stay center but lead her to downstage left
she crosses ramp
make soft curve to bending shot at the green line (stage left)
cut to "legs" (three whips)
jump back to stage left (middle) - (red line)on cut
cut to "that's it" first faust break - tanya center stage - close in with her - watch helen
tanya crosses downstage right ramp goes over to downstage left - lead her
when she crosses ramp - cross to green line to prepare for pov
do pov (two twirls)
then horizontal crosses each marked with a whip
go down center for close up of olga to downstage right - whip - turn to left
get distracted by helen
get grabbed by kate - start scene
"o, go to hell" - turn cross to center stage (middle) - wait for tanya to stumble
twirl around her as she crosses to stage right lifting rubber band for ari and roy
cross to sheena (center stage middle) criss cross with her
cut to rein grabbing freeze facing stage left
give reins to kate
cross around stage right ramp to stage left stool/table area
dance around to tv - whipping
follow kate to center mic - go up behind her head
go back to stage left stool/table area
follw kate to center mic again - go up behind her head again - get flicked off
go back to stage left stool/table area
when kate goes downstage right and moves stool - double her
then meet her center stage for her scream
cut to close up of olga looking down smiling "proud day for olga"
make clicking noise
make clicking noise again at "now there were two"
make clicking noise again at end of voice over
twirl around and exit to downstage left stool
adjust mic
say "no listen to me take her with you do i will make you young"
kate says "is it true i can be young"
say "yes"
breathe and say "always deceived' with tape
exit downstage left on "curtain"

the end

Roy House/Lights (spring '99)
Props preset:

handkerchiefs in pants and jacket pocket
tie, harness, battery pack, earphone, etc.
left pant tie untied

SL:

2 pillows
glass bottle (behind "couch" flat)
glass bottle (behind "2nd" flat)
rubber hose (now "preset" by Suzzy)
tree w/ tie ring
full bed waves
water bottle

SR:

ballet shoes
fake fur sleeves
black waist thing
green coat
vest
gun
tree
small bed waves
water bottle

ON TV:

cigarettes and matches
grommeter
pincher

RUNNING:
enter after Ari
Move ramp to home w/ Ari
pointing (Nick on TV)
enter w/ Ari, x up and do Elaine running
go to DSL mic (when Olga appears in bottem left corner of tv), fake narration ("How much longer...")
All right then the ballet
added: back up "chinese step" when camera zooms back
sneak along bar to center, do Nick head moves and run SL of US TV and back down to tables
look left, the right then down for "close up" etc. Nick on TV, exit pushing SR table
X to USR wings
enter through open platform and come around 1/2 bed, diagonal with Ari to front bar, spin over to Tanya, do big step diagonal USL, mimic Suzzy when Olga touches rock on TV and then exit to SL mic and put earpiece in Ari's ear,
Mouth words with Ari: "The day begins today, The day, The mon begins the day, There is no moon today"
give him treat "there is not moon today"
diagonal DSR, jump ramp, and move ramp in clockwise circles
push ramp down , walk up ramp, jump off table, move in circles
drop table/ramp stagger diagonal UR, hand up and fall towards R of center mic and the spin to SR mic, fake narration

move ramp for Elaine's POV
X USC w/ Nick's feet
circle around to DSR, rush on to center track and run upstage pushing Kate and off R
come running on, "leap" from small platform, X to DC look left and then freeze
exit to end of SR ramp, move w/ Ari
X on diagonal when Nic appears on screen, run between Suzie and Kate and go past SL small TV and hide behind big upstage TV
Run to behind big TV pop up look left(?) jump, move ramp at diagonal by pushing table
Run to Kate, throw tie over Kate's shoulder, pick her up and drag to Tanya at computer, get tie caught, spin offstage L
goes almost immediately into:
ENJOY SWIM
Kate finishes Faust at SR mic "Thank you," light change
roll stool to DC mic, adjust mike
pick up grommeter
light cigarette
pick up grommeter again
and again
grab cock on "you promise"
pick up pincher
both hands w/ cigarette and matches in frame
give cigarette to Kate
X L go over ramp and do "tap" dance at green line
run off L when Ari sweeps on
Roy H/L page 2
"hunter rather than the hunted"
come on with turn after Ari throws away cigarette when Kate kicks Suzzy
X to SL green line "tap"
X to SR green line "tap"
X to Center fall towards Kate, slap, spin, tap at SL green line
X off when Ari sweeps L

CLUMPING
sit on couch
look back 3 times when Kate does
Have big part of tie pulled down long hang over arm of couch
(have string of left pants leg untied)
roll on couch with Peyton on behind
couch to center, talk to Suzzy as she steps over couch, then roll down to spike mark
caught tie bit
roll stool to Kate
move table down to mark, lift Kate by knees, lift legs
turn when Kate screams, hold her by legs, "tap" and let go of her when she opens her legs
move stool to SL of couch after fall
X off SL (all exits from "frame" are thefoot out pop head and upper body up thing)
X up to back bar w SL tree and double what Ari's doing with phonograph, lamp, etc. then SR tree then off SL with both
X down to back of couch, place bottle on stool, put legs over back of couch and slide into place
fragmented seated dance
entire seated dance, unzip left pants leg (1st or 2nd "dance"?)
DS with Ari to phonograph
3 spins taken off tv
remove needle from record when Suzzy signals
jerk back to sofa when Suzzy makes noise with mic

"Running," *House/Lights*, Act 1

follow Christine on TV
X SL ("move over next to Christine"

"ready to go the limit... call me later and we'll play" fall in with "SR" tree and place SR of SL table
return for other tree and place in front of SL small tv
When Kate rolls stool back, zip pants, and strike "SR" tree off SL, "call" Ari/dog to couch, lie down, pet and give dog a treat, wake up on dogs barking, "calling Dr. Faustus..." first knock go to table (SL), 2nd knock lean on table, 3rd knock move table almost to green line
FRANKENSTEIN ORPHE DANCE
"Where's the girl"
repeat "cure her cure her cure her" until...
RING OF FIRE
Stein "What difference does it make" vamp until squeal of tires, rubber hose throw

computer: "one minute pause"
pick up rubber hose & take off small heavy platform
bring ramps to home and place pillows on tables
put SL waves on bed (who puts SR waves on short bed? Me?)
exit SR
Adjust SR lighting insturment, remove stove pipe

change into ballet slippers, tie on head and fur sleeves
tie left leg tie beneath zipper
LUCY BALLET (all the way through)
'the ballet rushes in and out" LUCY BALLET only up to 123 123 X OSR

WATER BALLET
change into "Nick outfit" (vest and Ari's coat) gun in right pants pocket

scene change (remove SR pillow from table, Helen and I strike waves?)
ELECTROCUTION

KISSING
enter when music begins
pelvis thrust walk in to DSC TV and switch switch from "Olga" to "mix"
show back of jacket to camera, reveal room (USC TV)
exit to SR green line
"Oh I didn't know you were undressed..." etc.
Stein: "Yes, there is no moon..."
to stool upstage for final lines and slap
complete laugh and exit SR
unzip and hook pants, pull up sleeves, tie bow tie

Kate announces entrance of Boy and Dog, fall in with Ari and cross to SL of Kate, lean on table and listen to Suzzy's song.
Take pillow(s) off with me SR
move table to end and ramp to mark (Once Kate has walked far enough DS to front pipe)

(Tanya takes pillows off tables)
angle plexiglass table
sit on stool slow ride of horse
lean back holding reins

HORSEY
recent changes
the ducking when Kate lifts gun
the turning when bulbs on TV burst
the exit from table to the back with Ari

 Above: **Boy/Nick score: Roy Faudree** Opposite: **"Kissing" and "Horsey,"** ***House/Lights*****, Act 3**

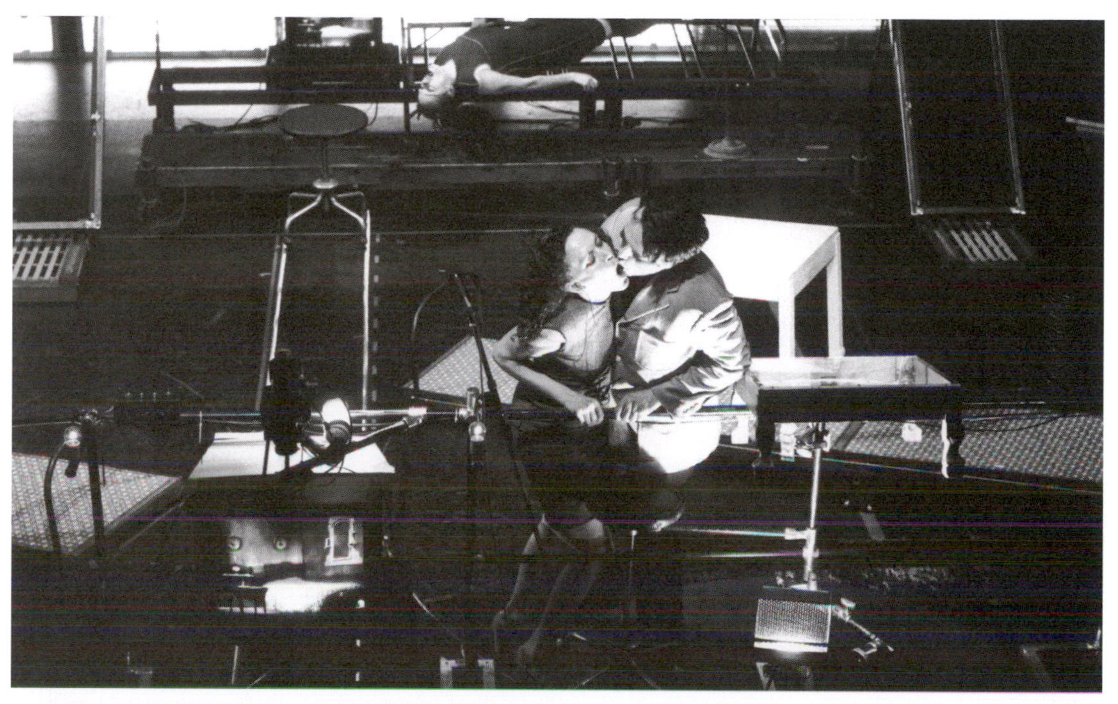

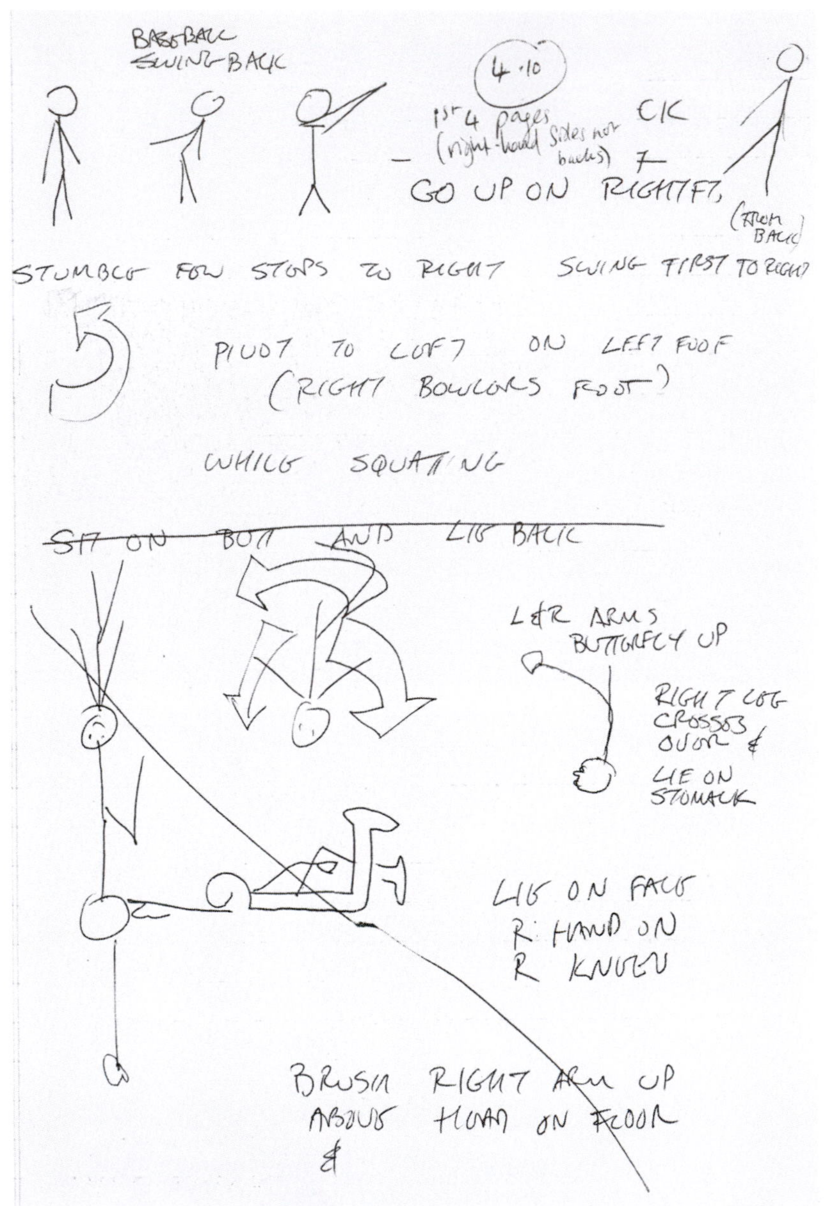

BASEBALL SWING BACK
4·10
1st 4 pages (right-hand sides not backs)
OK
GO UP ON RIGHT FT,
(FROM BACK)
STUMBLE FOW STEPS TO RIGHT
SWING FIRST TO RIGHT
PIVOT TO LEFT ON LEFT FOOT
(RIGHT BOWLERS FOOT)
WHILE SQUATTING
SIT ON BUTT AND LIE BACK
L&R ARMS BUTTERFLY UP
RIGHT LEG CROSSES OVER &
LIE ON STOMACH
LIE ON FACE
R HAND ON
R KNEE
BRUSH RIGHT ARM UP
ABOVE HEAD ON FLOOR
&

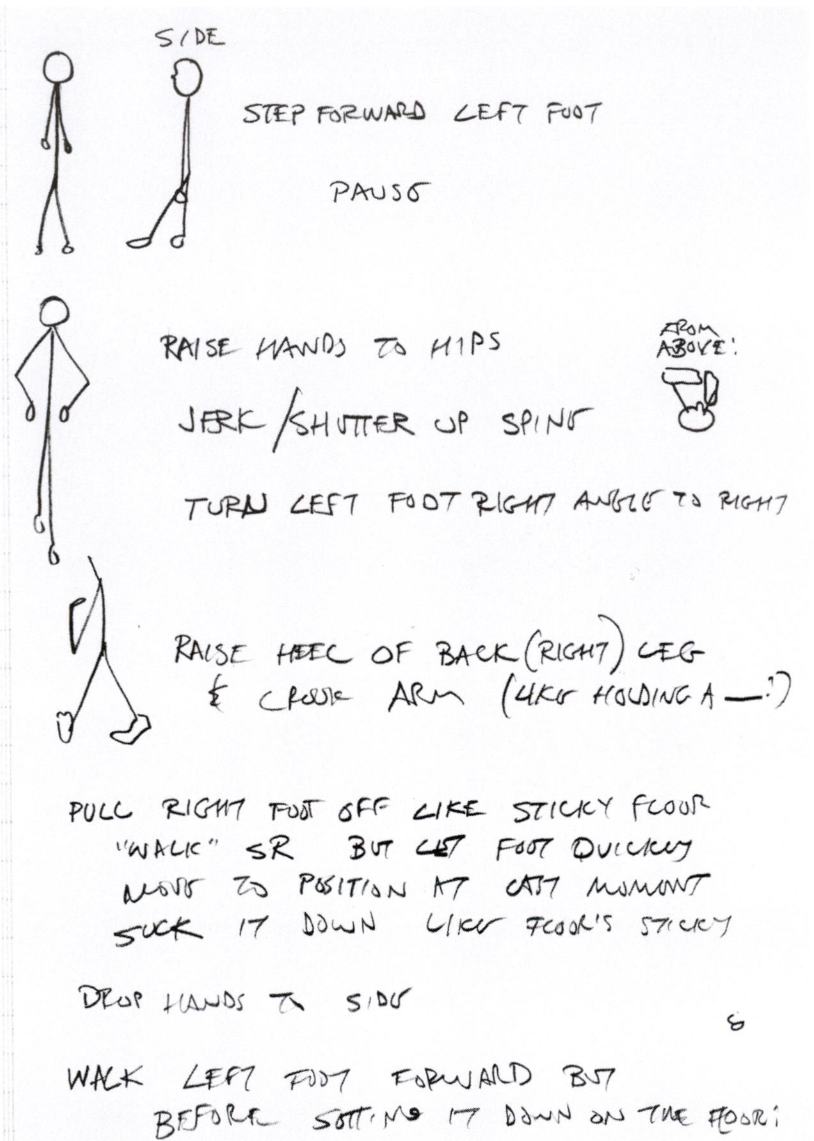

SIDE
STEP FORWARD LEFT FOOT
PAUSE
RAISE HANDS TO HIPS
FROM ABOVE:
JERK/SHUTTER UP SPINE
TURN LEFT FOOT RIGHT ANGLE TO RIGHT
RAISE HEEL OF BACK (RIGHT) LEG
& CROOK ARM (LIKE HOLDING A —!)
PULL RIGHT FOOT OFF LIKE STICKY FLOOR
"WALK" SR BUT LET FOOT QUICKLY
MOVE TO POSITION AT LAST MOMENT
SUCK IT DOWN LIKE FLOOR'S STICKY
DROP HANDS TO SIDE
8
WALK LEFT FOOT FORWARD BUT
BEFORE SETTING IT DOWN ON THE FLOOR:

 Above and opposite: **"Act 1 Special Dance (to *Young Frankenstein*),": notation: Roy Faudree**

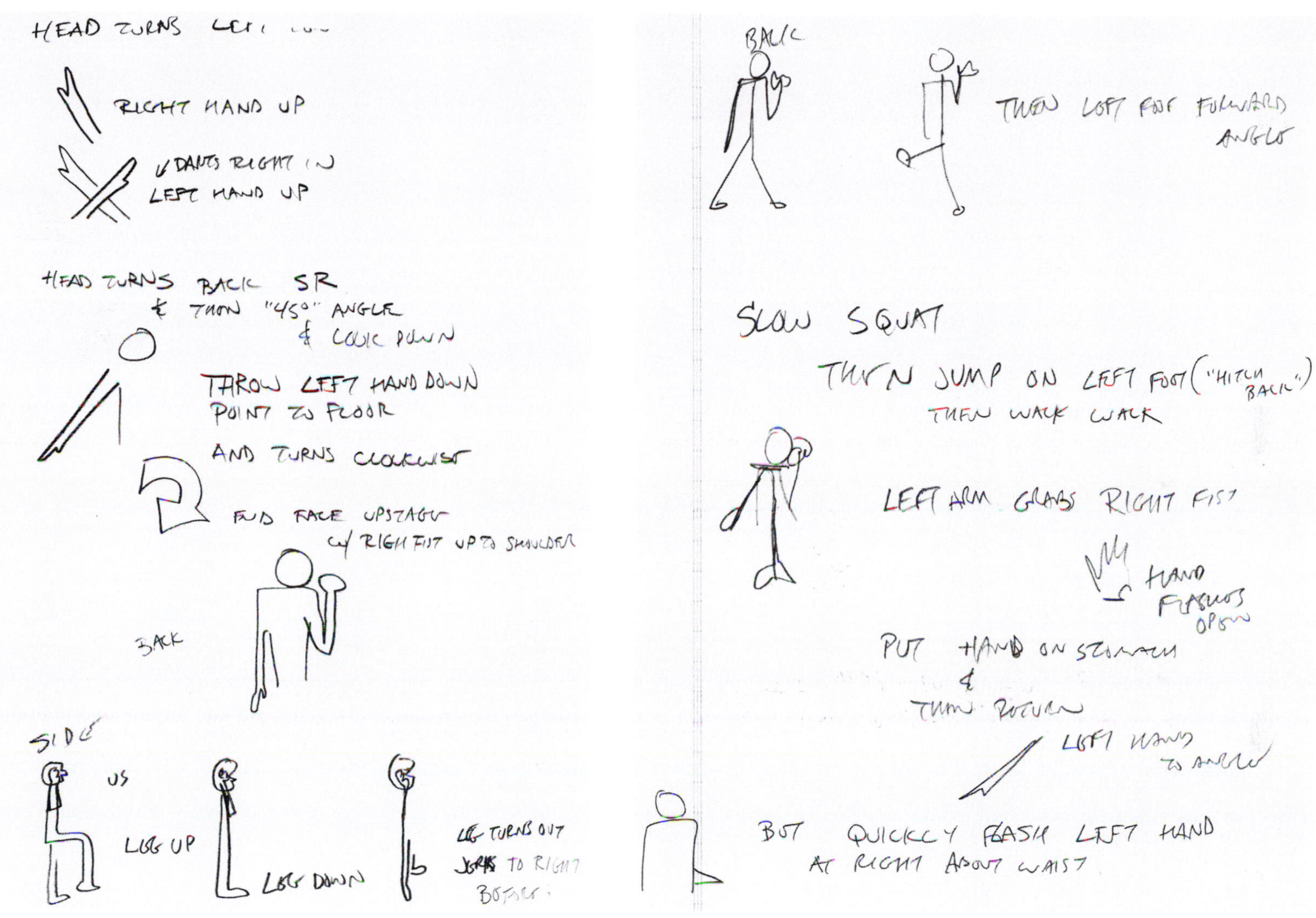

HEAD TURNS
RIGHT HAND UP
LEFT HAND UP
HEAD TURNS BACK SR
& THEN "45°" ANGLE
THROW LEFT HAND DOWN
POINT TO FLOOR
AND TURNS CLOCKWISE
END FACE UPSTAGE
W/ RIGHT FIST UP TO SHOULDER
BACK
SIDE
US
LEG UP
LEG DOWN
LEG TURNS OUT
TO RIGHT
BACK
THEN LEFT FOOT FORWARD
ANGLE
SLOW SQUAT
THEN JUMP ON LEFT FOOT ("HITCH BACK")
THEN WALK WALK
LEFT ARM GRABS RIGHT FIST
HAND
OPEN
PUT HAND ON STOMACH
&
THEN RETURN
LEFT HAND
BUT QUICKLY FLASH LEFT HAND
AT RIGHT ABOUT WAIST

Running

Begin UL behind screen
XDR ("arm flail"), collapse on Tanya, spin to DR wall on cut
follow Olga to miidle of right frame as Nick, over ramp (pointing) on cut, DC right frame on cut
XUC right frame on green line to platform, turn (holding stomach) as Elaine w/ Roy and Kate
Spin off R on cut
After Kate close-up w/ Stein, take position on ramp.
Move ramp in relation to Peyton's adjust. Ramp to home.
On Cut after Peyton colse-up, ramp down for Peyton's table move DR. XUC right frame doubling Kate. Stutter diagonal UL, Reach for stupid (right leg out), X around right frame monitor, right leg over metal frame w/Kate, XD on L of table, look quickly over right shoulder, push ramp UL with table, climb on table, jump off and spin off R.
On Roy's approach DC, take position on ramp. On Roy's extreme close-up, angle ramp so table moves with Roy. Ramps to home on cut. Double Peyton circling UR and DR to right of right frame monitor. Exit off R.
Peyton crosses ramp. After Kate crosses ramp, right frame table to center, L of ramp push upstage. Continue scan into left frame pushing table to SL and angling L of ramp upstage.
Double Kate/Elaine back onto table, arm on forehead head side-side.
On cut around table, X UR of left frame getting ready to double Roy.
X DL as Nick, spin R on cut, "foot walk" off L.
Approach bar and take position at mike. Take receiver in ear from Roy and follow Dog/Boy lines as Walken.
Double Roy in Left frame, as Nick X D of ramp to almost C, leap over ramp and swing ramp for POV. Stand on ramp at cut, XL on ramp as Nick, crashing table down with ramp, jump off on cut.
Swing stupid with camera sweeps. On cut take position in center of left ramp. Double Roy UR as Nick, walk DL on next shot, table to center, mirroring Roy UR.
Guide ramp D to make room for Kate and Peyton on stool. When Kate moves out of way, ramp to home, sneak into position at center of left frame (green line). On cut to blank sky, rush to bar as Nick (hands up in half-fists). Follow Nick off L with arm flourish.
Move stupid w/ camera for final water scene.
Take position at mike, taking Dog/Boy lines as Walken

End.

Transition: Stupid rope to second position, straighten L ramp and to couch with Roy.

Clumping

On couch w/ Roy. Roy takes cue off video and moves couch C. Off couch guiding it over track, stool DC, stumble to edge of ramp just off center frame. Cigarette. After Kate's side shot on tables, double Roy, pushing right table DC, pick up Kate. Drop Kate when cued by Kate, stumble back to ramp. Follow shots of girl in black not on couch. Turn UR when Kate moves UC. Towards end of scene, move with Roy as he leaves couch and prepare to give Kate US mike for "glass" shot"
End.

Transition: Stupid rope back to first position. Table in right frame to R of ramp. Check that stools are all to left, bar tables in same position. Jacket to Roy.

Kissing

Begin DR. When Roy opens ramps, scan stools to angle UR. Wait off L with hand on wall (Play with dog?) On cut to no Nick, scan ramps D, stubling over ramps after move and off R. Righ back on to double Roy as Nick on table. After second move to R of bar table and breathing into Mike, scan ramps closer to home and tables a little to L while crossing L. XR on Roy/Kate's move to table. "Echo" Roy's table shift on L ramp and double movement on R. Off R. Immediately back on to double Roy on table again. Double Roy up to bar. On Roy's move back US, X off R.
End.

Transition: Ramps to green tape marks on both frames, raise and secure both bar tables. Get jacket from Roy.

Horsing Around

Begin on stool to R of bar table in left frame. Whisper sweet nothings to Tanya. Doubling Roy, stagger to right of ramp and swing ramp home, X to table, duck under rope and pratfall onto table. On video, as Olga reaches forward w/ whip, table to L Ramp. On Olga's close-up, ramps up and echo crash w/ head jerks. As Tanya moves L along ramp, table to R Ramp, now mirroring Roy. On Roy's cue, back US under Peyton/Tanya rope, wait until Tanya moves out of path and then double with roy to crash bar tables. Mimic Roy's position at mike, do two "horse shit shuffles", bar table move to R on 1st POV (table just above bar for crash at end of POV).
Bar table move to L on secon POV. Crash table, stagger to L stool and swing over and back with Roy. After Tanya's little Stein moment, crash back to table, swing body and head L around on 3rd POV. Spin around descending lights on dummy for 4th and spin to ramps opening channel for Tanya and then reversing channel for Tanya.
Froog/run on froog/run shot. Use POV to spin over ramp to URamp, pause and dive under Kate/Tanya reins, push R ramp table D, step over ramp to D ramp and exit off R

End of story.
See you in August.

Left: **"Kissing," *House/Lights*, Act 3** Right: **"Running," Act 1**

Pre-set: Middle stool 1ft away from back ramp
Center front mic
Boom mic in rear hole → full extension video position

Enter Stage R front

CAR BALLET
1st turn to left
Dead on Car
2nd turn to Right

First
Faust Faust up front ...
When head turns Elaine gets picked up (after) roll back instead of front
exit Stage left back

RUNNING Video roll is my cue

(set SR floor)
Running ends with end of Scene 1
Wait till light changes
Look to Computer screen then Tanya

Get White Rope for Nick/Elaine

CLOSE WINDOWS + pick up white

REPRISE

NICK / ELAINE unhook + move SL
ELAINE / OLGA

Microphone, CLOSE WINDOWS

198 Faustus/Elaine score: Kate Valk

"Nick/Elaine Interrogation," *House/Lights*, Act 1

pos 1 pos 2
cig out/skirt down/on table hit Roy. Tussle Hint Hint Fake Toss SL SR

~~Look to Tanya + Nod "Scene 2"~~

Take time to settle
(Hit on head cues JJ) Phillip cues J.J.

CLUMPING

Scene 2 to "wild, wild"

Stand up into breasts

Dance w/film

On CU before going upside down

~~2 dance moves with couch~~ — Set mic down for scream

After boys drop me get up and pull SR TV top to green tape + flatten w/Helen

~~1c when guys slide down~~

Resume Olga

on Marianna's 2nd close-up

~~2 – on edit after va zip shot~~

video freezes + ~~snap~~.

JJ Rolls when I'm in place

"and I I am not there I am here

oh dear. I am not there." but

Keep going till
(Stay until tape rolls)

~~Overlap Faustt with Olga~~

to just before "She lets out a shriek"

while on way to couch take off top black

Center self on couch for
But + she lets out a shriek
"I am not there...."

Come up behind Peyton + Tanya

look at Camera on 2nd

"there is a rustling under the leaves..."

Continue Faust until "No, not really"

Look over couch as P+T reveal film

Join Marianna dancing again

Move back + forth with Marianna to ~~head move~~ in ~~center~~? — SR of center line

Making Ooh's + AAh's Stomach ache

When Marianna is about to drop skirt

Center head in glass

Begin Faust section after Pour

~~Remove Black top right away on~~

Roy takes ~~Flask~~ mic ~~black~~ move stool in position in center

Go to front for

MIHA/County woman scene w/head freezes

Leave stool front right up till "And so she disappears" → where is there Nobody says nobody is there tape rolls

against TV ~~right Move stool back / Boys move in~~ across front

Left: **"Clumping,"** ***House/Lights***, **Act 1** Right: **"Water Ballet,"** ***House/Lights***, **Act 2**

set mic upright
on girls' first flip say where
JJ Rolls somebody
turn back or Knock
Frankenstein
Dance

Elaine's CU – Faust break from Scene 3

Elaine exits Mic to full ext. upside down
swing to near SL Stool

After Roy laughs Swing w/ mic in front
as curtain for next Faust break
then

More Stool all the way front for Peyton
SL Window to Trees (just black up + down)
SR Window same
Place mic in Rear hole
SR Window again to reveal Country Woman

stay until move across when Ari moves

After Peyton + Ari ll + Roy swirl behind get mic lay on couch
1st Intro line of "Ring of Fire" say The country woman w/ the sickle ...

"Ring of Fire"
join in on choruses

Continue Faust after song dissolves be on text already
MIHA's lines to "bitter viper" "cue me"
Then put mic on couch Stagger forward
after Peyton does "Thank you's"
in time for Leg up over Peyton puff of cigarette
"And at the last – center head in screen
In a low whisper After line head will get small then go to sleep
She says
I am Margarite Ida and Helena Annabel
And Enough said I am not dead"

+ Say The chorus sings and thought is not... when she lights smoke

Stagger back to couch
wake Ari up

ACT II → pre-set glove
Viper head
Stick + hypo

HORSEY

Unhook mic
bring front
re hook
viper head on mic
glove on Begin

Faust CODA

Faustus/Elaine score: Kate Valk

"Horsey," *House/Lights*, Act 3

02/18/98 WED 11:45 FAX 212 742 1653 Ms. Foundation for Women

HOUSE/LIGHTS

Score for
Tanya Selvaratnam

February 1998

Clay--
The computer score I've developed is comprised of "sounds" and "voices." I hope that the outline below is clear. Call me if you have questions.

Love,
Tanya

Pre-Show
Set up computer on downstage right plexiglass table. Plug in power and sound cable; make sure the wires are not touching the metal bar foundations. Turn on the computer. Open up the text boxes and alert sounds control panel. Then put the computer to sleep.

Set the horsey gear, i.e., bit and girdle, offstage left.

I.

Enter space following Peyton and Kate. Enter stage behind Kate.
Open Computer, hit key to turn on.
Sit at stool before computer

Car Ballet
"klink" and "blip" sounds.

Faust Front and Center
(Faust, Scene 1)
When Kate begins speaking downstage center, begin typing. Type as if taking dictation. Riff on words with computer sounds (beeps, mostly; a few quacks).
Kate ends with "unless the devil tells you so..."; "quack" sound

Car Ballet Continues
Voiceover of Olga Movie--"klink" and "blip" sounds throughout, and "crow" sound used when Olga is in the frame.

Faust at Boom
Type as if taking dictation
Kate reaches "but have I a soul to pay for it"; end with 2 "quack" sounds

Running
Begin typing rapidly; where the elevator shaft noises are, mimic the rhythm with your hands.
(Freeze of Elaine) Kate is downstage front and center; stop typing, echo breathing; "Simple Beep" sound and "quack" sound.

02/18/98 WED 11:46 FAX 212 742 1653 Ms. Foundation for Women

--"The Ballet"--
Remove hands from keyboard
Swivel backwards to face downstage bar
Hold bar with both hands.
Mimic action on tv monitor in booth.
Feel for the whip-cracks by Peyton; hop slightly upward when the whip cracks.
Adjust.
To mimic motion where she turns around, swivel on stool from left to right and right to left.
Cantonese Opera snippet ends.
Swivel back to computer.

Running continues.

"At that moment the electric lights begin..."
Ari is at downstage left microphone.
Echo "thank you" in Fred voice from the computer. Echo "leave me alone" in Good News voice.

Running continues.

Kate will put her hands on your shoulder--this is a clue that the end is approaching. Become alert for when Roy comes to downstage center microphone. Stop typing in freeze of Nick.
When Olga has Elaine at the river bank...
Swivel back with one push of the right foot.
Left hand on downstage bar.
Both hands on downstage bar.
Fall to right side over bar.
Roy lifts Kate...
Kick up legs, and around to floor left.
Walk myself back to computer.
Put hands on the keyboard.
Kate will fall on my back, caress my leg, then move to downstage right microphone.
Type as if taking dictation "As he says the last might be, the dog says thank you"
Echo "thank you" in Fred voice.

Nick and Elaine
"droplet" and "attach" sounds
intermittently, rhyme words (day, obey, hay, pay) in Whisper voice
As Elaine exhales, "insert" sound

--In transition--
type

Olga and Elaine
"simple beep" sound, "blip" sound
intermittently, rhyme words (day, obey, hay, pay) in Whisper voice

Holly / Jenny
SHEENA SCORE

House/Lights

ENTER slightly after Kate + TANYA

SIT ON COUCH w/ Dog puppet (improvise w/ puppet)

"And now the Ballet" - Follow moves of Chinese opera

when Ballet tape is over - get up + wag butt - then go off UPSL

(SIT BACK STAGE UNTIL -)

? Kate - "Dog says thank you" - Kate moves toward around TANYA @ computer

ENTER from SL - CREEPING ON (TIP TOE)

Go between TV Ramp holders - First-fold up TV FLAP place hands in rope +

Stand until Roy says "I'll go get OLGA"

Pull TV DOWN ~~on~~ TO Lower yellow mark

run under TV and stagger for a moment UPstage

then off left.

At end of OLGA + ELAINE SCENE - "Nice to be hunter instead of hunted" -

lurch on - stand in place - small running when Ari + Roy run. Stop

when Suzzy comes back - move forward after She clears

back fixture -

go up beside TV - wait until Kate throws Dog toss Rope for real

Start flips

at end of flips - "creep" off STAGE R.

["clumping" scene] AFTER BITE, + DROP - when Kate touches table -

enter (funny low walk) to SR TV

Sychronize w/ Helen - put leg over TV ramp bar

Pull TV Down to GREEN TAPE -

Straighten TV - eye contact with Helen - move to

end of ramp (with TABLE) down Stage R

-2-

move ramp when Olga film shot moves.

Hold + imitate girl on Olga film -

move down Stage right to bar when girl in Olga film with

arm behind her head comes on TV

imitate her.

imitate girls on Olga tape as each comes on

eventually take off top + hang it on mike

leaning over TANYA TABLE - look over right

Shoulder at Ari -

Kate: "her voice rises to a shriek - make "eeeep" sound into

mike.

TANYA HANDS HER TOP

(END OF SCENE) When lights dim - take 2 tops - go over ramp - take

lamp off STAGE LEFT - FARTHEST UPSTAGE STill.

~~CUE FOR ENT~~ Computer says - paging Dr. Faustus for 2nd time.

"creep" on stage - quickly - go up on small ramp

by TV - immediately straighten TV - Then put black

flip up then down -

watch Helen - go up w/ her with black flipper -

do Flips.

when finished Knocks come up pretty quickly -

watch Helen - step down onto TV ramp

Frankenstein dance on Ramp - (See Helen's dance notes)

ON → "not the 3rd switch" put right leg back thru TV ramp

turn + go upstage - continue Frankenst. dance

See Helen's dance notes -

"Electrocution," *House/Lights*, Act 3

 Left: **"Act 1 Special Dance (to *Young Frankenstein*)," *House/Lights*** Right: **"Clumping," Act 1** Opposite: **Video cue sheet/performer track: Tara Webb**

House/Lights
Video CUEs

ACT I

	Time Code D1 Tape
Scene 1: Car Ballet cross	7.45
Opening	
Where's the Girl	20.02
Running	
Voiceover	
Scene 2: Nick/Elaine	
Short Running Reprise	
Olga/Elaine interrogation	
Flip flops	
Scene 3: Clumping	
Wild Woods	24.10
Country woman	26.07
Scene 4: Frankenstein-Dance	34.17
Scene 5: Ring of Fire	35.35

ACT II

Scene 6: Kate still	39.00
Viper Improv	
Scene 7: Stein with Chorus	39.16
Singing Kate	
Martha	
Ballet	
2nd Ballet/Water Ballet	43.08
Phone	
"Let's see, where were we?"	46.35

ACT III

Scene 7a: Electrocution	48.07
Scene 8: Kissing	51
Scene 9: Horse Dance	53
Scene 10: Torso Finale	53.44

T. Webb 1 04/20/99

 Above and opposite: **Stills from center video monitors (live and pre-recorded mix)**

 Stills from center video monitors (live and pre-recorded mix)

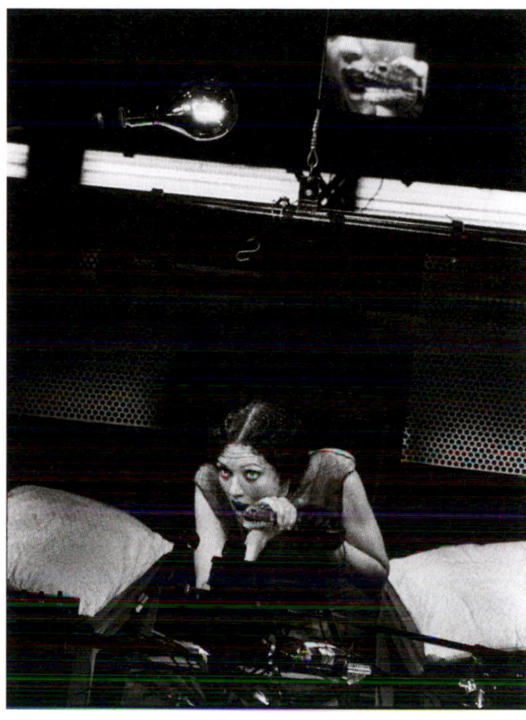

House/Lights, Act 2: Mr Viper Transcript:
10th April 2005, St. Ann's, Warehouse, N.Y., last performance.

Kate Valk: Yeah, just a second.

Mr Viper (*Voice by John Collins, live from the sound booth*): Don't put that glove on.

Kate: OK. Alright. Are you ready?

Mr Viper: (*as Kate puts viper puppet head onto mic.*) Yeah. Ohh… Careful. Oww, Ohh, Oww.

Kate: Ohh.

Mr Viper: Oow. That's better.

Kate: I need to sit down. That was difficult.

Mr Viper: Yeah, for you. For me, easy.

Kate: Hmm.

Mr Viper: What? What's the matter, don't you feel good?

Kate: No.

Mr Viper: No?

Kate: No.

Mr Viper: Oh yeah, somebody told me you catch cold last night.

Kate: Dis morning.

Mr Viper: Dis morning?

Kate: Yeah.

Mr Viper: Oh. Feel bad?

Kate: Yeah.

Mr Viper: Oh, feel bad. Let me see (*inspects Kate's face*). Yeah. Aha. Yep. Yep. Uh hum. Feel bad no?

Kate: No.

Mr Viper: No?

Kate: No.

Mr Viper: Shooz, no? Oh, OK. Open up your mouth please, let me see inside your throat.

Kate: Ah.

Mr Viper: Open up just a little more.

Kate: Ahh.

Mr Viper: Just a little more.

Kate: AAHH!

Mr Viper: No. That's too much. (*Bell rings*)

Kate: Oh. I think… I think we're all set down here.

Mr Viper: Oh, OK.

Kate: Why don't I call up to the booth and see if they're ready.

Mr Viper: Yeah. Call them on the phone.

Kate: (*On telephone*) Hello? Yeah. I know. We're all set. Yeah. He's here. Uh huh. OK. Yeah. You too. Alright. Bye bye. OK.

Mr Viper: Are they all OK up there?

Kate: Yes. OK. Mr Viper?

Mr Viper: Yeah.

Kate: Places.

Mr Viper: (*as he is being hidden*) Ohhh. Aahh. OK.

Kate: Thank you. Just wait for your cue.

Mr Viper: OK.

Kate: Here we go.

Source: Señor Wences: Spanish ventriloquist popular on American TV variety shows of the 1950s and 60s.

Left: **"Mr Viper,"** ***House/Lights*, Act 2** Right: **"Mr Viper,"** ***House/Lights* (prelim. to Act 2)**

Neither behind, nor ahead: animating *House/Lights*

An interview with Elizabeth LeCompte and Kate Valk (Oxford, Maine, July 9th, 2005)

Andrew Quick (AQ): How did you become interested in Gertrude Stein's *Doctor Faustus Lights the Lights* (1938) for the making of *House/Lights*?

Kate Valk (KV): We already had the idea to stage the Olga's House of Shame *(1964) film and we were even using this material to sketch something out in the space. We already had some notion of how the set might work, but we knew we needed some weight, something to counter the film, that would give it bottom. Then, we found out that the anniversary of Gertrude Stein's death was about to come up.*

AQ: Was it also about getting funding, tying the project into Stein's anniversary?

KV: Yes, it was kind of pragmatic, but you never know about these kinds of things. Someone made a suggestion and Liz picked up on it immediately — "Of course, Olga's House of Shame *— a female dominant/submission film — Gertrude Stein": Stein's relationship with Alice B. Toklas; Stein's whole world alongside the world of the film.*

Elizabeth LeCompte (EL): And lumpy women, for me.

KV: We didn't come to that specific text at first. It was Gertrude Stein as a persona/writer that we were interested in. Everyone brought in all the Stein material they had on their shelves, most of which they had never really read, and pictures and recordings. We listened to Stein reading and then we all took turns reading. There was a fantastic recording about death that Stein read. When it came to the opening encounter with Faust and the Devil, Liz just got the glazed over look. Her eyes swelled up and she was like, "this is it."

AQ: Was there something about the story of Faust that was interesting?

KV: Yes. On one level it went seamlessly into the Olga's House of Shame *film because of the relationship with Olga as leader of the girl-gang. The voice-over even calls Olga "the devil herself." And then there's the power struggle with Elaine and Olga and Faust and the Devil. It had a symmetry to it.*

AQ: What was it about the tone of *Olga's House of Shame* that you liked?

EL: Well, initially we were working on something different. We were working on a film and we needed some torture footage for a dream sequence, so we went to Dennis Dermody, our "cinematurg." He showed us a whole bunch of films and we watched a section of *Olga's House of Shame*, and we said, "Go back to the beginning," and we watched the whole film. There was just something about the simplicity of the voice-over, its language, which had a lot of room in it. It could mean a lot, or nothing. It was both funny and touching. At first, I was thinking about attaching the film to something else.

AQ: It's a well-made film, in a strange way.

EL: Yes, and the cinematography is in the mode of the late 1960s/early 1970s, although it predates that period of independent cinema: odd angles, strange edits, jump cuts, even a couple of shots from way above the rooms.

AQ: Did you begin by attempting to translate the film into a physical score?

KV: Well, we also knew that we didn't have any men for the project. Willem (Dafoe) was going off to do a long stint of making movies and so we were looking for things about women. It seemed more like a surprise to me when we came across the Olga's House of Shame *film because it was such a good vehicle for us, for the women in the company — the film has this girl-gang element to it. I guess I'm just selfish, but Peyton really loved it too. She had just played Olga in* Brace Up!. *Well that was it; she was going to be Olga. That's why it was so entertaining, because it really was a titillating extension of the power dynamics between Peyton, Liz and Kate.*

AQ: This sense of absent men, of men leaving, it's there in *Brace Up!* as well.

EL: Yes, it's in *Point Judith* (1979) too. It's in *St. Antony* (1987) as well. All of the pieces are about men leaving — it's a common theme in literature. It's even true of *To You, the Birdie!* (2002): Theseus is away and then he returns.

AQ: You seem to be concentrating on the film in the earliest rehearsal tapes.

EL: I think before we got hold of the film, we looked at playing with the set. We spent a week just rearranging all the pieces of set from *The Emperor Jones* (1993) and *The Hairy Ape* (1995).

AQ: What's really evident from the early rehearsal tapes is how quickly you arrived at a basic concept for the set: the ramps, the section at the back, the TVs that could go up and down. It doesn't change that much as you develop the piece. Was this early definition of the space unusual?

EL: I think this was the earliest that we defined the space. Usually, I would need to have something built. This means that there is always a period of time between when I have the idea of the set and when we physically start work on it. In this case we didn't have much money, so we just had to use what we already had.

AQ: You were ransacking previous sets?

EL: Yes. We just made it up. I said, "Let's just take apart the set and see where it lands." So, we laid out what interested us on the floor and reassembled it.

AQ: The large swinging lights were first used in *St. Antony*, weren't they? They seem so appropriate to the design for *House/Lights*...

EL: I know. We were all surprised too.

AQ: And the costumes? You just mentioned this thing about lumpy women. Did you have a specific costume designer for this piece?

EL: Yes. Usually, we don't work with a costume designer, but this time I just had no idea how to costume the piece. I think this was because I was caught between the 1950s and the 1930s. I didn't want it to be kitschy 50s and I didn't want it to look like period 30s. But, I knew I wanted lumpy. So, I just said to Elizabeth (Jenyon), "Lumpy," and that is what she came up with.

KV: You also talked about those dolls with seams on their shoulders and their heads —those dolls that have plastic arms and heads, but have a stuffed cloth body, giving them that lumpy, unstructured look.

AQ: I wanted to ask you about Stein's use of language. I'd never really thought of her as an American writer. I suppose I'd always thought of her as being within a European tradition—with her spending so much of her life in France. Then, when I saw *House/Lights*, it struck me how quintessentially American Stein is and that, perhaps, it was only the fact that she was an American living abroad that could have allowed her to create that attitude to language.

EL: Absolutely.

AQ: It was the same with *Olga's House of Shame*, where else but in America could the B-movie meet art?

EL: America doesn't have the hierarchy of European high art.

KV: And it doesn't have a hierarchy in language where meaning is at the top.

EL: Stein had such a strong sense of the rhythm of modern language. She really listened to it, to get its rhythm and sound.

AQ: And there's little or no conventional syntax in her writing, very little punctuation. She plays with the language at some profound level and it struck me that while you were letting this play of language unravel in the piece, you were also playing with other core elements of theater, like space and time.

EL: Those two pieces worked so well together: Stein's language and that simple language that Elaine has with Olga. The two of them bounce off each other really nicely. Because, again, there is air in her language, just like there was in the film language, about "What could this mean?" Some of the voice-overs in the film were so beautiful. There was a close relationship between the two languages, the way she was using language and the way that the film was using language.

AQ: You use the structure of film, the editing, camera angles, close-up, foreground and background and so forth, as a way to construct the physical score in *House/Lights*.

KV: Yes, that's how we started. When we sketched out our physical score from the film it was more like a translation. There weren't strict rules. It was like being in a playing field where you had to imagine where the camera was. It wasn't always in relation to the live camera in the center of the stage. When we were developing the movement, you could make the camera be anywhere. So, if there was a close-up, you had to find it for yourself. You had to decide how to mark something as a close-up and it was the same thing for medium and long shots. Then there was the way the camera moved, you had to translate this to the theater space too. Liz also divided the space with the center aisle, and the two areas either side of it made it look like two frames or squares next to each other. So, we played a lot with the idea of passing from one frame to the other, or scanning, or doubling somebody in the other square. These were some of the parameters Liz set up at the beginning.

EL: I thought of it a bit like when you're editing a Super 8 film. You see the film running through the editing machine and you watch the two frames go by. It was like that. You see the same action in the next frame—just a fraction of a second later.

AQ: So, it's off the beat. It's never really synchronized is it?

EL: Right—just off.

AQ: When you're searching for this physical score in *House/Lights*, the rehearsals are very raucous and chaotic. I remember Peyton saying at one point, "I want it to be just a bit stiller. Can we have it a bit calmer?" And Liz replies, "I have trouble with stationary." I wanted to ask what that trouble was.

EL: Peyton always liked to make a picture of herself in a space and be "placed" and I always like to see something transforming. I like to see things between the picture and the next picture. I like to make sure that nothing gets stuck, that it's always changing. Even now, as I'm working with dance (*Poor Theater* [2004]), I like to see how they get in and out of their moves, rather than the move itself.

AQ: So, it's actually getting to the point of doing something and then leaving it?

EL: Exactly, and then leaving it. Peyton was very good at assembling herself as a picture and very good at striking a very comfortable one-to-one relationship with the audience.

AQ: You can see this at work in *Fish Story* (1994).

EL: In many ways that was set up specifically for her.

AQ: You also continually break up that stillness in *Fish Story*. You create a series

of frames she has to get into and out of.

EL: Yes, but that was almost impossible for her. She couldn't even bear that. She just wanted to stand in front of the audience in the position that she always creates for herself and have them love her and they did. I had to find ways to give her different frames so that she was always having to make transitions. It was the tension of her wanting to stay still but having to move to the next position that I found interesting to watch.

AQ: Returning to *House/Lights*. Was this the first time that you'd used the in-ear device, where the performer had to respond to what was being heard on a recording?

EL: No, that was in *L.S.D.* (*L.S.D. (...Just the High Points...)* [1984]): Nancy Reilly listens and speaks the recording of Leary's babysitter. *House/Lights* was the first time we had access to that particular piece of equipment — the in-ear receiver. But people had used similar devices in other pieces: Peyton in *Fish Story* and *Brace Up!*. She used this device whenever she had to speak and there was a lot of other stuff going on. She'd get a bit rattled and she was unable to center herself, like in the fire scene in *Brace Up!*, with everybody running around with all that noise. So we recorded her speaking her lines and at that moment she's listening to the lines and just saying them back as she spoke them originally on the recording.

AQ: So, the in-ear is always pragmatic?

KV: The only way we could make the Stein work was to have it recorded and to say it, not ahead, not behind, but to stay with it. And I was listening to somebody else reading the text. It was the only way we could get Stein to feel more effervescent in the space and not purely dredged up from some memory.

AQ: You were being receptive to the language in the moment.

KV: Yes, so I could channel it.

AQ: Transcription and translation is one of the signatures of The Wooster Group's work. It's used in *Route 1 & 9* (1981) with the Pigmeat Markham routines and I assume that you have used these techniques in earlier works as well.

EL: Ron (Vawter) in *Rumstick Road* (1977), lip-synching the conversation between the father and Spalding Gray.

AQ: Then, there's the opening monologue in *St. Antony*, where Ron is working directly off the "Channel J" videotape.

EL: He improvised that section by listening to Nancy Reilly — this was before we had the in-ears. We couldn't do it like that then. I had to put Nancy Reilly far away from him, almost in another room. Then I had her read Flaubert's *The Temptation of Saint Anthony* and have Ron just pick out whatever he could hear and to make up the rest. The situation was a talk show. So, he knew he was either talking to the audience beyond the camera, or to the person in the frame with him and he would riff off what he heard from Nancy Reilly.

AQ: It's like those broadcasters who are receiving information as they are delivering the news. Some are very good at it, but others really struggle.

EL: Yes, they can't take in that information. I always love that, when I see them and realize that they are getting information while they are interviewing someone. They are getting a whole lot of information about other things. In a weird way they are acting — they are not listening to what is being said. They are presenting it to the audience, because they can't be listening and getting something else — they can't really be engaging.

AQ: There's something about time here isn't there — about being in two time zones in the same instance? This would seem to break up any psychologically based acting, where you have a very clear sense of where you are, where your impulse lies.

EL: What you just brought up about broadcasters, I hadn't really thought of it like this. But, it's very similar to when you're on the in-ear because you have to be very aware of the room and I think this awareness is in that part of the brain that's engaging on some kind of psychic or visual level — it's not intellectual. I don't think you can process two things at once, what's in the space and what's coming in through the ear. So, you have to deal with what you're hearing and what's happening then and there in the room with you.

KV: Yes, it's different every night because the feeling in the room is different.

EL: Exactly. The audience is different.

AQ: Do performers who are new to the company find this approach difficult?

KV: Yes, some people do find this difficult. There's a certain anxiety that goes with being fed information through your ear, a type of anxiety that makes that state that Richard Foreman talks about — a state of awareness. It's interesting to watch somebody dealing with and channeling information, responding to stimulus and also negotiating the room, the whole room, with a kind of presence.

AQ: It's not just the in-ear that you have to be able to negotiate in *House/Lights* — you have to respond to all the other dynamics in the space, the sound, the other performers and, of course, the video...

EL: We're moving more and more in that direction. *House/Lights* is more like a machine with the video, the lights and the sounds and everybody working together to make the cues. I would say that *To You, the Birdie!* is even more video driven, because we had two different kinds of videos we were responding to. There was the live scratching of the video material and there were also the video tracks that we honed and selected for our physical score, much like in *House/Lights*—but the live scratching of the video in *To You, the Birdie!* added something else, because we had to physically keep up with it.

AQ: So, you are working off the video operators' improvisation with the visual material?

EL: Yes, a little bit. The biggest thing for us in *House/Lights* was that thing about learning not to anticipate what you are going to see on the televisions—in the same way that a lot of acting teachers talk about not anticipating how you are going to feel in a certain scene and to always be open and responsive. You know that the performers are going to do the same thing because they have a particular blocking and the task is to somehow make this new every night. To do this with a television, you have to turn the television into another actor, a participator in the scene with you, one that you can't ever take for granted. You have to imagine, when you look at the TV, that it's for the first time and take on whatever is presented to you at that moment, so that you don't prepare for it. I'm taking what's a normal discipline in theater and applying it to the TV—people think of TV as a mechanized thing, but you can't do that here. For me, there are so many impulses that can be generated by a visual picture. One day you might respond to the way the camera moves and the next day you might respond to the fact that the person on the film looks in a certain direction. Katie, you can talk about this better than me. You know how you respond to the same picture over and over again.

KV: Yes, it's always a challenge. I have one of the worst performer tendencies, which is to generalize. It's the detail that's amazing; that's what we find in rehearsal—that there's always more detail and also that there's a tendency to generalize and a desire to control and shape things, which comes out when you say, "Oh yes, I did that really well tonight." But, Liz sets up a situation that liberates you from these tendencies. You have to approach it like a game or like an athlete. You have to approach the text, the words, the physical score, your relationship with the video, sound, lights and then just respond, just be in the moment with the material. You have to try to be open enough, so that you can surprise yourself. That's the best state—when you surprise yourself and it's not the way you ever did it before and who knows how it's going to feel? There's always more detail to be discovered and usually you need somebody else to point this out to you. Liz is incredible for keeping the whole thing tweaked, rehearsing certain transitions or cues, keeping us tweaked as an ensemble. Also, everyone in the room has access to this process. Some people have to work hard to think ahead to be where they have to be for the video—because they don't think ahead enough. Some people think ahead too much and imagine they're there. It's something about your personality, but I think that's true of all performing, any kind of performing. It's just that the video gives you lots of different kinds of stimuli.

AQ: Is one of your main functions, once the piece is being performed to a public, to stop it becoming too rigid?

EL: Well, by relinquishing a certain kind of control there's an electricity in the whole space, because there are these things that are being played that you can, in the best sense, channel or make a response to. I don't think this is really different from any good production, where a performer, no matter how big or small their role is, has to work out what his or her relationship is to the scene. I'm trying to get the same effect, just using different means. Only it's more abstract here because the performers are working off something that's a little more abstracted. The movements that you make up from the TV don't look natural and they feel a bit more random, which is more fun for me. And if the two tracks are humming next to each other, the vocal text and the physical world, then they play off each other and then it becomes surprising—you can always do something that you never thought of.

AQ: Watching the rehearsal tapes of *House/Lights*, I was struck by how much laughter there was. You played with the material a bit like the way children play with the adult world—imitating it, jagging off it, taking things in strange directions.

KV: I think this is to do with the way we work. Liz didn't come from a theater background and most of the performers aren't specifically trained in theater. I think that what you are sensing might be the approach of the non-expert, which is based on how much fun it is to be able to think you could do anything and be anybody. You can be interested in Japanese Noh Theater, and then you play with it, a bit like a child does. Liz always has this bottom line which is us encountering the material. I think that with any of the things we take on we keep, in the best sense, a beginner's mind, or, at least, the attitude of a divine amateur.

AQ: There was a lot of laughter in rehearsal, but I am aware there were moments of real struggle as well, especially with getting the right tone for Stein's text. Why was it so difficult to deal with Stein's language?

EL: It sounded pretentious. It was hard to listen to. Often, we would make meaning out of it and I heard it as music. So, it was very hard to find a style of performing that would let the language be free of meaning. It's only thirty-four pages long, but the problem was how to sustain the language. I would separate the text out into segments and I'd say, "I hear this with this." Then, I'd say, "Well, we will skip all of this," but Katie was so good at remembering what happened, what the order was, and she'd take me back to certain things.

KV: I think I had a compulsive relationship with the text during the early rehearsal period. I memorized it and it's hard to memorize. So, I knew the text and the different parts and so I'd be, "We need something here" — "I remember this" — "this section for here."

AQ: But you never changed the order of Stein's text, you didn't break it up completely.

EL: I didn't want to take it out of order. And Katie knew the whole of the Stein. So, we'd skip a huge section and we would get to a place in our score and I'd go, "What have we missed here that could go next to this image or these words from the film? Is there anything we can use, because it needs Stein here?" It's like playing around with colors — we needed the Stein color at that point and Kate would be able to go through the Stein and come up with, "Well, what about this?" She was emotionally connected to the text. She and I really depended on Clay (Hapaz), who was on both scripts all the time.

KV: I also transcribed Olga's House of Shame, *so I got quite familiar with the film. It always helps to have the parts transcribed when you actually start working with the material.*

AQ: Is this notion of transcription ghosting in Tanya's (Selvaratnam) role, when she's at the computer at the front edge of the stage? She's a bit like the scribe. She seems to be writing what's happening on stage around her, then adding sound effects.

EL: She's also on the text and she is putting in things that I couldn't incorporate verbally. Tanya puts the text in the MacInTalk computer program when I go, "I don't want to miss these lines here," and Katie can't say them because she's doing something else.

AQ: Doesn't Tanya make the lines into a song at one point?

EL: She may also make songs out of the text as well. She takes some of the phrases and some of the words and just repeats the words, so she's like a chorus. Also, the whole thread of assisted suicide — that's all done though the computer. She has a whole track of her own.

AQ: She functions a bit like the character of Sue in *St. Antony* or Nancy Reilly's role in *L.S.D.* — on the edge of the action, but following the whole story. Marianne Weems also had the text of *Three Sisters* with her at the back table in *Brace Up!*.

EL: That has to do with the bottom line — the whole text on the computer. Nancy was originally in *St. Antony* too, several people took her role, but she had the book and they were always following the book.

AQ: So you have the source on or very near the stage. It's a bit like the old-fashioned stage manager, who was always on the book, who would give you the cue when you forgot your lines.

EL: Exactly, to have somebody in a direct physical relationship with the text. It might not even be the person who's speaking it.

AQ: I wanted to ask you about the function of the men in *House/Lights*. They never seem to hold the center of the space, like the women do. They're always crashing about; they don't really seem to have any hold on the language either.

EL: I just think this is because we didn't have any men at the beginning. There's no reason why one of the men couldn't have been playing Faust, it's just that we set off without the men. Anyhow, what's so much fun about the Stein is that she makes Marguerite Ida and Helena Annabel the central crisis of the piece. But I never thought about limiting the men. Roy (Faudree) refused to say any lines of the Stein — he hated it. It took a long time to get him to say the few lines that he says, that he listens to, because he would sabotage them: he would make fun of them or he would do them as an actor. He would try to get away from Stein and so I couldn't give him any lines. It wasn't saying, "Men don't control the space."

AQ: We're back to pragmatics again. It's clear in the rehearsal tapes that Roy loves playing the role of Nick from *Olga's House of Shame*.

EL: Yes and it's humorous and funny, which is what he's great at. As for Ari (Fliakos), I just don't remember why he doesn't have any language. Oh, because he's a dog and all the dog says is, "Thank you." With Ari, I was fascinated by his physicality. It was the first time I saw what a wonderful physical performer he was.

AQ: He has an incredible energy in the piece. The piece buzzes, hums, to use your expression, with contrasting energies and tensions. It's very noisy...

EL: A lot of this is to do with putting a room together that contains that kind of tension, which I used to love to work with. Oddly enough, in *Poor Theater* I just wanted to get rid of all that tension and get to a room that was peaceful.

AQ: I suppose that tension can't help but return.

EL: Yes, it does. But *Poor Theater* has a different feel about it, because there isn't that tension in the room. You get a little tension when you feel you're not doing it well, but I don't like that kind of tension. The tension I usually like is with people competing with each other, "I can do that better, I can do that better." That kind of tension, I like.

AQ: You give the performers a great deal of freedom, certainly in the early parts of the rehearsal process, when you're really developing the piece. You often use this phrase in response to what you are watching: "I don't know what it is. I know it's not this, but when you do it, I'll know it works." This is a very particular directorial approach.

KV: When I worked with Richard Foreman, it was the exact opposite. He would tell you where to go, what to do and what to say. He would like things that you did, but if you ever said, "I could do this while I say the line," he'd say, "No, what about this."

AQ: He admits to a certain sado-masochistic tendency as a director.

KV: But I've never really worked with another theater director and I've never seen how other directors, except Foreman, work. But I think you're right, Liz does place an emphasis on the relationship with the performers, where they bring something into the room.

AQ: I get a sense it was really difficult to complete *House/Lights*.

EL: I remember thinking that this was the closest we ever came to abandoning a project. *To You, the Birdie!* was really hard, but I never came as close to abandoning *To You, the Birdie!* as I did to giving up on *House/Lights*. With *To You, the Birdie!* I had a story to complete, whereas with *House/Lights* there wasn't a story. I had to construct the story for myself as we were going on, which makes it easier to abandon for me. And Peyton (Smith) was leaving the company at the time, so that was another kind of ending.

AQ: Were you sustained by the energy and tension in the room, did it keep the rehearsal process going?

KV: Well, it was a kinetic room. This is an important point. Liz would always be in despair because of the amount of side-text we had to bring in. But, when we were blocked, we could always go back to the "running" section, which we took from the film, and she would be laughing again. We would get back to having a good time, because we always had that section, like the badminton in To You, the Birdie!. *There was always a physical thing that could animate the space and make it kinetic.*

EL: Usually, this comes very early in the process, along with the architectonics of the space, before we have even read the text. We set something up that creates a game, or we take an already established game, using all the material we have—the video and the technology, which animates the space.

AQ: It's the play between all these different things, the technology, the game, the design, that creates this animation?

EL: Yes, it makes the space kinetic. If I get stuck, I want to go, "Oh please, do something, anything," because then my mind keeps going. But, if they all sit on the side and go, "Next," my mind goes dead too, because I have completely invested in what is happening with them.

AQ: So, how do you make decisions about what works and what doesn't?

EL: When I see what I like, whatever that means. What makes me laugh, what makes me cry (laughs).

AQ: What made you want to carry on with *House/Lights*?

EL: I guess it's just the daily thing; because I had to come back every day. If we worked in some other way, I think I would have given up on it. If we'd had to rent the rehearsal space, then, maybe, I would have gone, "Oh, this doesn't work," and not finished it. But because I have The Performing Garage, I keep coming back and sometimes I'll fool myself into thinking, "Alright, I'm not going to do this piece but we'll do a little work on something else that I like." And this will take me back into the piece. I'll put something up on the stage that I like. Sometimes it takes a while. I might have to watch what I like for a long while—it's like a meditation. Then, something comes out of this process.

AQ: And then you run with that thing that comes out?

EL: When I come to what you'd call writer's block, the only thing to do is to go back in the room and have the performers do something—anything. And there are times when you might hear me say, "Do something and I don't care what it is, just move in the space;" and then I'll start thinking again.

AQ: So, it's almost like you are sculpting with the people playing in the room. If they keep moving, your mind keeps moving.

EL: And then, of course, I go home and think of zillions of things I want to do. I write this and that down and I turn it into some kind of psychological meaning for myself. And then, I go back in with this information and it doesn't work. It never works because it's in my mind, it's separate from them: it's a residue of what they have given me. Then I bring it back and it's just repeating something that's already there in a language that they don't relate to. It's not theirs and then I have to throw it away. But this is all part of the process of throwing away the duff layers. I don't go home and say, "Don't bother writing this down because you are not going to use it anyway." I still write it down, because, somewhere, it animates something underneath. It gives me a thicker experience to bring back into the space. And my telling them what I thought, even though they can't act it out and we have to throw it away, they still have it—it's there.

AQ: It hangs in the room somewhere?

EL: They have shared with me what is the most personal thing for me about the piece. I'm on the outside, so it gives them something next to their performance, which they don't own themselves. There's something bigger in the space.

To You,
the Birdie!
(Phèdre)

 Rehearsals: Spring 2000

3/13/00 Phèdre Rehearsal Starts

1st day of movement workshop. Francesca taught two modern dance phrases, one with fast, sharp arm movements and a wonderful head-balancing act at the end. The second was a foot pattern that turned in rough inward squares and ends with three squatted steps.

The space was open with a few lights up, the video projector going and a sound system. Liz wants to leave the space open but wants set piece to play with before she starts working with the text. She pulled the set apart for *House/Lights* and built from its elements; but does not know where to go with this one.

Liz seeks a combination of early 20th century modern architecture and the faux classicism of the early 17th century. We should see the steel structures of underlying modern architecture but with an ostentation that has no purpose other than its own existence. She sees a wide short playing area, roofed by light and a background table that rolls upstage and down. The projections must be bright and do not need to be huge. Not using TVs as lights.

Willem questioned the usefulness of the movement. Liz said that it would work. She wants the actors to have a common vocabulary that they can riff off, no matter what the difference in qualities. She sees this used in attempts to play sport, badminton or volleyball.

3/14/00

Production Meeting and Movement Workshop:

Liz and Jim (Findlay) presented the ideas for the set, which Jim had drawn on the floor. We are extrapolating from old Wooster Group pieces, early Californian modern architecture, and Kabuki Theater. Have 36′ x 10′ platform that can pivot upstage / downstage. This will be mechanically controlled but give the illusion of free balance.

A ramp will run along the downstage edge of the platform with a piece that extends off into an unknown unused area. A gang plank, left over from Kabuki's hanamichi. This plank will pivot and be able to flank the platform so that entrances and exits can be made on it. Projections will be cast down on the platform to give it many different looks.

Upstage will be a light box with fluorescent and incandescent lights. Make 60s modern interior drawn from Pierre Koenig. This box moves right to left and will have a 50cm table on the stage right half. This box will look like windows and have a front and back. The stage right table can have musicians set-up: also functions as an interrogation center, because it ghosts other Wooster Group pieces.

Liz wants to look at videotape from Martha Graham, Paul Taylor and Erick Hawkins. Plan to have working model of set by the time we work with the text on 3/29.

3/16/00

Liz had the actors work with dance phrases as they play badminton. She told them not to move the dance toward the sport nor the sport toward the dance: the two were to stay apart and see how they related. All movement has to relate to physical necessity. Either dance or game or personal emergency/accident—like tripping up or pants falling down. Move from an abstraction into a game, a goal orientated, rule-defined action. Liz does not want to compromise the dance to fit the badminton. She needs to establish the rules of each form of movement and play by these rules first to see what comes out.

3/17/00

Liz calls an end to initial movement workshops.

3/20/00

We begin by playing badminton. The rules were very important because they constitute the form: form over content. We put a wireless microphone on the rackets and listened to the resounding hollow whack that came with shuttle contact.

Then the actors sat on the upstage table and read the play (Paul Schmidt's translation of Racine's *Phèdre*) using microphones. A sense of humor came through that I had not heard before. First reading was simple, clear and properly half-loaded.

Liz directed people to read quickly and throw lines away, to not emote or worry about the content but to listen to how the words flowed together. "A day of irony," Liz said. She loved keeping the text under control by keeping the emotion out. She also liked its brevity: less than 35 minutes.

Opposite: ***To You, the Birdie! (Phèdre)*, Rehearsal, Act 1** Above: **Early rehearsal log: Jim Dawson**

Plenty of spaces exist in the text as it is and will be good ground for dance and music, which will carry the main content of the play and keep the words in motion. Liz's only worry is how to keep things as light and thrown away as they were today.

3/22/00

Played badminton with lines marked out and following the rules. A couple of people played announcer, which completed the scene.

We then watched Merce Cunningham, Martha Graham and some Kabuki. The Cunningham is strong and beautiful, not clichéd. Liz thought the Kabuki was too overblown and gaudy, but loved the openness of the set, the ramped entrances with dramatic lighting. Also really liked the stand-and-deliver quality of the acting. She connects this with the stand-and-deliver style of the Racine and wants something similar.

Liz spoke of getting the play up quickly; working on what is in the Paul Schmidt translation and add layers in later. Work like they did on *Fish Story*. Action should stay to just what is in the text. Don't invent things.

3/24/00

Liz started the day wanting two people to move in the space, she liked the sound of the miked racket and had the actors work on volley, then jump/hit while volleying, then spin/jump/hit. She wanted the playing to be bigger. Asked Tara to keep up with the officiating and calling the score, pronouncing the ruling.

Projected Cunningham's *How to Pass, Kick, Fall and Run* (1965) while the actors played badminton and Jim and I read from Antonin Artaud, Valère Novarina and Roland Barthes. Actors tried to gain momentum from Cunningham to build vocabulary that could be used to play games but still retain its look as dance. Several sections were learned or begun to be learned from the tape.

Also read the play. Liz looking for a dual reading that is on one level light and ironic where the words are thrown away and also wants the horror of these horrendous people to come through. Connected with 30s movies, full of cliché and yet with a weight to it at the same time.

Liz wants to hear the words first and the emotion to follow, as if they are racing ahead of what they say and get into it only later. The words and emotion should synch up in certain places. The action should be fast but can down-shift into moments of textual connection. She sees the play as always moving and never static except in moments of punctuation. Repeated that she only wants to keep things to what's in the text and that she is unsure how to deal with the largeness of the text. Normally she attacks from the backside or underside.

She does not yet know how to handle the sexual tension. She sees no shame in the bodies or the physical sex, like a boring porn film, blatant and clinical. Shame only exists in the missed moments, the non-communication, like Phèdre thinking Hippolytus betrayed her.

Liz sees these people as full of greed.

****

3/29/00

Ping Pong — 4 players. Badminton — same exercises.

Liz had the actors do the play with entrances and exits looking for explosive moments of emotion. She stopped them after the first scene, saying they were doing what she doesn't want. What she wants to do is tell the story first without emphasizing the acting. Usually, people act to tell the story; they become the people that tell the story. Liz wants the story first. Tell it instead of inhabiting it. Don't tell it from the body, let it go. Keep the body lax and let the words come from the head. Liz is looking for a 30s film emotion that is intact but repressed. Kate said that she has no image for this. Liz says play the shame not as your shame or the character's shame. It's just shame.

****

4/7/00

Went back to slapstick, Three Stooges and Marx Brothers. Liz has no image for the men and everything she tries moves them towards melodrama. They have no power and she spoke of returning to *House/Lights* movement.

 Above and opposite: **Early rehearsal log: Jim Dawson**

4/10/00

Music meeting with Liz. Work can complement or oppose. Liz spoke of 30s film sound effects, Three Stooges and using music to fill in the huge emotion of the piece. May use The Marx Brothers for rhythm riffs like the Soap Operas that were used in the BBC version.

Liz had the actors work with the Schmidt translation with The Marx Brothers. Use The Marx Brothers' riffs or movements to take them out of the character and somewhere else. So that it is unclear where the naturalism comes from, if it ever happens. Liz likes the way performers switch which Marx Brother character they are following on the tape and how they pass each other during the change over. Also, she told them they can stop when who they are following goes off screen. They can stop and wait as long as the Schmidt continues.

By the end of the day, she wanted them to interpolate more and not take things so directly from the tape. Be influenced by little movements and take into other directions.

4/11/00

Keep two tracks running, vocal and movement. Men do Cunningham movement. Worked on always facing front. The idea is that you move from self, so your front is always forward, no matter where the audience is.

4/13/00

Liz had them work without the voice in their ear and got them to try and riff off the movement as much as possible. Doesn't want them working off each other or the video in a literal way. They get it at times and it reads more literally than straight naturalism. And sometimes it drifts into abstraction that can be evocative or boring.

She also asked for feedback because she wants them to have fun, wants to find the things they enjoy and go with them. If they are not having fun switching out into these other places, these explorations will never work.

People can drop out of the movement but they need to stay with the lines from the script. If you follow a character that is no longer on screen, you can be some one else or drop out, physically step back from that layer, but keep the word flow.

Liz stopped them to say that she does not want literal movements. Don't start from the hand because you get caught waving or emphasizing a detail. Figure out the focus, the center of the body, and flow with that.

Some of the actors shadowed others and it had a beautiful resonance with the badminton.

****

4/17/00

Worked with Marx Brothers tape and Liz told them to perform like a player having to return a ping pong ball. You may go out of place to return a shot but then you have to go back to where you were. Also, don't just hit it straight back. Put a spin on it. If you take a move from the film, don't copy it exactly. Make it work for your scene and pass it on to your partner. Make another form. Don't simply hit the ball back.

Liz wanted to see how a fractured story could combine with outside influences and still hold together. Again, take the movement or vocal rhythm from the tape or work with the camera shot and editing.

Change facings with each other. Don't all look at the same monitor. Find another screen to watch. Only signal sitting. Don't actually sit when the screen characters sit. Same for all movements taken from the TVs. Don't use them literally. Use them as a direction and then flow through them. Then go on to the next thing.

Things were beginning to work, but still not flowing well overall. Liz missed the text and it all came to a stop too often. Everything needs to continue, needs to go somewhere. It must move. It must have the pong after each ping.

****

4/26/00

Almost gave up on the project today. Liz couldn't stand Theseus's big entrance and she can't find a way to make the material work beyond naturalism. Says she hates naturalism... Really stuck... No frame to put the play into.

Tried acting out *Sex: The Annabel Chong Story*, feeding it to the actors through the in-ear device and video tape, which was very amusing but did not work for Liz.

Kate thought we should scrap it as well, if Liz can't see anything in it. Then Kate admitted that she really wants to do this piece, but doesn't know why. But she is attached to it. Liz suggests that Kate do the play with the rest of us and she'll come in once in a while to see what works. But she can't do a play that she feels is just layer and layer of affectation. She would rather not work on it. She gets hits, sees things that make sense… But when it hits the stage, it falls flat. She doesn't know what to do or where to go.

Ended the day deciding to put the lines to music—like songs. Kate says we have given up looking for a frame and are now working on a style, after all. Liz agrees.

4/27/00

Set—Liz wants roofing material on the deck to make it look like high European design. The idea is that this is the roof of the house, and it has a pool. She wants suspended glass that we can project on to. Use the TVs and the glass surfaces, that's all. The big screen is out.

Gone was the idea of scoring the play and putting the men to music.

4/28/00

Big day. Kate found acting style that can carry the first scene… Kate found a flat, straight style that shows everything a beat after the word arrives. Not an over the top diva, but a small direct reading that slices fun while delivering the words with no trappings.

****

5/3/07

Searched for physical relationship with the men. Played with them sitting down front and Theramenes working chiropractics on Hippolytus. Small moves worked and Liz wants a sound score to play subtly underneath. When things got too big, Liz felt they overwhelmed the words and eventually nothing seemed to work. Either the word makes the movement or the movement must wait for space.

5/4/07

Worked text the entire rehearsal. Began with yesterday's version of the first scene with the nude boys doing body work, with them upstage center and Phèdre and Oenone downstage center. Liz had Phèdre watching them. The plexi-glass mirror became a window through which Phèdre watches the boys and Oenone helps her hide with myrtle leaves on her racket.

Game begins the play with everybody involved. A collapse and tilt deliver Phèdre and Oenone to the front and the boy's towel off stage… The girls clear up and then play… Temptation of Phèdre happens down stage center in the mirror. Applying make-up as Oenone lays out the course of action. Seduction happens with Hippolytus. Oenone down stage center reading and giving advice to Phèdre, who leans heavily on the young boy.

As far as we got, but a physical score for the first third of the play was finally set.

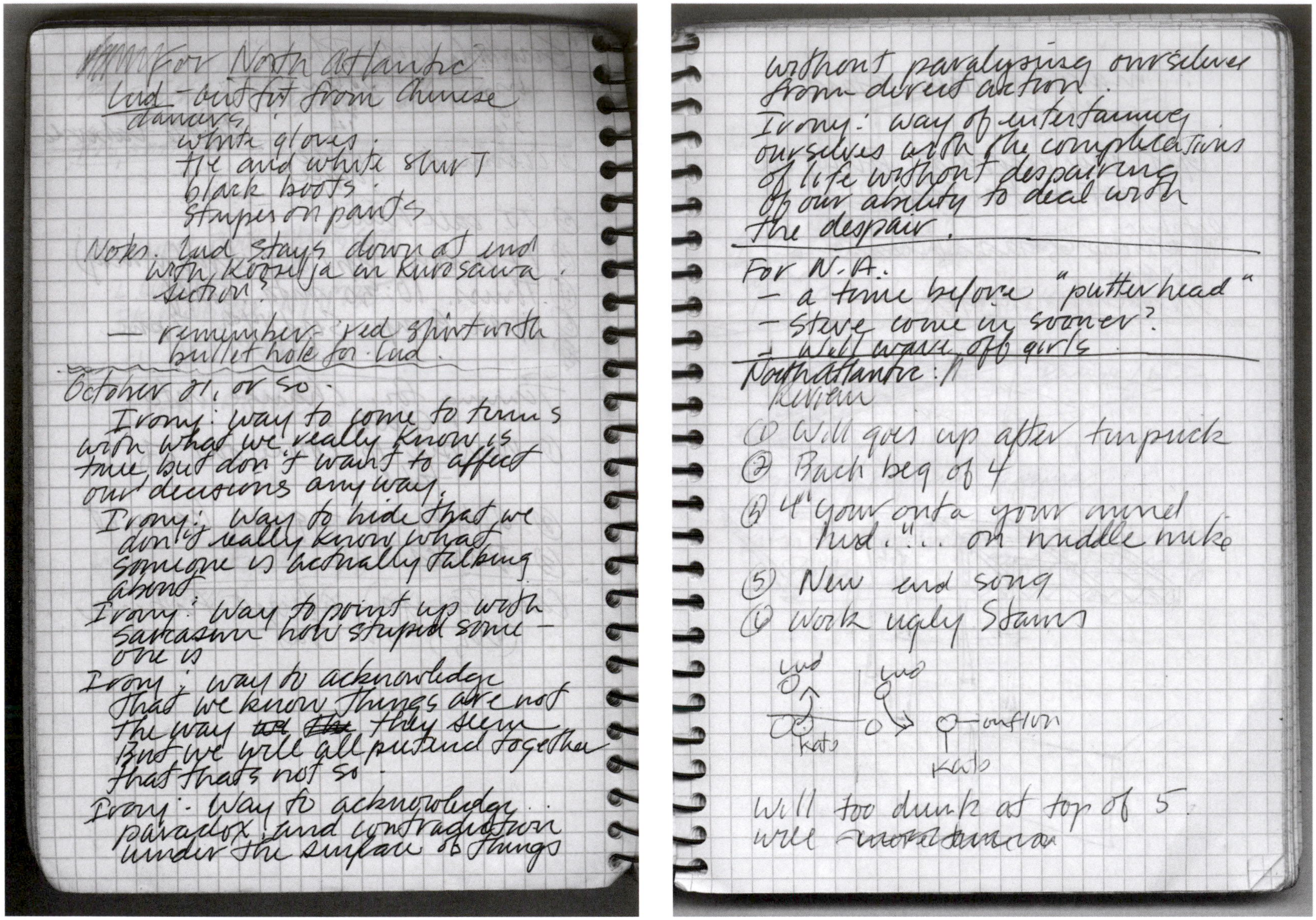

For North Atlantic
Lud – outfit from Chinese dancers,
white gloves
tie and white shirt
black boots
stripes on pants
Notes: Lud stays down at end
with Kozelja in Kurosawa section?
— remember: red shirt with bullet hole for Lud.

October 01, or so.
Irony: way to come to terms with what we really know is true, but don't want to affect our decisions anyway.
Irony: way to hide that we don't really know what someone is actually talking about
Irony: Way to point up with sarcasm how stupid someone is
Irony: way to acknowledge that we know things are not the way ~~the the~~ they seem But we will all pretend together that that's not so.
Irony: Way to acknowledge paradox and contradiction under the surface of things without paralysing ourselves from direct action.
Irony: way of entertaining ourselves with the complications of life without despairing of our ability to deal with the despair.

For N.A.
– a time before "putterhead"
– Steve come in sooner?
– Will wave off girls

North Atlantic: II
Review
(1) Will goes up after tin puck
(2) Back beg of 4
(3) 4 "your outa your mind kid." .. on middle mike
(5) New end song
(6) Work ugly Stairs

Lud
Lud
Kato
on floor
Kato

Will too drunk at top of 5.
Will ~~[illegible]~~

 Above and opposite: **Elizabeth LeCompte: journal entries**

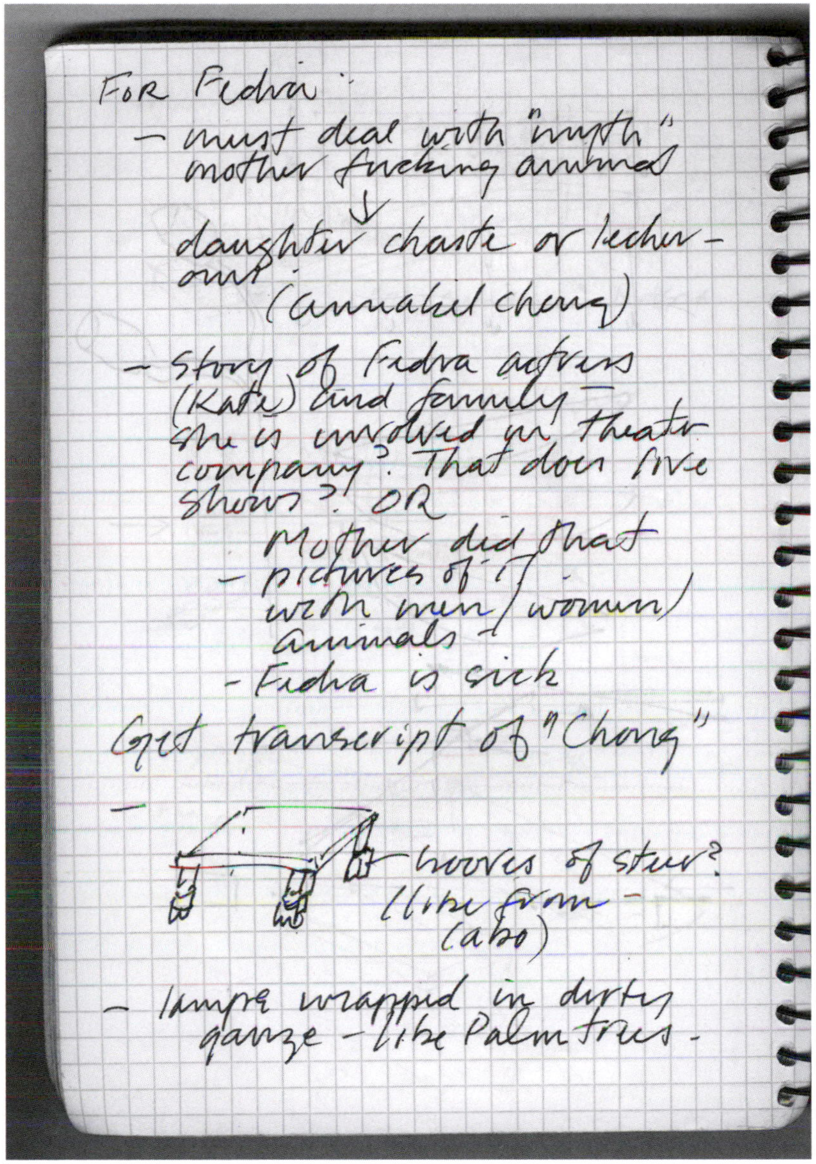

For Fedra:

– must deal with "myth"
mother fucking animal
↓
daughter chaste or lecher-ous
(Annabel Chong)

– Story of Fedra actress (Kate) and family –
She is involved in theater company? That does live shows? OR
Mother did that
– pictures of T with men / women / animals –
– Fedra is sick

Get transcript of "Chong"

–

hooves of steer? (like from – Cabo)

– lamps wrapped in dirty gauze – like Palm trees –

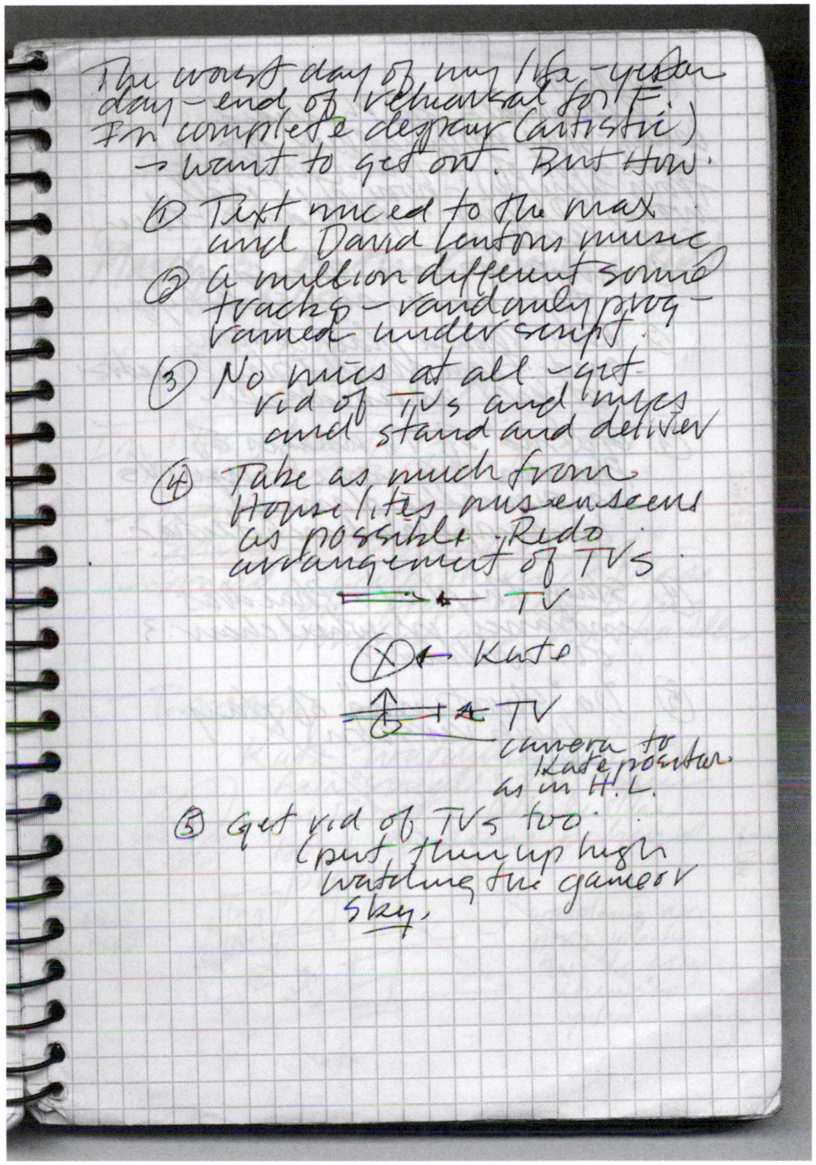

The worst day of my life – yesterday – end of rehearsal for F.
I'm complete despair (artistic)
→ want to get out. But How.

① Text miced to the max and David Linton's music

② A million different sound tracks – randomly programmed under script.

③ No mics at all – get rid of TVs and mics and stand and deliver

④ Take as much from House/Lites mise-en-scene as possible. Redo arrangement of TVs.

TV

Kate

TV

camera to Kate position as in H.L.

⑤ Get rid of TVs too. (put them up high watching the game or sky.

2. click
low engine throb
buzzer chaser
computer bleeps from
70.

piano lesson sound change

For Phedra
(1) Annabel chong
Porn. Pam 251 men
Myth of Phedras mother
(2) Get documentary —
(3) Phedra sick, with
aids
asshole & vagina
are destroyed
Nurse must carry
her everywhere
Can't walk
Still must be debased
carves up her arms
jealous of everyone
Aricia = new
porn queen.

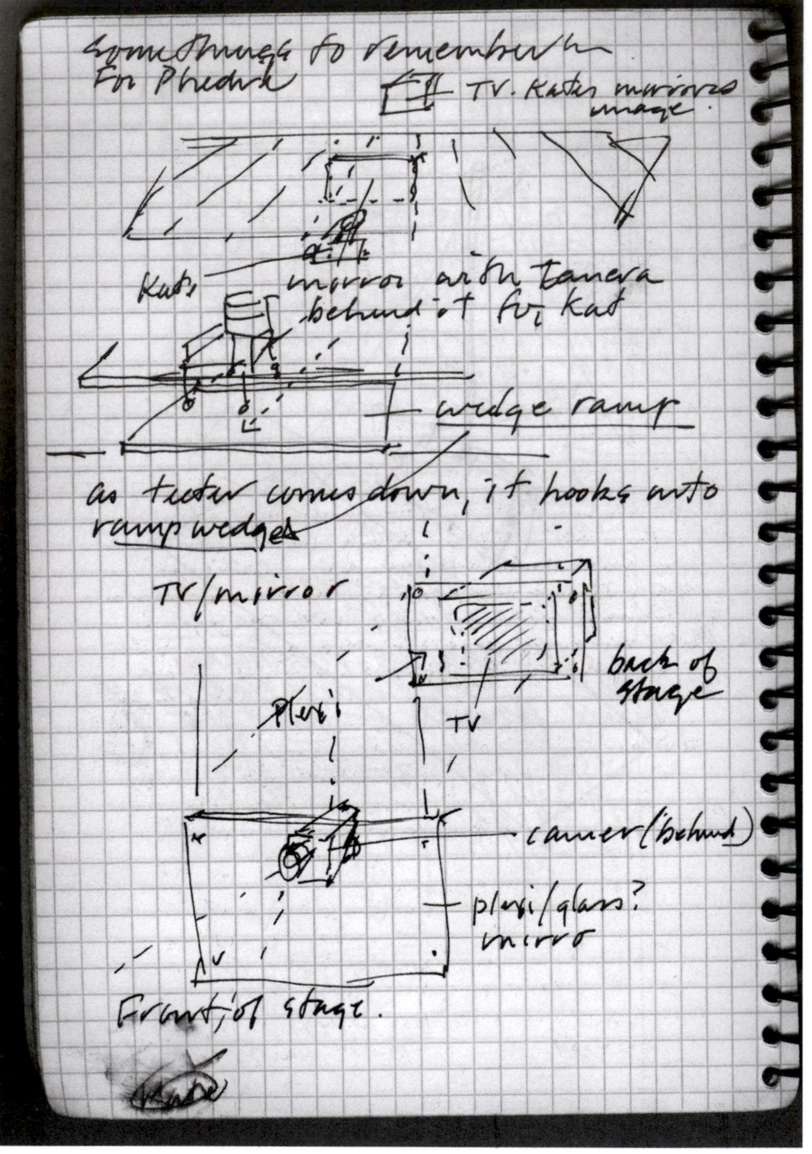

 Above: **Elizabeth LeCompte: journal entries** Opposite: **Video still:** ***To You, the Birdie! (Phèdre)*****, Act 1**

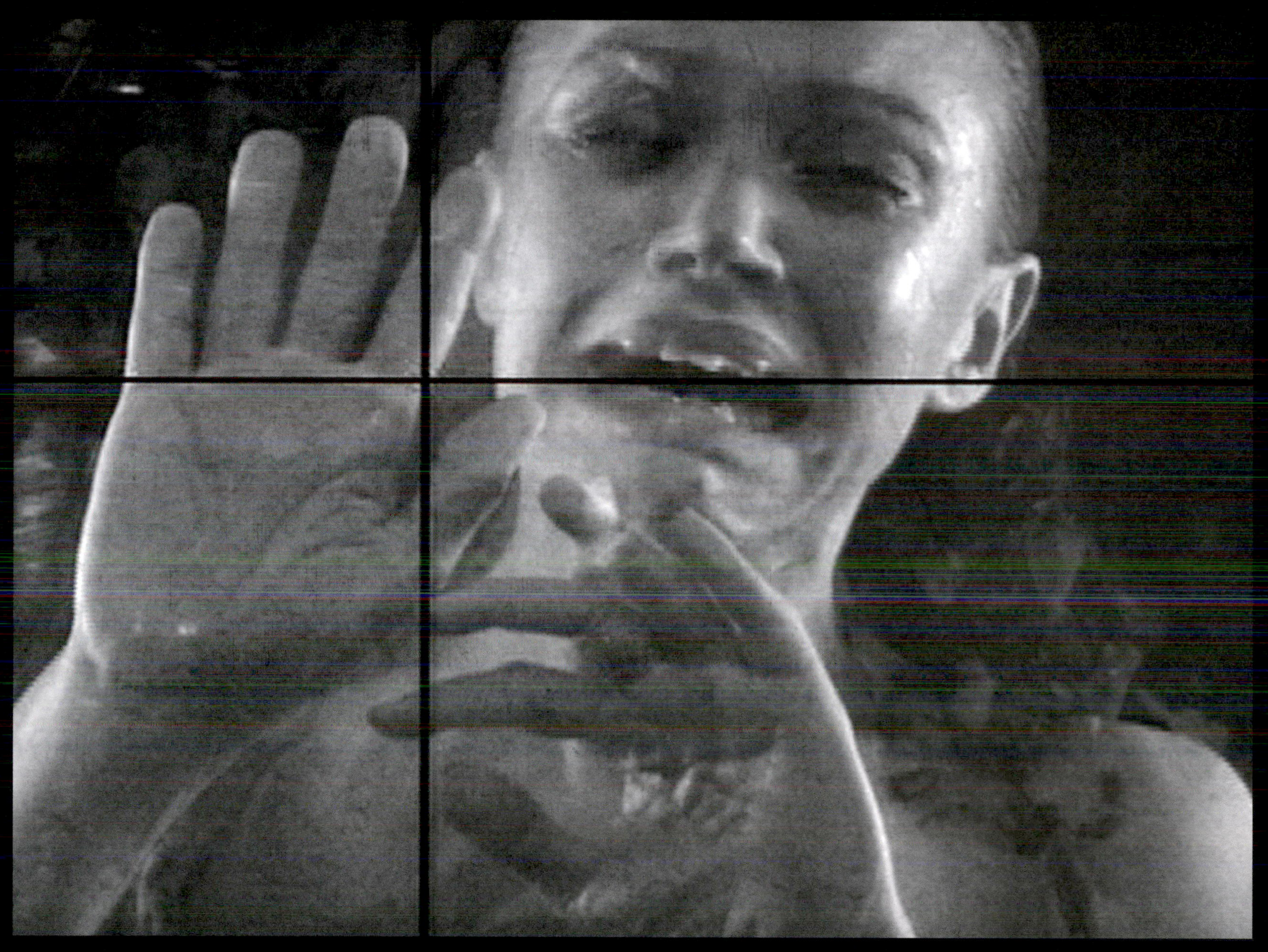

9/22

LIZ SEZ:

- "Big clunker" of text - how to make evanescence - lightness
- Reality of game - BUT also unreal
- connection through hands
- window of images. Palm Pilot - scroll through - [stop that = stop looking at that]
- 2 primary actions:
  - playing of badminton
  - giving of enema
- whispering + kibbitzing - can repeat, can work w/ role acting class within scene
- Back g - fore g relationship how to nail down - back as interesting as front
- dislocation in game - there's an impossible unreal score that must be completed

10/3

- to find a mode on stage which unites elements
  - badminton
  - groucho
  - Schmidt text
  - Greek myth
  - Racine
  - Scott S. voice

But not so codified that audience gets it (or gets ahead of it)

MUST BE A SECRET

- MODERNISM: the thing uncommented - not contemporary - the first discovery of modern forms

- accumulation of tiny quotidian awkwardness to begin scene
- KV gets FMD to adjust in car levels, w/ track
- game / S.R. in deep bkgrnd sound - crying babies H_2O trickle

 To You, the Birdie! (Phèdre), badminton practice

10/3

- Specificity + tempo within the game structure. How to keep both tight —
- w/AF text – we need to hear inner monologue throw off lines – it's the acting/reacting visible in body
- All the games + tricks are pasteons until the fundamental transaction: tension: source of energy is identified. Can be discovered through outside → in – but must be discovered
- has to be something more at stake than just getting through the scene
-

10/24

Now we improvise physically w/ sound, desperately hunting for something, anything, that can help us define the way of being on stage. But it seems like so much ambling … we need a structure or a big idea, or something central to hang on to that tracks through the entire piece. Badminton, yes, but that collision w/the text – at least directly – has been assayed + found not to work. So what is it that we can together find that will allow us to work, for at the moment it feels we're on an arbitrary, unproductive tangent. But then again, as Kate reminds me before rehearsal today everything always comes back, nothing is for naught. So this grab bag, collage of techniques with no glue, will find its form. But what will it take to get there?

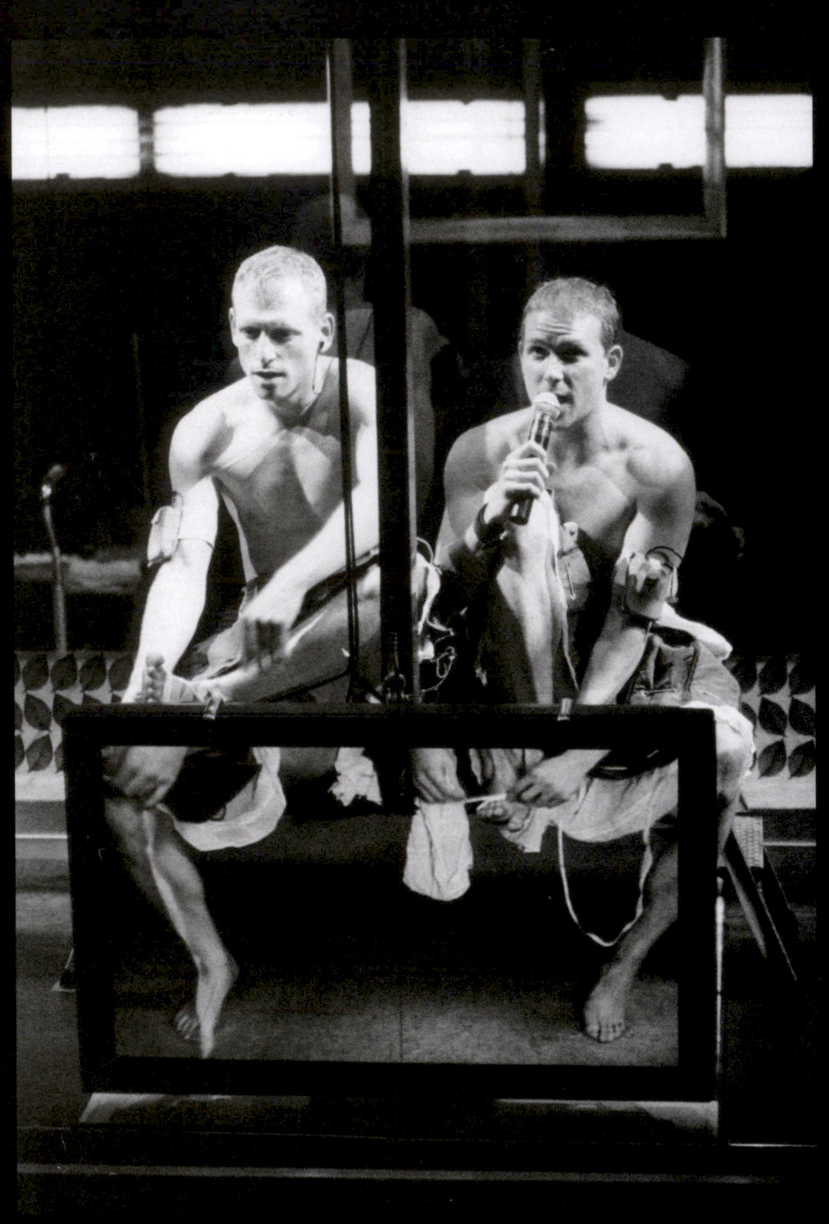

REHEARSAL REPORT

Production: Phèdre
Begin: 1:35pm **Break:** 2:50pm
Break: 4:30pm **End:** 5:30pm
Next Rehearsal: Wed., April 18, 1:30pm

Rehearsal 5 of 38
Date: April 16, 2001
Stage Manager: Judy Tucker

Distribution: Richard Kimmel, Elizabeth LeCompte

General:
Special note: Next Thursday, April 26, we need an all day work call; talk to performers about schedule. Freight should be in by Wednesday, April 25.

1:30pm-2:50pm Rigorous badminton warm-up with Chi-Bing.
2:50pm-3:05pm 15-minute break
3:15pm-4:30pm Text/Sound/Video Work

Bring out old work with Fran, DC shaking Kate, weaving through DS TV.
We have a new Merce Cunningham compilation video.
Same video monitor set up: Marx Bros. offstage DL, DR, underneath SR bench
Martha Graham offstage L,R
Merce Cunningham offstage CS
Work with Fran on naturalism on stage as an interruption, double lines if she wants to.
Work with Suzzi in the house on getting into the play, starting badminton game, blowing whistle Q's. Remember the Marx Bros. tape: when Harpo blows the whistle everyone pauses to give him the space. Suzzi is the Harpo element, not psychologically, but find the interruptions.

In working with videos, use camera moves (i.e., come to foreground and background as camera moving), and to imitate movement of characters. It's an internal thing, where your concentration is, not the main focus or movement. Take the last thing with you to find the bridge into the next thing you do. Where does concentration go until you pick it up again?

There should always be 2 people onstage. If someone drops out then someone else should take their place.
Dominique and Koosil-ja will do panel moves for US entrances and exits.
Also use benches, clamber across from stage to benches.
Marx Bros., Martha Graham, Merce Cunningham videotapes run from beginning of videotape.

Suzzi to speak when Karen talks on referee videotape; blow whistle when she blows whistle, then say something from badminton phrases. Everyone do some kind of take (think of Marx Bros.) in a short pause, not too long, then go back to play until next whistle. Can this be used as a way to get to badminton? Note: Performers can't hear whistle. beats Make a visual Q. On whistle: FREEZE VIDEO for 5 beats. All look @ US TV. Follow Suzzi's instructions, play to next whistle, go back to text/movement when whistle to end game is blown (women continue cleaning birdies, raquets). End whistle followed by angelic chorus.

Find places to use panels. Fran and Scott back off mics when screen is moved in front of them to give a sense of separation.
A monitor was put on the floor near DR for Kate to hear Fran.
Willie to lip sync. Scott speaking text as the US panel opens to SR, mirrored by panel open SL for Scott's lines (pp. 11, 17)

Kate pointed out that it is difficult to work on movement and concentrate on text, they need to be worked on separately for now. Liz wants to work on entrance and exit physicality, less on lip sync., choosing lines, etc. It's too frantic.

REHEARSAL REPORT

Production: Phèdre
Begin: 1:30pm **Break:** 4:04pm
Break: 4:32pm **End:** 6:00pm

Rehearsal 38 of 58*
Date: June 2, 2001
Stage Manager: Judy Tucker

*Rehearsal schedule TBD for June, schedule to follow in the next report.

Next Rehearsal: Wed., June 6, 1:30pm

Distribution: Richard Kimmel, Elizabeth LeCompte, Kim Whitener
General:
Rehearsal tapes #204, #205

2:00pm-2:35pm Notes:

Liz was in the show last night (on mic), so she has no idea what the first part is about.
The piece has developed in a strange way. We need to find a balance between showing and inhabiting it. Pull back and try other things.
The piece has many tones sitting next to each other like a collage, there are many styles. We need to pick areas to work on. There's great stuff.
Wait until next week to move forward; use Scott for Willie's role.

How did people feel in it?
•confused
•top of the show only done once before, disorienting
•Fran was tonally much lower (from nerves); save that for only a few places. It sounds very serious, great. We need to find another way to say "Oh, help me, help me" (transition I.1.-I.2., pp. 6).
Mic check worked in a great way, it's showy. The idea works with the text; the idea and what we're doing are separate. Deal with it as a more direct address.

•Incorporate the Venus monologue more.
•Incorporate badminton more, see how much establishment we need with the players in I.1., make it clearer that they are in a badminton game (watching). Hold a racquet? Put birdies on the court, SL, SR.
•Work on establishing crying; use video tape with only crying, no text.
•The sound mixes will work out over time; the audience, nerves may have changed some of the way things sound. Will continue working out the Qs.
•Fran smoking is tonally beautiful, but it takes her into a totally comic place. Try to make it more personal. Stay in it just a little more.
People don't see the psychology (of the relationship between Fran, Kate; they see the TV and tech. which makes them confused and titllated until they see Fran smoking, and the Queen doesn't like it.
Liz is looking at the physical thing happening. Need to find a balance between physical, and Phèdre waiting for Oenone and she's nervous, it's too far out of the story.
When Fran loops back on "...your situation's desparate...", Kate circle back on "I hate him! Hate him!" (III.2., pp. 18).

•Sound mix for first badminton needs to be more wild, big. Last night it was tepid, beautiful, but Liz needs to see it blown out, not careful.
•There were many stops, it was hard to keep the volley going. Try warm up moves and moving more like when you're being shadowed.
•Mic sounds are missed; try to add one volley with the racquet mics-the sound connects exactly rather than sampling the sound, which is a different thing.
•Need to work on the mix for the Suzzy Venus dance.
•Many scenes are really beautiful, really starting to work.

Hipp.....That was then. But everything has changed,.....
left us with that woman..... Phaedre → whistle "Service judge Signal"

1

Act One

SHE WOULDN'T WANT ** TO SEE ME ANYWAY WHISTLE

I am Venus, the referee. I am the most important of
all the referees among the service judges and line judges
and everyone is going to listen to what I say.
Now I will quickly tell you the truth of this story

Phadre saw Hypolytus, son of Theseus, by that Amazon
and her heart was filled with the longings of love
This was my work (door close) PAUSE

But her love will not remain a secret
I will reveal the matter to Theseus and all will come out
Father will slay son with a curse

BIG OVER MUSIC

Look, here is the son of theseus, hyppolytus
he has just entered the court (JUMPS)—PAUSE
he does not know that the doors of death are open for him
that he's looking on his last sun

(whistle) are you ready?

play! -game

warning for misconduct player X or Y

you slung the birdie, is the birdie ok?, you are
standing in the wrong court, the birdie has failed to
pass the net, serving out of turn, if both sides commit
and error it shall be a let, you received out of turn,
do not change the birdie, the birdie touched you,
you distracted your opponent,marker, check the birdie

X to serve TIME CALLED

A 40 second interval has been claimed.

REHEARSAL REPORT

Production: Phèdre
Begin: 1:30pm
Break:

Break: 4:32pm
End: 6:00pm

Rehearsal 40 of 58*
Date: June 6, 2001
Stage Manager: Judy Tucker

*Rehearsal schedule TBD for June.

Next Rehearsal: Thurs., June 7, 2:00pm

Distribution: Richard Kimmel, Elizabeth LeCompte, Kim Whitener
General:
Rehearsal tapes #207, #208

1:30pm-1:40pm Continue clean up, Chi-Bing arrives
1:40pm-2:45pm Badminton warm up: Chi-Bing racquet feed, overhead (smashing)/underhand. Everyone was pretty tired.
2:45pm-3:00pm 15-minute break.
3:00pm-3:50pm Figure out what we should do on a day like today, in a year like this year, in this political climate…

Priorities:
Liz has notes on performance style and Qing, just a little but they have to do with the tone of the piece. Working these notes tends to take time away from the piece, which we don't need right now. We will do these notes later.

Talk about the setting for the piece, how we're setting up the whole piece:
•Scott coming on to do Phèdre's lines. We have to figure out who he is. Why did Liz choose him saying the lines at the UL bench on the mic?
•Instinctive; Liz doesn't like to see a woman kill herself because she's guilty. She doesn't like the character, the person, the piece. Now she sees madness beyond the psychological, she sees someone superhuman.
•Paul (Schmidt) is a man, it's a man's voice.
•Liz doesn't like Kate's voice for the character, it sounds weak, she doesn't want any pretense.
•Liz didn't choose the project, but she loves Paul. She partly chose it for Paul.
Don't know what that means. Does it mean
•Scott is Paul? Liz?
•Doesn't want it to be a psychological drama.
•Fool people?
•Kate pointed out that Liz likes the separation of voice and body for the character. Set Scott up as the one who tells the story.
•Liz empasized that is hard to do without losing or overexplaining the story.
•Bunraku: People on the side say the lines, the puppets move. We go back and forth between them. In our piece, only the main character is in that place.
•Jim F. pointed out that there is something in the text that sets this up: Theremenes is the storyteller at the end, the guy who's seen it all, the witness. It is positioned that way in the text.
•Fran suggested that it might help to do it with other characters.
•Liz wants to work on the Prologue which sets up the story, not our structure. We have to make it (the prologue) up. She's not in a rush to deal with this.
•Scott as Kate's voice is a little abstract in the shoe scene, but it could be connected in a stronger way.

•Here's the crux of it: To the audience this man is speaking for Kate so they can listen, it doesn't destroy other ambiguities in the piece.

•Dom brought up the example of Noh theater, in which 2 real people (Shite, Waki) come out and have an initial conversation about what the play is about, then the characters come in as ghosts.
•Liz: how to do this unpretentiously? If the story is in Paul's voice, this will not reveal itself in the end; we have to say it's Paul's story at the end. Afraid to front load the story, but back loading is OK.

Work with Suzzy, Ari, Scott on Euripides invocation for the top of the piece.
See about what Phèdre is at the beginning.
•Illness has to be on video. See if there is an image of a torso with a skin virus which causes the skin to consume itself (Liz and Tara looked at some pictures on the internet).
•Can we construct a screen of those images to put on the front TV, over Kate's body (Philip-yes).
•That story is revealed early on.

Pale Fire.
•Liz read the beginning of Pale Fire aloud. About Paul (as the translator):
We think we know what Paul wants.
We're pretending that we're doing it for Paul.
We're doing it for ourselves (not 1940's noire).
In the writing, there's confusion of the person who interprets, not the person who creates. Paul translated the French Phèdre for TWG, then did a longer version for Liz Diamond at A.R.T.; the translations are removed from the original.
•For Liz this isn't Phèdre, it's TWG, it's Paul. Anything you do is going to change the play so radically. How you tell the story is the story. Myths are born from this.
•Adan Sandoval sent Liz dramaturgy notes from Phèdre from Guatemala. He saw a production of Phèdre in Strasbourg, France, and tried to learn how to say the play in French, but couldn't find a recording in French. He sent a translation from the programme, which is comparable to the strange writing of Pale Fire.

For today:
•Work on Suzzy's prologue.
•See where we go with the torso (of Theseus, we will work on Kate's more on Thursday. Tara has info.)
On Thursday:
We will do performance notes before the show.

Set for the top.
3:50pm-4:25pm •Create a loop of Scott and Ari's feet, and put the red curtain over them just revealing their feet on the front TV.
•Sound bed: Court sounds, and Jim Dawson tried various gentle music underneath at certain points.
•Kate helped Suzzy organize the monologue text to fit in with the text for the piece.
•Scott and Ari come into the video of them sitting on the bench wrapping their feet.
•Try Suzzy reading the monologue first, then the curtain lifting on video into I.1. at the end of the monologue with Scott and Ari on.

I. Suzzy read monologue she transcribed from rehearsal, stay on the video to blow the whistle and feed instructions.
II. Suzzy read instruction monologue.
III. (After searching…) Suzzy read the "Freedom flowing from the mirror" monologue, which is a combination of Paul Schmidt and Martha Graham, which Liz really liked from last week.
IV. Suzzy read Jim D.'s intro, "…the Goddess of Love and Desire…"

TO SHOOT (SPECIFIC):

- For Kate w/gals & chair meeting Fran in center during acc. tape (I.2) – need something for front monitor

- Suzzy → pool and Pool → Suzzy transitions (II.1)

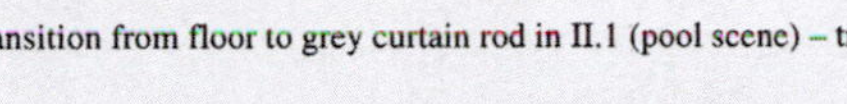

- Transition from floor to grey curtain rod in II.1 (pool scene) – travel up curtain

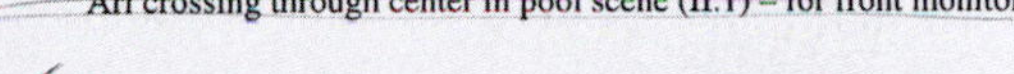

- ~~Ari crossing through center in pool scene (II.1) – for front monitor~~

- After enema (II.1) – shot of Koosil-ja knees, hands w/enema tube?
- ~~Fran running through center before knife fight (II.1) – need something for front monitor~~

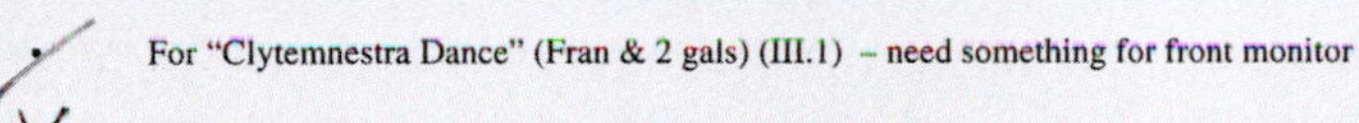

- For "Clytemnestra Dance" (Fran & 2 gals) (III.1) – need something for front monitor

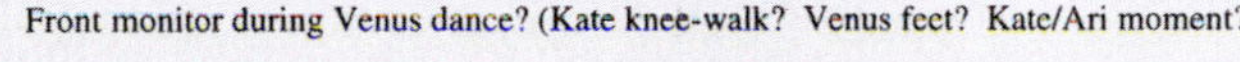

- Front monitor during Venus dance? (Kate knee-walk? Venus feet? Kate/Ari moment?)

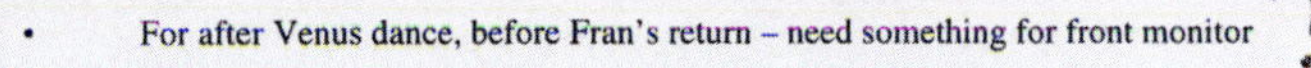

- For after Venus dance, before Fran's return – need something for front monitor ?
- ~~Fran's knees/Willem's head (IV.1)~~

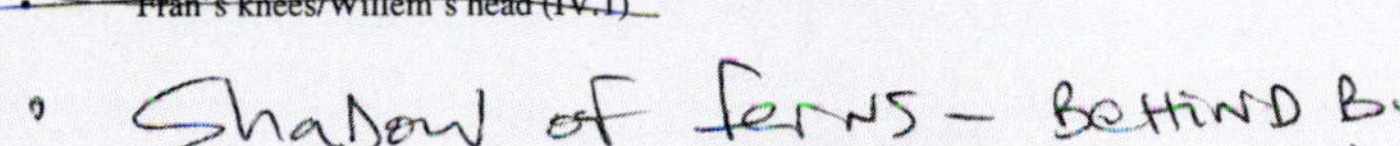

- Shadow of ferns – Behind busts (IV.2)

- ~~Reshoot HEAD?~~

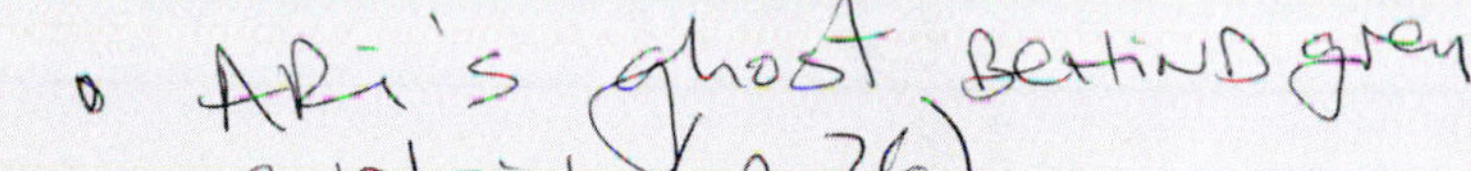

- Ari's ghost behind grey curtain (p. 26)
- "Writing" in the Frost (IV.4)
- When W rises out of Leaf – eyes "go out"

Opposite: ***To You, the Birdie (Phèdre)*, Act 4** Above: **Early video shoot list**

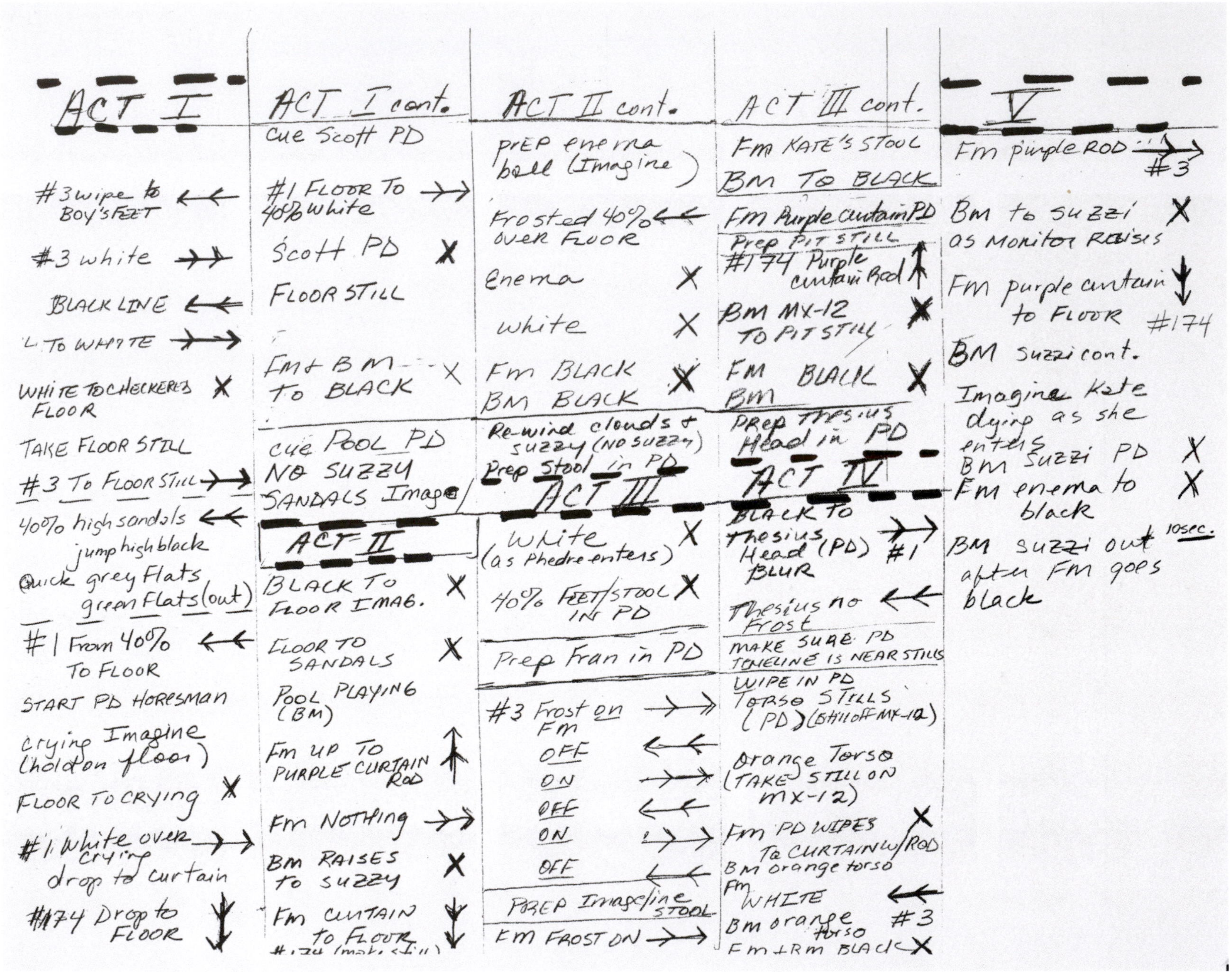

ACT I

#3 wipe to Boy's FEET ←←

#3 white →→

BLACK LINE ←←

L TO WHITE →→

WHITE TO CHECKERED FLOOR X

TAKE FLOOR STILL

#3 To FLOOR STILL →→

40% high sandals ←←
jump high black

Quick grey Flats
green Flats (out)

#1 From 40% ←←
To FLOOR

START PD HORESMAN

crying Imagine
(hold on floor)

FLOOR TO CRYING X

#1 White over crying →→
drop to curtain

#174 Drop to FLOOR ↓

ACT I cont.

Cue Scott PD

#1 FLOOR TO 40% white →→

Scott PD X

FLOOR STILL

FM + BM TO BLACK X

cue POOL PD
NO SUZZY
SANDALS Image

ACT II

BLACK TO FLOOR IMAG. X

FLOOR TO SANDALS X

POOL PLAYING (BM)

FM UP TO PURPLE CURTAIN ROD ↑

FM NOTHING →→

BM RAISES TO SUZZY X

FM CURTAIN TO FLOOR ↓
#174 (make still)

ACT II cont.

prep enema ball (Imagine)

Frosted 40% over FLOOR ←←

enema X

white X

FM BLACK X
BM BLACK

Re-wind clouds + suzzy (NO SUZZY)
Prep Stool in PD

ACT III

white (as Phedre enters) X

40% FEET/STOOL IN PD X

Prep Fran in PD

#3 Frost on FM →→
OFF ←←
ON →→
OFF ←←
ON →→
OFF ←←

PREP Imageline STOOL

FM FROST ON →→

ACT III cont.

FM KATE'S STOOL
BM TO BLACK

FM Purple curtain PD

Prep PIT STILL

#174 Purple curtain Rod ↑

BM MX-12 TO PIT STILL X

FM BLACK X
BM

Prep Thesius Head in PD

ACT IV

BLACK TO Thesius Head (PD) #1 →→
BLUR

Thesius no Frost ←←

MAKE SURE PD TIMELINE IS NEAR STILLS

WIPE IN PD Torso STILLS (PD) (BM off MX-12)

orange Torso (TAKE STILL ON MX-12)

FM PD WIPES TO CURTAIN W/ROD X
BM orange torso

FM WHITE ←←

BM orange torso #3

FM + BM BLACK X

V

FM purple ROD →→ #3

BM to suzzi as Monitor raises X

FM purple curtain to FLOOR ↓ #174

BM suzzi cont.

Imagine Kate dying as she enters

BM suzzi PD X

FM enema to black X

BM suzzi out after FM goes black 10sec.

Early video cue sheet

Video stills: *To You, the Birdie! (Phèdre)*, Acts 1–2

 Above: **Video stills:** ***To You, the Birdie! (Phèdre)*****, Acts 3–5** Opposite: **Elizabeth LeCompte: journal entries (undated)**

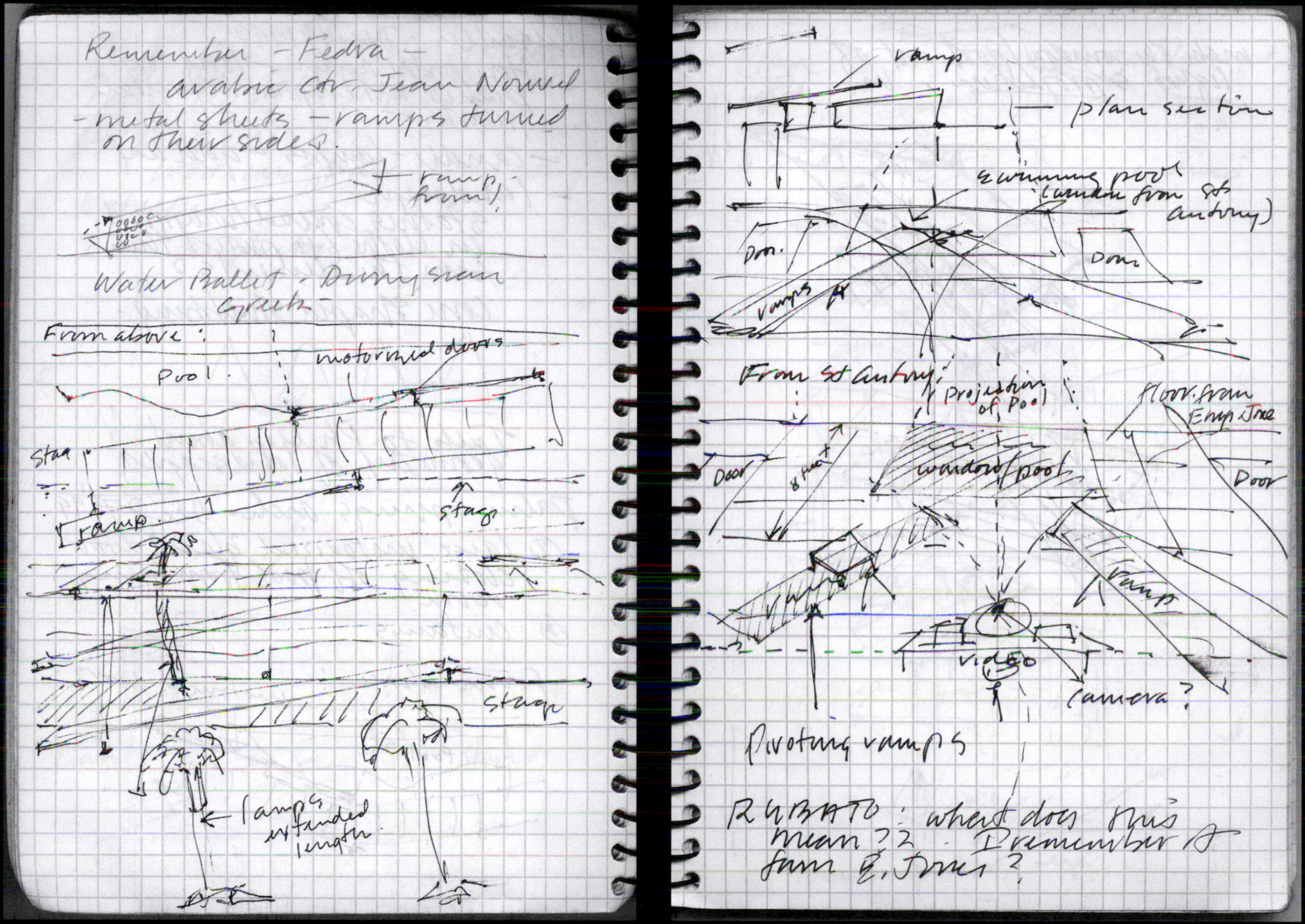

Remember – Fedra –
arabic ctr. Jean Nouvel
– metal sheets – ramps turned
on their sides.

ramp,
front)

Water Ballet – Diving scene
Greek

From above:

Pool

motorized doors

stag

ramp

stage

stag

stage

ramps
extended
length

ramps

plan section

swimming pool
(window from St
Antony)

Door.

Door

ramps

From St Antony:

Projection
of Pool

Floor from
Emp Tree

Door

8 feet

window/pool

Door

ramps

video

camera?

Pivoting ramps

RUBATO: what does this
mean?? I remember it
from E. Jones?

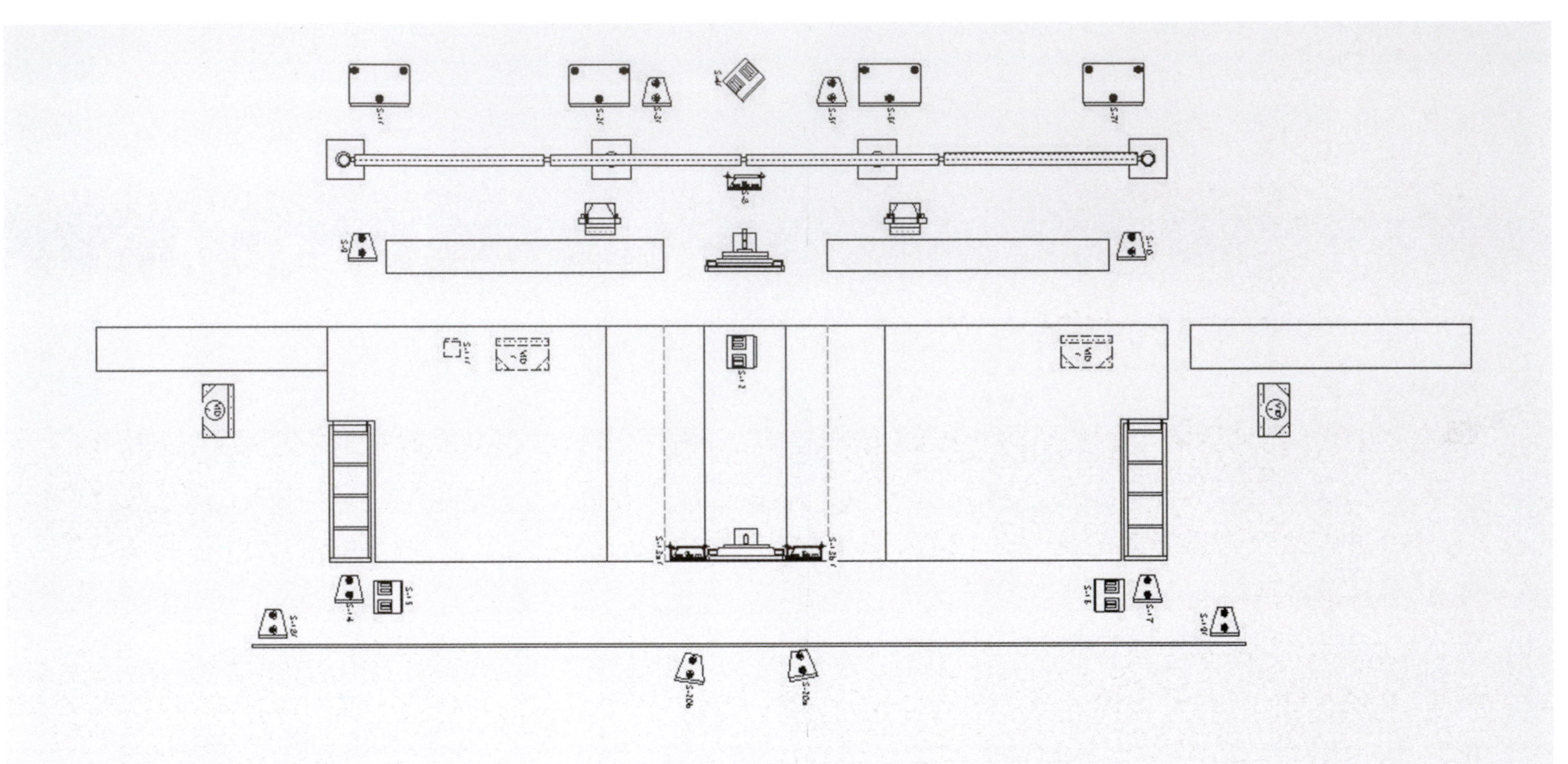

 Above: **Final set drawing: Jim Findlay** Opposite: ***To You, the Birdie! (Phèdre)*, Act 1**

 Top: ***To You, the Birdie! (Phèdre)***, Act 3 Bottom: Act 4

Left: ***To You, the Birdie! (Phèdre)***, Act 1 Right: Act 2

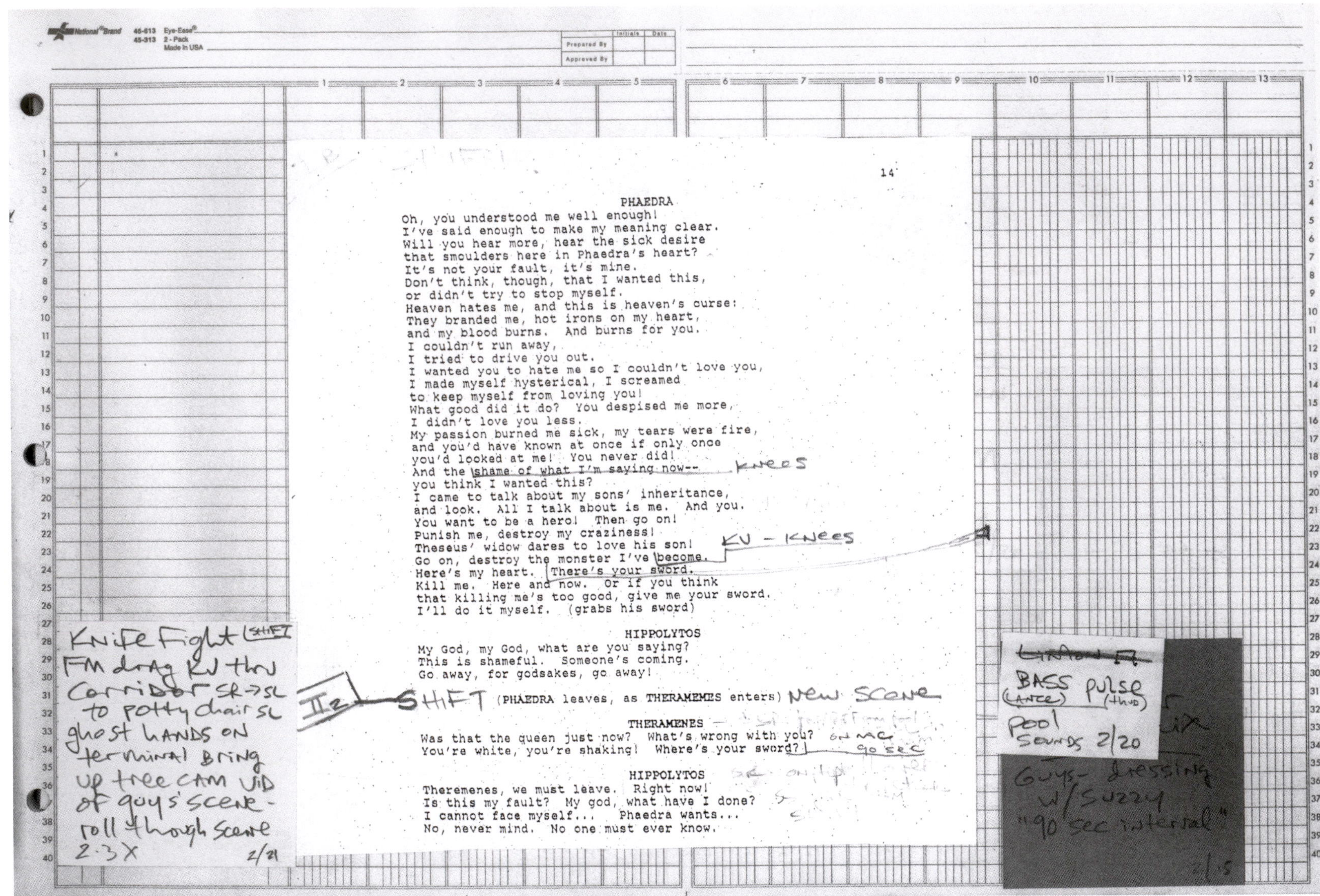

14

PHAEDRA

Oh, you understood me well enough!
I've said enough to make my meaning clear.
Will you hear more, hear the sick desire
that smoulders here in Phaedra's heart?
It's not your fault, it's mine.
Don't think, though, that I wanted this,
or didn't try to stop myself.
Heaven hates me, and this is heaven's curse:
They branded me, hot irons on my heart,
and my blood burns. And burns for you.
I couldn't run away,
I tried to drive you out.
I wanted you to hate me so I couldn't love you,
I made myself hysterical, I screamed
to keep myself from loving you!
What good did it do? You despised me more,
I didn't love you less.
My passion burned me sick, my tears were fire,
and you'd have known at once if only once
you'd looked at me! You never did!
And the shame of what I'm saying now-- KNEES
you think I wanted this?
I came to talk about my sons' inheritance,
and look. All I talk about is me. And you.
You want to be a hero! Then go on!
Punish me, destroy my craziness!
Theseus' widow dares to love his son! KV - KNEES
Go on, destroy the monster I've become.
Here's my heart. There's your sword.
Kill me. Here and now. Or if you think
that killing me's too good, give me your sword.
I'll do it myself. (grabs his sword)

HIPPOLYTOS

My God, my God, what are you saying?
This is shameful. Someone's coming.
Go away, for godsakes, go away!

II2 SHIFT (PHAEDRA leaves, as THERAMEMES enters) New Scene

THERAMENES

Was that the queen just now? What's wrong with you? on mic
You're white, you're shaking! Where's your sword? 90 sec

HIPPOLYTOS

Theremenes, we must leave. Right now!
Is this my fault? My god, what have I done?
I cannot face myself... Phaedra wants...
No, never mind. No one must ever know.

Knife Fight (SHIFT)
FM drag KV thru corridor SR→SL to potty chair SL
ghost hands on terminal bring up tree cam vid of guys' scene - roll through scene 2-3X
2/21
BASS pulse (Lance) (thud)
Pool sounds 2/20
Guys- dressing w/ Suzzy
"90 sec interval"

Above: **Assistant director score: Richard Kimmel** Opposite: ***To You, the Birdie! (Phèdre)***, Act 2

 To You, the Birdie! (Phèdre), Act 1

Off Stage hook tent to Kate's skirt pull it out as walks exit Enter in trough X to USR cane

16

ACT THREE

PHAEDRA

(she holds Hippolytos' sword)
Take it all away! Crowns and kingdoms,
what do they mean to me now?
I won't see anybody; tell them that.
I've said too much already, things
no one should ever have to hear.
He understood! Oh God! But how he tried
to make believe he didn't! And tried
to get away! My shame was choking me,
and he... I watched his face grow pale.
I wanted him to kill me but he wouldn't.
Wouldn't even kill me!
Wouldn't touch his sword, because I'd touched it!
I tried to kill myself. You stopped me.

follow hand tape

after 2nd hand reach

roll up tent toss to Koosilja

OENONE

You are a danger to us all, you know?
You feed a fire that will destroy you!
You're Minos' daughter, you have greater things to do!
Leave this place and that rude boy behind;
Take the crown of Athens! Go be queen.

knee pivot off at cane

PHAEDRA

Queen of Athens! How can I rule
a country when I can't control myself!
I've lost the empire of my common sense,
and choke on shame and unrequited lust!
I want to die!

OENONE

The sooner you leave here,
the better.

PHAEDRA

Leave? And leave him here behind? I can't.
Don't ask me. It's too late anyway,
he knows, he knows me now, I make him sick!
I shock his adolescent modesty!
I shook my shame before his very eyes
and watched him turn away. It's all your fault!
You flattered me! You lied!
You tried to make me think all this would work!

OENONE

I thought it would. Please, don't blame me!
Blame him! Why not? He treated you like dirt,
that look he gave you, holier-than-thou.
I hate his pride. It's worse than yours.

17

PHAEDRA

sit on edge of following tape

Oenone... if I'm wrong? After all,
he grew up in the woods, an animal
almost. And no one ever spoke of love
to him before. Perhaps he wasn't angry,
just surprised. Perhaps I'm being too hard...

OENONE

His mother was hard, that Amazon--

PHAEDRA

Still, she must have loved him...

OENONE

She taught him to hate women. Where does that leave you?

PHAEDRA

I'll never have a rival for his love,
at least there's that! Don't try to reason with me.
His heart is closed to love? All right then,
let's find something else. The talk of Athens
seemed to move him; he couldn't hide it...
that's it, Oenone! Call him back,
I'll offer him the sacred crown of Athens,
I'll put it on his head myself!
Let him be regent for my son, perhaps...
Oh God... he'll want to take his father's place...
Go on, go find him, try to make him see
we need him here. Say anything. I'll wait.

— Q tosses knife — stand X R wait in front of Scott

(Exit OENONE)

Scoosh off at cane get crown from Kja

PHAEDRA

Follow Graham tape

Relentless Venus! See the shame I've fallen to.
Are you content to see me in despair?
Your cruelty has gone as far as it can go.
Your triumph is complete, you win it all.
If that's the glory you desire, why not
destroy someone who hates your name?
Go find Hippolytos, he scorns your power,
he runs away from anyone who speaks
of love. Avenge yourself on him, not me!
Make him love me! Punish him with love,
make him--

X to window watch 2 lunges then join for 2 more. Watch Q until she screams

— Knee Scoosh — throw yourself at her feet

hear Graham X to SL cane follow B+W dress to racket

(Enter OENONE)

Oenone. What did he say? He hates me,
doesn't he? He wouldn't listen, he said no--

VENUS dance

Scoosh to R to get sword Tell Kja to get crown Scoosh L to Q - put sword in belt scoosh towards cane

Mirror pass

1st doorbell – panel slides
Step X out
panel slide – drop out

2nd doorbell – panel slides
Step X out
panel slide – drop out

3rd X to SR cane w/
crown in R hand
longer wait – footsteps
doorbell panel slides
X in + out panel slide
pass to crown to Dom
Go behind plant – unbend
hook up skirt

End of Venus Dance "Fault" – drop racket
kneel bow w/Ari
Stand, + pass to Dom
and Exit to floor at cane
Go behind plant – unhook skirt
light cig – Dom whispers

doorbell – X to SR edge of panel
panel slides – On mirror

18

OENONE
Get rid of it! Forget Hippolytos!
Stop feeling what you're feeling! X to SL of Mirror
Theseus is alive,
He's back, he's asking for you!
You can't afford emotion now. X off follow mirror tape

PHAEDRA
My husband is alive! Then I must die!
Don't tell me any more. It's all your fault!
I followed your advice, and look!
He'll hate me, and I'll die.

OENONE
You'll die? What for?

PHAEDRA
Because of what I've done! My husband's on his way,
his son beside him; can I go welcome him
with my adultery in the air between us?
You think he won't tell Theseus everything?
He loves his father, honors him; of course
he will. He's too honest not to.
I won't know how to look them in the face!
I'm not a woman who can cheat and then
think nothing of it; I know myself. My desperate
passion shows itself in everything I do.
I'd rather die. How easy that would be!
Death is what I dream of, better than the misery
I live in now. But what will my children do?

OENONE
I wondered when you'd think of them. Look, X in following mirror tape.
your situation's desperate, but why give up
so soon? You die, you leave Hippolytos
to snatch up everything! He rejects you, SR to cane
then you die and leave the throne to him?
Do you love him that much? X out ~~after brushing hair~~ ~~away~~

PHAEDRA
I hate him! Hate him!

OENONE
Then make him suffer too! // Go straight to Theseus; meet her in front of panel
accuse Hippolytos of rape
before he mentions your adultery.
Why shouldn't he believe you? The evidence
is all against Hippolytos; you have his sword, ("I don't" give it to her hard)
everyone can see that you're upset, hysterical;
Accuse him of rape. Theseus will disown him,
and you're home free.

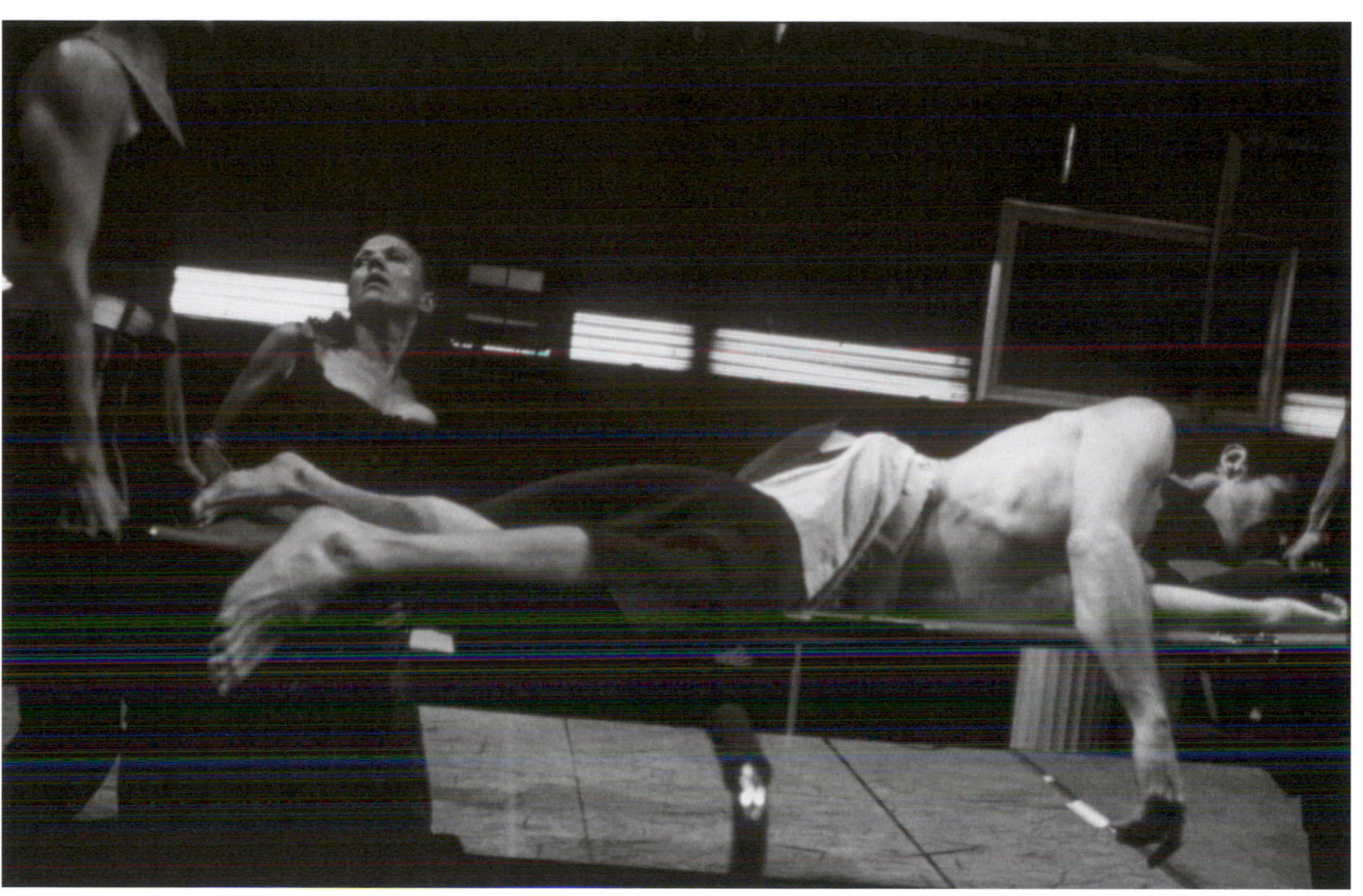

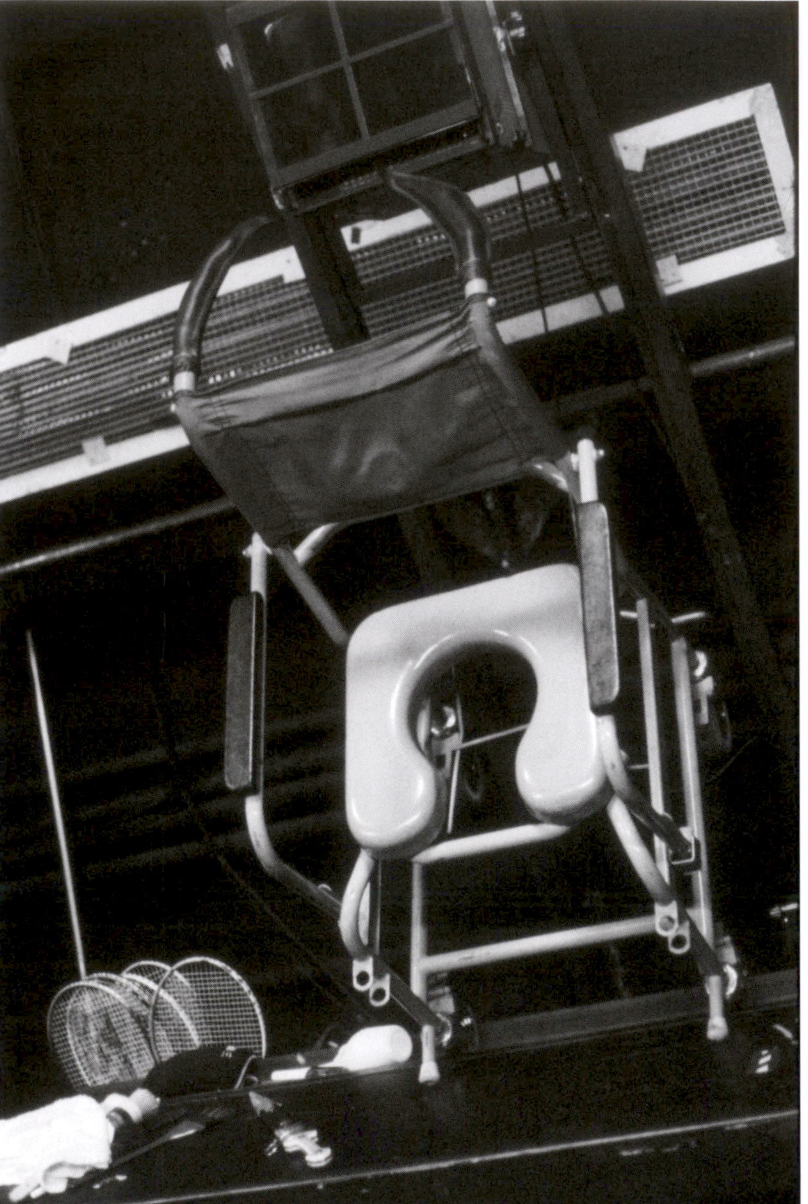

 Props: *To You, the Birdie! (Phèdre)*

① We are working on this piece thru June and in Sept. planning to open in Jan for an extended run

(in progress)

② Tonite we'll show about 1 hr of material which includes, text mainly from Paul Schmidt's Phaedra but also from Martha Graham & a manual called the rules of badminton.

③ New material – may have to stop

THE WOOSTER GROUP
NEW WORK

Non-Profit Organization
U.S. Postage
PAID
New York, NY
Permit N° 5827

based on
Paul Schmidt's *Phèdre*
(from the play by Racine)

June 1–July 1
Thursday–Sunday, 8 pm
19 performances only
Tickets $20
(212) 966-3651

The Performing Garage
33 Wooster Street, SoHo
www.thewoostergroup.org

The New Work has been made possible with generous support from the National Endowment for the Arts; the New York State Council on the Arts, a State Agency; The Rockefeller MAP Fund; and Étant donnés, the French-American Fund for the Performing Arts.

please bear with us and come back.

~~air conditioning~~ – ~~apologize~~

For tonite ~~please~~ have a good time

6/23/01

Taking it off center: perspectives on *To You, the Birdie! (Phèdre)*

An interview with Elizabeth LeCompte (New York, September 24th, 2006)

Andrew Quick (AQ): What drew you to the text of *Phèdre* for the making of *To You, the Birdie!* (2002)?

Elizabeth LeCompte (EL): At first, nothing. I remember we read a version of the play ten or fifteen years ago when Paul Schmidt first wrote it and the text wasn't interesting to me. It seemed all plot and the writing just didn't grab me, so I let it go. Then when Paul died in 1999 Katie became interested in the play again and she began working on it—she did a radio version for the BBC. I thought, "OK, since so much work has already been done on the play, why don't I take a look at it." Paul had rewritten it since I'd first read it, but I didn't feel very excited about the text when I started working on the piece.

AQ: So, you felt very distanced from the play text from the start?

EL: Yes, but I wasn't afraid of that. I'd been like that with *St. Antony*. I knew I would find something. But, it wasn't until I found the connections with Martha Graham, Merce Cunningham, sickness and popular music that I really got a hook into it.

AQ: Did these connections come early in the process?

EL: The Martha Graham came pretty quickly because I had been thinking about doing a ballet for a long time. Also, we started looking at all the different productions of *Phèdre* we could get hold of and, of course, we found Martha Graham's dance version of *Phèdre* and I focused on her work for a while.

AQ: Did the initial physical development start from Martha Graham? In the rehearsal tapes, you get the actors to work from video projections of her dances.

EL: Yes, but the earliest physical work was the badminton.

AQ: Did you know right from the start that there was going to be a physical motif, that this game structure would play such a central part in the piece? In some early rehearsal tapes you even have the actors playing table tennis.

EL: No, I didn't have any idea. I just knew that I was very far away from how I was going to approach this material. When this happens I usually need some kind of distraction, so I can think in the space. I'll get people doing something that I can watch in the space and this lets me consider the possibilities without them all sitting around waiting for me, because I'm much slower than they are. So, I'll often start with a game or something like that. So no, I had no idea how the badminton was going to work out. I was just pretending that I knew what I was going to do with it.

AQ: Looking back, it seems that badminton is the perfect frame for this piece.

EL: Yes, but I didn't know this then. I didn't really find out until we were six months into the badminton, when I looked into the history of badminton and tennis and discovered that they played these games at the French court. When I found this out I got hold of the pictures of the original badminton court and this really influenced how I developed the piece. I became interested in the original rules and that's where I found the phrase "to you, the birdie." The actors had already started to learn how to play badminton the modern way, but I had them return to the original rules—who played who and why they played in the French court. Mind you, this was some time into the rehearsals, although badminton had been integrated into the beginning of the piece very early on.

AQ: Did you have a sense of the overall structure of the piece at the beginning of rehearsals?

EL: Well, at the beginning I thought that I would have two distinct sections. That I would start with a dumb-show that would include the badminton. This would tell the whole story in the dumb-show style. And the second section would be a really fast run through of the script, thirty minutes at most.

AQ: I remember in one of the early rehearsal tapes that you say that you really need some other text to put alongside *Phèdre*. I think you start playing with the documentary *Sex: The Annabel Chong Story* (1999). You say something like, "This is fantastic, but it doesn't work against the *Phèdre*."

EL: I was desperately looking for something else to put against the text. I went through lots of possibilities and it was only when I took Katie's voice out that I finally realized that it would work.

AQ: It's a key moment when Scott (Shepherd) takes on the different voices in the text of *Phèdre*.

EL: I would hear Scott say the lines and I'd say, "Perfect." He was able to throw them away; he was totally comfortable with them being funny.

AQ: In one of the early rehearsals you get him to imitate or work off the dialogue from a film that he's watching on a TV monitor. I think it's an old black and white movie. You actually coach him for a while about how to throw the lines away and then you go, "Yes, that's it."

EL: I remember hearing him and saying, "That's the tone." Once I had that tone I didn't have to worry about cutting it with something else.

AQ: What was the tone?

EL: It's a kind of cross between old silent films and early American comedians — The Marx Brothers, The Three Stooges, that kind of thing.

AQ: Scott's role echoes Kate's function as the narrator in *Brace Up!* (1991). He's a kind of *benshi*, isn't he?

EL: Absolutely.

AQ: In so many of your pieces you have this person on the edge of the stage, sometimes at the front, sometimes at the back, who works between you and the piece itself. They have the voice that channels everything we hear and Scott seems to have this function in *To You, the Birdie!*.

EL: Yes, and when he got this role I felt free. It just freed me up to do whatever I wanted physically because I realized that there was no way that Katie was going to be able to do all the physical movement I wanted and still say the lines. When she tried to combine the two you couldn't see any of the physical stuff. All you could see was her trying to say those lines.

AQ: Struggling with that weird melodrama in *Phèdre*.

EL: Exactly, and I didn't want it to be naturalistic. It had to be bigger than life.

AQ: This notion of being larger than life is in the text of *Phèdre*.

EL: Yes, except that the text is so clunky, in a really interesting way. But, it's very clunky.

AQ: It feels a bit like soap opera...

EL: Soap opera, exactly — with bits of purple prose thrown in as some kind of fillip. So, I had to cut, or rather play down the purple prose, and the way to do this was through Scott saying Katie's lines. This left her being able to physicalize the passion, the purple prose, without you wanting to say, "Oh, my God, who is this?" I had to move it beyond the ordinary, somehow.

AQ: You also juxtapose this with Frances McDormand playing the servant Oenone in what seems to be a relatively naturalistic style.

EL: Well, I realized that this was what Frances was good at and I also knew that Katie wasn't at all comfortable with this type of naturalism as a performer. And this was the problem: with Frances being natural, Katie looked very awkward and uneasy in the language. Whenever I tried to get Frances to do what Katie is so good at, moving and saying the lines in a lifted, heightened, way, it just didn't work. So, I had to set them off against each other. I had two kinds of performer that were an absolute anathema to each other. I solved this problem by having Scott provide a third voice that was the bigger voice.

AQ: The framing voice?

EL: Yes.

AQ: You often have this figure of the servant or the maid, don't you?

EL: Always. It's my favorite character. I wanted Katie to play that character in *To You, the Birdie!*, but she didn't want to do it.

AQ: She wanted to be the queen?

EL: Yes.

AQ: However, the character of Phèdre is rendered subservient when Theseus arrives. There is a very clear hierarchy in the piece, who has the power. The power is in the language, in its strange rhetorical style.

EL: Yes, well it was written by Racine.

AQ: You play with this to great comic effect when Theseus finally arrives in Act 4. I found the use of video and sound here — the stills of Theseus's sculptured body combined with his amplified footsteps and his exclamations, "Look at this" — very funny. I remember thinking, when I saw the piece for the first time, how this way of dealing with the power relationships on the stage seemed so appropriate.

EL: I have to say I enjoyed that section. However, what made it so hard for me to be interested in this text as whole, and I said this to Katie, was "Why would you want to kill yourself in this piece, why would you want to do this when the language isn't very good — it's not Shakespeare?"

AQ: I remember this discussion coming up in the rehearsal tapes. In reply to this question, Katie says that she's interested in Phèdre's shame.

EL: That's interesting because I think that's what she tapped into with Paul Schmidt.

AQ: That's how you respond in the rehearsal: "It's about Paul."

EL: I remember that now — you're right — that's what she was interested in.

AQ: In the same rehearsal you seem almost at a point of despair with this piece. You say, "I don't know what to do with this damned text."

EL: That's true...

AQ: ...And people are throwing lots of ideas at you and in response you say, "I know it's not that, so I must be attached to this."

EL: Well, I was attached to it, that's why I stuck with it. I had to work it through.

AQ: On reflection, it seems that *To You, the Birdie!* is very different in style to *House/Lights* (1999). Yet, now that you're working on *Hamlet* and having seen some of the ways you're currently staging this play, *To You, the Birdie!* feels like a bridge between *House/Lights* and *Hamlet*, a kind of natural progression in your approach.

EL: I was thinking this today when I was watching *Hamlet* this morning. The same ideas are coming up and I am blending *To You, the Birdie!* and *House/Lights* together in some way.

AQ: I want to ask you about the design of *To You, the Birdie!*. In an earlier interview we touched on it and you made a connection with the design of *House/Lights*.

EL: Well, actually it's more like *Brace Up!*. With *House/Lights* I went back to the *Brace Up!* set and just pulled it out sideways to give it the feel of Panavision—we were watching a lot of films in Panavision at the time.

AQ: In the early rehearsals of *To You, the Birdie!* it's clear that you are interested in certain forms of modernist architecture as a source for the set.

EL: I was very interested in Californian modernist architecture at the time. I was looking at the Joseph Eichler houses, the work of Rudolf Schindler, modular houses, that kind of thing.

AQ: Was it because this architecture had a certain look or tone to it?

EL: I'm not sure why. It was just something that I was exploring visually at the time and I brought it into the process. I trusted that it would work itself out in the piece. When I bring what I'm interested in visually, it doesn't necessarily have anything to do with the text. Often, I am working on something completely different and then I bring this material to the text I'm looking at.

AQ: The design works so well in terms of the openness of the space and the flat screens and sliding doors. In some ways it connects to the earlier Japanese aesthetic that we've talked about. Yet, it's very American in terms of space and light. There's a sort of grandeur to that Californian architecture.

EL: Well, it's not only that. I was thinking about where the biggest artistic ego was, with Merce Cunningham and Martha Graham and all of those sorts of people. It seemed like modernism in dance, the movement in dance, and modernism in architecture were all linked together in a way. But there is also something about that text that was so bald and bare. When I looked at pictures of some of those Californian houses that were mainly made of glass there would often be women posing with big 1950s skirts. There was something about this that resonated with Paul's translation: a 50s piece with a big swimming pool—I think he was indicating this with his language. So, I think I followed this route to see where the language would take me.

AQ: Were there any other influences that determined the look of this piece?

EL: Yes. While I was looking at this architecture I also spent some time looking at the Palace of Versailles. I became very interested in the techniques of creating perspective. I was interested in that singular view, that one-to-one voice and I put it just off center.

AQ: You often do this, don't you, create a point of contact that's a little off-center?

EL: Yes, I just slide it a little. Except with *House/Lights*, where I put it right on the center. Everything in that piece is pulled from the center.

AQ: And this one-to-one voice is filtered through cinema. Scott filtering the text through the language of The Marx Brothers and similar popular films from the 1920s and 1930s. There's a sense of the cinema being a hall of mirrors, like in Versailles, which constantly reflects a certain language, a certain voice, back at you again and again.

EL: Yes, and it's the voice of television too, which is an offshoot of what you're describing. You see, for me, television is such a huge influence.

AQ: And this is the first time that you use flat screen TVs in your work.

EL: Yes. We took the TV and went (clap), we squashed it. As soon as I saw one of the those flat-screen TVs, I thought it looked as if somebody had stepped on it and smashed it up. These TVs were like the see-through walls, the glass windows, where you can see everything through them and then this becomes the world. These TVs also captured something about reflections, something around the way light works in our reflections—because you see the flat-screen as a plate of glass at the same time as you see it as something that has depth in it. And I play with this idea.

AQ: When you first opened *To You, the Birdie!* I remember you telling me that the video technology available to you at the time had limited certain ideas that you were wanting to explore.

EL: This often comes back to the problem of money—things being very expensive. You see, I love technology and I'm around it all the time, but I don't know the ins and outs of how it all works. So, often I'll see something that I like and then I'll be told that the technology can't do it. Then, I try desperately to get something close to the idea I had. With *To You, the Birdie!*, I wanted to make the TVs look as though they were completely transparent so you could see through them, as if you could put your hands through the screen and get into the space behind. I wanted them to be like glass, to be transparent and reflective. This was because I wanted to video tape from a certain perspective: the center of the space, from the audiences' point of view. I was interested in the idea that the whole audience could be aware that there was someone at the center who would see directly through or along this line of perspective.

AQ: So, this goes back to the Palace at Versailles and the French court.

EL: Yes. Now, not all the audience would have access to that particular perspective I'd set up, but they would know it was there. This is just like when you're a tourist in Versailles—you know it's created for somebody, even if it's not specifically made for you. Anyhow, it was so difficult to create this sense of transparent glass. We would film material and then it would go through different processes and different software, which would degrade the images. So, in the middle of the rehearsal process I had to rethink this and soften all the imagery, as though the windows might have been frosted. I just changed everything, so you could see through the screen as if the glass was slightly blurred. It worked fine, but now we have the ability to make the screen transparent. The last time we did *To You, the Birdie!* it was clear and it was beautiful.

AQ: How did you create the soundtrack for *To You, the Birdie!*? It feels very intricate and complicated. Was it difficult to put together?

EL: I create the sound by having a lot of different people making contributions —well, I make all the pieces hoping that people will contribute (laughs). When it comes to the sound, most of the ideas aren't mine, they're somebody else's, and I just go, "Oh, I like that." One of the problems in creating the sound for *To You, the Birdie!* was the fact that we had too many cooks at the beginning of the process. We had the guy who had worked on the radio version with Katie, but he found it difficult to work with some of the other people that I wanted to bring in, like David Linton. I wanted to create an overall score, so I brought in Jim Dawson. Then, Jim and I worked with all the music that we had collected together during the rehearsal process, this included a lot of the early material, and we blended it with David Linton's electronic music. Overall it was a very hard process—a big learning experience.

AQ: Watching the rehearsal tapes you rely on the ability of people having certain energies, on their ability to risk bringing ideas in and not worrying about them being accepted or dropped—people being brave enough to bring material in and risk whatever might happen to it.

EL: I depend on this. Every time I approach a project, I am like "Why?" Then, the people in the room tell me why. If they're not there, I am not there.

AQ: There are a couple of moments in the rehearsals of *To You, the Birdie!* where you are clearly frustrated with the fact that people weren't offering ideas to you.

EL: Yes, yes. People weren't coming forward so much, and that made it very difficult. Katie was trying, but every time she would come forward, I wouldn't want what she was bringing, which was very painful. I was battling to get some irony into a sincere performance and an idiotic text.

AQ: This comes back to this problem of finding the right mask for the performance.

EL: I think that was the struggle there.

AQ: Kate has talked about the liberating moment of using the in-ear device. It's fascinating that in one of the rehearsals Frances is trying to persuade Kate to take the in-ear out.

EL: Fran was going around to everyone and saying, "Take the earpiece out—rebel, rebel!," which I loved. That was exactly what I was looking for in Frances' performance.

AQ: Because Oenone is so rebellious in the play?

EL: Yes. So, I needed to channel this rebellious energy in her actual performance. Frances would be great in rehearsals, because she was really rebelling against me. But then, when we would go into a performance, she would suddenly become an actress and all that fun and naughtiness, which was directed at me, would disappear. I would say, "What happened to that energy you had in rehearsal?" I knew she was acting, that she was kidding me. I wanted to retain that quality she had in rehearsal in the performance. I always plan on keeping something of the rehearsal and something of the performance and bringing them into play together to create that energy, which is the link between rehearsals and performance.

AQ: The fact that it's you giving the instructions to the performers via the in-ear device seems to make perfect sense in *To You, the Birdie!* ...

EL: I don't do it in any other piece; I have no desire to.

AQ: This device seems connected to the operations of reflection and perspective that we touched on earlier. You know, the point of view of the director, the ideal spectator in the audience: the King's seat, as it were. I know it's a secret, the way you talk directly to the performers—it's not like you're at the edge of the stage conducting the action like Kantor did.

EL: It's all a secret, even from the people sitting next to me.

AQ: In the interview with Kate she says that she realized that she missed the presence of your voice, that your voice, that your instructions, were the most vibrant and most interesting thing in the room and that's why she

needed the in-ear: to hear this voice live in performance.

EL: I think this came out of a certain frustration, because Katie was insecure about who she was on stage. Because of this insecurity, she didn't trust that she could dance at the beginning. I think she felt exposed when she didn't have the actual language. But you know, it kind of started because I was desperately trying to teach everyone certain dance moves as a way to watch the badminton. I wanted them to watch the game as if it were happening for real—I wanted the head move, you know, as it follows the shuttlecock, to have a certain torque. But, this couldn't be acted. When they did the move on their own it lacked something. You could see thought instead of reactive instinct.

AQ: This notion of the reactive impulse, it's very important in your work. There's something real here, isn't there?

EL: Yes. So I needed to get them to turn so it looked like it wasn't controlled, like they weren't planning it like actors showing the audience that they were pretending to watch the shuttlecock. I wanted it to be so organic, so spontaneous, that the audience would look in the same direction as the turn, as if they had missed something. The only way I knew how to create this was to get on the in-ears and give the actors a specific signal. When I did this it was like magic. In this extremely turgid piece, I could now bring in this sort of impulsive action. The audience would not be aware of how this was actually being created, but they would get an overall sense of it and feel the lack of control that comes with this impulsive action. I like to set things up and steer them out of control.

AQ: I remember you talking about this in relation to the actors responding to the material that's on the TV monitors that the audience doesn't get to see. You describe it as something between imitation and sketching. You seem to want the performer to be working off the material in a way that allows them to bring a certain abstraction to their response. The relationship is natural, but a little off-kilter, but always done in real time.

EL: Yes, doing something in real time.

AQ: It's hard for actors, isn't it?

EL: Well, it depends on the actors. It's not hard for Scott or Ari (Fliakos); it's not hard for Katie. They do it naturally because it's really the basis of great acting. I think the problem for a lot of stage acting is that it's so often concerned with the actor's desire to make sure that he or she is connecting with the audience. So, there's always this little thing, this patronizing thing, that they are always one little second ahead of the audience, telling them what they should feel and what is coming next. I don't want performers to be responsible for this. This should be the responsibility of the piece as whole, it's not down to individual performers.

AQ: So the ego of the performer has to push to the back?

EL: In some ways, in other ways it's pure narcissism. You have to have a certain kind of narcissism because you have to trust that the audience will watch whatever you do. A lot of actors have egoism, but they don't have this kind of narcissism. Maybe, the egoism comes from film, where the actors always want to make sure that they are doing something important—this so different to the narcissist, who simply doesn't care.

AQ: This is quite a demand that you're making of actors—to relinquish that control.

EL: A lot of people I work with can't do it, especially performers new to the company. For instance, Frances wouldn't wear the in-ear device, she refused point blank—not that I demanded it of her. It was offered to everyone and everybody wanted to use it, except Frances. But for me, the fact that she didn't take up the offer was brilliant.

AQ: Because of the role she was playing?

EL: Partly, yes. But also because, without the in-ear, she's the only one who doesn't know what's going on. She's not in control because I can tell people on stage that she's in the wrong place and I can have them move her, change her position—so she has to respond to the impulse.

AQ: So, you are getting her to do it anyway.

EL: Yes, but don't tell her (laughs).

AQ: That's a great director's trick.

EL: It was for me. She will never forgive me for it, but she knows now.

There for the taking

An interview with Elizabeth LeCompte (New York, September 24th, 2006)

Andrew Quick (AQ): I wanted to close by asking you some general questions about your work, which spans some thirty years or so. I'm intrigued as to the way your approach is so pragmatic: the different ways in which you always use what's in the room with you. But, I'm wondering if there are other things, maybe general principles, that you never make compromises with—I'm thinking of things that might be outside or beyond the rehearsal room.

EL: Well, there are certain things I notice that I am attracted to and I guess I make lots of compromises all of the time. I mean, this is such a ragged business and there is no idea of perfection.

AQ: Theater can't be perfect?

EL: No. You cannot control it. If I have learned anything over the years, it's that you have to let things go. In answer to your question, the one thing that I really enjoy is that I like to watch people do what they like to do, when they don't know that they like to do it. If people say that they like a text and then all they do is show me the text, I'm not interested. But if they are deeply involved in and really interested in the text, like its ideas, I could listen to them forever: it doesn't matter what they do. And it's the same with their bodies. If they are really interested in their bodies and do something that they really have to do—not, "this is what I have got to do as an actor"—I could watch them do anything on stage. So, this is the only thing I kind of try to look for. I try to look for what they want to do and they might not even be aware of it.

AQ: I think this is evident in one of the first rehearsal tapes that I watched. When you had people throw bean bags at the performers in the earliest stages of making *St. Antony*.

EL: Well, if you throw bean bags you see what the performers have to do to survive. And you see what their bodies do when they're not in control of the situation. For me, it's a way of getting to know them.

AQ: Maybe you're always throwing bean bags at the performers in different ways in every piece that you make...

EL: In different ways. Exactly. It's the only way for me to find out what they will do naturally, without them thinking about what they look like. I like to get at what's at the root: where's the real pleasure, where's the real impulse? I mean this is not an intellectual thing for me, I suppose I just think it's natural.

AQ: I am aware that people, especially academics, are always keen to ask you about your use of technology, to find a general principle or theoretical reason for the way you engage with technology in your work. This is interesting, because I can now see that you have a very pragmatic relationship to technology.

EL: I think the problem here is that I don't come from a theater background; I connect much more to art, television and popular culture. It never occurred to me that you had to have an idea why you wanted to use technology: for me, it's just if you like it, you use it. I also think one of the problems, especially when I first started, is that a lot of the people in theater weren't ever interested in technology—that's why they went to theater. And if it did get used it was to reveal how terrible it was, how it was destroying the world. Whereas for me, it's just another thing in the room, it's another thing we are dealing with all the time in our lives. So, why keep it out?

AQ: It seems that you're often drawn to the televisual, rather than to theater.

EL: Well, that's what I had as a child growing up in southern New Jersey: TV and books. I mean, my mother took us to Broadway shows, but, you know, I didn't even see many films as a child. So, in some specific way, television was very important to me—it's important to a lot of Americans. It's strange, because most people who were involved in theater, they didn't like television, they were interested in higher art. They were focused on the writing, what the text said. You see, I just sort of stumbled into the theater—probably because of Spalding (Gray). I don't think I would have ever chosen to do this without Spalding—it was him that basically hooked me into all this. I was attracted to Spalding because he was in this weird thing too: theater. I was constantly saying, "What is this?" In other words, my way into all this, my approach, wasn't at all traditional. I think this is a good way to find new forms, to find a new way of seeing.

AQ: Something of what you're saying reminds me of Andy Warhol. His work seems deeply connected to books and to TV.

EL: Absolutely, and popular culture. In some ways his background was very similar to my own. He was in Pittsburgh, a small town. My mother sent me to the local art school because I could draw and so I think I went in a similar direction. You know, I had the same kind of weird feelings about myself in that small town and also I had the same impulse and input. My mother tried to get me to study literature, but I couldn't write, I would draw.

AQ: Although you're nearly always working with texts, you don't actually write text do you?

EL: Never. I can't even read texts before we do them because I get so bored.

AQ: But you always get people to read them for you in the space. This seems to be repeated in every piece that I have looked at. I remember you saying somewhere, "I need people who allow me to look up and not down at the script."

EL: That's right. I look at the script, but not until very late on in the rehearsals —when I have got the overall picture. Then I go to the script. But it's usually a year into rehearsals before I really look at the script—I looked at the script of *Hamlet* four months ago, after I'd been working on it for a year and a half. So, I've been watching *Hamlet* and saying, "Where is that? What does that mean? I didn't get that." Instead of reading it, I go, "I didn't understand that." And it's not an intellectual thing. It's boredom. I can't read these texts. It's also a form of problem solving. I guess I have said this many times, "How do I hear it? How do I hear it—me—personally? How can I hear it?" I haven't read it, so I can't understand it that way. I want to hear it in order to understand it. I want to hear it because I don't approach it intellectually.

AQ: But there is method in your approach.

EL: Yes, but it's not intellectual—Katie's much more intellectual than me. She'll say, "We're missing a vital part of the plot if we cut this." And I'll go, "Oh, really? I don't hear it that way." I am not looking for logic in the text. I am listening for me—this isn't necessarily logical. Katie's very logical and if I miss something she goes, "Whoa, we can't do that." And then we have this thing where I say, "Well, do we really need it?" And sometimes she will drag me back, so I will put it in. Scott's (Shepherd) the same. He'll say, "We can't lose that," and I say, "Why not?" I feel like I am a computer, if stuff gets deleted I go, "Tut, tut—did it ever exist?" This isn't intellectual. I don't know quite what it is. I just don't hang on to that particular part of the meaning.

AQ: This isn't random...

EL: No, I don't just cut things out randomly. I mean, I definitely hang on to the words. But I don't mind losing certain things to make the whole better. And that is what I think I am saying: that I am very aware, unlike Scott or Katie, of the whole. They like every detail. But I feel if it interferes with the whole, which I try to take from the writer or whatever the source is, then I can let it go.

AQ: Is this because for you theater is a visual medium where the writing isn't always at the center?

EL: I don't think theater is about writing, but a lot of people do. And these people make good work as well, but it's not my way.

AQ: It seems strangely appropriate that after thirty plus years that you have come to *Hamlet*: the play that many people claim marks the beginning of modern theater.

EL: I know. I would never have got to *Hamlet*, except through Scott. It's the same with Katie. Katie has taken me to almost everything that I have looked at. She took me to the Eugene O'Neill plays. I'd never have gone to *The Emperor Jones*, without thinking about her identification with the blackface. You see, I get taken to things. Often, the things that I do for myself just aren't as interesting (laughs).

AQ: But you organize the material in a very particular way, don't you?

EL: Yes. I am just saying that I wouldn't be doing all this if people didn't say, "I want to do this." I would be drawing alone in the studio.

AQ: But there is a definite sense of a signature to this work, isn't there?

EL: Well, sort of. I have a certain way of working and it comes through in all my work, it affects everything I make. But when I say me I mean me as part of this collective thing, which is The Wooster Group. The collective mutates all the time; this is the nature of The Wooster Group. It is always a reflection of me and Katie and now Ari and Scott and whoever is closest to the center of making the work. The group is always changing and mutating.

AQ: But, you have been the one person who has constantly been there from the start.

EL: Yes, I'm the only one who has been constantly there from the beginning, so that dominates. But as the people who were originally in the group have fallen away the work has been infiltrated by other's sensibilities. Now Katie, Scott and Ari are incredibly influential in the same way that Spalding and Ron were when we first started out. It's not me alone—it's the world that I make, that I gather together, with the others.

AQ: And The Performing Garage has been a constant space for you?

EL: It's been a huge thing. I think one of the main reasons we are as we are is because I initially developed as a kind of visual artist. So, there's this idea of working in a studio alone and making something. It's funny because when I am working at the Garage I feel that I am working alone. I feel that I am alone in there and that all these people are... like... ideas in my head—like the way people worked in studios in the past. In many ways it's thanks to Richard (Schechner) that I'm here—Spalding, as well. They showed me that I could do with other people what I had previously tried to do on my own. They took me here.

Only pragmatics?

Andrew Quick

> **Elizabeth LeCompte** Is it that you want to know how we construct the set? I can answer that.
> **Questioner** That's only pragmatics.
> **Elizabeth LeCompte** *Only* pragmatics?[1]

A workbook is always going to focus on pragmatics, on everyday practices that are somehow brought into play when putting a performance together. As the questioner above illustrates, there is often a skeptical response to pragmatics, especially within academic circles, as if a direct engagement with the processes of making work, what might be called the "doing" of performance, is avoiding those larger issues of meaning and context. LeCompte's playful retort, "*Only* pragmatics?" which so disarmed the dramaturg that was attempting to locate The Wooster Group's work within what he termed "the socio-cultural contexts of downtown New York," can be interpreted as the conventional refusal of the experimental artist to explain their work. However, LeCompte's insistence on engaging with the pragmatics of making and doing, as a means to speak about her practice, gestures towards significant ways in which we might critically encounter the five performances that make up this book that have often been overlooked in previous attempts to negotiate The Wooster Group's work.

Across the interviews that accompany each of the enclosed documentary sections, LeCompte and Valk repeatedly describe a performance making practice that is primarily based on problem solving. Work takes place around who is in the room, the material brought into the room and what constitutes the history of The Wooster Group during any particular (often lengthy) period of rehearsal. History is rarely thought of in abstract terms. It is made manifest in the materiality of objects, in the skeletal structures of the sets that are continuously returned to and re-worked across many of the performance pieces. Each rehearsal period begins with the almost ritualistic act of laying out the set design of the previous work and re-orientating it in some dynamic way. Words such as stretched, lifted, dropped, rotated and reversed describe how the footprint of the room, or the double room, which has dominated LeCompte's vision from the very beginning, appears again and again. This return to the specific designs of past works can be seen in LeCompte's journal entries for *House/Lights* (1999) (p. 181) where, although separated by eleven years, the basic scenic layout of *Frank Dell's The Temptation of St. Antony* (1987) is revealed as a reference point around which design choices are being negotiated.

In this sense, each new Wooster Group set is as a kind of palimpsest, where the clean straight lines of metal and light are, in fact, built on top of the scar tissue of all the previous works. Scratch away at these designs and you inevitably find the faint imprint of the architectural layout of The Performing Garage itself: The Wooster Group's home for close to thirty years and the space in which all the work has been made. And the archaeological digging does not end here, because written into The Performing Garage is also the model and history of theater, with its spatial divisions, its mechanisms of representation, its traditions, its manipulation of sound and light, its practices of play and its complex relationship to the operations of illusion. Digging deeper still, we might speculate that theater somehow harks back to the rooms, real and psychological, out of which we make and imagine ourselves, those domestic spaces (the houses) that fashion and shape how we begin and what we become.

Animating the room

Looking back at the accounts of The Wooster Group's first body of work – LeCompte's collaborations with Spalding Gray and others in *Three Places in Rhode Island* (*Sakonnet Point* [1975], *Rumstick Road* [1977], *Nayatt School* [1978])—it appears that this interplay between theater and domestic space has been there right from the beginning. In these pieces, the various domestic places of Gray's childhood are superimposed upon and interwoven with LeCompte's engagement with the mechanisms of theatricality as a practical means to "confront," rather than represent, the material generated and negotiated in the rehearsal process.[2] The house/theater is not organized as a site of quiet contemplation, a place where personal memory, conflict and tragedy can be easily identified, communicated and resolved. In these works, the interleaving of house and theater prompts a disorientating form of animation. Here, memories and events are encountered through the practical interaction of texts, bodies and objects in and with space, in and with time. This animation, this making mobile, in which all the elements in play are rarely permitted to synchronize, not only undermines the foundations of domesticity (the site of our identity creation) but also the possibility of theater as a system to secure or ground representation (as form or meaning).

This delicate imbrication of house and theater is clearly evident in all the works documented in this book. It is there in the split levels that make up the scenic design of *Frank Dell's The Temptation of St. Antony* (1987), where the downstairs hotel room occupied by Frank is juxtaposed with the room upstairs in which a magic show is being performed. It ghosts in *Brace Up!* (1991), as Chekhov's domestic space is transformed into a kind of micro-theater—a steel-framed box, which facilitates a practical engagement with the text of *Three Sisters* (p. 85). The idea of a theater company attempting to stage *Three Sisters*, which forms a barely discernable layer in *Brace Up!*, becomes much more explicit in *Fish Story* (1994), where shards of the last act of Chekhov's play are interwoven with *Geinin* (1977), a documentary account of the day-to-day activities of the Sentaro Ichikawa Troupe from Japan. In *To You, the Birdie! (Phèdre)* (2002), the domestic drama of Racine's royal court is played out on a stage constructed from an elongated version of the *Brace Up!* set, which echoes not only the Noh-influenced scenography of the earlier work, but also the streamlined grandeur of modernist Californian architecture. In *House/Lights* (1999) the concept of domesticity is invoked through the use of television monitors as windows, the sofa that slides on and off the set and the coffee tables that balance precariously on the ends of the pivoting ramps. The separation of the stage into two film-like frames, created by the placing of parallel dotted lines across the depth of the space (a reference to the sprocket holes in a spool of cine-film) also reworks the juxtaposition and overlaying of rooms that is a feature of these and earlier works.

What might be at stake in this doubling, in these acts of destabilization, in this apparent emphasis on confrontation and encounter? One response to this question is to suggest that the different works contained and referred to in this book explore the various ways in which we fashion ourselves in the world: how we are formed, and form ourselves, as subjects. After all, if being is a form of dwelling (to borrow from Heidegger), then the shaking of the foundations of domestic and theatrical space would seem to speak of some profound displacement of selfhood.[3] This would be a convenient thematic in which to "house" The Wooster Group's work. It would certainly link with those approaches that have attempted to place their performances within particular philosophically informed critiques of presence. It would also mirror the many attempts to explain their work through the twin lenses of deconstruction and postmodernity—approaches that have always placed a certain emphasis on the idea of the de-centered subject.[4] Similarly, to engage with theater's failure as a representational system would probably return us to these very same critical reference points. After all, so much deconstructive energy has been expended in order to expose the limits of representational systems, to reveal how these systems function to make everything intelligible and how they exclude and erase all that cannot be contained within their various operations.

Without wishing to dismiss such contextualization, I want to identify what I consider to be less iconoclastic and more affirmative practices in The Wooster Group's work. LeCompte's insistence on pragmatics in relation to her performance practice draws our attention to the activities of doing, rather than undoing, to the processes of production, rather than reproduction and to the experience of negotiation, rather than explication. Indeed, what is at stake in these works is the attempt to create a direct and lived relationship with material as it is encountered. This accounts for why LeCompte and Valk, in their different ways, insist on a suspension of the performer's ego, why a particular emphasis is constantly placed on the performer being open to what is happening in the room (p. 162). Consequently, The Wooster Group's pragmatics engage with the mechanisms of theater to produce what, for want of a better word, we might call experience: experience that presents itself as a series of happening nows, as occurrences, as presences that resist being folded back into meaning (what LeCompte refers to as the "ordinary" or, the "literal").

This insistence on being open to the materiality of performance, to everything that is confronted within the performance, to the extraordinary, is distinctly ethical. It is built on the performers' ability to relinquish themselves entirely to what is happening in the room, to respond without the safety blanket of predetermined thinking: in short, to "be" in relation to what is encountered. This seems a long way from those descriptions of a post-modern stage in which truth is banished, forsaken for the ironic play of endless simulation. In these performance works, the truth, the "to be" of the encounter, emerges in the *act* of confronting the material, rather than in an excavatory practice that would pull the truth from hidden depths. As LeCompte explains in an early interview, "I don't learn, I search."[5] This searching is founded on a deep respect for the material that is brought into the room. This includes the dramatic texts that are always put to work in the performances: in this book, these are the words and dramaturgical structures of Flaubert, Chekhov, Stein and Racine. Far from overpowering this material, this demand for openness entails an engagement that is not prescribed. It is a searching for those multiple possibilities and outcomes, which are identified, explored and shared in rehearsal and, most important of all, in front of and with the audience as well.

The art of confrontation

Confrontation should not be seen as an act of aggression towards the material that makes up the work or audience that watches it, although, in the past, The Wooster Group have sometimes been accused of this.[6] Confrontation is a mode of dealing with the material at hand, keeping it on the move and always, somehow, alive in the very process of its negotiation. As Valk puts it, "Liz always has this bottom line, which is us encountering the material" (p. 217). It is a doing that arises out of a practical encounter with everything that finds itself in the rehearsal space during the work's making. This matter of (and in) performance cannot be reduced to the dramatic text, although a specific play-text is often one of the key components. It is produced by, and attaches itself to, whomever and whatever is brought into the room. It circulates around the personal histories of all those involved in the making process and it is generated through the ways in which these participants interact with the texts, props, costumes, technologies (audio and televisual) and specific performance practices, which are often returned to and developed in each of the individual pieces. This explains why LeCompte is always at pains to acknowledge the collective nature of The Wooster Group, how it is energized by the shifting sensibilities that work within its compass. For LeCompte, the worlds that are made are never created in isolation: "it's not me alone." Rather, these worlds are always gathered together, "with the others" (p. 268).

The Wooster Group's multiple interactions with the texts, props, technologies, costumes and so forth ensure that the materials and objects used in these performances are always marked by use. This is evident in the repeated appearance of particular props that often have a utilitarian, rather than a decorative, function. These include tables, televisions, lamps, fabrics, costumes, screens, chairs, as well as the more obvious recycling of the larger scenographic elements outlined above. Many of these objects are also marked by histories that indicate a life before and outside of The Wooster Group. This can be seen, for example, in the antique lamps used on-stage in *Brace Up!*, *Fish Story* and *House/Lights* (these lamps also appear in *Point Judith* [1979] and *Route 1 & 9* [1981]), which seem to invoke a period of North American vernacular design that combined forms of classicism and modernism (perhaps, a nostalgic nod to an America that was confident in expressing how it had superseded an older and less economically successful Europe). These objects are marked by a history of domestic use that precedes the formation of The Wooster Group. They carry the imprints of the everyday activities of other users, which, although having had a life before the rehearsal process, inevitably ghost into the Group's work. Such objects also function to remind us that in the encountering of props, bodies, technologies, sounds, texts and televisual/film images in these performances, we not only confront their various material presences, but the wider social and public histories that have formed them as well.

It should come as no surprise, then, that much of the documentation that makes up this book is similarly marked by use. Each of the documentary sections is made up of texts, performance scores and choreographies that are the outcomes of a constant rewriting, re-scoring and re-editing. These re-writings, which can be seen in the multiple examples of scribblings, notations, jottings, listings, sketches, in the patchwork of post-it notes and the thick tracery of amendments on performance scores, explicitly mark the temporal development of each work as it constructed, layer by layer. These are the textual and visual relics of a performance making process that is constantly in flux; a process that, as is made evident in the transcripts and accounts of LeCompte's notes to the actors (p. 53), continues throughout the work's performance to audiences and also across the histories of individual pieces. This demand to keep everything that is developed in rehearsal in play, in motion, in what Valk calls "the present," accounts for the seemingly obsessive recording of actions and decisions that scar so many of these documents. Consider, for example, the Assistant Director's scores for *House/Lights* (pp. 174–180) and *To You, the Birdie! (Phèdre)* (pp. 252–254), which depict not only the intricate relationship that exists between the different components of the performance (sound, video, performer actions etc.) but also how the work is continually tuned and tweaked as it is composed. Often, the writings on these documents seem to bear the signs of their author's energetic engagement with the compositional process. This is starkly apparent in the scribblings that make up the early technical score for *Brace Up!* (pp. 88–90). Here, Chekhov's script is almost obliterated by the chaotic tapestry of sound and video cues, which is etched onto its pages. Similarly, the Post-it notes that crowd around Paul Schmidt's translation in the score of *To You, the Birdie! (Phèdre)* seem to be a documentary response to the complex process of layering and juxtaposition that forms the structure of the piece, where all the major elements can be re-arranged and re-ordered as they are developed and tested out in rehearsal.

It is possible to view the documentation in this book as the by-product of the individual and collective attempts to impose a system on a process that is, by its very nature, difficult to control. What is fascinating about many of these documents are the ways in which they illustrate the desire to choreograph and place absolutely everything: to enforce some sense of order, or sustain a lost presence. This should not come as a surprise because theater production is, by necessity, highly disciplined. It relies on the capacity to repeat with a great deal of accuracy. This is especially true of its technologies, which impress certain types of logical systems on all genres of performance: these logics are evident in the many sound and video cue sheets, in the props lists, in the performance scores that juxtapose live action against the running orders of sound, light and video. If these documents stage an attempt to control material, they also reveal, through the signs of their constant scorings and amendments, how the process of composing the performance is never entirely fixed. It is important to point out that these documents also have a practical relationship to The Wooster Group's organizational make up—how the Group, although economically able to sustain a full-time company across the long period of an individual piece's development, are often faced with the problem of having to change both on and off stage personnel because their basic wages are relatively low (people have to supplement their income by other means). Documentation becomes a key mode of record-keeping and communication that helps solve the difficulty of having different people entering and leaving the making process. The function of documentation does not end here, however. The documents in this book also reveal how important the activity of documentation is to The Wooster Group's compositional methodology, how the practices of notation, recording, transcribing and copying are put to use in constructing the work. In this sense, the documents that make up this book are not merely illustrations or representations of the multiple and complex ways in which these performances are put together. They are much more than the residues, or the leftovers, of practice. These documents signal the ways in which the practices of documentation are used as key tools for creating and composing the work. In short, documentation has an important creative purpose.

One very obvious example of this is given by Valk in her explanation of how the Group arrived at the idea of using LeCompte's live spoken directions, via the in-ear transmitter/receiver, in the performance of *To You, the Birdie! (Phèdre)* (p. 162). As LeCompte and Valk both acknowledge, the speaking of simultaneously heard text has featured in many of the performance pieces: it is at work in Ron Vawter's lip-synching of the recorded conversation between Spalding Gray and his father in *Rumstick Road*; Nancy Reilly speaks the lines of Ann Rower, Timothy Leary's babysitter, as she hears them through a Walkman in *L.S.D. (...Just the High Points...)* (1984); Vawter and other performers periodically repeat, and improvise from, Reilly's reading of Flaubert's *The Temptation of Saint Anthony* in the making of the "Channel J" video, which forms the opening monologue of *Frank Dell's The Temptation of St. Antony*; Kate Valk is listening to a recording of *Doctor Faustus Lights the Lights* (1938) via an in-ear transmitter as she says Gertrude Stein's lines in *House/Lights*. In all these pieces, this technique is used to bring documentary material directly into play in the rehearsal and/or performance, providing a source text that can be mediated via the performer, or used as a basis for improvisation. In the case of *To You, the Birdie! (Phèdre)*, Valk describes how she uses the video recording of a particular moment in a rehearsal in order to learn and repeat a set of specific moves. While watching the tape, she realizes that it is LeCompte's directions, which are being shouted from the back of the space, that are making the room "dynamic." It is through a careful scrutiny of the rehearsal tape that she comes to comprehend what, as she describes, "was really happening in the room." To re-create this "happening", she requests that LeCompte's voice be introduced to feed live responses and directions into the ears of performers as they move and speak on the stage. In this performance, it is LeCompte's whispered instructions that Valk finds liberating, that provide the impulse for her to have a "present" relationship with the material.

Valk's account of how the Group arrived at the decision to make use of LeCompte's live instructions in *To You, the Birdie (Phèdre)* provides a very useful insight, not only into the complex ways that documentation is put to use in The Wooster Group's work, but also as to what might be at stake in the need to be present in these performances. Valk returns to the director's voice at this vital stage in the development of the piece in order to free herself from the act of repetition that is making the performance feel forced and constraining. LeCompte's directions, made in response to what she is watching, oblige the performer to react impulsively, without recourse to doing something that is learned or habitual. It is somewhat ironic that it is the words of the director, traditionally *the* authoritarian figure in the theater, who initiates these unrehearsed and spontaneous actions. Of course, LeCompte's scenic landscapes are often organized to keep the key performance elements in motion, to ensure that the room is "kinetic," as Valk puts it (p. 219). This begins to explain why the sets are often constructed like obstacle courses, why they are arranged as spaces in which it is difficult for the actor to find secure points of rest. Consider, for example, the performers who are tied to the doors in *St. Antony*; the two ramps that are continually swiveled (and "crashed") across the space of *House/Lights*; the actors' feet that are fastened to their backs by bungee cords in *Fish Story* (p. 145); the bound arms and physical restraints imposed on the performers in *To You, the Birdie! (Phèdre)*. The performer's relationship in these spaces is always one of active negotiation, an encounter in which the scenic landscape is never fully mastered. The demand that the performer relinquish certain key elements of control is an important feature in this work. Nowhere is this more tellingly revealed than in the description of the actors having to perform while having beanbags hurled at them during a rehearsal of *St. Antony*. In doing this, as LeCompte explains, you learn what performers have to "do to survive," you "see what their bodies do when they're not in control of the situation" (p. 267).

Survival practices

Across the five pieces of work documented in this book, LeCompte returns to a number of key practices that compel the performer to relinquish their control in the playing space, which induce the production of "survival" techniques. She often sets up choreographic rules that performers have to follow while they deliver the lines, participate in the dramatic narrative, or be in the space. For example, in *Brace Up!* LeCompte tells us how she divided the space into three separate sections: middle, back and foreground. These spaces demanded a different type of movement that had to be dropped and then adopted as a performer passed through each division (this separation of the space is clearly marked out on LeCompte's sketch of *Brace Up!* on p. 83). Specific movement sequences taken from Noh Theater books were also used to construct choreographic patterns (described by Valk as "the grammar of the feet"), which were interwoven with *Three Sisters*. According to LeCompte, the demands made by following these choreographic rules stopped the action from becoming literal; they prevented the performer from always having a psychological (and, by implication, a readable) relationship to Chekhov's text.

It is clear, however, that the introduction of Noh movement patterns also worked to disorientate the performer in the space. This might sound contradictory, as one would expect the strictly organized choreographic structures of Noh Theater to impose order (establish orientation), rather than create disjuncture and displacement. The performer's disorientation, it seems, arises out of the discontinuity that is created from having to move between the highly focused demands made by the Noh choreography and the spatial rules imposed upon the performing area and the representational logistics of Chekhov's dramaturgy, where character and psychological motivation are still in play. It is the move between these distinct modalities of performance that creates the kinetic energy that Valk and LeCompte both invoke. It is an energy that arises from the performers having to navigate their way through the scenic landscape, continually having to re-orient themselves as a reaction to the shifting demands made upon them as they move and/or speak within the space. Hence, the emphasis placed on completing physical tasks, on the act of doing, rather than on what the action represents. This mode of performance necessitates, as Ron Vawter (who played Vershinin in *Brace Up!*) explains, "such consciousness and such concentration." Crucially, it is this concentration, created by the obligation to fulfill and embody the physical tasks, and to follow the complex and layered score, that keeps the work "open" for Vawter. As he describes, it is the very difficulty of the physical demands made by the work and the mental effort required to perform it that keeps it "open and alive."[7]

Similar choreographic structures are put into play in *House/Lights*, where the text of Gertrude Stein's *Doctor Faustus Lights the Lights* is interwoven with Joseph Mawra's B-movie *Olga's House of Shame*. As in *Brace Up!*, the stage is divided into sections, although in this performance the separations are two adjacent spaces marked by dotted lines, which are taped across the depth of the playing area (see LeCompte's journal entries on p. 181 and the set diagram on p. 182). These areas are used by the performers to mirror actions, sometimes choreographing their movements in response to what another performer is doing in the parallel space, often imitating the physical actions of *Olga's House of Shame*, seen on TV monitors that are placed to the sides and above the audience. During rehearsals, as both LeCompte and Valk explain (p. 217), performers were encouraged to create physical action while watching the film in a number of ways. They could respond and channel an element of the film's composition at a particular moment: close-up, long shot, camera movement, edits and so forth (for example, a close-up might generate a move to the front of the stage, a long-shot a move to the back). Or, they could imitate a movement of a character on the film (this could be a move of the head, a particular gesture, or action). In her journals, LeCompte notes that the necessity to channel their response to the film always positions the performer as either being a little behind the action and having to follow it; or, in a state of anticipating the action: being a little ahead of it (p. 170). LeCompte seems to be identifying with, and producing a practical response to, Stein's observation that action on the stage is usually "syncopated," where the spectator's emotional relationship to the scene is of a different temporal order to that which is taking place on the stage. Stein writes, "I say your emotion concerning that play is always either behind or ahead of the play at which you are looking and listening. So your emotion as a member of the audience is never going on at the same time as the action of the play."[8] LeCompte's introduction of delayed and/or anticipated responses into the scenic landscape moves the performer into a similar emotional and temporal relationship to the action that is occurring on the stage. In this sense, LeCompte produces an extraordinary reversal, where the performer is put in the position of Stein's spectator, becoming a looker and a listener, rather than being a master of the material. This is a state of syncopation, not synchronization. Here, the performer is always on the offbeat and always out of time, arriving, like a jazz musician, at the unexpected accent. It is the emotional sensation, an embodied affect, produced by being in this state that, as Stein reminds us, "makes one endlessly troubled about a play."

LeCompte extends this interplay with technology a little further in *To You, the Birdie! (Phèdre)*. At specific points in the performance, the performers compose physical actions by imitating particular sequences extracted from dance pieces by Martha Graham and Merce Cunningham that are played on TV monitors, which are positioned out of the audience's sight. In these instances, however, a new dynamic is introduced. The video operator can manipulate, or "scratch" the images. This ensures that the performer always has to react to the moment-by-moment technical improvisation with this visual material, which, in turn, compels a spontaneous and impulsive reaction to take place on the stage. Once again, the interaction with technology is instrumental in keeping the performers in a state of heightened awareness, as they have to channel a shifting array of stimuli (visual image, director's voice, the actions of other performers, audio and so forth). In describing how the performer interacts with the television images in *House/Lights*, LeCompte makes it clear that technology is not a mechanical device for her, one that is used to illustrate or explain what is occurring on the stage. She describes how technology always has to be dealt with and negotiated, likening the live interaction with the televisual image to that of encountering another person on the stage: "you have to turn the television into another actor, a participator in the scene with you, one that you can't ever take for granted." Consequently, the performer has to look at the TV as "if it's for the first time" and engage with what is presented without premeditation (p. 217). In rehearsal, the flow of TV images can stimulate a range of responses that can change with each encounter: "One day you might respond to the fact that the camera moves and the next day you might respond to the fact that the person on the film looks in a certain direction" (p. 217).

LeCompte makes it clear in this statement that the performer is not in the thrall of technology, always compelled forensically to reproduce or follow the information that flows from the TVs, through the in-ear devices, that is generated by the soundscape and by the interaction with the set. Rather, the performer has an embodied relationship with the technology and uses it as a means to be present in the space. This is not to say that anything can happen in response to the information that technology produces. The performer's ability to be responsive to the impulses that the interaction with technology generates is always framed within a highly organized choreographic and scenic structure. The presence LeCompte invokes is one that is based on the performer being open to the multiple and complex stimuli that the technology offers, to channel the information and respond experientially and somatically to the encounter with it. Valk describes this process as one that works against "the tendency to generalize and a desire to shape and control things." According to Valk, the systems that LeCompte sets up in the space ensure that rehearsals and performances are approached in the manner of an athlete or game-player. Consequently, you have "to approach the text, the words, the physical score, your relationship with the video and then just respond, just be in the moment with the material." As Valk explains, this induces a state of disconcertion (disarrangement) in the performer, which arrives when something completely new is being experienced: "That's the best state—when you surprise yourself and it's not the way you ever did it before and who knows how it's going to feel" (p. 217). What Valk emphasizes here is the veracity that arises when you let go, or move beyond, predetermined limits. This is the risk that these performances demand: the state of surprise that arrives when one surrenders to the indeterminate.

The ethics of listening

Risk always implies danger. What is imperiled when the performer interacts in the scenic landscapes described above? It would seem that the performer always has to let go of certain habitual ways of being on the stage in order to bear the impress of the experiential and to discover what might really be there. As LeCompte explains in the final interview in this book: "I like to get at what's at the root: where's the real pleasure, where's the real impulse?" (p. 267). When Valk speaks about what might be at the 'root' of her own mode of performance in these works, she often invokes the metaphor and the physical reality of the mask to describe a means for moving beyond her own desire to generalize and control. According to Valk, the mask can appear in many guises. It is most obvious in the use of blackface in *Route 1 & 9* (1981), *L. S. D. (...Just the High Points...)* and *The Emperor Jones* (1993), but it is also at work in the persona of the facilitator in *Brace Up!* and *Fish Story*, and in the on-stage relationship with the video camera, the TV monitors and in-ear technologies in *House/Lights* and *To You, the Birdie! (Phèdre)*.[9] The mask, however, is not solely a device that disguises and hides the personality of the performer. Nor can it be explained as a Brechtian device to expose how the operations of power and ideology shape social structures through the non-psychological medium of *gestus*. The mask has three functions. It establishes a sense of distance between the performer and the audience, creating a barrier between a two-way process of potential psychological identification: the performer with the audience and the audience with the performer. The mask also pushes aside the burden of always having psychologically to embody the character that is formed in the fictional world being negotiated on the stage. Finally, and perhaps most important of all, the mask works to displace the performer's construction of their own subjectivity, the requirement *psychologically* to be themselves on stage. In this sense, the mask operates as a means through which the performer is able to let certain notions of the self fall away. This leaves the performer free to engage as immediately as is possible with what the stage presents to them. In an unpublished interview from 1991, Valk explains this process by referring to the function of the mask in Noh Theater: "They say the mask is the device that allows for 'spiritual possession' because you deny your own self by donning the mask, and then you deny the existence of the mask." In the Noh tradition, the mask acts as a barrier to the representation of a performer's subjectivity. Then, in a crucial second stage, where the mask itself is denied, the performer moves into the complete state of dispossession (thus able to be spiritually possessed), which allows contact with the immediacy (the reality) of the on-stage experience. This is why the use of the mask is such a liberating device for Valk: "You truly discover through this two-step process of denial—first by denying your own physicality, and then by going a step further within your own consciousness to deny the existence of the mask." [10]

The worlds created by The Wooster Group are places for discovery, for searching and for finding out. In the act of surrendering a certain construction of selfhood something else is created in its place. What is being described here is not the eviscerated or dehumanized performer, where the will of the actor is always subjugated by the machinic operations of LeCompte's scenic organization. In her program notes written for the performance of *Fish Story* at the Vienna Festival in 1993, LeCompte describes one of the functions of the mask in her work in the following terms: "Actors are searching for masks of themselves—not of character. Who they are on stage is who they are on stage—period. They must be more 'themselves' than in life." [11] The implication here is that the interaction with the scenic landscape might reveal something profound about the performer: that it somehow exposes who and what they really are. The "more" of the self is the self that the performance induces, one that, because of the acute demands made by being on the stage, is always more intensely there, always more present, than in everyday life. In short, the act of having to perform on The Wooster Group's various stages produces a profound revelation of self in the very activity of having to give up what the subject thinks s/he knows about her/himself. This notion of heightened awareness (the "more" of the self), that there is always something new to be discovered through the act of performance, is elaborated by Vawter in relation to his performance in *Brace Up!*:

> It wasn't about my ability to impersonate or "be" Vershinin. What was very important was that I find ways of being myself, as best I could, publicly... It's a very difficult thing to describe; I don't even know what this process is. In some ways it's the mystery of my life, and I sort of hope that I die before i discover the answer to it. It's sort of the thing that still makes me want to go on the stage because I'm still trying to figure out what it is I'm doing in front of an audience. There are no lessons to be learned, but I'm still interested in finding out who I am in front of an audience.[12]

For Vawter, his work with The Wooster Group is always concerned with a process of self-revelation, with the need to test out who he is (how to be) in relation to the material that is encountered in the various pieces. His search, which he claims is identical to that of LeCompte's, is "to figure out what's there." What LeCompte, Vawter and Valk are each invoking here is the necessity to have an ethical relationship with what takes place on the stage with and before audiences. The relationship is ethical because to "figure out what's there" entails a willingness (an openness) to surrender themselves to the immediacy that is the experience of what is being encountered. To do this they have to abandon all predetermined modes of thinking, to set aside the rules through which the world might be known (this would be a moral order), to be receptive to what is really happening in the room. Ethics is not necessarily a mode of discovery, although finding out is inevitably part of the ethical process. The openness to experience, to being present provokes a practice of judgment: what to do next, now that I know this; how to be in the future, now that I have had this experience? It is a mode of judgment that proceeds without criteria, one that demands an imaginative or inventive way of responding to the immediacy—the occurrence—of the event that is the performance. This form of ethics, of thinking the future, like the work itself, is always a matter of pragmatics.

In the closing interview in this book, LeCompte tells us how she always has to create an environment in which she is looking into the space, not down at the script or score. Tellingly, she often describes her attention to the space as one of listening, rather than seeing: "How do I hear it? How do I hear it—me—personally?" (p. 268). This explains why all the texts under consideration for a particular performance have to be played with, heard and explored in the space. However, the effort of listening implies something that's markedly different to the act of seeing. This emphasis on the ear indicates that there is something about the present, the experiential, the "thereness" of performance that cannot be accounted for just by the eye. Listening demands an openness to the rhythm, the timbre and to the audible plasticity of occurrences, to what might be taking place beneath the surface appearance of things, to the fullness (the noise) of what is there in the room. This begins to explain how vital The Performing Garage is to The Wooster Group, why LeCompte continually places such an emphasis on engaging with what occurs in the rehearsal space, on the pragmatics of the work's creation. The Garage becomes the epicenter for this process of discovery, of searching, of listening, which is shared by all participants (performers, technicians, composers, stage managers and so forth). The Garage not only produces the sense of continuity and history that a home for the company inevitably provides. It also creates the time for a prolonged enquiry, the time to shift in and out of projects, the time to leave and then return to the room when rehearsals get difficult, the time it takes to search and listen. These kinds of temporality are very precious in a contemporary culture in which time is constantly measured, commodified and fixed by financial exchange. The time needed to explore, to imagine and to listen is becoming increasingly scarce.

Of course, the ultimate aim of engaging with these processes of finding out is to share the experience with audiences: this is the goal of all performance. The presence of the audience also affects what happens in the room. They have to be listened to as well. In some ways, as an audience member, I undergo a similar sense of disorientation to that of the performer as I also watch, listen and feel the effects of the constant movement of sounds, bodies and images that occur on The Wooster Group's stage. Yet, perhaps more importantly, in the act of being in front of these performances, what I bear witness to is the obligation to experience what might be there, to encounter what might be present not only in this room (the theater), but all the rooms and places I inhabit and interact in. What I am reminded of in acknowledging this obligation is that I too might have to be prepared to give up on who I think I am and what I know. Perhaps, this is the work of all performance and of thinking itself: always to be considering what might be possible and then to live up to this imagining. Something of this notion of work is echoed in the closing lines of *Fish Story*. Looking at the nearly empty stage I see Vawter, who is playing Vershinin, on the TV screen, his eyes moist from the glycerin that he has recently dropped into his eyes. Just before he kisses Masha he speaks the following lines, taken from the final act of *Three Sisters*: "We must find a way to join love of work to love of higher things, mustn't we? Well now I must go... I came to say goodbye." The prolonged kiss between Vershinin and Masha that immediately follows these words ends with Olga saying, "Now, now, that's enough" (p. 156). Vawter's image then slowly fades away. This beautiful and moving final moment reminds me to acknowledge not only the transitory nature of performance but also how the work of performance, like thinking itself, is rarely brought to a neat or fully resolved conclusion.

Notes

1 "Enacted Arts Seminar," Kanon Hallen, Copenhagen, Denmark, 1997, transcribed by the author.

2 For an excellent account of the processes and approaches in making *Three Places in Rhode Island*, see David Savran, *Breaking the Rules: The Wooster Group*, New York, Theatre Communications Group, 1988, pp. 47–157.

3 See Martin Heidegger, *Poetry, Language, Thought*, New York, Harper and Row, 1971, pp. 156–157.

4 See, for example, Philip Auslander, *From Acting to Performance: Essays in Modernism and Postmodernism*, London, Routledge, 1997; Michael Vanden Heuvel, *Performing Drama/Dramatizing Performance: Alternative Theater and the Dramatic Text*, Michigan, University of Michigan Press, 1991; Nick Kaye, *Postmodernism and Performance*, London, Palgrave MacMillan, 1994.

5 Lenora Champagne, "Always Starting New: Elizabeth LeCompte," *The Drama Review*, 25: 3, New York, 1981, p. 28.

6 See, for example, Herbert Blau's description of *Route 1 & 9* in *The Audience*, Baltimore, Johns Hopkins University Press, 1990, pp. 267–270.

7 Unpublished interview with Marianne Weems and Cynthia Hedstrom, The Performing Garage, New York, 1991.

8 Gertrude Stein, "Plays," *Last Operas and Plays*, Baltimore, Johns Hopkins University Press, 1995, p. xxix.

9 It is important to acknowledge the different specific uses of the mask in these performances, particularly in relation to blackface. I do not have the space in this conclusion to engage in an analysis of the Group's performance of blackface, although much has been written on the relationship between mask and race in terms of performativity and masquerade that could be pursued in relation to this work. See especially, Homi Bhabha, "Of Mimicry and Man: the Ambivalence of Colonial Discourse," *October* 28, Spring, Cambridge (MA), 1994, pp. 125–133; Gail Ching-Liang Low, *White Skins/Black Masks: representation and colonialism*, London, Routledge, 1996. See also, Frantz Fanon, *Black Skin, White Masks*, London, Paladin, 1970. For an excellent review of The Wooster Group's *The Emperor Jones*, see Charles Isherwood, "An Emperor Who Tops What O'Neill Imagined," *The New York Times*, 14th March, 2006 (http://theater2.nytimes.com/2006/03/14/theater/reviews/14empe.html).

10 Unpublished interview with Marianne Weems and Cynthia Hedstrom, The Performing Garage, New York, 1991.

11 Elizabeth LeCompte, "Notes on Form," originally published in the program for The Wooster Group's performance of *Fish Story* at the Wiener Festwochen in 1993. A version is published in *Felix: A Journal of Media Arts and Communication*, Vol 1, No. 3, New York, 1993. For an electronic version see: www.efelix.org/issue3/Lecompte.html

12 Unpublished interview with Marianne Weems and Cynthia Hedstrom, The Performing Garage, New York, 1991.

Select Wooster Group Bibliography

(for further information and extensive bibliography see www.thewoostergroup.org)

Aronson, A. (1975) "*Sakonnet Point*," *The Drama Review*, 19: 4, 27–35.

______ (1985) "The Wooster Group's *L.S.D. (...Just the High Points...)*," *The Drama Review*, 29: 2, 65–77.

______ (2000) *American Avant-garde Theatre: a history*, London: Routledge.

Auslander, P. (1987) "Toward a Concept of the Political in Postmodern Theatre," *Theatre Journal*, 39: 1, 20–34.

______ (1992) *Presence and Resistance: Postmodernism and Cultural Politics in Contemporary American Performance*, Ann Arbor: University of Michigan Press.

______ (1997) From *Acting to Performance: Essays in Modernism and Postmodernism*, London: Routledge.

Bell, P. (2005) "Fixing the TV: Televisual Geography in the Wooster Group's *Brace Up!*," *Modern Drama*, 48: 3, 565–584.

Bierman, J. (1979) "*Three Places in Rhode Island*," *The Drama Review*, 23: 1, 13–30.

Bottoms, S. (2004) "Wooster Group *Poor Theater*, a Series of Simulacra," *Theatre Journal*, 56: 4, 693–695.

Calhoun, J. (1989) "*The Road to Immortality* and Europe: The Wooster Group Tours *L.S.D. (...Just the High Points...)*," *Theatre Crafts*, 23: 46–49.

Callens, J. (1998) "FinISHed Story: Elizabeth LeCompte's Intercultural Take on Time and Work" in W. Huber & M. Middeke (eds.) *Anthropological Perspectives. Contemporary Drama in English* Vol. 5, Trier: Wissenschaftlicher Verlag, pp. 143–158.

______ (2004) *The Wooster Group and Its Traditions*, Brussels, Belgium: Peter Lang.

Champagne, L. (1981) "Always Starting New: Elizabeth LeCompte," *The Drama Review*, 25: 3, 19–28.

Coco, W. (1982) "Wooster-Group *Route 1 & 9 (the Last Act)*," *Theatre Journal*, 34: 2, 249–251.

Elton, H. (1991) "New City of Angels," *Dance Connection*, 8: 4, 26–39.

Etchells, T. (1999) "Replaying the Tapes of the Twentieth Century: An Interview with Ron Vawter" in T. Etchells *Certain Fragments: Contemporary Performance and Forced Entertainment*, London: Routledge, pp. 84–93.

Euridice, A. (1992) "Island Hopping: Rehearsing the Wooster Group's *Brace Up!*" *The Drama Review*, 36: 4, 121–142.

Foreman, R. and LeCompte, E. (1999) "Off-Broadway's Most Inventive Directors Talk About Their Art" in G. Rabkin (ed.) *Richard Foreman*, Baltimore, MD: Johns Hopkins University Press, pp. 133–142.

Giesekam, G. (2002) "The Wooster Group" in H. Bertens & J. Natoli (eds.) *Postmodernism: The Key Figures*, Oxford: Blackwell, pp. 327–333.

Goulish, M. (2000) *39 Microlectures: In Proximity of Performance*, London: Routledge.

Gray, S. (1978) "Playwright's Notes," *Performing Arts Journal*, 3: 2, 87–91.

______ (1979a) "Perpetual Saturdays," *Performing Arts Journal*, 4: 1, 46–49.

______ (1979b) "About *Three Places in Rhode Island*," *The Drama Review*, 23: 1, 31–42.

______ (1980) "Children of Paradise: Working with Kids," *Performing Arts Journal*, 5: 1, 61–74.

Gray, S. and LeCompte, E. (1978) "*Rumstick Road*," *Performing Arts Journal*, 3: 2, 92–115.

Heathfield, A. Templeton, F. and Quick, A. (eds.) (1997) *Shattered Anatomies: Traces of the Body in Performance*, Bristol: Arnolfini Live.

Isen, K. P. (1987) "Theater of Resistance: The Wooster Group's *The Road to Immortality*," *High Performance*, 10: 2, 30–33.

Kaye, N. (1994) *Postmodernism and Performance*, New York: St. Martin's Press.

______ (1996) *Art into Theatre: Performance Interviews and Documents*, Netherlands: Harwood Academic Publishers.

______ (2005) "Hardware in Real Time: Performance and the Place of Video," *Contemporary Theatre Review: An International Journal*, 15: 2, 203–218.

______ (2007) *Multi-Media: Video, Installation, Performance*, New York: Routledge.

Klaver, E. (2000) "Scenes from the Popular Culture Debate: The Wooster Group's *Route 1 & 9 (the Last Act)*," *Essays in Theatre—Etudes Theatrales*, 19: 1, 21–32.

Knowles, R. (2000) "The Wooster Group: *House/Lights*, Landscapes, and the Politics of Nostalgia," *Essays in Theatre—Etudes Theatrales*, 19: 1, 33–43.

LeCompte, E. (1978) "An Introduction," *Performing Arts Journal*, 3: 2, 81–86.

______ (1979) "Who Owns History?" *Performing Arts Journal*, 4: 1, 50–53.

______ (1985) "The Wooster Group Dances: From the Notebooks of Elizabeth LeCompte," *The Drama Review*, 29: 2, 78–93.

Leverett, J. (1982) "The Wooster Group's 'Mean Theatre' Sparks a Hot Debate," *Theatre Communications*, July/August: 16–20.

MacDonald, E. (1993) *Theater at the Margins: Text and the Post-Structured Stage*, Ann Arbor, MI: University of Michigan Press.

Marranca, B. (2003) "The Wooster Group—a Dictionary of Ideas," *Performing Arts Journal*, 74, 1–18.

Mee, S. (1992) "Chekhov's *Three Sisters* and the Wooster Group's *Brace Up!*" *The Drama Review*, 36: 4, 143–153.

Murray, T. (1997) *Drama Trauma: Specters of Race & Sexuality in Performance, Video & Art*, Abingdon: Routledge.

Rabkin, G. (1985) "Is There a Text on This Stage? Theatre/Authorship/Interpretation," *Performance Research*, 9: 2/3, 142–159.

Reilly-McVittie, N. (1999) "Writing for a Cyborg Who Prepares (Part One)," *Performance Research*, 4: 2, 92.

Rosten, B. (1998) "The Gesture of Illogic," *American Theatre*, 15: 3, 16–19.

Savran, D. (1985) "The Wooster Group, Arthur Miller and *The Crucible*," *The Drama Review*, 29: 2, 99–109.

______ (1987) "Adaptation as Clairvoyance: The Wooster Group's Saint Antony," *Theater*, 18: 1, 36–41.

______ (1988) *Breaking the Rules: The Wooster Group*, New York: Theatre Communications Group.

______ (1991) "Revolution... History... Theatre: The Politics of the Wooster Group's Second Trilogy" in S.E. Case & J. Reinelt (eds.) *The Performance of Power: Theatrical Discourses and Politics*, Iowa City: Iowa University Press, pp. 41–55.

Schechner, R. (1982) *The End of Humanism: Writings on Performance*, New York: Performing Arts Journal Publications.

Schechner, R. and Vawter, R. (1993) "Ron Vawter: For the Record: An Interview," *The Drama Review*, 37: 3, 17–41.

Schmidt, P. (1992) "The Sounds of *Brace Up!* And the Wooster Group's Staging of *Three Sisters*: Translating the Music of Chekhov," *The Drama Review*, 36: 4, 154–157.

Vanden Heuvel, M. (1991) *Performing Drama/Dramatizing Performance: Alternative Theater and the Dramatic Text*, Ann Arbor, MI: University of Michigan Press.

______ (1995) "Waking the Text: Disorderly Order for the Wooster Group's *Route 1 & 9 (the Last Act)*," *Journal for Dramatic Theory and Criticism*, 10: 1, 59–76.

Wooster Group, The (1996) "*Frank Dell's The Temptation of St. Antony*" in B. Marranca (ed.) *Plays for the End of the Century*, Baltimore, MD: John Hopkins University Press, pp. 261–314.

Chronology

1985

January 5–12 *L.S.D. (...Just the High Points...)* at The Performing Garage (TPG)
January 26–27 *L.S.D.* at Yale University, New Haven, Connecticut
February Work begins on Flaubert's *La Tentation de Saint Antoine*, a text suggested by Peter Sellars
February 19–25 *Frank Dell's The Temptation of St. Antony* rehearsals at MIT, Cambridge, Massachusetts
Mid-March, April, May rehearsals for *Miss Universal Happiness*, a collaboration with Richard Foreman/Ontological-Hysteric Theater
May *Route 1 & 9* rehearsals
May 14–June 22 *Miss Universal Happiness* at TPG
June 25–30 *Route 1 & 9* at the Bastille Theatre, Paris, France
August, September, October *St. Antony* rehearsals. *Channel J* first video draft
November The Wooster Group (TWG) residency at the Kennedy Center, Washington, D.C. begins
November, December *Channel J* video shoot. *Flaubert Dreams of Travel but the Illness of his Mother Prevents It*, a film shoot with Ken Kobland (later incorporated into *St. Antony*)
December 7–22 *North Atlantic* at The Playwrights Theatre, Washington D.C.

1986

January 4–19 *L.S.D.* at the Kennedy Center Lab, Washington, D.C.
January 23–26 *St. Antony* open rehearsals at the Kennedy Center Lab, Washington, D.C.
March While in Australia, Michael Kirby writes *White Homeland Commando* for TWG
March 1–15 *L.S.D.* in Adelaide, Australia
April 28–May 4 *L.S.D.* and *St. Antony* rehearsals filmed for ITV's *South Bank Show*
May *St. Antony* rehearsals, *Hofstra Pool* video shoot
May 26–June 30 *St. Antony* at TPG
August 12–18 *L.S.D.* in Edinburgh, Scotland
August 21–September 6 *L.S.D.* and *White Homeland Commando* public readings at the Riverside Studios, London, England
September 9–14 *L.S.D.* in Cardiff, Wales
October 5–11 *L.S.D.* at the Ancienne Belgique, Brussels, Belgium
October 15–19 *L.S.D.* in Theatre Am Turm, Frankfurt, Germany
October 28–November 2 *L.S.D.* in Milan, Italy
November: *Route 1 & 9* rehearsals at The Kitchen, NYC—run postponed due to illness

1987

December 26 (1986)–January 18 *Route 1 & 9* opens at The Kitchen, NYC
January 22–February 10 *L.S.D.* at TPG
February, March *St. Antony* rehearsals
April 1–26 *St. Antony* work-in-progress at TPG
May 5–10 *St. Antony* at MIT, Cambridge, Massachusetts
June 4–7 *L.S.D.* at the Montreal Festival, Montreal, Canada
Mid-June–mid-August TWG residency in North Hampton, Massachusetts, sponsored by No Theater
June 18–21 *L.S.D.* at Smith College, North Hampton, Massachusetts
June 25–28 *St. Antony* at Smith College, North Hampton, Massachusetts
July, August *Rehearsal Tapes: WG* a video shoot with Ken Kobland
August 13–14 *Wrong Guys* at Thornes, North Hampton, Massachusetts
September 6–13 *L.S.D.* at the L.A. Festival, Los Angeles, California. *Cubby in L.A.* video shoot (later incorporated into *St. Antony*)
September 17–21 *L.S.D.* at On the Boards, Seattle, Washington
Late September, October *St. Antony* rehearsals
October 8–November 9 *St. Antony* at TPG
November, December rehearsals for *Symphony of Rats*—a second collaboration with Richard Foreman/Ontological-Hysteric Theater

1988

January 6–February 22 *Symphony Of Rats* at TPG
January–April Script work on *This Will Kill That* film project
May 23–28 *L.S.D.* at The Jerusalem Festival. *Cubby in Jerusalem* video shoot (later incorporated into *St. Antony*)
June 5–30 *North Atlantic* at TPG
July *St. Antony* rehearsals
September *Cubby as Jesus* video shoot in Venice (later incorporated into *St. Antony*)
September 16–October 15 *St. Antony* at TPG
November 5–28 *St. Antony* at TPG
December *White Homeland Commando* pre-production and rehearsals at TPG

1989

January *White Homeland Commando* video shoot
February 1–5 *L.S.D.* in Toronto, Canada
February, March rehearsals begin on new work, later to be titled *Brace Up!*
April *White Homeland Commando* post-production work
May 15–20 *St. Antony* in Antwerp, Belgium
June 1–4 *St. Antony* in Montreal, Canada
June, July *Brace Up!* rehearsals
September 14–October 29 *St. Antony* at TPG

November 6 "Episode One" of *St. Antony* at The New Museum, NYC
December Script work on *Love Affair* film project

1990
January–April *Brace Up!* rehearsals
March 24–26 *Brace Up!* excerpts shown at The Guggenheim Museum, NYC
May 10–13 *St. Antony* and *Brace Up!* in Frankfurt, Germany
May 21–27 *St. Antony* and *Brace Up!* in Vienna, Austria
June *Geinin (Today I Must Sincerely Congratulate You)* pre-production
July 1–3 *Geinin* film shoot at TPG
August 30–September 4 *St. Antony* at the Temporary Contemporary, Los Angeles, California
October 4–19 *L.S.D.*, *St. Antony*, and *Brace Up!* at The Tramway Theater, Glasgow, Scotland
November, December *Brace Up!* rehearsals

1991
January 18–March 9 *Brace Up!* at TPG
March 21–24 *Brace Up!* in Seattle, Washington
April *White Homeland Commando* rough picture edit
April 3–6 *Brace Up!* in Minneapolis, Minnesota
April 19 *Geinin* "bathroom shoot" at TPG
April 24–28 *Brace Up!* in Frankfurt, Germany
May 4–9 *Brace Up!* at the Hebel Theatre, Berlin, Germany
May 14–20 *Brace Up!* in Amsterdam, The Netherlands
May 25–29 *Brace Up!* in Vienna, Austria
June, July *White Homeland Commando* final picture edit
August 26–28 *Kisser* film shoot (later to become part of the MTV "Art Break")
September 12–October 26 *Brace Up!* at TPG
November 6–14 *Brace Up!* in Frankfurt, Germany
November 19–27 *Brace Up!* at the Kaaitheater, Brussels, Belgium
December *White Homeland Commando* sound edit. MTV "Art Break" film shoot

1992
January–February *Peggy Carstairs* video sessions
January–March Work on material for a new piece (later to be titled *Fish Story*)
February *White Homeland Commando* sound edit
February–March rehearsals for *Dances From The Wuji Islands*
March *Brace Up!* rehearsals
March 27–April 25 *Brace Up!* at TPG
April 1 Rae Whitfield and The Johnsons perform *Dances From The Wuji Islands* at the Whitney Museum of American Art at Phillip Morris, NYC
May *Brace Up!* in Zurich, Switzerland and Lisbon, Portugal
June *Rhyme 'em to Death* pre-production
July *Rhyme 'em to Death* film shoot
August, September *The Emperor Jones* rehearsals at TPG
October *Rhyme 'em to Death* edit work begins
October 8–17 *The Emperor Jones* at TPG
October 28–November 1 *Brace Up!* in Glasgow, Scotland
November 10–14 *Brace Up!* in Bordeaux, France
November 19–22 *The Emperor Jones* in Frankfurt, Germany

1993
January 28–February 6 *The Emperor Jones* at TPG
February, March, April *Fish Story* rehearsals
March–June *White Homeland Commando* included in The Whitney Biennial, NYC
April 15–May 1 *The Emperor Jones* and *Fish Story* as a double bill at TPG
May 16–19 *The Emperor Jones* and *Fish Story* in Vienna, Austria
May 27–June 4 *The Emperor Jones*, and *Fish Story* in Brussels, Belgium
June 9–13 *Brace Up!* in Antwerp, Belgium
June 18–27 *Brace Up!*, *The Emperor Jones*, and *Fish Story* at Theatre de Welt Festival in Munich, Germany
July 2–6 *Brace Up!* at Riverside Studios in London, England
August Script work on *The Black Hole* film project
September 7–11 *The Emperor Jones* and *Fish Story* in Aarhus, Denmark
September 15–19 *The Emperor Jones* and *Fish Story* in Stockholm, Sweden
October 15–23 *The Emperor Jones* and *Fish Story* in Frankfurt, Germany
November 11–December 5 *St. Antony* at TPG
October, November Rehearsals for revival of *St. Antony*

1994
December 29 (1993)–January 29 *Fish Story* at TPG
March 3–6 *Brace Up!* at The Hong Kong Arts Festival, Hong Kong
March 24–April 9 *The Emperor Jones* at TPG
April 29–May 8 *St. Antony* at The Hebbel Theatre, Berlin, Germany
May 13–17 *Fish Story* at Maison des Arts, Creteil, France
June, July *The Hairy Ape* rehearsals begin
August 30–September 9 *The Hairy Ape* rehearsals
September 23–28 *Brace Up!* and *Fish Story* in Hamburg, Germany
October *Brace Up!* at TPG
November *Fish Story* at TPG
December *The Hairy Ape* rehearsals

1995
January *The Hairy Ape* rehearsals
February 1–March 5 *The Hairy Ape* at TPG
March *St. Antony* in São Paulo, Brazil
March–June *Rhyme 'em to Death* included in The Whitney Biennial, NYC

April *The Hairy Ape* rehearsals
April 22–June 14 *The Hairy Ape* at TPG
June *Wrong Guys* preparation work
July *Wrong Guys* filming in Maine
September 13–October 15 *The Emperor Jones* at TPG
October filming of *The Emperor Jones* video at TPG, filming of the "Sugar Shack" scene from *Wrong Guys* at TPG
November, December editing begins on *Wrong Guys*
December 11 *Wrong Guys* work-in-progress showing and reading by Jim Strahs at Matthew Marks Gallery, NYC

1996
January *The Hairy Ape* rehearsals
January 24–February 18 *The Hairy Ape* at TPG
February–March *Fish Story* rehearsals
March 21–25 *Fish Story* in Bogota, Colombia
April 18–May 4 *Fish Story*, *The Emperor Jones*, *The Hairy Ape* at The Luna Theatre, Brussels, Belgium
May editing and sound recording on *Wrong Guys*, editing begins on *The Emperor Jones* video
June rehearsals begin on new work, later to be titled *House/Lights*
June 10–16 preparation and filming of the "motel" scenes from *Wrong Guys*
September editing continues on both *Wrong Guys* and *The Emperor Jones* video
October–December *House/Lights* rehearsals. *Wrong Guys* editing continues. *Love Affair* script work
December 15–22 Rehearsals with Vincent Dunoyer for *Dances With TV And Mic* at the Wexner Center, Columbus, Ohio
December 28–31 *Dances With TV And Mic* rehearsals at TPG

1997
January–February *House/Lights* rehearsals
February 27–March 2 *House/Lights* (then subtitled *Dances with TV*) at TPG
March–June *Wrong Guys* included in The Whitney Biennial, NYC
March 21–May 25 *The Hairy Ape* at the Selwyn Theatre, NYC
June 4–9 *The Hairy Ape* at The Weiner Festwochen, Vienna, Austria
June 14–16 *The Hairy Ape* at Theatre Am Turm, Frankfurt, Germany
June 22–30 *The Hairy Ape* at The Hebbel Theatre, Berlin, Germany
September *House/Lights* rehearsals
October 8–12 *House/Lights* at The Wexner Center, Columbus, Ohio
November 2 *House/Lights* at Kanonhallen, Copenhagen, Denmark
November 12–16 *House/Lights* at The Museum of Contemporary Art, Chicago, Illinois
December 20–23 *House/Lights* at the Walker Arts Center, Minneapolis, Minnesota
December *House/Lights* rehearsals

1998
January 2–10 Trisha Brown, with Diane Madden, conducts a workshop with the company from which a dance phrase is later incorporated into *House/Lights*
January *House/Lights* rehearsals
January 29–February 15 *House/Lights* at TPG
March 4–April 26 *The Emperor Jones* at TPG
May work on BBC Radio 3 presentation of *The Emperor Jones*
May 28–June 1 *House/Lights* at Kunstfest, Weimar, Germany
June 7–16 *The Hairy Ape* and *House/Lights* at The Holland Festival, Amsterdam, the Netherlands
June 25–July 3 *The Hairy Ape* at The Bavarian State Opera, Munich, Germany
July 11–15 *The Hairy Ape* at The Murgulho No Futuro Festival (Expo '98), Lisbon, Portugal
September *House/Lights* rehearsals
October 3–25 *House/Lights* at TPG
November 20–24 *The Emperor Jones* at The Queen's Festival, Belfast, Northern Ireland
December 2–6 *House/Lights* at deSingel, Antwerp, Belgium
December 9–12 *House/Lights* at Kaaitheater, Brussels, Belgium

1999
January 10–March 28 *House/Lights* at TPG
April–May rehearsals begin for the revival of *North Atlantic*
May 27–31 *House/Lights* at The Montreal Festival des Amerique, Montreal, Canada
June–July Work on the BBC Radio 3 presentation of *Phèdre*. Editing of *The Emperor Jones* video continues
July 16 Showing of *The Emperor Jones* video at The New York Video Festival, NYC
September–October *North Atlantic* rehearsals
October 14–November 18 *North Atlantic* at TPG
December 8–18 *House/Lights* at Theatre de la Bastille, Paris, France

2000
January 11–February 20 *North Atlantic* at TPG
March, April, May Rehearsals begin for *Phèdre*, later to be titled *To You, the Birdie! (Phèdre)*
May 27–31 *House/Lights* at The Bergen International Theatre, Bergen, Norway
June 7–10 *House/Lights* at Tramway, Glasgow, Scotland
June 23–27 *North Atlantic* at Kaaitheater, Brussels, Belgium
September–October *To You, the Birdie! (Phèdre)* rehearsals
November 15–19 *North Atlantic* at On The Boards, Seattle, Washington
November 28–December 2 *North Atlantic* at The Wexner Center, Columbus, Ohio
December 7–10 *North Atlantic* at The Walker Art Center, Minneapolis, Minnesota

2001

January–February *To You, the Birdie! (Phèdre)* rehearsals
March 14–17 *House/Lights* at La Rose des Vents, Lille, France
March 21–24 *House/Lights* at Theatre Garonne, Toulouse, France
March 28–31 *House/Lights* at Le Maillon, Strasbourg, France
April–May *To You, the Birdie! (Phèdre)* rehearsals
June 1–July 1 *To You, the Birdie! (Phèdre)* at TPG
August work begins on the *House/Lights* DVD
September 21–23 *To You, the Birdie! (Phèdre)* at TPG
October 19–November 6 *The Hairy Ape* at Melbourne Festival, Melbourne, Australia
November 14–17 *North Atlantic* at the Festival D'Automne, Paris, France
November 22–26 *The Hairy Ape* at The Festival D'Automne, Paris, France
November 28–December 7 *To You, the Birdie! (Phèdre)* at The Festival D'Automne, Paris, France

2002

February 1–March 30 *To You, the Birdie! (Phèdre)* at St. Ann's Warehouse, Brooklyn, NYC
April–May Work on BBC Radio 3 presentation of *The Peggy Carstairs Report*
May 9–May 23 *To You, the Birdie! (Phèdre)* at Riverside Studios, London, England
May 31–June 5 *To You, the Birdie! (Phèdre)* at International Istanbul Theatre Festival, Istanbul, Turkey
June 13–19 *To You, the Birdie! (Phèdre)* at Kaaitheater, Brussels, Belgium
September recording and editing of the "fake commentary" for the *House/Lights* DVD
October 15–19 *To You, the Birdie! (Phèdre)* at The Wexner Center, Columbus, Ohio
October 25–31 *To You, the Birdie! (Phèdre)* at On the Boards, Seattle, Washington
November 8–17 *To You, the Birdie! (Phèdre)* at UCLA, Los Angeles, California
December rehearsals begin for the revival of *Brace Up!*

2003

January *Brace Up!* rehearsals
February 19–April 13 *Brace Up!* (2003) at St. Ann's Warehouse in Brooklyn, NYC
March–May rehearsals of "new work" (later to be titled *Poor Theater*)
May 30–June 3 *To You, the Birdie! (Phèdre)* Teatr Dramatyczny, Warsaw, Poland
June 11–June 15 *To You, the Birdie! (Phèdre)* Holland Festival, Amsterdam, the Netherlands
June 26–June 30 *To You, the Birdie! (Phèdre)* Hebbel Theater, Berlin, Germany
July 8–August 29 "By the Sea" and "The Nun's Home Movie" from *Point Judith (an epilog)* included in the exhibit *Half Air* at the Marianne Boesky Gallery, NYC
September, October, November rehearsals of "new work" (later to be titled *Poor Theater*)
November 19–December 19 performances of *Poor Theater* at TPG

2004

January–February *Poor Theater* rehearsals
February 18–April 24 *Poor Theater* at TPG
April work with Joji Inc. on *Erase-e(x)*
June 17–20 *To You, the Birdie! (Phèdre)* at Bonn Biennale, Halle Beuel, Bonn, Germany
July 12–16 *To You, the Birdie! (Phèdre)* at GREC Festival 2004, Theater Lliure, Barcelona, Spain
August 19–22 *To You, the Birdie! (Phèdre)* at Welt in Basel Festival, Reithalle, Basel, Switzerland
September 15 Selections from The Wooster Group archive in honor of Spalding Gray at TPG
September 22–26 *Poor Theater* at Cal Arts/Red Cat, Los Angeles, California
October 5–10 *Poor Theater* at Hebbel am Ufer Theater/Hau II, Berlin, Germany
October 16–20 *Poor Theater* at Festival of Theater Festivals, Teatr Dramatyczny, Teatr Warsaw, Poland
November *House/Lights* DVD goes into distribution
November 10–December 19 *Poor Theater* at TPG

2005

January rehearsals for the revival of *House/Lights*
February 2–April 10 *House/Lights* at St. Ann's Warehouse in Brooklyn, NYC
March, April, May, June rehearsals begin for *Hamlet*
June 23–July 2 *Poor Theater* at Kaaitheater, Brussels, Belgium
July *Hamlet* rehearsals
September 14–October 15 *Poor Theater* at TPG
October, November, December *Hamlet* rehearsals

2006

January, February rehearsals for *Hamlet* and for the revival of *The Emperor Jones*
March 1–April 2 *The Emperor Jones* at St. Ann's Warehouse, Brooklyn, NY. *Hamlet* rehearsals
April, May, June rehearsals for *Hamlet* and a "new opera project" and for *Who's Your DADA?!*
June 27–July 1 *Hamlet* at Festival Grec, Barcelona, Spain
July 16–19 *To You, the Birdie! (Phèdre)* at Hellenic Festival, Athens, Greece
August, September *Who's Your DADA?!* rehearsals.
September 6, 7, & 9 Performances of *Who's Your DADA?!* at The Museum of Modern Art, NYC
September, October *Hamlet* rehearsals. Rehearsals for a "new opera project"—*La Didone*
October 22–25 *To You, the Birdie! (Phèdre)* at Territory Festival, Moscow, Russia
November 4–10, 16–20 *Hamlet* at Festival D'Automne, Paris, France and at The Hebbel Theater, Berlin, Germany
November, December work on a "new media project." *La Didone* rehearsals

Production credits

Frank Dell's The Temptation of St. Antony

Frank Dell Ron Vawter (1986–93), Willem Dafoe (1994)
Phyllis Peyton Smith
Onna Kate Valk
Eva Anna Köhler
Jacques Michael Stumm (1986–90), Dave Shelley (1993–94)
Sue Nancy Reilly (1986), M.A. Hestand (1987–89), Valerie Charles (1989), Cynthia Hedstrom (1990, 93–94)
Dieter Jeff Webster (1986–90), Christopher Kondek (1993–94), Michael Nishball (1994)
Tracy Leipold Herself (1993–1994)
J.J. Himself
On video Nancy Reilly, Willem Dafoe, Irma St. Paule
Director Elizabeth LeCompte
Set Jim Clayburgh
Sound Jeff Webster, James "J.J." Johnson, John Collins (1993–94)
Light Paula Gordon (1986–90), Clay Shirky (1993–94)
Video Elizabeth LeCompte
Additional Video Christopher Kondek (1993–94)
Film Ken Kobland
Additional Text James Strahs
Assistant to the Director James "J.J." Johnson (1986–88), Marianne Weems (1988–93), Clay Hapaz (1994)
Dramaturg Norman Frisch (1986–87)
Set Assistant Michael Nishball
Master Carpenter Ruud van den Akker (1993–94)
Sound Consultants John Erskine, Janet Kalas
Engineering Consultant Bill Ballou/No Radio
Technical Director Eric Dyer (1993–94)
Special thanks Peter Sellars, Jo Andres, Lenora Champagne, Matthew Hansell, Michael Kirby, Roy Faudree and Sheena See/No Theater, and Elion Sacker for their contributions to the piece.

Frank Dell's The Temptation of St. Antony is dedicated to Ursula Easton.

Brace Up!

Olga, Andrei's sister Peyton Smith (1990–94, 2003), Sheena See (2003)
Masha, Andrei's sister Joan Jonas (1990–92), Karen Lashinsky (1992–94), Kate Valk (2003)
Irina, Andrei's sister Beatrice Roth
Andrei Sergeyevich Prozorov Willem Dafoe (1990–94), Scott Renderer (1992–94), Ari Fliakos (2003)
Natalya Ivanovna, Andrei's fiancée, later his wife Anna Köhler
Bobik, Andrei's son Jack Frank (on video)
Anfisa, the Prozorovs' old nurse Josephine Buscemi (on video)
Fyodor Ilyich Kulygin, Masha's husband Roy Faudree (1990–94), Paul Lazar (2003)
Colonel Alexander Ignatyevich Vershinin Ron Vawter (1990–93), Paul Lazar (1992–94), Willem Dafoe (2003)
Baron Nikolai Lvovich Tusenbach Jeff Webster (1990–94), Scott Shepherd (2003)
Doctor Ivan Romanovich Chebutykin Paul Schmidt (1990–94), Roy Faudree (2003), Joel Bassin (2003)
Vassily Vasilievich Solyony Michael Stumm (1990–91), Clay Shirky (1992–94), Gary Wilmes (2003)
Rohde, Second Lieutenant Dave Shelley (1991–94, 2003)
Fedotik, Second Lieutenant Scott Renderer (1992–94), Ruud van den Akker (1992–94), Michael Stumm (1994), Steve Cuiffo (2003)
Street Musician Michael Stumm (on video)
Stage Manager/Servant Linda Chapman (1990–94), Clay Hapaz (1994), Dominique Bousquet (2003)
Narrator Kate Valk
Anton Chekhov's *Three Sisters* Translation Paul Schmidt
Director Elizabeth LeCompte
Set Jim Clayburgh
Video and First Camera Christopher Kondek, Reid Farrington (2003)
Sound James "J.J." Johnson, John Erskine (1990–94), Andrew Bellware (1992), John Collins (1993–94, 2003), Geoff Abbas (2003)
Lighting Jennifer Tipton
Costumes Elizabeth Jenyon
Assistant Director/Dramaturg Marianne Weems (1990–94), Clay Hapaz (2003)
Production Manager Clay Shirky (1990–94), Iver Findlay (2003)
Master Rigger Ruud van den Akker
Master Electrician Tad Yenawine (1990–93), Eric Dyer (1993–94), Gabe Maxson (2003)
Costume/Video Assistant Tara Webb (2003)
Doctor's Camera Roy Faudree (1990–94), Clay Shirky (1990–94), Iver Findlay (2003)
Original Music John Lurie, Lawrence "Butch" Morris, Suzzy and Terre Roche
Additional Music Evan Lurie
Dance Director Kate Valk
Dance Consultant Jo Andres
Special thanks to Steve Buscemi, Ruth Maleczech, Bill Ballou, Scott Breindel, Bob Cardelli, Paula Gordon, Michael Kirby, David Linton, Michael Nishball, Ellen Spiro, Elion Sacker, Leslie Thornton, Ken Watt, and Bob Wisdom for their contributions to the piece.

Fish Story

Asako Kate Valk
Eiji/Irina Beatrice Roth
Hiroko/Kulygin Roy Faudree
Sensaburo/Tusenbach Jeff Webster
Sensha/Olga Peyton Smith
Sentaro/Rohde Dave Shelley
Taro Christopher Kondek
Yukio/Andrei Scott Renderer (1993–94), Willem Dafoe (1996)
Masha Karen Lashinsky
Stage Assistant Cynthia Hedstrom/Jack Frank/Ari Fliakos (1996)
Vershinin Ron Vawter (on video)
Masha Karen Lashinsky (on video)
Natasha Anna Köhler (on video)
Ferapont Elion Sacker (on video)
Director Elizabeth LeCompte
Video Christopher Kondek
Sound James "J.J." Johnson, John Collins
Set Jim Clayburgh
Light Clay Shirky (1993–94), Jennifer Tipton (1994–96)
Assistant Director Marianne Weems (1993), Clay Hapaz (1994–96)
Production Manager Clay Shirky (1993–94), Georg Bugiel (1996)
Technical Director Eric Dyer (1993–94), Jim Findlay (1996)
Master Carpenter/Rigger Ruud van den Akker
Video Assistant Victor Morales (1993), Philip Bussmann (1996)
Follow Spot Operator Clay Hapaz (1993), Ruud van den Akker (1994–96)
Choreography The Wooster Group
Costumes The Wooster Group, Elizabeth Jenyon, Ellen McCartney
Dance Consultant Jo Andres
Additional Music Evan Lurie, John Lurie, The Roches
Texts Act IV of Anton Chekhov's *Three Sisters*, as translated by Paul Schmidt; *Geinin*, a documentary film, 1977
Special thanks Vincent Dunoyer and Annie Iobst for their contributions to the piece.

House/Lights

Faustus/Elaine Kate Valk
Mephistopheles/Olga Peyton Smith (1997–98), Suzzy Roche (1998–2001, 2005)
Boy/Nick Roy Faudree
Dog/Johnny Ari Fliakos
Christine & Nadja Tanya Selvaratnam
Susie & Ellie Helen Eve Pickett (1997–2001, 2005), Natalie Thomas (2005)
Holly & Jenny Sheena See (1998–2001, 2005)
Paula White & Black Karen Lashinsky (1997–98)
Mr. Viper John Collins
Director Elizabeth LeCompte
Sound James "J.J." Johnson, John Collins, Geoff Abbas (2005)
Set Jim Findlay
Video Philip Bussmann
Additional Video Christopher Kondek
Lighting Jennifer Tipton
Costumes Elizabeth Jenyon
Choreography The Wooster Group
Music Hans Peter Kuhn, John Lurie
Assistant Director Clay Hapaz
Dramaturg Kate Valk
Technical Director Jeff Sugg (1997–98), Guy Larkin (1999), Geoff Abbas (1999), Jim Dawson (2000–01), Iver Findlay (2005)
Rigging Engineer Ruud van den Akker
Master Electrician Scott Gillette (1997), Georg Bugiel (1997–99), Jeff Sugg (1999–2001), Gabe Maxson (2005)
Video Operator Reid Farrington (2005)
Assistant Video/Wardrobe Ellen Hofmann (1997), Tara Webb (1998–2001)
Assistant Video Margaret Mann (2005)
Assistant Sound Operators Lance Dann (1999), Mark "Muttt" Huang (1999–2001)
Production Manager Bozkurt Karasu (2005)
Production Assistant Lori Chodos (1998–99)
Sound Consultant Martin Desjardins
MacIntalk/Powerbook 520 Tanya Selvaratnam
Texts *Doctor Faustus Lights the Lights* by Gertrude Stein, 1938; "Olga's House of Shame," a film by Joseph Mawra, 1964
Additional choreography Act 1 Special Dance (to *Young Frankenstein*) by Trisha Brown with Diane Madden; Act 2 Ballet (*I Love Lucy* recreation) by Helen Eve Pickett
Special thanks Dennis Dermody, Andrew Schneider, Eve Schuffenecker, Ariana Smart, Martin Weisenhofer and PRADA for their contributions to the piece.

To You, the Birdie! (Phèdre)

Hippolytos Ari Fliakos
Theramenes/Reader Scott Shepherd
Oenone Frances McDormand (2001–02), Sheena See (2002–06)
Phèdre Kate Valk
Theseus Willem Dafoe (2001–02), Roy Faudree (2002–06)
Venus/Referee Suzzy Roche/Fiona Leaning
Marker 7 Koosil-ja Hwang
Marker 4 Dominique Bousquet
Video Venus Suzzy Roche
Director Elizabeth LeCompte
Text Paul Schmidt
Set Jim Findlay
Sound John Collins, Geoff Abbas, Jim Dawson
Video Philip Bussmann
Lighting Jennifer Tipton
Original Music Tracks David Linton
Original Songs Koosil-ja Hwang, Suzzy Roche, Kate Valk
Costumes The Wooster Group with Elizabeth Jenyon
Assistant Director Richard Kimmel
Video Totems Ruud van den Akker
Stage Manager Ariana Smart (2000), Judy Tucker (2001)
Technical Director Geoff Abbas, Iver Findlay
Master Technicians Ruud van den Akker, Jeff Sugg (2001)
Production Manager Bozkurt Karasu (2003–06)
Master Electrician Reid Farrington (2001), Lara Wilder (2002), Gabe Maxson (2003–06)
Video Operator Reid Farrington (2002–06)
Assistant Costumes/Video Tara Webb (2001–04)
Assistant Video Anna Henckel-Donnersmarck (2006)
Assistant Video/Editor Max Finneran (2001)
Sound Consultant Lance Dann, Dan Dobson
Badminton Master Chi-Bing Wu
Dramaturgy Jim Dawson, Dennis Dermody
Special thanks Phyllis Carlin, Constantine Fliakos, Austin Guest, Kimberley Hassett, Margaret Mann, Geraldine Swayne, and PRADA for their contributions to the piece.

This piece is dedicated to Paul Schmidt (1934–1999), who wrote this version of Racine's *Phèdre* for The Wooster Group in 1993.

Photo credits

Frank Dell's The Temptation of St. Antony

Page 16 (l–r): Ron Vawter, Peyton Smith. Photo: © Louise Oligny

18 (l–r): (on video monitor) Anna Köhler and Ron Vawter, Ron Vawter. Photo: © Paula Court

24 *top left*, (l–r): Elizabeth LeCompte, Ron Vawter, Cynthia Hedstrom. Photo: © Mary Gearhart; *top right*, (l–r): Michael Stumm, Peyton Smith, Kate Valk. Photo: © Paula Court; *bottom left*, Kate Valk. Photo: © Mary Gearhart; *bottom right*, Ron Vawter. Photo: © Paula Court

25 *top*, (l–r): Mary Hestand, Anna Köhler, Michael Stumm, Ron Vawter, Kate Valk, Jeff Webster (obscured), Peyton Smith. Photo: © Paula Court

34 Ron Vawter. Photo: © Paula Court

39 center and left, Ron Vawter. Photo: © Paula Court

46 (l–r): Kate Valk, Anna Köhler, Ron Vawter, Michael Stumm, Peyton Smith. Photo: © Paula Court

47 *left*, (l–r): Ron Vawter, Kate Valk. Photo: © Paula Court; *center*, (l–r): Kate Valk, Ron Vawter. Photo: © Paula Court; *right*, (l–r): (on video monitor) Willem Dafoe and Kate Valk, Ron Vawter. Photo: © Paula Court

48 *left*, (l–r): Peyton Smith, Ron Vawter. Photo: © Paula Court; *center*, (l–r): Kate Valk, Dave Shelley. Photo: © Paula Court; *right*, Anna Köhler. Photo: © Paula Court

49 *top left*, (l–r): Kate Valk, Ron Vawter. Photo: © Paula Court; *top right*, Ron Vawter. Photo: © Paula Court; *bottom left*, (l–r): Ron Vawter, Jeff Webster. Photo: © Paula Court; *bottom right*, (l–r): Michael Stumm, Peyton Smith, Kate Valk, Jeff Webster, Ron Vawter. Photo: © Paula Court

52 Michael Stumm. Photo: © Paula Court

Brace Up!

62 Photo: © Mary Gearhart

64 (l–r): Beatrice Roth, Elizabeth LeCompte, James "J.J." Johnson, Kate Valk. Photo: © Mary Gearhart

70 (l–r): Willem Dafoe, Elizabeth LeCompte, Anna Köhler, Paul Schmidt, Linda Chapman. Photo: © Paula Court

72 (l–r): Jeff Webster, Roy Faudree (obscured), Kate Valk, Peyton Smith, Joan Jonas, Willem Dafoe. Photo: © Paula Court

74 (l–r): Anna Köhler, Jeff Webster, Dave Shelley, Michael Stumm (obscured), Beatrice Roth, Ron Vawter, Willem Dafoe (obscured), Peyton Smith, Kate Valk, Linda Chapman. Photo: © Paula Court

78 (l–r): Paul Schmidt, Kate Valk. Photo: © Mary Gearhart

81 *top*, (l–r): Beatrice Roth, Kate Valk. Photo: © Paula Court; *bottom*, (l–r): Kate Valk—carrying Paul Schmidt (on video monitor), Jeff Webster (on video monitor), Paul Schmidt, Beatrice Roth. Photo: © Mary Gearhart

82 Paul Schmidt. Photo: © Bob van Dantzig

86 (l–r): Beatrice Roth, Peyton Smith, Ron Vawter, Roy Faudree, Joan Jonas, Kate Valk, Paul Schmidt. Photo: © Bob van Dantzig

87 (l–r): Peyton Smith (on large video monitors), Beatrice Roth, Roy Faudree (on small video monitor). Photo: © Paula Court

92 Photo: © Mary Gearhart

93 (l–r): Scott Shepherd, Willem Dafoe, Kate Valk, Peyton Smith (on video monitor), Ari Fliakos. Photo: © Paula Court

95 *top*, (l–r): Beatrice Roth, Anna Köhler, Kate Valk, Dave Shelley, Peyton Smith, Roy Faudree, Linda Chapman, Joan Jonas. Photo: © Paula Court; *bottom*, (l–r): Beatrice Roth, Anna Köhler, Michael Stumm, Kate Valk, Ron Vawter, Peyton Smith, Willem Dafoe, Roy Faudree, Linda Chapman, Joan Jonas, Dave Shelley. Photo: © Paula Court

99 *top*, (l–r): Jeff Webster, Michael Stumm, Christopher Kondek, Willem Dafoe, Beatrice Roth (obscured), Kate Valk, Linda Chapman, Joan Jonas, Roy Faudree, Paul Schmidt. Photo: © Paula Court *bottom*, (l–r): Christopher Kondek, Kate Valk, Roy Faudree, Willem Dafoe, Steve Buscemi, Jeff Webster, Michael Stumm. Photo: © Mary Gearhart

101 (l–r): Kate Valk, Peyton Smith, Roy Faudree, Willem Dafoe (x2), Chris Kondek, Michael Stumm, Paul Schmidt, Jeff Webster, Anna Köhler. Photos: © Paula Court

103 (l–r): Scott Shepherd, Dominique Bousquet (obscured), Jack Frank (on video monitors), Anna Köhler, Roy Faudree, Willem Dafoe, Kate Valk, Paul Lazar, Beatrice Roth, Dave Shelley (obscured), Peyton Smith, Ari Fliakos. Photo: © Paula Court

105 *top left*, Beatrice Roth. Photo: © Mary Gearhart; *top right*, Ron Vawter. Photo: © Mary Gearhart; *bottom left*, (l–r): Paul Schmidt, Karen Lashinsky. Photo: © Mary Gearhart; *bottom right*, (l–r): Peyton Smith, Beatrice Roth, Jeff Webster. Photo: © Mary Gearhart

Fish Story

116 *left*, Jeff Webster. Photo: © Mary Gearhart; *center*, Scott Renderer. Photo: © Mary Gearhart; *right*, Dave Shelley. Photo: © Mary Gearhart

117 *left*, Peyton Smith. Photo: © Mary Gearhart; *center*, Roy Faudree. Photo: © Mary Gearhart; *right*, Chris Kondek. Photo: © Mary Gearhart

118 *left*, Kate Valk. Photo: © Mary Gearhart; *center*, Beatrice Roth. Photo: © Mary Gearhart

120 (l–r): John Collins, Chris Kondek, Kate Valk, James "J.J." Johnson. Photo: © Mary Gearhart

125 (l–r): Peyton Smith, Kate Valk, Roy Faudree. Photo: © Mary Gearhart

129 *top left*, (l–r): Scott Renderer, Jeff Webster (on video monitor). Photo: © Mary Gearhart; *top right*, (l–r): Jack Frank, Chris Kondek. Photo: © Mary Gearhart; *bottom left*, Peyton Smith. Photo: © Mary Gearhart; *bottom right*, Scott Renderer. Photo: © Paula Court

132 *top*, Kate Valk. Photo: © Mary Gearhart; *bottom*, (l–r): Dave Shelley, Kate Valk, Scott Renderer, Roy Faudree. Photo: © Mary Gearhart

136 (l–r): Jeff Webster, Kate Valk, Scott Renderer. Photo: © Mary Gearhart
138 (l–r): Willem Dafoe, Beatrice Roth. Photo: © Mary Gearhart
139 (l–r): Roy Faudree, Kate Valk, Jeff Webster, Beatrice Roth, Ari Fliakos. Photo: © Mary Gearhart
145 Kate Valk. Photo: © Paula Court
147 *top*, (l–r): Peyton Smith, Jeff Webster. Photo: © Mary Gearhart;
bottom, (l–r): Roy Faudree, Beatrice Roth, Scott Renderer. Photo: © Mary Gearhart
149 (l–r): Peyton Smith, Willem Dafoe. Photo: © Mary Gearhart
151 (l–r): Karen Lashinsky (obscured), Jack Frank, Scott Renderer, Peyton Smith.
Photo: © Mary Gearhart
152 Dave Shelley. Photo: © Mary Gearhart

House/Lights

164 (l–r): Suzzy Roche, Kate Valk. Photo: © Paula Court
166 (l–r): Tanya Selvaratnam, Elizabeth LeCompte, Roy Faudree, Natalie Thomas, Suzzy Roche.
Photos: © Paula Court
178 (l–r): Peyton Smith (on video monitor), Kate Valk. Photo: © Mary Gearhart
179 (l–r): Peyton Smith, Ari Fliakos, Tanya Selvaratnam, Kate Valk, Roy Faudree, Karen Lashinsky.
Photo: © Paula Court
183 Clay Hapaz. Photo: © Mary Gearhart
185 (l–r): Ari Fliakos, Tanya Selvaratnam, Roy Faudree, Kate Valk. Photo: © Paula Court
187 *left*, Suzzy Roche. Photo: © Paula Court; *center*, Suzzy Roche. Photo: © Paula Court;
right, (front l–r): Tanya Selvaratnam, Suzzy Roche (back): Kate Valk. Photo: © Mary Gearhart
191 Roy Faudree. Photo: © Mary Gearhart
193 *top*, (l–r): Peyton Smith, Kate Valk, Roy Faudree. Photo: © Mary Gearhart;
bottom, (l–r): Roy Faudree, Kate Valk. Photo: © Mary Gearhart
197 *left*, Ari Fliakos. Photo: © Paula Court; *right*, (l–r): Roy Faudree, Ari Fliakos. Photo: © Paula Court
199 (l–r): Kate Valk, Roy Faudree. Photo: © Paula Court
201 *left*, Kate Valk. Photo: © Mary Gearhart; *right*, (l–r): Kate Valk (upside down), Suzzy Roche,
Ari Fliakos. Photo: © Mary Gearhart
203 (l–r): Sheena See, Helen Eve Pickett, Kate Valk, Roy Faudree, Tanya Selvaratnam, Suzzy Roche.
Photo: © Paula Court
205 Tanya Selvaratnam. Photo: © Paula Court
207 (l–r): Sheena See, Kate Valk. Photo: © Paula Court
208 *left*, Helen Eve Pickett. Photo: © Paula Court; *right*, (l–r): Helen Eve Pickett, Suzzy Roche.
Photo: © Paula Court
213 Kate Valk. Photo: © Paula Court

To You, the Birdie! (Phèdre)

220 (l–r): Koosil-ja Hwang, Willem Dafoe, Ari Fliakos, Suzzy Roche, Dominique Bousquet.
Photo: © Paula Court
222 (l–r): Dominique Bousquet, Ari Fliakos, Suzzy Roche. Photo: © Paula Court
227 Scott Shepherd. Photo: © Mary Gearhart
234 *left*, (l–r): Willem Dafoe, Ari Fliakos. Photo: © Paula Court;
right, (l–r): Koosil-ja Hwang, Kate Valk, Dominique Bousquet. Photo: © Paula Court
236 (l–r): Scott Shepherd, Koosil-ja Hwang, Fiona Leaning, Ari Fliakos. Photo: © Mary Gearhart
238 (l–r): Scott Shepherd, Ari Fliakos. Photo: © Mary Gearhart
242 (l–r): Willem Dafoe, Koosil-ja Hwang, Ari Fliakos, Dominique Bousquet. Photo: © Mary Gearhart
249 (l–r): Frances McDormand, Kate Valk, Suzzy Roche (on video monitor). Photo: © Paula Court
250 *top*, (l–r): Koosil-ja Hwang, Roy Faudree. Photo: © Mary Gearhart
bottom, (l–r): Willem Dafoe, Kate Valk, Koosil-ja Hwang. Photo: © Paula Court
251 *left*, (l–r): Frances McDormand, Kate Valk, Ari Fliakos. Photo: © Paula Court
right, (l–r): Scott Shepherd, Sheena See. Photo: © Mary Gearhart
255 *left*, (l–r): Frances McDormand, Koosil-ja Hwang, Kate Valk. Photo: © Mary Gearhart;
right, (l–r): Kate Valk, Ari Fliakos, Dominique Bousquet. Photo: © Mary Gearhart
256 (l–r): Frances McDormand, Scott Shepherd (on video monitor), Kate Valk.
Photo: © Mary Gearhart
259 (l–r): Koosil-ja Hwang, Kate Valk, Willem Dafoe. Photo: © Paula Court
260 *left*, photo: © Paula Court; *right*, photo: © Paula Court

Index